A HISTORY OF THE
ITALIAN REPUBLICS

WALLACE K. FERGUSON, Professor of History at the University of Western Ontario, was born in Toronto, Canada, in 1902. He received his BA degree from the University of Western Ontario in 1924, and continued his studies at Cornell University, receiving his MA in 1925 and his PhD in history in 1927. He taught at New York University for many years. Professor Ferguson is the author of *Europe in Transition, 1300–1520; The Renaissance;* and *The Renaissance in Historical Thought* as well as several essays and monographs.

A HISTORY OF THE ITALIAN REPUBLICS

BEING A VIEW OF THE
ORIGIN, PROGRESS AND FALL
OF
ITALIAN FREEDOM
BY
J. C. L. DE SISMONDI

INTRODUCTION BY
WALLACE K. FERGUSON

ANCHOR BOOKS
DOUBLEDAY & COMPANY, INC.
GARDEN CITY, NEW YORK

Anchor Books edition: 1966

Library of Congress Catalog Number 66–17451
Introduction Copyright © 1966
by Doubleday & Company, Inc.
All Rights Reserved
Printed in the United States of America

INTRODUCTION

THE appearance of Sismondi's *Histoire des républiques italiennes au moyen âge* in sixteen volumes between the years 1807 and 1818 was an event of major importance in the history of European historiography. It was the first—and the last—attempt to write the history of medieval Italy with its manifold political divisions as a single story. It was also one of the first histories to present the Middle Ages in a favorable light and to suggest that in that hitherto despised period there might be values worthy of admiration and which had since been lost. The edition here presented is a condensed version made by the author himself and published simultaneously in French and English in 1832. It was the product of a lifetime of thought on the subject and was written at a time when, as he remarked in the Preface, he "no longer felt that influence of novelty by which petty facts often seduce authors into the belief that every notion which it has cost them much labour to acquire must have a proportionate value with the reader." Seen from this more distant perspective the individual trees merged into the general shape of the woods and the picture as a whole took on clearer outlines. Though shorn of many details and episodes which the author now felt he could sacrifice without regret, the general theme of his history and the basic ideas underlying it remained the same as in the earlier and longer edition.

Sismondi belonged to the generation which felt the full impact of the French Revolution and its Napoleonic aftermath, followed by the restoration of the old regime in France and the introduction of an era of conservative reaction throughout Europe. It was also the generation which experienced the scarcely less revolutionary cultural manifestations that collectively make up what, for lack of a better name, is known as the Romantic movement. In every aspect of intellectual life this was a period of crisis, not least in the field of historical thought and writing. The circumstances of Sismondi's personal life, moreover, were such as to expose him to the most varied ideological currents of his age. To place his great historical work in its proper setting, then, we must first consider briefly the major currents of contemporaneous thought and then turn to the story of Sismondi's life and trace the personal experiences which conditioned his activity as a historian and at the same time furnished the motive force that carried him through two decades of incredibly arduous labor.

The intellectual atmosphere into which Sismondi was born, and from which he never completely departed, was that of eighteenth-century rationalism, modified in his case by the surviving Calvinism of his native Geneva. The "Enlightenment" of the middle years of the eighteenth century had its origins in a combination of the growing tendency toward a secular Weltanschauung, which accompanied the emergence of the educated bourgeoisie as a cultural force, with ideas drawn from the scientific thought of the preceding century. From the latter the philosophes drew their basic conception of a mechanical universe, created by God in the first instance, but operating independently of any supernatural cause and in strict accord with unchanging and universally applicable natural laws. That these laws could be discovered by the use of reason, exact observation, and experiment had been demonstrated by such pioneers of modern science as Harvey, Galileo, Kepler, and Newton. Before the scientific method could be transferred from the physical universe to man and to human society, however, a further step was needed. This was supplied by John Locke, whose psychological theories assumed that man is born with-

out inherent ideas and that his mind is formed exclusively by the action of external stimuli upon his
senses. It followed, therefore, that basic human nature,
until conditioned by experience, is universally similar
and unchanging. Human society accordingly could be
assumed to be subject to the operation of natural laws,
and it was the primary aim of the philosopher to discover these laws and, having discovered them, to apply
his knowledge for the betterment of the human race.
For, if man's character is conditioned by his environment, it seemed logical to assume that it could be im-
proved by improving his environment through enlightened legislation and governmental institutions.

The principal value of history for the philosopher
was to provide the necessary data with which to work.
As Sismondi put it in the Introduction to the present
edition, "It should be explored, not for scenes of carnage, but for instructions in the government of mankind." History, in short, was to serve a didactic purpose, not to be studied for its own sake but for the
lessons it could teach. To quote our author again, "history has no true importance but as it contains a moral
lesson." It was an approach which rendered almost impossible any true understanding of the past. The
assumption of the basic similarity of human nature in
all times and places in itself tended to get in the way
of a sympathetic understanding of men who lived under
different conditions from their own. If men in the past
acted in ways that to the enlightened philosopher
seemed unreasonable, it could only be because they
were the victims of ignorance and superstition or of
unjust institutions and irrational laws. In any case, the
historian *en philosophe* seemed often less concerned
with attempting to understand than with his duty to sit
in judgement on the actions of men in the past. This attitude was particularly evident in the approach of the
rationalist historians to the Middle Ages. By all the
standards of the Enlightenment, medieval men were
hopelessly sunk in ignorance, superstition, and barbarism, victims of every form of oppression. Moreover,

the elements in the society of the old regime which the French rationalists were endeavoring to overthrow —the dominant position of the Church and the privileged position of the nobility—were all legacies from the Middle Ages. Their attitude toward that benighted period, then, could only be one of undiluted condemnation. In the words of Voltaire: "It is necessary to know the history of that age only in order to scorn it."[1]

Among the French rationalists of Voltaire's generation, who had little faith in the rationality of the masses, there was a tendency to assume that the application of reason to the amelioration of social conditions would come through the legislative activity of enlightened rulers, aided and instructed by the philosophers who had read the lessons of history aright. The doctrine enunciated by Rousseau in the *Contrat social,* on the contrary, vested sovereignty in the people and substituted dependence on the enlightened ruler by a new faith in the infallibility of the collective will. At the same time the emotional force of his matchless prose introduced a new note of passionate conviction into the struggle for liberty and gave the revolution its fighting faith. In a more general way the emotionalism and heightened sensibility of the *Nouvelle Héloïse* served as one of the sources of inspiration for the new stirrings of Romanticism in England and Germany and eventually for the Romantic movement as a European phenomenon.

The Romantic movement took a variety of forms, but it was in almost all respects a reaction against what was most characteristic of the Age of Enlightenment. We are here concerned primarily with its effect on historical thought. Under the influence of Herder, who was himself influenced by Rousseau, the Romantic historians replaced the rationalist belief in the universal similarity of human nature with that of the funda-

[1] Voltaire, "Essai sur les moeurs et l'esprit des nations," *Œuvres complètes* (Paris, 1883–85), XII, 180.

mental differentiation of nations, each of which has its own peculiar character, its *Volksgeist*. This peculiar national character remains constant, but it is not unchanging. Rather it develops through stages of growth analogous to the developing yet constant character of the individual person. It is this national spirit that imposes a special form upon all the institutional and cultural manifestations of a people. At each stage in its development it produces the institutions and the culture that are right for it at the time. The effect of this doctrine was to produce a radically new attitude toward the past. Instead of condemning as barbarous and irrational the civilizations of earlier ages, the Romantic historians strove to understand them and to value them as stages in the organic growth of the nation. The most immediate effect of this new attitude was a rehabilitation of the Middle Ages as the period in the growth of the nation when the national character could be found in its purest form, unspoiled by foreign influences. Here the critics of literature and art were at one with the historians. Rebelling against the classical rules and emotional aridity of eighteenth-century culture, they found in medieval folk poetry and Gothic art a natural and spontaneous quality much more to their taste. In short, the Romantics valued in the Middle Ages just those qualities that the rationalists had condemned —religious faith, literature and art unhampered by rigid classical rules, chivalrous idealism, and all the charm of the far away and strange. That the Middle Ages they discovered had never existed was for the moment irrelevant.

Such in brief outline were some of the more important intellectual currents in the years around the turn of the century when Sismondi was beginning to turn his attention to the writing of history.

Jean Charles Léonard Simonde, for such was the family name by which he was still known as a young man, was born in 1773 in Geneva, the son of a pastor

of the Reformed Church.[2] Although his later experience made him a cosmopolitan and an agnostic, he
retained throughout his life qualities engendered by his
upbringing in a Calvinist church and a free bourgeois
republic. A long tradition of political self-government
and Calvinist morality tended to make Genevans—and
our author not the least—moralists and doctrinaire political theorists. If faith in responsible self-government
came naturally to Sismondi as heir to the Genevan
tradition, it was also to a fellow-Genevan, Jean-Jacques
Rousseau, that he owed the passionate devotion to the
ideal of political liberty that remained the core of his
political philosophy. Years later one of his friends related how young Charles Simonde as a schoolboy used
to meet with two or three chosen friends under the
statue of Rousseau to make imaginary constitutions for
an ideal republic.[3] If one may judge from his later
comments on the Florentine constitution,[4] one may
safely assume that his ideal republic was one in which
all citizens should have some share in the government
—"such a share as may be necessary to preserve them
from oppression"—but in which effective political power
would be safely vested in a prosperous and educated
bourgeois patriciate. If, at any rate, he had ever had
any faith in the "false equality" of unrestrained democracy, he lost it with the advent of the Reign of Terror.
His first personal experience with the Revolution was
discouraging. In 1792 a revolutionary movement overthrew the Genevan government, and the Simonde family, who were classed among the patrician aristocracy,
felt it advisable to emigrate to England.

The year and a half his family spent in England
marked an important stage in the intellectual and cultural development of the young Genevan. He was soon
thoroughly at home in the English language and had

[2] The best biography of Sismondi is: Jean R. de Salis,
Sismondi, 1773–1842, 2 vols. (Paris, 1932).

[3] Cf. J. C. Herold, *Mistress to an Age, a Life of Madame
de Staël* (London, 1959), p. 288.

[4] See below, pp. 216–18.

acquired a sound working knowledge of the English political constitution. He never ceased to be a republican, but he learned in England that political liberty could exist under a constitutional monarchy. Here, too, his lifelong interest in economic theory was first aroused by the writings of Adam Smith.

Young Charles was apparently quite happy in England, but his mother was not, so in 1794 the family returned to Geneva just in time to be caught in another, more violent outbreak of the Terror. Many family friends were imprisoned and some executed. Young Charles and his father were both imprisoned for a time and most of their remaining fortune was confiscated. Forced once more to emigrate, Simonde *père* sold his estate in Geneva and departed for Italy where he bought a small farm near Pescia in Tuscany. Here Charles spent the next six years as a gentleman farmer, trying to make the farm pay, studying the advanced agricultural methods prevailing in Tuscany, and occupying his spare time in research into local history. During these years Italy became for him a second *patrie*, and one that was to hold his affection for the rest of his life. There were troubled years when Bonaparte was engaged in the conquest of Italy, and in the shifting political situation that followed Charles found himself more than once in prison. The event left him with a strong dislike for the Bonapartist dictatorship, but did not sour his feeling for his newly adopted country. When he returned to Geneva in 1800, leaving his family behind in Tuscany, he was already an Italian patriot and had added an Italian name to his native patronymic.

It was a matter of family history that the Simondes had come to Geneva from Dauphiné a century earlier as Protestant refugees from the persecution that followed the revocation of the Edict of Nantes. During his historical research Charles discovered that the ancient and aristocratic Pisan family of Sismondi, which had played an important and often heroic role in the history of medieval Pisa, had in the sixteenth century emigrated to Dauphiné and settled there. The similarity of the two family names, together with the fact that they had the same coat of arms, was sufficient to convince Charles, who had a broad romantic streak running through the solid core of his Genevan common sense, that the Sismondi were indeed his ancestors. When he returned to Geneva it was as Jean Charles Léonard Simonde de Sismondi. Some aristocratic eyebrows may have been raised at this *"anoblissement un peu arbitraire,"* as Sainte-Beuve has called it,[5] but the name was accepted, and it was as Sismondi that he gained international fame as historian, economist, literary critic, and man of letters.

As a first step in launching his career as a writer, Sismondi published in 1801 an extensive study of Tuscan agriculture, followed two years later by a two-volume work, *De la richesse commerciale*, which had a considerable influence in introducing the economic liberalism of Adam Smith's *Wealth of Nations* to a French-speaking audience. These books gained him recognition in Geneva and abroad, but most important of all they gained him admission to the entourage of Mme. de Staël. Napoleon having quite understandably decided that there was not room enough in Paris for that woman and himself, Necker's famous daughter was spending her years of exile holding a court of her own in the family chateau of Coppet on Lake Geneva. Here a constant stream of distinguished visitors from every country in Western Europe came to stay for a few days—or weeks—and talk and talk and talk. To Sismondi, a shy, awkward young man, of rather unprepossessing appearance and almost entirely self-educated, this brilliant cosmopolitan society was a revelation. Germaine de Staël, herself, was from this time on a decisive influence in his life. He became, and remained until her death in 1817, her devoted admirer. Together with Benjamin Constant and August

[5] C.-A. Sainte-Beuve, *Nouveaux Lundis* (Paris, 1908), VI, 29.

Wilhelm Schlegel, he was one of the most permanent members of her court and her traveling companion on long tours through Italy and Germany. On her part, Germaine took Sismondi's career firmly in hand, wooed him away from economics, in which she had little interest, and directed his literary activity into fields she found more congenial. The greater part of the *History of the Italian Republics* was written during the years when he was closely associated with her, and it is safe to say that without her his *History of the Literature of the South of Europe* (4 vols., 1813)[6] would never have been written.

Aside from the stimulus provided by her daemonic energy and masterful personality, Mme. de Staël's most important contribution to Sismondi's intellectual development was to introduce him to German thought at a time when the Romantic movement had as yet scarcely touched France. It was at Coppet in 1804 that Sismondi met Johannes von Müller, the historian of the Swiss Confederation. The two men were drawn together at once by a common Rousseauian devotion to the ideal of political liberty, while Müller's Romantic enthusiasm served to arouse Sismondi's latent nostalgia for the Middle Ages. Sismondi was too much the rationalist to adopt Müller's emotional style or his predilection for local color, but the popular success of his history of the struggle of the Swiss cantons for freedom encouraged Sismondi to do the same for the Italian communes. At Coppet Sismondi was also brought into daily contact with one of the high priests of Romantic literary theory, A. W. Schlegel, but since he and Schlegel loathed one another on sight, the contact probably served to inoculate Sismondi against the Romantic virus rather than otherwise. His tour of Germany with Mme. de Staël in 1808, however, gave him a more sympathetic understanding of German thought, especially as it was interpreted by Madame herself in

---

[6] For full discussion of this work, see C. Pellegrini, *Il Sismondi e la storia delle letterature dell' Europa meridionale* (Geneva, 1926).

her most important book, *De l'Allemagne*. Although Sismondi never fully accepted the conception there presented of the fundamental difference between the spirits of the Latin and Teutonic nations, its influence was evident throughout his *History of the Literature of the South of Europe* and in his intention, never carried out, to write a similar history of the literature of the northern nations.

The *History of the Italian Republics in the Middle Ages,* which Sismondi began writing in 1804, occupied the major part of his time and energy for the next fourteen years. In the opening paragraph of the first volume, published in 1807, he laid down one of the basic principles of his philosophy of history. Though slightly modified under Romantic influence in later volumes and finally omitted from the condensed version of 1832, it is essential to an understanding of his work and may therefore be worth quoting.

One of the most important conclusions that we can draw from the study of history [he wrote] is that government is the prime cause of the character of peoples; that the virtues or vices of nations, their energies or their weaknesses, their talents, their enlightenment or their ignorance are almost never the effects of climate or the attributes of a particular race, but the work of laws; that everything has been given to all men by nature, but that government takes from or guarantees to men who are subjected to it the heritage of the human species.

This faith in the power of government and laws to shape the character of a people comes straight out of the philosophy of the eighteenth-century rationalists. It formed a necessary premise to a second article of faith, which Sismondi owed more to Rousseau than to the philosophes of Voltaire's generation. This was the conviction that political liberty is not only the highest achievement of any nation, but is an essential prerequisite to any real greatness of heart or mind. From beginning to end it is the theme which gives form and coherence to what might otherwise have been a loosely

organized and formless narrative. It was the loss of
liberty under the emperors that led to the decline of
ancient civilization, and it was the recovery of liberty
by the medieval communes that made possible the
flourishing civilization of the twelfth and thirteenth
centuries. To their form of government the citizens of
the free republics owed not only their courage and
public spirit, but also their economic prosperity and
their brilliant literary and artistic culture at a time
when the rest of Europe was still barbarous. And it
was the gradual loss of liberty, beginning in the fourteenth century, becoming more evident in the fifteenth
and almost total thereafter, which was the basic cause
of that catastrophic decline in every aspect of her
civilization from which Italy had never since recovered. Only thus could Sismondi explain the rhythm of
Italian history. The race and the climate remained
constant. Only the government, and hence the people,
had changed.

Sismondi's attention was naturally focused primarily
on the republican communes, but the scope of his work
was much broader than that. It was in fact a history of
the whole of Italy, including the Kingdom of Naples,
the States of the Church, and the despotic states of
Lombardy. The history of these was, indeed, necessary to demonstrate his thesis by describing the miserable condition of those states which did not enjoy liberty. For Sismondi the problem was fundamentally a
moral one. As he strove to demonstrate, liberty and a
high standard of public and private morality were in-
separable. When one was lost the other necessarily
declined. And in this respect the states ruled by the
pope were no exception. Sismondi had all the French
rationalists' dislike for the secular authority of the
Church, reenforced by the prejudices retained from his
Protestant upbringing, "Law and order [he declared]
seemed incompatible with the government of priests."[7]
The Republic of Florence furnished another example

[7] Below, p. 314.

of his favorite theme. So long as it remained free it was morally sound and led the rest of Europe in all intellectual and artistic activity. But, unlike Voltaire and most other earlier historians, he did not regard the age of the Medici as the high point of Florentine history. On the contrary, he accused the Medici of deliberately undermining Florentine morality as a means of seizing dictatorial power. Lorenzo de' Medici was "a bad citizen of Florence, as well as a bad Italian,"[8] an opinion which involved Sismondi in a heated controversy with William Roscoe, the hero-worshiping biographer of Lorenzo.

Despite the prevailing rationalist tone of Sismondi's work, it encouraged certain Romantic tendencies in contemporary historiography. His idealization of the medieval communes gave an additional stimulus to the rehabilitation of the Middle Ages, especially in France, while his insistence on the moral decline which followed the loss of communal freedom in the fourteenth and fifteenth centuries supplied documentation for the Romantic conception of the "wicked Renaissance" as a period of unrestrained vice and crime. He was in agreement with the Romantic historians of literature, too, in his attitude toward the revival of antiquity. While recognizing the valuable service performed by the Italian scholars who revived knowledge of the classics, he felt that on the whole their activity had had a disastrous effect on the development of the national literature. "The imagination was extinguished; genius disappeared; and even the language retrograded."[9] In one respect only does his view of Italian history seem to foreshadow the conception of the Renaissance formulated a generation later by his fellow Swiss historian, Jacob Burckhardt—that is, in his emphasis on the importance of the cities in shaping the Italian character.

It was the doctrinaire liberalism of Sismondi's history, however, rather than any Romantic overtones,

[8] Ibid., p. 273.
[9] Ibid., p. 152.

that made the widest appeal during the following generation or two, especially since, good republican though he was, he had come to recognize that "It is the participation of numbers in the government, and not the name of republic as opposed to monarchy, that constitutes liberty: it is, above all, the reign of the laws; publicity in the administration, as well as the tribunals; equality; the removal of all shackles on thought, on education, and on religion."[10] This was a conception of liberty that could appeal to English Whigs, to French statesmen of the July Monarchy like Guizot, and to the leaders of the Italian Risorgimento, whether republicans like Mazzini or constitutional monarchists like Cavour. Sismondi had been prepared to accept the possibility of liberty under a constitutional monarchy by his early interest in the English constitution, but his full conversion came only with the fall of Napoleon and the restoration of the reactionary Bourbon regime in France and the equally reactionary Austrian domination in Italy. Until 1814 Sismondi had remained consistently anti-Bonapartist, but the restored Bourbon monarchy soon persuaded him that the Napoleonic empire had been the lesser of two evils. Then, when Napoleon, on his return from Elba, promised to inaugurate a liberal constitution, Sismondi joined his friend Benjamin Constant in journalistic attempts to rally public support to the imperial side. Many of his friends blamed him for his apparent change of front, but he was in reality acting, if somewhat naïvely, in accord with his lifelong convictions, and was simply too honest to fear the appearance of inconsistency. Later visits to Italy, once more under Austrian rule, served to convince him that the governments established there by Napoleon had been at least relatively free. In the 1832 edition he hailed the French invasion at the end of the eighteenth century as having "restored to Italy all the advantages of which their invasion at the end of the fifteenth had deprived her."[11]

[10] Ibid., p. 357–58.
[11] Ibid., p. 357.

The concluding paragraphs of this edition, written late in 1831 after the failure of the incipient revolutions of that year, were an impassioned call to the nations of Europe to aid the Italians in regaining their freedom. The French interlude had revived in Italians a desire for liberty, and they had shown themselves willing to fight for it; but before they were strong enough to defend it the victorious coalition had taken it from them. "And [he concluded] Europe will know no repose till the nation which, in the dark ages, lighted the torch of civilisation with that of liberty, shall be enabled herself to enjoy the light which she created."

The story of the remaining years of Sismondi's life may be irrelevant to our task of introducing his *History of the Italian Republics*, but a few words about his later career may serve to round out the picture of this remarkable man. Scarcely had he finished his Italian history than he began to write a massive *Histoire des Français*, which occupied the last twenty-two years of his life and was finally completed in twenty-nine volumes just before his death in 1842. As "the first detailed and comprehensive survey of the whole field of French history,"[12] it was a respectable work, but it lacked the verve of his Italian history. Moreover, he now had to compete with such masters of historical writing as Guizot and Michelet, and by comparison his work, founded though it was on immensely laborious research, seemed dull and insufferably long-winded. The standard by which Sismondi judged the past had not changed, but whereas in the history of the Italian communes he had found much to praise, in the history of the French monarchy there was little that he did not condemn. To quote Gooch's final comment: "His first book was a hymn to liberty, his second a philippic against the despotism of kings and priests."[13] A work of such magnitude could not, however, be ignored, and

[12] G. P. Gooch, *History and Historians in the Nineteenth Century* (London, 1935), p. 167.
[13] Ibid.

it is pleasant to relate that just before his death he accepted from King Louis Philippe the cross of the Legion of Honor, which many years before he had felt obliged to refuse when it was offered him by Napoleon during the Hundred Days.

Meanwhile, after the completion of his *History of the Italian Republics,* Sismondi had also returned to his earlier interest in economic theory. A second visit to England in 1818–19 gave him an opportunity to observe the workings of industrial and commercial capitalism in a period of economic crisis. Sismondi's warm heart and eighteenth-century humanitarianism were outraged by the condition of the workers in the capitalist industries. The result of his observations was to destroy his faith in the economic liberalism of Adam Smith and the doctrine of laissez faire. He was now convinced that unrestrained competition could result only in the impoverishment of the workers and in periodic crises of overproduction due to the imbalance between increased production and the shrinking purchasing power of the masses of the population. He therefore suggested, though with some hesitation, the necessity for governmental control of production and profits in the interest of both capitalists and workers. He also urged, more strongly, the necessity for laws to protect the workers from exploitation, to enable them to form unions in self-defense, to shorten working hours and abolish child labor, and to ensure workers against the periodic unemployment resulting from the shutting down of factories. Once more, as in the political crisis of the Hundred Days, he had reversed his former position in accord with his lifelong devotion to the ideal of liberty, for it now seemed to him that the freedom of the workers was being imperiled by the extraconstitutional power of the capitalists to enslave them. These ideas, expressed in a two-volume work entitled *Nouveaux principes d'économie politique* (1819) and in numerous articles thereafter, were too radically opposed to the orthodox theories of classical economics to have much immediate influence.

They were, however, taken up by various groups of social reformers after the middle of the century, and he has been recognized by modern economists as an original thinker well in advance of his age.[14]

The circumstances of Sismondi's personal life, as well as his economic theories, changed radically during his visit to England in 1818. He had always had a number of female friends, with whom he corresponded and maintained a quite blameless and rather low-keyed emotional relation, among them the Countess of Albany, widow of the Young Pretender, Charles Edward Stuart. He seems to have been quite content with his bachelor state, however—at least until the death of Mme. de Staël, who admittedly did not like her friends to marry, removed that powerful influence from his life. However that may be, he now at forty-six married an English gentlewoman in her thirties, whom he had met and courted assiduously when she was traveling in Italy two years earlier. There can be no doubt that he had fallen deeply in love with Jessie Allen, and the marriage was apparently a happy one, with no more than the slight frictions to be expected under the circumstances. Jessie was occasionally grieved by her husband's critical attitude toward the Church of England and by his failure to recognize the superiority of all things English. Her numerous family, which included Wedgwoods and Darwins, found him at first disturbingly un-English, though most of them were soon won over by his sweet temper and essential goodness. For his part, accustomed as he was to the surcharged emotional atmosphere and cosmopolitan company of Coppet, they may at times have seemed rather too English.

[14] See, e.g. R. Jeandeau, *Sismondi, précurseur de la législation sociale contemporaine* (Bordeaux, 1913), where the author argues that in the works of Sismondi one can find in germ the greater part of the social legislation of the late nineteenth and twentieth centuries. For Sismondi's economic theories, see among others, H. Grossman, *Simonde de Sismondi et ses théories économiques* (Warsaw, 1924) and Mao-Lan Tuan, *Simonde de Sismondi as an Economist* (New York, 1927).

After his marriage, Sismondi lived a more settled life, mostly in Geneva. He had by now achieved international recognition, and the need to make a name for himself and a place in society was no longer so urgent. The habit of research and writing, however, had become second nature to him, and his Calvinist self-discipline drove him to continuous labor. Even during the last two years of painful illness he continued to write his *History of the French*, and he was busy correcting the final proofs on his deathbed. The volume and scope of his literary production is indeed staggering. Any fair assessment of his achievement must also take into account the fact that each of his major works was a pioneering venture. At the same time, he was one of the last historians to write history *en philosophe* in the eighteenth-century manner, and with the development of academic historiography his work fell somewhat out of fashion. Generations of research in medieval history have exposed errors of detail in his *History of the Italian Republics*, but it has yet to be superseded as a whole, and it is doubtful if it ever will be.

WALLACE K. FERGUSON

AUTHOR'S PREFACE

"WOULD it be possible to comprise the history of the Italian Republics in a single volume?" This question, addressed to me by Dr. Lardner, the learned editor of the Cabinet Cyclopædia, gave birth to the present work. It was flattering to me to be associated, in a great historical undertaking, with the most distinguished English writers; but, at a moment when the rights of nations are weighed anew in the balance of public opinion, when diplomacy and war have been invoked, in turn, to give or take away from nations the faculty of advancing without limit in civilisation, under their respective laws—at such a moment, it was still more flattering and precious, in my eyes, to lay before the two powerful nations which glory in being without a master, the claims of ill-fated Italy to enjoy the same freedom. I thus found the opportunity of presenting, in the two languages of freemen, the memory of what Italy was the first to achieve for obtaining the greatest of blessings—the memory of the impulse and example which she gave, and which all others but followed—and, at the same time, the memory of those crimes of her oppressors which have robbed her of the advantages with which she has endowed the rest of the human race. It seemed to me that the more rapid my recital of the starting up of Italy from her slumber —of her struggles, her misfortunes, and her glories—the stronger would be the impression, and the greater the facility with which I could seize, in the history of Italian freedom, that unity of interest which escapes in the simultaneous existence of a hundred independent states. I was already familiarised by long study with this history, in all its details. After having presented it in

sixteen volumes, I no longer felt that influence of novelty by which petty facts often seduce authors into
the belief that every notion which it has cost them
much labour to acquire must have a proportionate
value with the reader. I could sacrifice details and
episodes without regret. I knew, in some sort, by experience, the vicissitudes which in Italy produced last-
ing results; and those which, on the contrary, produced
none. I undertook, then, not an abridgment of my great
work, but an entirely new history, in which, with my
eyes fixed solely on the free people of the several
Italian states, I have studied to portray, within a compass which should be compatible with animation and
interest, their first deliverance, their heroism, and their
misfortunes. I have confined myself within the limits
assigned to me: it is for the reader to judge whether I
have employed them with due advantage.

J. C. L. DE SISMONDI

London, January, 1832

CONTENTS

ANALYTICAL AND CHRONOLOGICAL
TABLE

INTRODUCTION

CHAPTER I

STATE OF THE POPULATION OF ITALY AT THE FALL OF
THE ROMAN EMPIRE IN THE FIFTH CENTURY   SUC-
CESSIVE INVASIONS OF BARBARIANS BY WHOM ITALY
WAS HARASSED FOR FIVE CENTURIES   THE FIRST
EFFORTS OF TOWNS TO DEFEND AND GOVERN THEM-
SELVES TO BE DATED FROM THE TENTH CENTURY

CHAPTER II

FREDERICK BARBAROSSA DETERMINED TO RESTRICT THE
LIBERTIES OF THE CITIES OF ITALY   THEIR RE-
SISTANCE   LEAGUE OF LOMBARDY   TRUCE OF
VENICE   PEACE OF CONSTANCE, WHICH SETTLED
THEIR RIGHTS

CHAPTER III

PROGRESS OF THE CITIES TOWARDS INDEPENDENCE FROM
THE PEACE OF CONSTANCE TO THE DEATH OF FRED-
ERICK THE SECOND   RELENTLESS STRUGGLE BE-
TWEEN THE GUELPHS AND GHIBELINES   THE FIRST
CHIEFS OF PARTIES WHO RAISE THEMSELVES TO TY-
RANNIC POWER. 1183–1250

CHAPTER IV

INTERREGNUM OF THE EMPIRE   DECLINE AND SUB-
JUGATION OF THE LOMBARD REPUBLICS   CHARLES
OF ANJOU CALLED TO THE SUPPORT OF THE GUELPHS
HIS POWER   HIS CRUELTY   SICILIAN VESPERS.
1251–1282

CHAPTER V

ITALY NEGLECTED BY THE EMPERORS, ABANDONED BY
THE POPES   COUNT UGOLINO AT PISA   THE
BIANCHI AND NERI AT FLORENCE   CLOSING OF THE
GRAND COUNCIL AT VENICE   EXPEDITION OF THE
EMPEROR HENRY VII INTO ITALY. 1283–1313

CHAPTER VI

GREATNESS OF SOME GHIBELINE CHIEFS — DISORGANISA-
TION OF THAT PARTY BY THE PERFIDY AND INCONSIST-
ENCY OF THE EMPEROR LOUIS OF BAVARIA — EFFORT
OF THE FLORENTINES TO MAINTAIN THE BALANCE BE-
TWEEN THE POWERS OF ITALY — THEY FALL UNDER
THE TYRANNY OF THE DUKE OF ATHENS — HIS EX-
PULSION. 1314–1343

CHAPTER VII

REVIVAL OF LETTERS   REVOLUTIONS ATTEMPTED BY
TWO MEN OF LETTERS   ITALY RAVAGED BY THE
PLAGUE AND BY COMPANIES OF ADVENTURE   POWER
OF THE HOUSE OF VISCONTI   WAR BETWEEN THE
MARITIME REPUBLICS   DANGER AND FIRMNESS OF
THE REPUBLIC OF FLORENCE. 1344–1364

CHAPTER VIII

THE FLORENTINES CALL UPON THE CITIES OF ITALY TO
RECOVER THEIR LIBERTY   GREAT WESTERN SCHISM
WAR OF CHIOZZA   INSURRECTIONS OF THE POPU-
LACE AGAINST THE CITIZENS   CONQUESTS OF GIAN
GALEAZZO VISCONTI DUKE OF MILAN   HIS DEATH.
1365–1402

CHAPTER IX

ANARCHY IN THE DUCHY OF MILAN — THE VENETIANS CONQUER PADUA AND VERONA — THE FLORENTINES, PISA — FLORENCE, MENACED IN TURN BY LADISLAUS KING OF NAPLES AND FILIPPO MARIA VISCONTI, MAINTAINS AGAINST THEM THE EQUILIBRIUM OF ITALY. 1403–1432

CHAPTER X

COSMO DE' MEDICI CHIEF OF THE FLORENTINE REPUB-
LIC   DEATH OF THE LAST VISCONTI   EFFORTS OF
THE MILANESE TO RECOVER THEIR LIBERTY   THEY
ARE SUBJUGATED BY FRANCESCO SFORZA   CON-
SPIRACY OF STEFANO PORCARI AT ROME. 1431–1454

CHAPTER XI

ITALY LOSES ALL THE GREAT MEN WHO SHONE IN THE
PRECEDING PERIOD   THE REPUBLIC OF FLORENCE
ENSLAVED BY THE MEDICI   WAR OF THE VENETIANS
AGAINST THE TURKS   CONQUEST OF CYPRUS. 1454–
1478

CHAPTER XII

FREQUENCY OF CONSPIRACIES   THE LAST RESOURCE
OF THE ITALIAN PATRIOTS   THEIR ILL SUCCESS
CONSPIRACY OF THE PAZZI   ADMINISTRATION OF
LORENZO DE' MEDICI   HIS DEATH. 1470–1492

CHAPTER XIII

CHAPTER XIV

THE FRENCH MASTERS OF MILAN AND GENOA   THE
SPANIARDS OF NAPLES   THE GONFALONIER SODE-
RINI AT FLORENCE   CONQUEST OF PISA   LEAGUE
OF CAMBRAY AGAINST VENICE   THE MEDICI RE-
ESTABLISHED AT FLORENCE. 1499–1512

CHAPTER XV

CALAMITIES WITH WHICH THE FRENCH, SPANIARDS, AND GERMANS OVERWHELM ITALY   PILLAGE AND RUIN OF ALL THE GREAT CITIES   OPPRESSION OF THE ITALIAN NATION, AND LOSS OF ITS INDEPENDENCE. 1513–1530

CHAPTER XVI

OPPRESSION OF ITALY DURING THE LAST THREE CEN-
TURIES   SUCCESSIVE FALL OF ALL THE REPUBLICS
THEIR LAST CONVULSIONS

A HISTORY OF THE
ITALIAN REPUBLICS

INTRODUCTION

THE republics which flourished in Italy during the middle ages have neither been attached by ancient alliances, nor opposed by long rivalries and wars, to the powers which divide Europe at this day. From this it might be supposed that their history is altogether of secondary importance, and that each people, after having studied its own, should give precedence over that of the Italians to the history either of hereditary allies, or of those who, by a prejudice of barbarism, are called natural enemies. It would be a great error: history has no true importance but as it contains a moral lesson. It should be explored, not for scenes of carnage, but for instructions in the government of mankind. The knowledge of times past is good only as it instructs us to avoid mistakes, to imitate virtues, to improve by experience: but the pre-eminent object of this study— the science of governing men for their advantage, of developing their individual faculties, intellectual and moral, for their greater happiness—that political philosophy, began in modern Europe only with the Italian republics of the middle ages, and from them diffused itself over other nations.

After the destruction of the Roman empire, which carried away ancient civilisation with it in its fall, power henceforth, through many generations, belonged only to barbarians, exercising with their brutal passions the rights of conquest over human society. There was no longer a government, no longer an association of all the inhabitants of a country organised for the common good: society was divided between the conquerors and the conquered. The former, indeed, had a spirit of independence: they were companions united under their chief, to satisfy in common their rapacity and luxury; it was their glory to be feared, to be obeyed, and to be revenged. After having exhausted their caprices on the vanquished, they delighted in hearing such feats celebrated by their poets at festivals, as great deeds in which they took pride. For those, on the contrary, who had fallen under the yoke of the barbarians, there was no protection to be expected, there was no government formed even partly for their advantage— in short, there was no social bond. They were compelled to labour, that their conquerors might enjoy— to suffer and be humiliated, that those might pride themselves on their domination. Such was the state of Europe for a long period after the fall of the Roman empire—a state of which the history offers but little real instruction, and on which perhaps it may be as well not to dwell. We are easily seduced by the display of energy: the courage of the barbarians, employed only in crime and devastation, attracts us; long rivalries sometimes appear to us as a reason for hatred between descendants; and a poetic hue still disguises ages which can only teach us one lesson—to avert at all price their return.

Useful history, that of which the knowledge should be universally diffused, begins only with the period when the victors and vanquished, inhabitants of the same country, were fused into one people; and still more decisively when they became united by a single bond, the public good, at the period when the government belonged to the people, and not the people to the government. The fusion of conquerors and conquered was more or less rapid in the different states of Europe: in some it lowered the former, in others it raised the latter; and public order cannot be considered as having been established till the people were no longer confounded with the property which they created for the use of their masters. After the invasion of the barbarians, the people every where belonged, in the first instance, to the army; but, as the army must preserve its organisation to remain powerful, it could not exist without a chief: the power of the chief was often confounded with that of his soldiers, who sometimes found it advantageous to invest him with almost despotic authority. Thus it frequently happened that the chief, called by the barbarians king, from having been no more than the deputy chosen by the army, became its master. He had ruled for the army, by the army, and finally he ruled the army itself: government from being military became patrimonial; the people and the army belonged alike to the king, and were governed solely for the advantage of the king. In the midst of these governments, either military or patrimonial, when Gaul belonged to the Franks, Spain to the Visigoths, England to the Saxons, and at a later period to the Normans, or when each of these countries belonged to a king of the dominant race, Italy began early to feel, and to declare, that she belonged only to herself—to assume authority, and to exercise it for her own advantage. Italy, invaded by the barbarians, like the other western states, pillaged, oppressed, and disorganised, could, no more than they, repel the invaders or expel them, and constitute herself a single state. There, as elsewhere, the ancient social body was annihilated; but there, more than elsewhere, the principle of life remained in the fragments of the broken colossus: the Italians succumbed as a nation, but the component parts of their grand social union, their cities and towns, the first elements in some sort of what forms a nation, arose and defended themselves on their own account; every smaller association of men, which had survived the great one, had the courage to exist for itself—to feel that it had interests to protect, sentiments above fear, and virtues that deserved success. The Italians sought the good of all, not that of masters at the expense of slaves. Their hearts first told them, and their reason confirmed, that they had still a country: for her they set the first example of those public virtues which became the pattern of Europe. From the moment they formed their own governments, and formed them for the common good, they prospered: while every other nation suffered, they rose in intelligence as well as virtue. The exercise of commerce and the arts augmented their wealth, and fixed on them the attention of other nations; their example enlightened the smaller associations framed in the towns of the rest of Europe, and imitating them at a distance; their experience directed the meditations of some superior minds formed in the government of the Italian republics, who rose from the practice to the theory of civil society, and showed, not only to their own country, but to future nations and ages, the object to which all human associations should tend, and the best means by which to attain it.

In the mean time, while the Italian republics increased in population, intelligence, virtue, and wealth, the patrimonial governments of the rest of Europe advanced also, but in another manner. Nations made some slow progress in civilisation; their chiefs increased in power, not by the development of the resources of their people, but by the agglomeration of new states; their kingdoms, subject to the laws of inheritance and primogeniture, which always cause, and in no long period, the extinction of rich families, had grown, as the patrimony of the wealthy grows, by inheritance, by marriage, and by the abuse of power. The ancient sovereign families had, for the most part, become extinct, if not in all their branches, at least in the eldest; and their territories had accumulated on a few survivors in the younger branches. About ten powerful succeeded a hundred feeble princes. Towards the end of the fifteenth century, the chiefs of the French, German, and Spanish nations were tempted to invade Italy, allured by the marvellous opulence of a country where the plunder of a single town afforded sometimes greater riches than they could wrest from millions of their own subjects. The most frivolous pretexts sufficed; and, during forty years of war, that prosperous and beautiful country was ravaged by all the various nations which could find their way into Italy. The insatiable brigandage of these new barbarians at length destroyed the opulence which had allured them; but the soldiers of the north and west carried into their own countries, along with the treasures of the Italians, the instruction and example of a more advanced civilisation: numerous germs of a better state of things, carried away from the Italian republics of the middle ages, were spread over the rest of Europe. Let us not, while we now reap the harvest, forget the parent soil.

It is this first development of the Italian nation, thus instructive to every other, that we here purpose shortly to retrace. We have endeavoured to include in a single volume a summary of the events of which the Italian peninsula was the theatre, from the fall of the Roman empire to the end of the Middle Age. This summary will not satisfy the philosopher, who wishes to distinguish in the mass of general history the peculiar genius of each people, to follow institutions from their birth, to know their action and their defects, to study man in his various circumstances, and to see depicted individuals as well as nations. We refer those who can bestow time and attention on historical studies to the much larger work which we have already published on the same subject: they will there find ample details, and they will be put in the way to obtain still more. Proposing to ourselves here only a summary of facts, and a more luminous view of the ideas they suggest, in order to satisfy the curiosity of those who can give only a limited time and attention to the study of history, we have abstained from all references; we have considered it useless to cite authorities which we have made known elsewhere; and, above all, we have endeavoured to make the following pages universally intelligible without the aid of any other book.

CHAPTER I

STATE OF THE POPULATION OF ITALY AT THE FALL OF
THE ROMAN EMPIRE IN THE FIFTH CENTURY   ITALY
TORMENTED DURING FIVE CENTURIES BY THE SUCCES-
SIVE INVASIONS OF BARBARIANS   FIRST EFFORTS OF
TOWNS, IN THE TENTH CENTURY, TO DEFEND AND GOV-
ERN THEMSELVES

ANCIENT Italy lost her freedom in the conquests of the
Roman republic. Her numerous and warlike people had
long defended themselves, either in the chain of mountains which, issuing from the southern Alps, crosses the
whole length of Italy; or in the vast and rich plains to
the east of that chain, formerly occupied by the Cisalpine Gauls. This people disappeared; their cities, enlarged and embellished by the Romans, lost all independence, all remembrance of nationality; the land was
no longer cultivated but by slaves; when the Roman
republic itself in its turn also lost its freedom. Rome
held sway over the greatest part of the known world;
but, under the necessity of employing despotic authority, in order to secure the obedience of the army, and
the distant provinces, she finally became herself the
property of the master whom she had imposed on
others. One of the early successors of Augustus had
granted to every Italian the rights of citizenship in
Rome; but those rights had ceased to confer a participation in the sovereignty of the republic. On the
other hand, the inhabitants of the municipalities of
Italy, in becoming Roman citizens, renounced no one
of the rights of their native cities, of which they might
be either jealous or proud.

Italy continued to decline rapidly under the emperors: the component parts were no longer in due proportion. Rome contained about two or three thousand
senatorial families, whose luxury and splendour surpassed all the pomp now displayed by the greatest
nobles of our richest monarchies; but whose effeminacy
and pusillanimity shrunk from all the active offices of

life. These families were often decimated by despotism; their property was frequently confiscated; and they became rapidly extinct: but others arrived from the provinces to take their place. They were surrounded by an immense population, lodged in miserable houses, almost the only property they possessed. Rome contained several millions of inhabitants: the smallest number only exercised the necessary arts and employments of life, and even this more active part of the population (composed chiefly of foreigners and freedmen) left the manual work entirely to slaves; the remainder, all those who gloried in the title of Roman citizen, who had long despised every vocation but the military service, henceforward rejected even that, and lived in absolute idleness: supported by distributions of corn and largesses from the public treasury, they passed their days in the bath, the circus, and the amphitheatre. The state not only supported them, but took upon itself the charge of amusing them by gratuitous public spectacles. Whole families became extinct from the vices engendered by idleness; but their place was continually supplied by the crowd which flocked from the provinces to enjoy a life of indolence, largesses, immunities, and public shows.

Italy was covered with cities: the greater number of those now existing flourished in at least equal splendour in the time of the Roman empire; some, such as Milan, Verona, Bologna, Capua, were so considerable as to present an image of Rome, with their circus, their amphitheatre, their tumultuous and idle population, their riches, and their poverty. Their administration was nearly republican, most commonly composed, after the example of Rome, of a *curia*, or municipal senate elected by the people, and of duumvirs, or annual consuls. In all these towns, among the first class of inhabitants were to be found the proprietors of the neighbouring land, lodged in palaces with their slaves and freedmen; secondly, the artisans and shopkeepers whom their consumption established around them; lastly, a crowd of idle people, who had preserved just enough of land to supply, with the strictest economy, the means of existence. It does not appear that there was any prosperous manufactory in Italy. All manual labour, as well in towns as in the country, was executed by slaves. Objects of luxury, for the most part, came from Asia. War had for a long time been the only occupation of the Italians; for a long period, too, the legions had been levied partly among the Romans, and partly among their allies in Italy: but, under the emperors, the distrust of the master seconded the luxurious effeminacy of the subject, the Italians finally renounced even war; and the legions were recruited only in Pannonia, Gaul, and the other provinces bordering on the Rhine and the Danube. At a later period, the barbarians who menaced Rome were seduced by liberal pay to engage in its defence; and in the Roman armies the enemies of Rome almost entirely replaced the Romans. The country could not, as in modern states, supply the place of cities in recruiting the armies with a class of men accustomed to the inclemencies of the weather, and inured to toil. The only labourers to be found were an oppressed foreign race, who took no interest in public affairs. The Romans cultivated their land either by slaves purchased from the barbarians, and forced by corporal punishment to labour, or by *coloni partiarii*, to whom was given a small share in the harvest as wages: but, in order to oblige these last to content themselves with the least possible share, they were attached to the land, and nearly as much oppressed as slaves themselves. The proprietors of land varied between these two systems, according as the price of slaves varied, or the *colons* (peasants, labourers) were more or less numerous: no cultivator of the land had any property in it. The greatest part was united in immense domains, sometimes embracing whole provinces, the administration of which was intrusted to freedmen, whose only consideration was, how to cultivate the land with the least possible expense, and how to extract from their labourers the greatest degree of work with the smallest quantity of food. The agriculturists, as well what were called freedmen as slaves, were almost all barbarians by birth, without any interest in a social order which only oppressed them, without courage for its defence, and without any pecuniary resources for themselves; their numbers also diminished with an alarming rapidity, partly from desertion, partly from new invasions of barbarians, who carried them off to sell as slaves in other Roman provinces, and, finally, from a mortality, the necessary consequence of poverty and starvation.

Italy, nevertheless, was supposed to enjoy a constant prosperity. During the entire ages of Trajan and the Antonines, a succession of virtuous and philosophic emperors followed each other; the world was in peace; the laws were wise and well administered; riches seemed to increase; each succeeding generation raised palaces more splendid, monuments and public edifices more sumptuous, than the preceding; the senatorial families found their revenues increase; the treasury levied greater imposts. But it is not on the mass of wealth, it is on its distribution, that the prosperity of states depend: increasing opulence continued to meet the eye, but man became more miserable; the rural population, formerly active, robust, and energetic, were succeeded by a foreign race; while the inhabitants of towns sunk in vice and idleness, or perished in want, amidst the riches they had themselves created.

It was into this Italy, such as despotism had made it, that the barbarians penetrated. Eager for the booty which it contained and could not defend, they repeatedly ravaged it during the last two centuries of the western empire. The mercenary troops that Rome had levied amongst them for its defence, preferring pillage to pay, frequently turned their arms against those they were engaged to defend. They vied with the Romans in making and unmaking emperors; and generally chose them from their own ranks, in order to secure to the soldier a greater share of the property of the citizen. The booty diminished as the avidity of these foreigners increased. The pomp of the western empire soon appeared, to an army thus formed, an useless expense. Odoacer, of the nation of the Heruli, chief of the mercenaries who then served in Italy, suppressed it by deposing, in 476, the last emperor. He took upon himself the title of king, and distributed amongst his soldiers one third of the land in the most fertile provinces: he governed during seventeen years this still glorious country, as a rich farm which the barbarians had a right to cultivate for their sole use.

The mercenaries united under the sceptre of Odoacer were not sufficiently strong to defend Italy against a new invasion of barbarians. The Ostrogoths, encouraged by the Grecian sovereign of new Rome, the emperor of the east, arrived in 489, under the command of Theodoric, from the countries north of the Euxine to the borders of Italy: they completed the conquest of it in four, and retained possession of the Peninsula sixty-four years, under eight successive kings. These new barbarians, in their turn, demanded and obtained a portion of land and slaves: they multiplied, it is true; but became rapidly enervated in a delicious climate, where they had suddenly passed from the severest privations to the enjoyment of every luxury. They were at last conquered and subdued, in the year 553, by the Romans of Constantinople, whom they despised as the degenerate successors of the same nation which their ancestors had vanquished.

The invasion of the Lombards, in 568, soon followed the destruction of the monarchy of the Ostrogoths. Amongst the various hordes which issued from the north of Germany upon the southern regions, the Lombards were reputed the most courageous, the most cruel, and the proudest of their independence; but their number was inconsiderable, and they scarcely acknowledged any social tie sufficient to keep them united: accordingly, they never completed the conquest of Italy. From 568 to 774, twenty-one Lombard kings, during 206 years, succeeded each other without establishing their dominion either on the Lagunes, at the extremity of the Adriatic gulf, where such of the inhabitants of

Upper Italy as were personally the most exposed had taken refuge and founded the Venetian republic; or on the shores of the Adriatic, now called Romagna, governed by a lieutenant of the emperor of Constantinople, under the title of exarch of the five cities of Pentapolis; or on Rome, defended only by the spiritual arms of the patriarch of the western church; or on the southern coast, where the Greek municipalities of Naples, Gaëta, and Amalfi governed themselves almost as independent republics. The Lombards, nevertheless, founded a kingdom in northern Italy, of which Pavia was the capital; and in southern Italy the duchy of Beneventum, which still maintained its independence two centuries after the kingdom was subjugated.

From the middle of the eighth century the Lombards, masters of a country where the great towns still contained much wealth, where the land had lost nothing of its fertility, where the example of the vanquished had taught the vanquishers the advantage of reviving some agricultural industry, excited the envy of their neighbours the Franks, who had conquered and oppressed the Gauls, who despised all occupation but war, and desired no wealth but what the sword could give. They by repeated invasions devastated Italy; and at length, in 774, completed the destruction of the Lombard monarchy. For more than twenty years the popes or bishops of Rome had been in the habit of opposing the kings of France to the monarchs of Lombardy, who were odious to them, at first as pagans, and afterwards as heretics. Chief of the clergy of the ancient capital, where the power of the emperors of Constantinople had been nominally established but never felt, they confounded their pretensions with those of the empire; and the Lombards having recently conquered the exarchate of Ravenna, and the Pentapolis, they demanded that these provinces should be restored to Rome. The Frank kings made themselves the champions of this quarrel, which gave them an opportunity of conquering the Lombard monarchy; but Charles, the king who accomplished this conquest, and who was the greatest man that barbarism ever produced, in treating with Rome, in subjugating Italy, comprehended all the beauty of a civilisation which his predecessors had seen only to destroy: he conceived the lofty idea of profiting by the barbarian force at his disposal to put himself at the head of the civilisation which he laboured to restore. Instead of considering himself as the king of the conquerors, occupied only in enriching a barbarous army with the spoils of the vanquished, he made it his duty and his glory to govern the country for its best interests, and for the common good: he did more. In concert with Pope Leo III, he re-established the monarchy of the conquered as a western Roman empire, which he considered the representative of right, in opposition to barbaric force: he received from the same pope, and from the Roman people, on Christmas-day in the year 800, the title of Roman emperor, and the name of Charlemagne, or Charles the Great, which no one before had ever so well deserved. As king, and afterwards as emperor, he governed Italy, together with his other vast states, forty years: he pursued with constancy, and with increasing ability, the end he proposed to himself, viz. establishing the reign of the laws, and a flourishing civilisation: but barbarism was too strong for him; and when he died, in 814, it was re-established throughout the empire.

Italy had eight kings of the family of Charlemagne, reckoning his son and grandson, who reigned under him, and were, properly speaking, his lieutenants. Charles le Gros, great grandson of Charlemagne, was deposed in 888; after which ten sovereigns, either Italian or Burgundian, but allied to the race of the Franks, disputed, for seventy years more, the crown of Italy and the empire. In 951, Otho I of Saxony, king of Germany, forced Berenger II, who then reigned, to acknowledge himself his vassal: in 961, Otho entered Italy a second time with his Germans, was crowned at Rome with the title of emperor, and sent Berenger II to end his days in a fortress in Germany.

Thus, nearly five centuries elapsed from the fall of the ancient Roman empire to the passing over of the renewed empire to the Germans. For a long space of time Italy had been pillaged and oppressed, in turn, by barbarians of every denomination, who wantonly overran the country only to plunder, and believed themselves valiant because, though in small numbers, they spread terror over a vast extent, and imagined by bloodshed to give a dignity to their depredations. The country, thus exposed to so many outrages, did not remain such as the Romans had left it. The Goth, Lombard, Frank, and German warriors, who had successively invaded Italy, introduced several of the opinions and sentiments of the barbarian race, particularly the habit of independence and resistance to authority. They divided with their kings the country conquered by their valour. They caused to be ceded to them vast districts, the inhabitants of which they considered their property equally with the land. The Lombard monarchy comprehended thirty dukedoms, or marquisates; their number diminished under Charlemagne and his successors: but, at the same time, there rose under them a numerous class of counts and *vavasors*, amongst whom every duke divided the province that had been ceded to him, under condition that they should swear fealty and homage, and follow him to the wars. The counts, in their turn, divided among the warriors attached to their colours the land apportioned to them. Thus was the feudal system, which made the possession of land the warrior's pay, and constituted an hereditary subordination, founded on interest and confirmed by oath, from the king down to the lowest soldier, established at the same time throughout Europe. The Lombards had carried into Italy the first germs of this system, which had been developed by the Franks, and invigorated by the civil wars of Charlemagne and his successors: these wars rendered it necessary that every feudatory should fortify his dwelling to preserve his allegiance to his lord; and the country, which till then had been open, and without defence, became covered with castles, in which these feudal lords established their residence.

About the same time—that is to say, in the ninth century—cities began to rebuild their ancient walls; for the barbarian kings who had every where levelled these walls to the ground no longer opposed their reconstruction, the danger of being daily invaded by the rival princes who disputed the throne made them necessary; besides, at this epocha new swarms of barbarians from all parts infested Europe; the inhabitants of Scandinavia, under the name of Danes and Normans, ravaged England and France; the Hungarians devastated Germany and Upper Italy; the Saracens, masters of Africa, infested the southern coasts of Italy and the isles: conquest was not the purpose of any of these invaders; plunder and massacre were their only objects. Permission to guard themselves against continual outrages could not be withheld from the inhabitants of towns. Several thousand citizens had often been obliged to pay ransom to little more than a hundred robbers: but, from the time they were permitted by their emperors to rebuild their walls, to purchase or manufacture arms, they felt themselves in a state to make themselves respected. Their long suffering had hardened them, had accustomed them to privations and danger, and had taught them it was better to defend their lives than yield them up to every contemptible aggressor; at the same time, the population of cities, no longer living in idleness at the expense of the provinces of the empire, addicted themselves to industry for their own profit: they had, accordingly some wealth to defend. The ancient curiæ and municipalities had been retained in all the towns of Italy by their barbarian masters, in order to distribute more equally the burdens imposed by the conquerors, and reach individuals more surely. The magistrates were the chiefs of a people who demanded only bread, arms, and walls.

From the time when towns were secured by walls, their power rapidly increased; the oppressed from all parts sought refuge in them from the oppressors: they

carried with them their industry, and arms to protect
the walls that defended them. Every where they were
sure of a good reception; for every city felt it had
strength only in proportion to the number of its citizens: each vied with its neighbour in efforts to augment the means of defence, and in the reception given
to strangers. The smaller towns imitated the greater,
the villages those in their turn; and each had a castle,
or at least a tower, where the population, in case of a
sudden attack, might retire with the most precious of
their effects.

In the mean time the dukes, marquises, counts, and
prelates, who looked on these cities as their property,
on the inhabitants as men who belonged to them, and
laboured only for their use, soon perceived that these
citizens were ill disposed to obey, and would not suffer themselves to be despoiled; since they had arms,
and could defend themselves under the protection of
their walls: residence in towns thus became disagree-
able to the nobles, and they left them to establish
themselves in their castles. They became sensible that
to defend these castles they had need of men devoted
to them; that, notwithstanding the advantage which
their heavy armour gave them when fighting on horseback, they were the minority; and they hastened to
enfranchise the rural population, to encourage their
growth, to give them arms, and to endeavour to gain
their affections. The effect of this change of rule was
rapid: the rural population in the tenth and eleventh
centuries increased, doubled, quadrupled in exact proportion to the land which they had to cultivate.

Otho I, his son Otho II, and his grandson Otho III
were successively acknowledged emperors and kings of
Italy, from 961 to 1002. When this branch of the house
of Saxony became extinct, Henry II of Bavaria, and
Conrad the Salic of Franconia, filled the throne from
1004 to 1039. During this period of nearly eighty years,
the German emperors twelve times entered Italy at the
head of their armies, which they always drew up in
the plains of Roncaglia near Placentia: there they held

the states of Lombardy, received homage from their
Italian feudatories, caused the rents due to be paid,
and promulgated laws for the government of Italy.
A foreign sovereign, however, almost always absent,
known only by his incursions at the head of a barbarous
army, could not efficaciously govern a country which
he hardly knew, and where his yoke was detested. During these five reigns, the social power became more
and more weak in Italy. The emperors were too happy
to acknowledge the local authorities, whatever they
were, whenever they could obtain from them their
pecuniary dues: sometimes they were dukes or marquises, whose dignities had survived the disasters of
various invasions and of civil wars; sometimes the
archbishops and bishops of great cities, whom Charlemagne and his successors had frequently invested with
duchies and counties escheated to the crown, reckoning that lords elected for life would remain more dependent than hereditary lords; sometimes, finally, they
were the magistrates themselves, who, although elected
by the people, received from the monarch the title of
imperial vicars, and took part with the nobles and prelates in the *Plaids* (Placita), or diets of Roncaglia.

After a stay of some months, the emperor returned
with his army into Germany; the nobles retired to their
castles, the prelates and magistrates to their cities:
neither of these last acknowledged a superior authority
to their own, nor reckoned on any other force than
what they could themselves employ to assert what
they called their rights. Opposite interests could not
fail to produce collision, and the war was universal. In
the time of Conrad the Salic, the prelates almost
throughout Lombardy joined the cities against the nobles; and from 1035 to 1039 there was a general war
between these two orders of society. Conrad put an end
to it, by a constitution which is considered to be the
basis of feudal law. By this the inheritance of fiefs was
protected from the caprices of the lords and of the
crown, the most oppressive conditions of feudal de-

pendence were suppressed or softened, and the few remaining slaves of the land were set free.

The crown of Conrad the Salic passed in a direct line to his son, grandson, and great grandson. The first, Henry III, reigned from 1039 to 1056; the second, Henry IV, from 1056 to 1106; the third, Henry V, from 1106 to 1125. The last two reigns were troubled by the bloody quarrel between the Empire and the court of Rome, called the war of investitures. Rome had never made part of the monarchy of the Lombards. This ancient capital of the world, with the territory appertaining to it, had, since the conquest of Alboin, formed a dukedom, governed by a patrician or Greek duke, sent from Constantinople. The bishop of Rome, however, who, according to the ancient canonical forms, was elected by the clergy, the senate, and the people of his diocese, had much more authority over his flock than this foreign magistrate. He considered himself, too, as patriarch of the West, and the head of all the Latin churches. This authority, it is true, was not indisputably acknowledged by orthodox prelates; and the barbarians, who professed either paganism or Arianism, held it in contempt. The pontiff, however, who now began to take exclusively the name of Pope, had more than once successfully defended Rome with his spiritual arms when temporal ones had failed. When, in the year 717, an *iconoclast*, or enemy of images, filled the throne of Constantinople, the popes, under the pretence of heresy, rejected his authority altogether: a municipality, at the head of which were a senate and consuls, then governed Rome nearly as an independent state; the Greeks, occupied with their own dissensions, seemed to forget it; and Rome owed to this forgetfulness fifty years of a sort of liberty. The Romans found once more a faint image of their past glory: sometimes even the title of Roman republic was revived. They approved, notwithstanding, of pope Stephen II conferring on the princes of the Franks the dignity of patricians, in order to transfer to them the authority which the Greek magistrate exercised in their city in

the name of the emperor of Constantinople; and the
people gladly acquiesced when, in the year 800, Leo III
crowned Charlemagne as Augustus, and restorer of the
western empire. From that period Rome became once
more the capital of the empire. At Rome the chiefs of
the empire were henceforth to receive the golden
crown from the hands of the pope, after having received
the silver one of the kingdom of Germany at Aix-la-
Chapelle, and the iron crown of Lombardy at Milan.

Great wealth and much feudal power were, by the
gratitude of the emperors, attached to the see of Rome.
The papacy became the highest object of ambition to
the whole sacerdotal order; and, in an age of violence
and anarchy, barons notorious for their robberies, and
young libertines recommended only by the favour of
some Roman ladies, not unfrequently filled the pontifical chair. The other bishops selected were often no
better. The German emperors, on arriving at Rome,
were sometimes obliged to put an end to such a scandal,
and choose among the competitors, or depose a pope
who put all Christendom to the blush. Henry III
obliged the people to renounce the right which they
had hitherto exercised, and so greatly abused, to take
part in the election of popes. He named, himself, four
successively, whom he chose among the most learned
and the most pious of the clergy of Italy and Germany;
and thus powerfully seconded the spirit of reform which
began to animate the church from the eleventh century.

Amidst the convulsions to which society was exposed,
the wealth of the clergy had remained intact. The
kings whom it tempted dared not seize it for themselves; but they distributed it, with the dignities of the
church, among their favourites, their creatures—servile
priests, who had nothing ecclesiastical but the name.
These promotions excited a general clamour. Religious
men pretended that kings introduced corruption into
the body of the clergy—that they destroyed the independence which ought to belong to the ministers of
God. An ardent desire to purify the priesthood, by preventing these dignities from being distributed in purely

temporal views, was manifested; but it belonged to one of the greatest characters produced in the middle age to agitate all Christendom for the attainment of this end.

Hildebrand, born at Soana, in Tuscany, a man of the most obscure condition, but from the moment when he entered into orders distinguished for his talents, was sent by his convent to pursue his studies at Cluny, in France. He conceived, in his solitude, the plan of revolution, by which he proposed to himself the subjugation of the world to the sacerdotal power. In the universe he saw but God, the priest his sole minister, and mankind obedient. He designed that the whole priesthood should be moved by one single will, should know only one passion—that of establishing the power of Heaven. The whole church appeared to him corrupted: he undertook to reform it in its head, in its members, in the whole body of the faithful under its control. He anathematised all intervention of the secular power in the distribution of the dignities of the church; it was, he said, simony—making a commerce of the gifts of the Holy Spirit. The crime was the same, whether the people in their public assemblies, or nobles, or kings, took part in the election of prelates, or attempted to confer on them the investiture of even the temporal power attached to their bishoprics. In 1059, he obtained of the council of Lateran that the election of popes should be vested in the cardinals; and the nomination of all prelates in the chapters, jointly with the pope. To detach the clergy from human society, he proscribed and punished with severity the marriage of priests, which, till then, had been permitted or tolerated by some provincial councils, particularly in Lombardy. Finally, concentrating all the power of the church in the pope, he taught the priests to consider him as an unerring being, who became holy by his election—who could alone name and depose bishops—assemble, preside over, and dissolve councils: he was, he said, in short, a god upon earth—absolute master of all princes, who were bound to kiss his feet, and whom he could depose at will, by releasing their subjects from their oaths of fidelity.

Hildebrand accomplished, at least for a time, the immense revolution which he had undertaken: he changed the spirit of the popedom, of the clergy, and the people; and he enslaved kings. He procured, by his influence, the election of the four popes who preceded him in the chair of St. Peter, which he ascended himself in the year 1073, taking the name of Gregory VII. The popes his successors continued, after his death in 1085, to act upon his maxims, and seemed as if still animated by his spirit. Nevertheless, he experienced from the clergy, above all from those of Lombardy, a prodigious resistance. He tormented Italy and Germany with a constant civil war; he called in against Rome the Normans, who burnt the city, and sold almost all the inhabitants into slavery; he compelled his heroic rival, the emperor Henry IV, to do penance before him in the open court of Canosa, whilst the ground was covered with snow; he obliged him to remain three days and three nights in the habit of a penitent, barefooted and fasting, before he would grant him absolution. The successors of Gregory VII excited the two sons of Henry IV successively to revolt against him, and depose him. Henry soon died of a broken heart. Henry V, the second of these unnatural children, whose cause the pope had espoused, after having obtained the crown by the aid of the priests, became their enemy in his turn. During sixteen years he made war against the church, to maintain the independence of the imperial crown, and the rights of secular sovereigns over the fiefs held by the clergy. The people at length, wearied and exhausted, forced these two rival powers to an agreement, in which the rights of both were curtailed. In the diet of Worms, 1122, the emperor abandoned to the pope the investiture of bishops by the ring and crosier; while he reserved to himself the transmission of the regal rights attached to each bishopric by the concession of the sceptre. These were only exterior ceremonies; in fact, the people alone were deprived of their rights in the choice of their pastor. Sovereigns retained almost exclusively the nomination of prelates in their respective dominions.

The war of investitures, which lasted more than sixty years, accomplished the dissolution of every tie between the different members of the kingdom of Italy. Civil wars have at least this advantage, that they force the rulers of the people to consult the wishes of their subjects, oblige them to gain affections which constitute their strength, and to compensate, by the granting of new privileges, the services which they require. The prelates, nobles, and cities of Italy obeyed, some the emperor, others the pope; not from a blind fear, but from choice, from affection, from conscience, according as the political or religious sentiment was predominant in each. The war was general, but every where waged with the national forces. Every city armed its militia, which, headed by the magistrates, attacked the neighbouring nobles or towns of a contrary party. While each city imagined it was fighting either for the pope or the emperor, it was habitually impelled exclusively by its own sentiments: every town considered itself as a whole, as an independent state, which had its own allies and enemies; each citizen felt an ardent patriotism, not for the kingdom of Italy, or for the empire, but for his own city.

At the period when either kings or emperors had granted to towns the right of raising fortifications, that of assembling the citizens at the sound of a great bell, to concert together the means of their common defence, had been also conceded. This meeting of all the men of the state capable of bearing arms was called a *parliament*. It assembled in the great square, and elected annually two consuls, charged with the administration of justice at home, and the command of the army abroad. The militia of every city was divided into separate bodies, according to local partitions, each led by a *gonfaloniere*, or standard bearer. They fought on foot, and assembled round the *carroccio*, a heavy car drawn by oxen, and covered with the flags and armorial bearings of the city. A high pole rose in the middle of this car, bearing the colours and a Christ, which seemed to bless the army, with both arms extended. A priest said daily mass at an altar placed in the front of the car. The trumpeters of the community, seated on the back part, sounded the charge and the retreat. It was Heribert archbishop of Milan, contemporary of Conrad the Salic, who invented this car in imitation of the ark of alliance, and caused it to be adopted at Milan. All the free cities of Italy followed the example: this sacred car, intrusted to the guardianship of the militia, gave them weight and confidence. The nobles who committed themselves in the civil wars, and were obliged to have recourse to the protection of towns, where they had been admitted into the first order of citizens, formed the only cavalry.

The parliament, which named the consuls, appointed also a secret council, called a *Consilio di Credenza*, to assist the government, composed of a few members taken from each division; besides a grand council of the people, who prepared the decisions to be submitted to the parliament. The *Consilio di Credenza* was, at the same time, charged with the administration of the finances, consisting chiefly of entrance duties collected at the gates of the city, and voluntary contributions asked of the citizens in moments of danger. As industry had rapidly increased, and had preceded luxury—as domestic life was sober, and the produce of labour considerable—wealth had greatly augmented. The citizens allowed themselves no other use of their riches than that of defending or embellishing their country. It was from the year 900 to the year 1200 that the most prodigious works were undertaken and accomplished by the towns of Italy. They began by surrounding themselves with thick walls, ditches, towers, and counter guards at the gates; immense works, which a patriotism ready for every sacrifice could alone accomplish. The maritime towns at the same time constructed their ports, quays, canals, and custom-houses, which served also as vast magazines for commerce. Every city built public palaces for the *Signoria*, or municipal magistrates, and prisons; and constructed also temples, which to this day fill us with admiration by their grandeur and magnificence. These three regenerating centuries gave an impulse to architecture, which soon awakened the other fine arts.

The republican spirit which now fermented in every city, and gave to each of them constitutions so wise, magistrates so zealous, and citizens so patriotic, and so capable of great achievements, had found in Italy itself the models which had contributed to its formation. The war of investitures gave wing to this universal spirit of liberty and patriotism in all the municipalities of Lombardy, in Piedmont, Venetia, Romagna, and Tuscany. But there existed already in Italy other free cities, of which the experience had been sufficiently long to prove that a petty people finds, in its complete union and devotion to the common cause, a strength often wanting in great states. The free cities which flourished in the eleventh century rose from the ruins of the western empire; as those in Italy which preceded them in the career of liberty rose from the ruins of the empire of the East.

When the Greeks resigned to the Lombards Italy, which a few years before they had conquered from the Ostrogoths, they still preserved several isolated ports and fortified places along the coast. Venice, at the extremity of the Adriatic; Ravenna, at the south of the mouth of the Po; Genoa, at the foot of the Ligurian mountains; Pisa, towards the mouths of the Arno; Rome, Gaëta, Naples, Amalfi, Bari, were either never conquered by the Lombards, or in subjection too short a time to have lost their ancient walls, and the habit of guarding them. These cities served as the refuge of Roman civilisation. All those who had preserved any fortune, independence of mind, or hatred of oppression, assembled in them to concert the means of resisting the insolence of their barbarian masters. The Grecian empire maintained itself at Constantinople in all its ancient pride; but, with oriental apathy, it regarded these re-

mains as still representing its province of Italy, while
it did nothing for their defence. From time to time, a
duke, an exarch, a patrician, a catapan, or other magistrate, was sent, with a title announcing the highest
pretensions, but unaccompanied by any real force. The
citizens of these towns demanded money and soldiers
to repair and defend their fortifications; whilst the emperors, on the contrary, demanded that the money and
soldiers of Italy should be sent to Constantinople. After
some disputes, the Greek government found it prudent
to abandon the question, and shut its eyes on the establishment of a liberty which it despised, but which
perhaps might be useful in the defence of these distant
possessions; finally, the magistrates, whom these towns
themselves nominated, became the acknowledged de-
positories of the imperial authority. The disposal of
their own money and soldiers was allowed them, on
condition that nothing should be demanded of the emperors, who were satisfied to see their names at the
head of every act, and their image on the coin, without
exacting other acts of submission. This policy was not,
however, exactly followed with respect to Ravenna, or
afterwards to Bari. In these cities the representative of
the emperor had fixed his residence with a Greek garrison. Ravenna, as well as the cities appertaining to it,
denominated the Pentapolis, was conquered by the
Lombards between 720 and 730. Bari became then the
capital of the *thema* of Lombardy, which extended over
a great part of Apulia. We have already shown how
Rome passed from the Greek to the western empire:
we suspect, rather than know, that Genoa and Pisa,
after having been occupied by the Lombards, preserved their relations with Constantinople. The *pallium,*
or silk flag, presented for some time to the emperors,
was considered by them as a sort of tribute; but Venice
on the upper sea, Gaëta, Naples, and Amalfi, on the
lower, advanced more openly to independence.

From the invasion by Attila in 452, the marshes
called *Lagune,* formed at the extremity of the Adriatic
by the slime deposed by seven or eight great rivers,

amidst which arose innumerable islands, had been the refuge of all the rich inhabitants of Padua, Vicenza, Verona, Treviso, and other great cities of Venetia, who fled from the sabres of the Huns. The Roman empire of the west survived this great calamity twenty-four years; but it was only a period of expiring agony, during which fresh disasters continually forced new refugees to establish themselves in the *Lagune*. A numerous population was at length formed there, supported by fishing, the making of salt, some other manufactories, and the commerce carried on by means of these many rivers. Beyond the reach of the barbarians, who had no vessels, forgotten by the Romans, and their successors the Ostrogoths, they maintained their independence under the administration of tribunes, named by an assembly of the people in each of the separate isles. The Venetians looked upon the Ostrogoths, and their successors the Lombards, as heretics; so that religious zeal strengthened their aversion to the dominant powers of Italy. On the other hand, the population of each island forming a little separate republic, jealousies arose; their tribunes disagreed. To put an end to these factions, the citizens of every island met in a single assembly at Heraclea in 697, and elected a chief of maritime Venetia, whom they called doge, or duke. This title, borne by the Greek governors of the provinces of Italy, seems to indicate that the doge was considered a lieutenant of the emperor of Constantinople. The Venetians, in fact, persisting in regarding themselves as members of the eastern empire, never acknowledged the pretensions of Charlemagne and his successors to the dominion of all Italy. It was in 809, in a war against Pepin, son of Charlemagne, that the Venetians made choice of the island of the Rialto, near which they assembled their fleet, with their wealth collected on board, and built the city of Venice, the capital of their republic. Twenty years afterwards they transported thither, from Alexandria, the body of St. Mark, the evangelist. They chose him patron of their state. His lion figured in their arms, and his name in their language, whenever they would designate with peculiar affection their country or government.

While the Venetians disputed with the Lombards, the Frank and the German emperors, the little land on which stood their houses, they had also to dispute the sea that bathed them with the Slavonians, who had established themselves for the purpose of piracy on the eastern side of the Adriatic. Amidst them, on the same coast, several little cities inhabited by Greeks, but forgotten by the empire, endeavoured in vain to defend their liberties and municipal governments. In 997, these small towns of Istria and Dalmatia made alliance with Venice; consented to receive judges chosen by the doge, and to fight under his banner. With their aid Venice vanquished the pirates of Narenta and Croatia; and the doge from that period took the title of duke of Venice and Dalmatia.

The first magistrate of the republics of Naples, Gaëta, and Amalfi bore likewise the title of doge. These three cities, forgotten by the Greek emperors, and receiving no aid from them, still held by the ties of commerce to Greece. The inhabitants had devoted themselves with ardour to navigation; they trafficked in the Levant, and covered southern Italy with its rich merchandise. The country situated beyond the Tiber had been exposed to fewer invasions than Upper Italy. It had not, however, entirely escaped. A Lombard chief entered it in 589, and founded the great duchy of Benevento, which comprehended nearly the whole southern part of the peninsula. This dukedom maintained itself independent of the kingdom of the Lombards at Pavia, and had not been involved in its fall. It defended itself with valour against Charlemagne and his successors, who attempted its conquest; but in 839, at the end of a civil war, it was divided into the three principalities of Benevento, Salerno, and Capua. The Saracens had established colonies, in the year 828, in Sicily, which till then had been subject to the Greek empire: these Saracens, a few years afterwards, passed into southern Italy. The three republics of Naples,

Gaëta, and Amalfi preserved their independence by exciting enmity between the Lombards and Saracens, who equally menaced them; but these barbarians soon sank into the languor produced by the charms of a southern climate. It seemed as if they had no longer courage to risk a life to which so many enjoyments were attached. When they fought it was with effeminacy; and they hastened the termination of every war, to plunge again into the voluptuous ease from which it had roused them. The citizens of the republics had the advantage over them of walls and defiles; and, without being braver than the Lombards, maintained their independence against them for six centuries.

Southern Italy, till the year 1000, was disturbed only by the petty wars between the Lombard principalities, the republics under the protection of the Greek empire, the *catapans* of Bari, and the wandering bands of Mussulmans, whom love of plunder more than religious zeal had brought into Italy. But about this epoch there arrived at Salerno, and afterwards in Apulia, Norman adventurers, the second or third generation of those terrible Danish corsairs who had so long and so cruelly ravaged France, and who were already, in 912, established in Neustria, where they adopted Christianity and the French language. They retained the valour of their ancestors, their love of adventure, and passion for voyages. They first came in great numbers to visit as pilgrims the sanctuaries of southern Italy, and afterwards entered as soldiers into the armies either of the princes of Lombardy, the republics, or the Greeks of Bari, who had recently reconquered the whole of Apulia. They proved so superior in valour to all those to whom they were opposed, that these mercenaries soon made all the small states, among which they had come to seek adventures, tremble. In 1041, they conquered Apulia from the Greeks; in 1060, Calabria; from 1061 to 1090, Sicily: about the same time they subjugated the three Lombard principalities of Beneventum, Salerno, and Capua. The three republics were the last states in southern Italy which fell under the Norman yoke. We do not,

indeed, know the date of the conquest of Gaëta, the
records of the history of the town being very scanty.
But Amalfi, illustrious for the foundation, in the Holy
Land, of the hospital and military order of St. John of
Jerusalem, for the invention of the compass, and for the
preservation of the pandects of Justinian, surrendered
to the Normans in 1131. The leader of these last was
then Roger II; to whom the antipope Anacletus had,
the preceding year, given the title of king of the Two
Sicilies. Roger besieged, in 1138, the city of Naples;
which though, in turns, succoured by the emperor of
Germany and the republic of Pisa, was compelled also
to surrender.

The republic of Pisa, which vainly sought to save
from ruin these first Italian republics of the middle
ages, was a city which navigation and commerce had
enriched. Genoa, which soon became its rival, had escaped the pillage of these northern conquerors, and had
preserved a constant intercourse with Constantinople
and with Syria; from whence the citizens brought the
rich merchandise which they afterwards dispersed
throughout Lombardy. The Pisans and Genoese, invigorated by a seafaring life, were accustomed to defend
with the sword the merchandise which they conveyed
from one extremity to the other of the Mediterranean.
They were often in conflict with the Saracens, like them
addicted to maritime commerce, to which these last
frequently added piracy. The Saracens pillaged Genoa
in the year 936. In 1005 they entered a suburb of Pisa;
and again invested that city in the year 1012. Their
colonies in Sardinia, Corsica, and the Balearic Isles,
constantly menaced Italy. The Pisans, seconded by the
Genoese, in their turn attacked Sardinia, in the year
1017; but completed the conquest only in 1050. They
established colonies there, and divided it into fiefs, between the most illustrious families of Pisa and Genoa.
They also conquered the Balearic Isles from the Saracens, in the year 1113.

When, towards the end of the eleventh century, the
western world took up the dispute with the Saracens

for the sepulchre of Jesus Christ, Venice, Pisa, and Genoa had already reached a high point of commercial power; these three cities had more vessels on the Mediterranean than the whole of Christendom besides. They seconded the Crusaders with enthusiasm. They provisioned them when arrived off the coast of Syria, and kept up their communication with the west. The Venetians assert that they sent a fleet of 200 vessels, in the year 1099, to second the first crusade. The Pisans affirm that their archbishop Daimbert, who was afterwards patriarch of Jerusalem, passed into the east with 120 vessels. The Genoese claim only twenty-eight galleys and six vessels: but all concurred with equal zeal in the conquest of the Holy Land; and the three maritime republics obtained important privileges, which they preserved as long as the kingdom of Jerusalem lasted.

Such were the changes which the space of six centuries from the fall of the Roman empire accomplished in Italy. Towards the end of the fifth century, the social tie, which had made of the empire one body, became dissolved, and was succeeded by no other. The citizen felt nothing for his fellow-citizen; he expected no support from him, and offered him none. He could nowhere invoke protection; he every where saw only violence and oppression. Towards the beginning of the twelfth century, the citizens of the towns of Italy had as little to expect from abroad. The emperor of the Germans, who called himself their sovereign, was, with his barbarian army, only one enemy more. But universally, where the circle of the same wall formed a common interest, the spirit of association was developed. The citizens promised each other mutual assistance. Courage grew with liberty; and the Italians, no longer oppressed, found at last in themselves their own defence.

CHAPTER II

WHEN the inhabitants of the cities of Italy associated
for their common defence, their first necessity was to
guard against the brigandage of the barbarian armies,
which invaded their country and treated them as enemies; the second, to protect themselves from the robberies of other barbarians who called themselves their
masters. Their united efforts soon ensured their safety;
in a few years they found themselves rich and powerful; and these same men, whom emperors, prelates, and
nobles considered only as freed serfs, perceived that
they constituted almost the only public force in Italy.
Their self-confidence grew with their power; and the
desire of domination succeeded that of independence.
Those cities which had accumulated the most wealth,
whose walls enclosed the greatest population, attempted, from the first half of the twelfth century, to
secure by force of arms the obedience of such of the
neighbouring towns as did not appear sufficiently strong
to resist them. These greater cities had no intention to
strip the smaller of their liberty; their sole purpose was
to force them into a perpetual alliance, so as to share
their good or evil fortune, and always place their armed
force under the standard of the dominant city.

The long war of the *investitures*, between the Fran-
conian emperors and the popes, had given the first impulse to this ambition: as general interests were involved, as it was a question of distant operations and
common danger, the cities felt the necessity of alliances,
and of an active correspondence, which soon extended
from one extremity of Italy to the other. The smaller
towns soon found that this general policy was beyond

their means, and that the great cities, in which commerce and wealth had accumulated knowledge, and which alone received the communications of the pope or of the emperor, naturally placed themselves at the head of the league formed in their provinces, either for the empire or for the church. These two leagues were not yet known in Italy by the names of Guelph and Ghibeline, which in Germany had been the war cry of the two parties at the battle of Winsberg, fought on the 21st of December, 1140, and which had previously distinguished, the former the dukes of Saxony and Bavaria, devoted to the pope; the latter, the emperors of the house of Franconia. But although these two names, which seem since to have become exclusively Italian, had not yet been adopted in Italy, the hereditary affection respectively for the two parties already divided the minds of the people for more than a century, and faction became to each a second country, often served by them with not less heroism and devotion than their native city.

Two great towns in the plains of Lombardy surpassed every other in power and wealth: Milan, which habitually directed the party of the church; and Pavia, which directed that of the empire. Both towns, however, seem to have changed parties during the reigns of Lothario III and Conrad II, who, from the year 1125 to 1152, placed in opposition the two houses of Guelphs and Ghibelines in Germany. Milan, having during the first half of the twelfth century experienced some resistance from the towns of Lodi and Como, rased the former, dispersing the inhabitants in open villages, and obliged the latter to destroy its fortifications. Cremona and Novara adhered to the party of Pavia; Tortona, Crema, Bergamo, Brescia, Placentia, and Parma, to that of Milan. Among the towns of Piedmont, Turin took the lead, and disputed the authority of the counts of Savoy, who called themselves imperial vicars in that country. Montferrat continued to have its marquises. They were among the few great feudatories who had survived the civil wars; but the towns and provinces were not in subjection to them, and Asti was more powerful than they were. The family of the Veronese marquises, on the contrary, who from the time of the Lombard kings had to defend the frontier against the Germans, were extinct; and the great cities of Verona, Padua, Vicenza, Treviso, and Mantua, nearly equal in power, maintained their independence. Bologna held the first rank among the towns south of the Po, and had become equally formidable on the one side to Modena and Reggio, and on the other to Ferrara, Ravenna, Imola, Faenza, Forli, and Rimini. Tuscany, which had also had its powerful marquises, saw their family become extinct with the countess Matilda, the contemporary and friend of Gregory VII. Florence had since risen in power, destroyed Fiesole, and, without exercising dominion over the neighbouring towns of Pistoja, Arezzo, San Miniato, and Volterra, or the more distant towns of Lucca, Cortona, Perugia, and Sienna, was considered the head of the Tuscan league; and the more so that Pisa at this period thought only of her maritime expeditions. The family of the dukes of Spoleto had also become extinct, and the towns of Ombria regained their freedom; but their situation in the mountains prevented them from rising into importance. In fine, Rome herself indulged the same spirit of independence. An eloquent monk, the disciple of Abelard, who had made himself known throughout Europe, preached in 1139 a twofold reform, in the religious and political orders; the name borne by him was Arnold of Brescia. He spoke to men of the antique liberty which was their right; of the abuses which disfigured the church. Driven out of Italy by pope Innocent II and the council of Lateran, he took refuge in Switzerland, and taught the town of Zurich to frame a free constitution; but in the year 1143 he was recalled to Rome, and that city again heard the words "Roman republic," "Roman senate," "*comitia* of the people." The pope branded his opinions with the name of "heresy of the politicians"; and Arnold of Brescia, having been given up to him by the emperor, was burnt alive before the gate of the castle of St. Angelo, in the year 1155. But his precepts survived, and the love of liberty in Rome did not perish with him. In southern Italy, the conquests of the Normans had finally smothered the spirit of liberty; and the town of Aquila in the Abruzzi alone preserved any republican privileges.

Such was the state of Italy, when the Germanic diet, assembled at Frankfort in 1152, conferred the crown on Frederick Barbarossa, duke of Swabia, and of the house of Hohenstaufen. This prince was nephew to Conrad III, whom he succeeded; he was allied to the two houses of the Guelphs and Ghibelines, which had contended with each other for the empire, and was regarded, with good reason, by the Germans as their most distinguished chief. Frederick Barbarossa was not only brave, but understood the art of war, at least so far as it could be understood in an age so barbarous. He made himself beloved by the soldiers, at the same time that he subjected them to a discipline which others had not yet thought of establishing. He held his word sacred; he abhorred gratuitous cruelty, although the shedding of human blood had in general nothing revolting in it to a prince of the middle ages: but the prerogatives of his crown appeared to him sacred rights, which from pride, and even from conscience, he was disposed to preserve and extend. The Italians he considered in a state of revolt against the imperial throne and the German nation; and he believed it to be his first duty to reduce them to subjection.

Frederick Barbarossa, accordingly, in the month of October, 1154, entered Italy with a powerful German army, by the valley of Trent. He proposed to himself not only receiving there the crowns of Italy and the empire, and reducing to obedience subjects who appeared to him to forget their duty to their sovereign; but also to punish in particular the Milanese for their arrogance; to redress the complaints which the citizens of Pavia and Cremona had brought against them; and to oblige Milan to render to the towns of Lodi and Como, which it had dismantled, all the privileges which

Milan itself enjoyed. On arriving at Roncaglia, where the diets of the kingdom of Italy were held, he was assailed by complaints from the bishops and nobles against the towns, as well as by complaints against the Milanese from the consuls of Pavia, of Cremona, of Como, and of Lodi; while those of Crema, of Brescia, of Placentia, of Asti and Tortona, vindicated them. Before giving judgment on the differences submitted to his decision, Frederick announced his intention of judging for himself the state of the country, by visiting in person Piedmont and Montferrat. Having to pass through the Milanese territory on his way to Novara, he commanded the consuls of Milan to supply him with provisions on the road. The towns acknowledged that they owed the emperors upon their journeys the dues designated by the feudal words *"foderum, parata, mansionaticum,"* forage, food, and lodging: but the Germans, retarded in their march by heavy and continual rain, took two days to reach a stage which the Milanese supposed they would reach in one: provisions of course failed; and the Germans avenged themselves on the unhappy inhabitants by pillaging and burning the villages wherever sufficient rations were not found. Frederick treated with kindness the towns of Novara and Turin; but those of Chieri and Asti had been denounced to him as entertaining the same sentiments as Milan; the inhabitants fled at his approach, and he plundered and burnt their deserted houses. Arrived next before Tortona, he ordered the inhabitants to renounce their alliance with the Milanese; but they, trusting to the strength of the upper town, into which they had retreated, while Frederick occupied the lower part, had the courage to refuse. The Germans began the siege of Tortona on the 13th of February, 1155. They could not prevent the entrance of 200 Milanese, to assist in its defence. For sixty-two days did this brave people resist the attacks of the formidable army of Frederick, the numbers of which had been increased by the armed force of Pavia, and the other Ghibeline towns. The want of water compelled them at last to surrender; and the emperor allowed them to retire to Milan, taking only the few effects which each individual could carry away; every thing else was given up to the pillage of the soldiers, and the houses became a prey to the flames. The Milanese received with respect these martyrs of liberty, and every opulent house gave shelter and hospitality to some of the unhappy inhabitants of Tortona. Frederick meanwhile placed on his head, in the temple of Pavia, the iron crown of the kings of Lombardy; and began his march on Rome, to receive there the golden crown of the empire.

But the Germans who accompanied the emperor, notwithstanding the ardour with which they had undertaken this distant expedition, began to be tired of so long an absence from their home. The licence extended to their pillage and debauchery no longer appeared to them a sufficient compensation for tedious marches and the dangers of war. They pressed the emperor to advance towards Rome, and to avoid all quarrel with the great towns by which they passed, although almost all refused to admit them within their walls—providing subsistence and lodging for them in the suburbs only. The impossibility of maintaining discipline in a rapacious army, which beheld for the first time the unknown riches of commerce and the arts; the difficulty of avoiding quarrels between two nations, neither of which understood the language of the other, perhaps justified this precaution. Frederick thus passed by Placentia, Parma, Bologna, and Florence. He was not received even into Rome; his troops occupied what was styled the Leonine city, or the suburb built round the Vatican: he was there crowned by the pope, Adrian IV; while his army was obliged to repel the Romans who advanced by the bridge of St. Angelo and the *borgo** of Trastevere to disturb the ceremony. Frederick withdrew from Rome the following day; conducting his army into the mountains, to avoid the great heat of summer. The citizens of Spoleto, not having supplied

---

* Borgo is the communication between Trastevere and the Vatican.

with sufficient haste the provisions he demanded, he attacked, took, and burnt their city: sickness, however, began to thin the ranks of his soldiers; many also deserted, to embark at Ancona. Frederick, with a weakened army, directed his march on Germany by the valleys of the Tyrol. The citizens of Verona, who would not admit the Germans within their walls, constructed for him a bridge of boats on the Adige, which he hastily passed over, but had hardly gained the opposite bank, when enormous pieces of wood, carried down by the impetuosity of the current, struck and destroyed the bridge. Frederick had no doubt that the Lombards had laid this snare for him, and flattered themselves with the breaking of the bridge whilst he should be in the act of passing over; but he was no longer sufficiently strong to avenge himself.

The emperor at length returned into Germany with his barbarian soldiers. He every where on his passage spread havoc and desolation; the line by which he marched through the Milanese territory was marked by fire; the villages of Rosate, Trecale, and Galiata, the towns of Chieri, Asti, Tortona, and Spoleto were burnt. But whilst he thus proved his barbarism, he also proved his weakness. He did not dare to attack the stronger and more populous cities, which congratulated themselves on having shut their gates, and refused submission to him. Thus a year's campaign sufficed to destroy one of the most formidable armies that Germany had ever poured into Italy; and the example of ancient times encouraged the belief that it would be long before the emperor could again put the Germans in motion. The Milanese felicitated themselves on having preserved their liberty by their courage and patriotism. Their treasury was indeed empty; but the zeal of their opulent citizens, who knew no other luxury than that of serving their country, soon replenished it. These men, who poured their wealth into the treasury of the republic, contented themselves with black bread, and cloaks of coarse stuff. At the command of their consuls, they left Milan to join their fellow-citizens in rebuild-

ing, with their own hands, the walls and houses of Tortona, Rosate, Trecale, Galiata, and other towns, which
had suffered in the contest for the common cause. They
next attacked the cities of Pavia, Cremona, and Novara, which had embraced the party of the emperor,
and subjected them to humiliating conditions; while
they drew closer their bonds of alliance with the towns
of Brescia and Placentia, which had declared for
liberty.

But Frederick had more power over Germany than
any of his predecessors: he was regarded there as the
restorer of the rights of the empire and of the German
nation. He obtained credit for reducing Italy from what
was called a state of anarchy and revolt, to order and
obedience. His vassals accordingly flocked with eagerness to his standard, when he summoned them, at the
feast of Pentecost, 1158, to compel the submission of
Italy. The battalions of Germany entered Lombardy at
the same time by all the passes of the Alps. Their approach to Brescia inspired the inhabitants with so much
terror, that they immediately renounced their alliance
with Milan, and paid down a large sum of money for
their ransom. The Milanese, on the contrary, prepared
themselves for resistance. They had either destroyed
or fortified all the bridges of the Adda; flattering themselves that this river would suffice to stop the progress
of the emperor; but a body of German cavalry dashed
boldly into the stream, and, swimming across the river,
gained in safety the opposite bank. They then made
themselves masters of the bridge of Cassano, and the
whole army entered into the Milanese territory. Frederick, following the course of the Adda, made choice of
a situation about four miles from the ruins of the former Lodi. Here he ordered the people of Lodi to rebuild their town, which would in future secure to him
the passage of the Adda. He summoned thither also
the militias of Pavia and Cremona, with those of the
other towns of Lombardy, which their jealousy of Milan
had attached to the Ghibeline party; and it was not
till after they had joined him that he encamped, on the

8th of August, 1158, before Milan. His engines of war, however, were insufficient to beat down the walls of so strong and large a town; and he resolved to reduce the Milanese by famine. He seized their granaries, burnt their stacks of corn, mowed down the autumnal harvests, and announced his resolution not to raise the siege till the Milanese had returned to their duty. The few nobles, however, who had preserved their independence in Lombardy proceeded to the camp of the emperor. One of them, the count de Blandrate, who had before given proofs of his attachment to the town of Milan, offered himself as a mediator, was accepted, and obtained terms not unfavourable to the Milanese. They engaged to pay a tribute to Frederick of 9000 marks of silver, to restore to him his regal rights, and to the towns of Lodi and Como their independence. On their side, they were dispensed from opening their gates to the emperor. They preserved the right of electing their consuls, and included in their pacification their allies of Tortona and Crema. This treaty was signed the 7th of September, 1158.

Frederick, in granting an honourable capitulation to revolted subjects, whom he had brought back to their obedience, had no intention of renouncing the rights of his empire. He considered that he had preserved, untouched, the legislative authority of the diet of his kingdom of Italy. The Milanese, on the contrary, regarded their treaty as definitive; and were both astonished and indignant when Frederick, having assembled, towards the 11th of November following, the *placita* or diets of the kingdom at Roncaglia, promulgated by this diet a constitution which overthrew their most precious rights. It took the administration of justice from the hands of the consuls of towns, to place it in those of a single judge, and a foreigner, chosen by the emperor, bearing the name of *podestà;* it fixed the limits of the regal rights, giving them much more importance than had been contemplated by the Milanese when they agreed to acknowledge them; it deprived cities, as well as the other members of the empire, of the right of making private war; it changed the boundaries of territories appertaining to towns, and in particular took from Milan the little town of Monza, and the counties of Seprio and of Martesana, which the inhabitants had always regarded as their own property. Just motives had made the emperor and the diet consider these innovations necessary for the public peace and prosperity; but the Milanese regarded them only as perfidious violations of the treaty. When the podestà of the emperor arrived at Milan to take possession of the tribunal, he was sent contemptuously away. The Milanese flew to arms; and making every effort to repossess the different passes of the Adda, prepared to defend themselves behind this barrier. Frederick, on his side, assembled a new diet of the kingdom of Italy at Bologna, in the spring of 1159, and placed Milan under the ban of the empire.

The emperor did not yet attempt to reduce the Milanese by a regular siege. His army was neither sufficiently numerous to invest so large a town, nor his engines of war of sufficient force to make a breach in such strong walls; but he proclaimed his determination to employ all his power, as monarch of Germany and Italy, to ruin that rebellious town. The Milanese, accordingly, soon saw their corn mowed down, their autumn harvests destroyed, their vine stocks cut, the trees which covered their country either cut down or barked, their canals of irrigation broken: but the generous citizens of this new republic did not allow themselves to be discouraged by the superior force of such an enemy, or by the inevitable issue of such a contest. They saw clearly that they must perish; but it would be for the honour and the liberty of Italy: they were resolved to leave a great example to their countrymen, and to future generations.

The people of Crema had remained faithful to the Milanese in their good and evil fortune; but the siege of that town presented fewer difficulties to the emperor than the siege of Milan. Crema was of small extent, and could be invested on every side; it was also more accessible to the engines of war, though surrounded by a double wall and a ditch filled with water. The Cremonese began the siege on the 4th of July; and on the 10th, Frederick arrived to direct it in person. Four hundred Milanese had thrown themselves into the town, to partake the combats and dangers of their allies. The emperor, who regarded the besieged only as revolted subjects, sought to terrify them by the spectacle of punishments. Hostages had been sent to him by Milan and Crema: he ordered several of them to be hung before the walls of the town. Some were children of the most distinguished families: he caused them to be bound to a moving tower, which was brought so close to the attack that the besieged could not repel it without killing or wounding their own children. A cry of despair resounded along the walls of Crema. The wretched parents implored death from their fellow-citizens, to escape witnessing the agony of their children, and at the same time cried out to their children not to fear giving up their lives for their country. The battle, in fact, was not interrupted; and the moving tower was repelled, after nine of the young hostages who covered it with their bodies had been killed. During six entire months did the small town of Crema resist the whole army of the emperor. Famine at length accomplished what force could not; and on the 26th of January, 1160, the heroic inhabitants capitulated, abandoning their wealth to pillage, and their houses to the flames. For themselves, wasted by famine and fatigue, they obtained permission to withdraw to Milan.

The siege of Crema exhausted the patience of the German army. At this period, soldiers were unaccustomed to such protracted expeditions. When they had accomplished their feudal service, they considered they had a right to return home. The greater number, accordingly, departed; but Frederick, with immovable constancy, declared he would remain, with the Italians only of the Ghibeline towns, to make war against the Milanese; and placing himself at the head of the militias of Pavia, Cremona, and Novara, carried on the war a whole year, during which his sole object was to de-

stroy the harvests, and prevent the entrance of any
kind of provision into Milan. In the month of June,
1161, a new army arrived from Germany to his aid.
His subjects began to feel ashamed of having abandoned their monarch in a foreign country, amongst a
people whom they accused of perfidy and rebellion.
They returned with redoubled animosity, which was
soon manifested by ferocious deeds: they tortured and
put to death every peasant whom they surprised carrying provisions of any kind into Milan. The rich citizens of the republic had aided the government in
making large magazines, which were already in part
exhausted: an accidental fire having consumed the remainder, hunger triumphed over courage and the love
of liberty. For three entire years had the Milanese,
since they had been placed under the ban of the empire, supported this unequal contest; when, in the beginning of March, 1162, they were reduced to surrender at discretion. In deep despair they yielded up their
arms and colours, and awaited the orders of the emperor. Frederick, harsh and haughty, was not ferocious:
never had he put to death by the executioner rebels
or enemies whom he had vanquished. He suffered
nearly a month to elapse before he pronounced his
final determination; perhaps to augment the anxiety of
the subdued—perhaps, also, to pacify his own wrath,
which he at last vented on walls and inanimate objects,
while he pardoned man. He ordered the town to be
completely evacuated, so that there should not be left
in it a single living being. On the 25th of March, he
summoned the militias of the rival and Ghibeline cities,
and gave them orders to rase to the earth the houses
as well as the walls of the town, so as not to leave one
stone upon another.

Those of the inhabitants of Milan whom their poverty, labour, and industry attached to the soil, were
divided into four open villages, built at a distance of at
least two miles from the walls of their former city. Others sought hospitality in the neighbouring towns of
Italy; even in those which had shown most attachment

to the emperor. Their sufferings, the extent of their
sacrifices, the recollection of their valour, and the example of their noble sentiments, made proselytes to the
cause of liberty in every city into which they were received. The delegates of the emperor also (for he himself had returned to his German dominions), the podestas whom he had established in every town, soon
made those Lombards who had fought with him feel
only shame and regret at having lent their aid to rivet
his yoke on their own necks. All the privileges of the
nation were violated; justice was sacrificed to party interest. Taxes continually augmenting had increased six-
fold; and hardly a third part of the produce of the land
remained to the cultivator. The Italians were universally in a state of suffering and humiliation; tyranny at
length reached even their consciences. On the death of
pope Adrian IV, in September, 1159, the electing cardinals had been equally divided between two candidates; the one a Siennese, the other a Roman. Both
were declared duly elected by their separate parties;
the first, under the name of Alexander III; the second,
under that of Victor III. Frederick declared for the
latter, who had shown himself ready to sacrifice to him
the liberties and independence of the church. The former had been obliged to take refuge in France, though
almost the whole of Christendom did not long hesitate
to declare for him. While one council assembled by
Frederick at Pavia rejected him, another assembled at
Beauvais not only rejected but anathematised Victor.
Excommunication at length reached even the emperor;
and Alexander, to strengthen himself against Frederick,
endeavoured to gain the affections of the people, by
ranging himself among the protectors of the liberties of
Italy.

Frederick re-entered Italy in the year 1163, accompanied not by an army, but by a brilliant retinue of
German nobles. He did not imagine that in a country
which he now considered subdued, he needed a more
imposing force; besides, he believed that he could at
all times command the militias of the Ghibeline towns;

and, in fact, he made them this year rase to the ground the walls of Tortona. He afterwards directed his steps towards Rome, to support by his presence his schismatic pontiff; but, in the mean time, Verona, Vicenza, Padua, and Treviso, the most powerful towns of the Veronese marches, assembled their consuls in congress, to consider of the means of putting an end to a tyranny which overwhelmed them. The consuls of these four towns pledged themselves by oath in the name of their cities to give mutual support to each other in the assertion of their former rights, and in the resolution to reduce the imperial prerogatives to the point at which they were fixed under the reign of Henry IV. Frederick, informed of this association, returned hastily into northern Italy, to put it down. He assembled the militias of Pavia, Cremona, Novara, Lodi, and Como, with the intention of leading them against the Veronese marches; but he soon perceived that the spirit of liberty had made progress in the Ghibeline cities as well as in those of the Guelphs; that the militias under his command complained as much of the vexations inflicted by his podestas as those against whom he led them; and that they were ill disposed to face death only to rivet the chains of their country. Obliged to bend before a people which he considered only as revolted subjects, he soon renounced a contest so humiliating, and returned to Germany, to levy an army more submissive to him. Other and more pressing interests diverted his attention from this object till the autumn of 1166. During this interval his anti-pope, Victor III, died; and the successor whom he caused to be named was still more strongly rejected by the church. On the other side, Alexander III had returned from France to Rome; contracted an alliance with William, the Norman king of the two Sicilies; and armed the whole of southern Italy against the emperor.

When Frederick, in the month of October, 1166, descended the mountains of the Grisons to enter Italy by the territory of Brescia, he marched his army directly to Lodi, without permitting any act of hostility on the way. At Lodi, he assembled towards the end of November, a diet of the kingdom of Italy, at which he promised the Lombards to redress the grievances occasioned by the abuses of power by his podestas, and to respect their just liberties; he was desirous of separating their cause from that of the pope, and the king of Sicily; and to give greater weight to his negotiation, he marched his army into central Italy. The towns of Romagna and Tuscany had hitherto made few complaints, and manifested little zeal in defence of their privileges. Frederick hoped that by establishing himself amongst them, he should revive their loyalty, and induce them to augment the army which he was leading against Rome. But he soon perceived that the spirit of liberty, which animated the other countries of Italy, worked also in these: he contented himself, accordingly, with taking thirty hostages from Bologna, and having vainly laid siege to Ancona, he, in the month of July, 1167, marched his army towards Rome.

The towns of the Veronese marches, seeing the emperor and his army pass without daring to attack them, became bolder: they assembled a new diet, in the beginning of April, at the convent of Pontida, between Milan and Bergamo. The consuls of Cremona, of Bergamo, of Brescia, of Mantua and Ferrara met there, and joined those of the marches. The union of the Guelphs and Ghibelines, for the common liberty, was hailed with universal joy. The deputies of the Cremonese, who had lent their aid to the destruction of Milan, seconded those of the Milanese villages in imploring aid of the confederated towns to rebuild the city of Milan. This confederation was called the League of Lombardy. The consuls took the oath, and their constituents afterwards repeated it, that every Lombard should unite for the recovery of the common liberty; that the league for this purpose should last twenty years; and, finally, that they should aid each other in repairing in common any damage experienced in this sacred cause, by any one member of the confederation: extending even to the past this contract for reciprocal security, the league resolved to rebuild Milan. The militias of Bergamo, Brescia, Cremona, Mantua, Verona, and Treviso arrived the 27th of April, 1167, on the ground covered by the ruins of this great city. They apportioned among themselves the labour of restoring the enclosing walls; all the Milanese of the four villages, as well as those who had taken refuge in the more distant towns, came in crowds to take part in this pious work; and in a few weeks the new-grown city was in a state to repel the insults of its enemies. Lodi was soon afterwards compelled, by force of arms, to take the oath to the league; while the towns of Venice, Placentia, Parma, Modena, and Bologna voluntarily and gladly joined the association.

Frederick, meanwhile, arrived within sight of Rome. The Romans dared to await him in the open field; he defeated them with great slaughter, and made himself master of the Leonine city. The inhabitants still defending themselves in the Vatican, he dislodged them by setting fire to Santa Maria, the adjoining church; Alexander, in his fright, escaped by the Tiber. After his retreat the Romans took the oath of fidelity to the emperor, without, however, receiving his army within their walls; but fever, and the suffocating heat of the Campagna, soon began, by its ravages, to avenge the Italians: from the first days of August an alarming mortality broke out in the camp of the emperor. The princes to whom he was most attached, the captains in whom he had most confidence, two thousand knights, with a proportional number of common soldiers, were carried off in a few weeks. He endeavoured to flee from the destructive scourge; he traversed in his retreat Tuscany and the Lunigiana; but his route was marked with graves, into which every day, every hour, he deposited the bodies of his soldiers. He was no longer strong enough to vanquish even the opposition of the little town of Pontremoli, which refused him a passage; and it was by roads almost impracticable that he at length crossed the Apennines. He arrived at Pavia about the middle of September, and attempted to assemble a diet; but the deputies of Pavia, Novara, Vercelli, and Como alone obeyed his summons. He harangued the assembly with great vehemence; and, throwing down his glove, challenged the rebellious cities to a pitched battle. He passed the winter in combating, with his small remaining army, the league of Lombardy; but in the month of March, 1168, he escaped from the Italians, and repassed Mount Cenis, to return and arm the Germans anew against Italy. After his departure, Novara, Vercelli, Como, Asti, and Tortona also entered into the confederation, which resolved to found, as a monument of its power, and as a barrier against the Ghibelines of Pavia and Montferrat, a new city, on the confluence of the rivers Tanaro and Bormida. The Lombards named it Alexandria, in honour of the chief of the church, and of their league. They collected in it all the inhabitants of the different villages of that rich plain, which extends from the Po to the Ligurian Alps, and secured to them all the liberty and privileges for which they themselves had fought.

Frederick had sacrificed more time, treasure, and blood, to strengthen his dominion over Italy than any of his predecessors: he had succeeded for a long period in associating the German nation in his ambition. He persuaded the Germans that their interest and their honour were concerned in the submission of the Italians. They began, however, to feel tired of a long contest, from which they derived no advantage: other interests, affairs more pressing, demanded the presence of the emperor at home; and Frederick was obliged to suspend for five years his efforts to subdue Italy. During this period the towns of Lombardy, in the plenitude of their power and liberty, corrected their laws, recruited their finances, strengthened their fortifications, and finally placed their militias on a better war establishment. Their consuls met also in frequent diets, where they bound themselves by new oaths to the common defence, and admitted fresh members into the confederation, which at length reached to the extremity of Romagna.

Frederick, however, did not entirely abandon Italy. He sent thither Christian, the elected archbishop of Mentz, and arch-chancellor of the empire, as his representative. This warlike prelate soon felt that there was nothing to be done in Lombardy; and he proceeded to Tuscany, where the Ghibeline party still predominated. His first pretension was to establish peace between the two maritime republics of Genoa and Pisa, which disputed with arms in their hands the commerce of the East. As he found a greater spirit of pride and independence in the Pisans, he caused to be thrown into a dungeon their consuls, who had presented themselves at the diet of the Tuscan towns convoked by him at San Ginasio, in the month of July, 1173; he arrested, at the same time, the consuls of the Florentines their allies, while he studiously flattered those of Lucca, of Sienna, of Pistoia, and the nobles of Tuscany, Romagna, and Ombria; promising to avenge them on their enemies: but, said he, "to do so more effectually, you must first co-operate with me in crushing the enemies of the emperor." He thus succeeded in persuading them to second him in the attack which he meditated for the following spring on Ancona. This city, the most southern of all those attached to the league of Lombardy, contained about twelve thousand inhabitants, enriched by maritime commerce, and confident in the strength of their almost unassailable position. Their town, beautifully situated on the extremity of a promontory, which surrounded a magnificent port, presented on the side open to the continent only precipitous rocks, with the exception of a single causeway. The citizens had accordingly repulsed successfully for ages all the attacks of the barbarians, and all the pretensions of the emperors. The archbishop, Christian, arrived before Ancona in the beginning of April, 1174, and invested the city with an army levied among the Ghibelines of Tuscany and Ombria. The people of Ancona repulsed their attack with their accustomed bravery. But hunger, more formidable than the sword, soon menaced them. The preceding harvests had failed; their granaries were empty; and an enemy's fleet closed their port. They saw the harvest ripen, without the possibility of a single sack of corn reaching them. All human subsistence was soon exhausted: undismayed, however, they tried to support existence with the herbs and shell-fish which they gathered from their rocks, or with the leather which commerce had accumulated in their magazines. Such was the food on which had long subsisted a young and beautiful woman. Observing one day a soldier summoned to battle, but unable from hunger to proceed, she refused her breast to the child whom she suckled; offered it to the warrior; and sent him, thus refreshed, to shed his blood for his country. But to whatever distress the people of Ancona were reduced, they rejected every proposal to capitulate. At length the succour invoked from the Guelphs of Ferrara and Romagna approached; Christian saw the fires which they lighted on the mountain of Falcognara, about four miles from Ancona; and, unable to give them battle with an army exhausted by the fatigues of a long siege, he hastily retreated.

In the beginning of October, 1174, Frederick, at the head of a formidable army, again re-entered Italy. He passed from the county of Burgundy into Savoy, and descended by Mont Cenis. Suza, the first town to which he came on his passage, was taken and burnt; Asti, in alarm, opened its gates, and purchased its security from pillage by a heavy contribution; but Alexandria stopped the progress of the emperor. This city, recently founded by the league of Lombardy, did not hesitate to enter into a contest with the imperial power, for the sake of its confederates; although its mud walls were an object of derision to the Germans, who first gave this town the surname of Alexandria *della paglia,* or of straw. Nevertheless these walls of mud and straw, but defended by generous and devoted citizens, resisted all the efforts of the most valiant army and the most warlike monarch of Germany. Frederick consumed in vain four months in a siege, which was prolonged through the winter. The inundation of rivers more than once threatened him with destruction, even in his camp; sickness also decimated his soldiers. Finally, the combined army of the Lombard league advanced from Placentia to Tortona; and on Easter Sunday of the year 1175 Frederick found himself obliged to raise the siege, and to march for Pavia, to repose his army.

This last check at length compelled the emperor to acknowledge the power of a people which he had been accustomed to despise. The chiefs of the Lombard army showed themselves well prepared for battle; but still respecting the rights of their monarch, declined attacking him. He entered into negotiation with them: all professed their ardent desire to reconcile the prerogatives of the emperor and the rights of the Roman church with those of liberty. Six commissioners were appointed to settle the basis of a treaty which should reconcile these several claims. They began by demanding that the armies on each side should be disbanded. Frederick did not hesitate to comply: he dismissed his Germans, and remained at Pavia, trusting solely to the fidelity of his Italian Ghibelines. Legates from the pope arrived also to join the commissioners; and the negotiations were opened. But the demands of Frederick were so high as to render agreement almost impossible. He declared that he desired only his just rights; "but they must be those," said he, "which have been exercised by my predecessors, Charlemagne, Otho, and the emperors Henry III and Henry IV." The deputies of the towns opposed to this the concessions of Henry V and Lothario; but even these could no longer satisfy them. For the Italians, liberty had advanced with civilisation; and they could not now submit to the ancient prerogatives of their masters, without returning to their own ancient barbarism.

The negotiations were broken off, and Frederick sent to Germany for another army, which, in the spring of 1176, entered the territory of Como, by the Grisons. The emperor joined it about the end of May, after traversing, without being recognised, the territory of Milan. It was against this great town that he entertained the most profound resentment, and meditated a new attack. He flattered himself that he should find the citizens still trembling under the chastisement which he had before inflicted on their city. On the 29th of May, he met the Milanese army between Lignano and Barano, about fifteen miles from Milan. Only a few auxiliaries from Placentia, Verona, Brescia, Novara, and Vercelli had yet joined them. An impetuous charge of the German cavalry made that of the Lombards give way. The enemy pressed forward so near the *carroccio,* as to give great alarm lest this sacred car should fall into their hands. But in the army of the Milanese there was a company of 900 young men, who had devoted themselves to its defence, and were distinguished by the name of "the company of death." These brave youths seeing the Germans gain ground, knelt down; and invoking God and St. Ambrose, renewed their vow to perish for their country; then rising, they advanced with such impetuosity that the Germans were disconcerted, divided, and driven back. The whole army, reanimated by this example, hastily pressed forward. The Germans were put to flight; their camp was pillaged; Frederick was separated from his companions in arms, and obliged to conceal himself; and it was not till he had passed several days, and encountered various dangers, that he succeeded in reaching Pavia, where the empress was already mourning his death.

The defeat at Lignano at length determined Frederick to think seriously of peace, and to abandon pretensions which the Lombards resisted with so much energy. New negotiations were opened with the pope; and Venice was chosen, in concert with him, as the place for holding a congress. This town had withdrawn its signature from the league of Lombardy; it was acknowledged foreign to the Western empire, and might be considered neutral, and indifferent in the quarrel between the emperor and the free towns. The pope,

Alexander III, arrived at Venice on the 24th of March, 1177. The emperor, whose presence the Venetians feared, first fixed his residence at one of his palaces, near Ravenna; approached afterwards as far as Chiozza, and finally came even to Venice. The negotiation bore upon three different points—to reconcile the emperor to the church, by putting an end to the schism; to restore peace between the empire of the West and that of the East, and the king of the Two Sicilies; and finally to define the constitutional rights of the emperor and of the cities of Lombardy. Frederick was ready to submit to the church; and he had few subjects of dispute with the Grecian emperor, or the Norman king of the Sicilies: these parts of the treaty were not difficult to terminate. But that part which related to the league of Lombardy must be founded on a new order of ideas: it was the first pact that Europe had seen made between a monarch and his subjects; the first boundary line traced between authority and liberty. After long and vain attempts, the negotiators separated, contenting themselves only with obliging the emperor and the Lombards to conclude a truce of six years, bearing date from the 1st of August, 1177. During its existence, the rights on each side were to remain suspended; and the freedom of commerce was re-established between the cities which remained faithful to the emperor, and those which drew still closer their bonds of union by a renewal of the league of Lombardy.

The six years of repose, however, which this truce guaranteed, accustomed the emperor to submit to limitations of his authority. Thirty years had passed since the contest had begun between him and the Italian nation; age had now tempered his activity and calmed his pride. New incidents had arisen to fix his attention in Germany. His son, Henry VI, demanded to be associated in the sovereignty of his two kingdoms of Germany and Italy. A definitive peace only could restore to Frederick his rights and revenues in Lombardy, which his subjects there did not dispute, but which the truce held suspended. The adverse claims were hon-

estly weighed at the diet of Constance; reciprocal concessions were made both by the monarch and his subjects, and the peace of Constance, the basis of new
public rights for Italy, was at length signed on the 25th
of June, 1183. By this peace the emperor renounced
all regal privileges which he had hitherto claimed in
the interior of towns. He acknowledged the right of
the confederate cities to levy armies, to enclose themselves within fortifications, and to exercise by their
commissioners within their own walls both civil and
criminal jurisdiction. The consuls of towns acquired by
the simple nomination of the people all the prerogatives of imperial vicars. The cities of Lombardy were
further authorised to strengthen their confederation for
the defence of their just rights, recognised by the peace
of Constance. But, on the other side, they engaged to
maintain the just rights of the emperor, which were
defined at the same time; and in order to avoid all
disputes, it was agreed that these rights might always
be bought off by the annual sum of 2000 marks of
silver. Thus terminated, in the establishment of a legal
liberty, the first and most noble struggle which the nations of modern Europe have ever maintained against
despotism.

CHAPTER III

PROGRESS OF THE CITIES TOWARDS INDEPENDENCE, FROM
THE PEACE OF CONSTANCE TO THE DEATH OF FRED-
ERICK II   RELENTLESS ENMITY BETWEEN THE
GUELPHS AND GHIBELINES   FIRST PARTY CHIEFS
WHO ATTAINED TYRANNICAL POWER

THE generous resistance of the Lombards, during a war
of thirty years, had conquered from the emperors political liberty for all the towns of the kingdom of Italy.
The right of obeying only their own laws, of being governed by their own magistrates, of contracting alliances,
of making peace or war, and, in fine, of administering

their own finances, with the exception only of a certain revenue payable into the imperial treasury, was more particularly secured by the peace of Constance to the confederate cities of the league of Lombardy. But the Germans easily comprehended the impossibility of refusing to their allies the privileges which their enemies had gained by conquest; the liberties, therefore, stipulated by the peace of Constance, were rendered common to all the towns of Italy: and those which had been most distinguished by their attachment to the Ghibeline party, were often found the most zealous for the establishment and preservation of all the rights of the people. The cities, however, did not consider themselves independent. They were proud of the title of members of the empire: they knew they must concur in its defence, as well as in the maintenance of internal peace; reserving only that it must be in pursuance of their free choice and deliberation. They were in a manner confederates of an emperor, who acted on them rather by persuasion than orders; rather as a party chief than as a monarch: and as he was habituated to this compromise with public opinion in his relations with the princes of the empire, he yielded with the less repugnance to his Italian subjects. It is a circumstance highly honourable to the princes of the house of Hohenstaufen, which continued to reign sixty-seven years after the peace of Constance, that during this long period they made no attempt to infringe the conditions of the compact. They admitted, with good faith, all the consequences of the concessions made; they pardoned liberty, which the vulgar order of kings always regarded as a usurpation of the subjects on the rights of the crown.

It was not long, however, before the struggle was renewed between the emperor and most of the towns. It was supported with not less devotion and not fewer sacrifices; it caused not less calamity, whilst it endured; and it was crowned, at its close, with results not less happy. But the cities did not, as in the preceding struggle, engage in it for their own immediate interest; they rather seconded the policy of the holy see, which sought the independence of the church and of Italy, and did not cease to fight for the attainment of this object till the extinction of the house of Hohenstaufen.

Frederick I survived the peace of Constance seven years. During this period he visited Italy with his son Henry VI: he remained some time at Milan, where he was received with respect, and gained the affection of all the inhabitants, towards whom he testified the utmost trust, confidence, and kindness. Instead of endeavouring to intimidate Lombardy, and recover by intrigues his former power, he was occupied only with the marriage of his son Henry, whom he had previously crowned king of Germany, with Constance, sole heiress of the Norman kings who had conquered the Two Sicilies. The union of this crown with that of Germany and of Lombardy would have reduced the pope to be no more than the first bishop of his states; it would have disarmed the two auxiliary powers which had supported the league of Lombardy against the emperor; and it alarmed the church, in proportion as it flattered his ambition. The endeavours to prevent or dissolve this union gave rise to all the wars of the period embraced in the present chapter. Frederick Barbarossa did not see the commencement of them. When the news of the taking of Jerusalem by Saladin, on the 2d of October, 1187, had thrown all Europe into consternation, Frederick, listening only to his religious and chivalric enthusiasm, placed himself at the head of the third crusade, which he led into the East by land, and died the 10th of June, 1190, of a stroke of apoplexy, caused by the coldness of the waters of the little river Salef in Asia Minor.

Henry VI had worn for five years the German and Italian crowns, when he received in Germany, where he then was with his wife, news of the death of William II, king of the Two Sicilies, to whom Constance was successor; and a few months after, that of his father Frederick I. He immediately began his journey towards southern Italy. Tancred, a bastard of the race of the Norman kings, put in opposition to him by the Sicilians, defended, for some time with success, the independence of those provinces, but died in 1194; and Henry, who had entered the kingdom as conqueror, and had made himself detested for his cruelty, also died there suddenly, on the 28th of September, 1197. He left by his marriage with Constance only one son, Frederick II, hardly four years old, who lost his mother in the following year; and was, under the protection of the pope, acknowledged, child as he was, king of the Two Sicilies: but the imperial and Lombard crowns were withheld from him for several years.

From the peace of Constance to the death of Henry VI the free cities of Italy had, for the space of fifteen years, no contest to maintain against the emperors; but their repose and liberty were, during this period, constantly endangered by the pretensions of the nobility. The growing grandeur of the cities, and the decay of the imperial power, had left the nobles of Italy in a very ambiguous position.

They in some measure no longer had a country; their only security was in their own strength; for the emperor in resigning his power over the towns had not thought of giving an organisation to the nobles dispersed in castles. All the families of Italian dukes, and almost all those of marquises and counts, had become extinct; those who remained had lost all jurisdiction over their inferiors; no feudal tenure was respected; no vassal appeared at the baronial court, to form the tribunal of his lord. The frontiers of the kingdom of Lombardy were called *marches*, after a German word adopted into almost all the European languages, and the commander of these frontiers was called marquis; but the families of the powerful Tuscan marquises were extinct, as well as those of the marquises of Ancona, of Fermo, of Camerino, of Ivrea, and of those of the Veronese and Trevisan marches. There remained, however, on these frontiers some families which bore the same title, and had preserved some wrecks of these ancient and powerful marquisates: such was the marquis d'Este, in the Veronese march; the marquises of Montferrat, Palavacino, Malaspina, in the march of Ivrea; but they were not acknowledged as lords paramount, or lords of counties and baronies: there was moreover no other organisation than that created by the spirit of party. The nobles were not united by the hierarchical connection of the feudal system, but by the affections or antipathies of the Guelphs or Ghibelines. In general, the most powerful families among the nobles, those who had castles sufficiently strong, lands sufficiently extensive, and vassals sufficiently numerous to defend themselves, listening only to the ambition of courts, were attached to the Ghibeline party. Those families, on the contrary, who possessed castles capable of but little resistance, situated on accessible eminences, or in plains; those whose castles were near great towns, and too weak to support a contest with them, had demanded to be made citizens of the towns; they had served them in the wars of the league of Lombardy; they had since taken a principal share in the government, and they thus found themselves attached by common interests to the party of the Guelphs. Independent nobles were no more to be found in all the plains of Lombardy; there was not one who had not become citizen of some republic; but every chain of mountain was thick-set with castles; where a nobility choosing obedience to an emperor rather than to citizens, maintained themselves independent: these, too, attracted sometimes by the wealth and pleasures of towns, and sometimes desirous of obtaining influence in the counsels of powerful republics, in order to restore them to the emperor, demanded to be made citizens, when they thought it would open the way to a share in the government; and as war was their sole occupation, they were often gladly received by the republics, which stood in need of good captains. It was thus the Ghibeline family of Visconti, whose fiefs extended from the Alps to the Lago Maggiore, became associated with the republic of Milan. The house of Este, allied to the Guelphs of Saxony and Bavaria, and devoted to the pope, possessors of several castles built on the fertile chain of the Euganean hills, joined the republic of Ferrara; the parallel chain, which serves as a base to the Tyrolese Alps, was crowned with the castles of Ezzel, or Eccelino, of Romano, a family enriched by the emperors, entirely devoted to the Ghibeline party, and in process of time attached to the republics of Verona and Vicenza. In like manner were situated on the northern side of the Apennines the fortresses of the Ghibeline nobles, who excited revolutions in the republics of Placentia, Parma, Reggio, and Modena: on the southern side were the castles of other Ghibelines, in turns citizens and enemies of the republics of Arezzo, Florence, Pistoia, and Lucca: lower in the valleys of the Po, or in the upper vale of Arno, were the castles of the Guelphs, who had become decidedly citizens of the same republics.

The more the social tie was weakened in the kingdom of Lombardy, the more eager the nobles became to be admitted into the cities. Their wealth and military education soon led them, by the suffrages of their fellow-citizens, to the magistracy in this their new country. But if they displayed more talent for war and politics, they evinced much less subordination or submission to the laws. Their aversions were more virulent, and they gloried in cherishing them as a family inheritance. Accustomed in their castles to decide every question by the sword, they brought the same habits to the towns. Retaining, when they became inhabitants of cities, the wild independence of their ancient fastnesses, their houses were fortresses; thick walls, high and narrow windows, a massive door of oak, secured with iron bars, promised to resist more than one attack; and if they were at last forced, a high square tower still served for refuge. From these palaces of the nobles bands of assassins were often seen issuing, to rob or murder citizens, who were treated as enemies: chains were prepared to be thrown across the streets, and in an instant form barricades; behind which were seen ranged several hundred warriors. The peaceable citizens, to whom these quarrels were indifferent, never knew whether the peace they then saw reign around them should not

in a few hours be changed into a general war. The
power of the consuls seemed insufficient to repress these
fiery passions. All the towns saw the necessity of adopting the institution of the *podestà*, which they had received from Frederick Barbarossa. Their custom was
accordingly to choose annually, by their *consiglio di
credenza*, a foreign knight of arms, a warrior chosen
from one of the confederate cities. This knight, whom
they named *podestà*, was accompanied by two or three
doctors in civil and criminal law, dependent on him,
and acting under him as judges. The podesta received
at the same time the command of the militia, and the
power of the sword of justice, or of pronouncing and
causing to be executed sentences on criminals. He was
bound to render, at the end of the year, an account of
the manner in which he had performed his functions
to commissioners chosen by the people, and called
syndics, before whom he remained a certain number of
days amenable to justice. The towns believed that this
foreign judge would remain impartial amidst their factions; but the podesta himself rarely escaped participat-
ing in the deep hatred of the Guelphs or Ghibelines:
he needed also a hand of iron to maintain order among
nobles, so turbulent and so vindictive; he was accordingly invested with almost unlimited authority, the republics preferring rather to submit to his despotic sway
than to anarchy. The violence of faction, nevertheless,
and its natural consequence, a severe administration of
justice, inspired the citizens universally with a deep
hatred of the nobles, who were alone accused of having introduced disorder within their walls; and before
the end of the twelfth century all the Lombard cities
rose successively against the nobles, excluded them
from all public functions, and even expelled them from
the towns. Brescia, Padua, and Modena were the first
to set the example; but, after a few months, private
affection triumphed over public resentment, and the
nobles were recalled.

The death of Henry VI was followed by a general
war throughout the empire, which gave fresh activity

to the passions of the Italian nobles, and greater animosity to the opposing parties. The two factions in Germany had simultaneously raised to the empire the two chiefs of the houses of Guelph and Ghibeline. Philip I, duke of Swabia, and brother of Henry VI, had been named king of the Romans by the Ghibelines; and Otho IV, son of Henry the Lion, duke of Bavaria and Saxony, by the Guelphs. Their contest was prolonged to the 22d of June, 1208, when Philip was assassinated by a private enemy. The Germans, wearied with eleven years of civil war, agreed to unite under the sceptre of his rival, Otho IV, whom they crowned anew. The following year he passed into Italy, to receive from the pope the golden crown of the empire. But though Otho was the legitimate heir of the Guelphs of Bavaria, so long chiefs of the opposition to the imperial prerogatives, yet now wearing himself the crown, he was desirous of possessing it with these disputed rights: every one was denied him, and all his actions controlled by the pope. There was soon a declared enmity between the emperor and the pontiff, who, rather than consent to any agreement, or to abate any of his pretensions, raised against the Guelph emperor the heir of the Ghibeline house, the young Frederick II, grandson of Frederick I, hardly eighteen years of age, and till then reigning under the pope's tutelage over the Two Sicilies only. Frederick, excited and seconded by the pope, boldly passed through Lombardy in 1212, and arrived at Aix la Chapelle, where the German Ghibelines awaited, and crowned him king of the Romans and Germans. Otho IV in the mean time returned to Germany, and was acknowledged by Saxony. The civil war, carried on between the two chiefs of the empire, lasted till the 19th of May, 1218, when Otho died, without any attempt by either party to despoil his rival of his hereditary possessions. It was this civil war that caused the names of Guelphs and Ghibelines to be exclusively substituted for those of party of the church, and party of the empire. In fact, each noble family, and each city, seemed to consult only their hereditary affection, and not their political principles, in ranging themselves under either standard. The Guelphs placed themselves in opposition to the pope, to repel his Ghibeline candidate; and Milan, Placentia, and Brescia braved even excommunication to resist him: while, on the contrary, the Ghibelines of Pavia, Cremona, and of the March armed themselves with zeal against an emperor of the Guelph blood.

During this period, while the minority of Frederick II left so much time to the cities of Italy to consolidate their independence, and to form real republics, the person most influential and most prominent in history was the pope, Innocent III, who reigned from 1197 to 1216. He was a Roman noble, count of Signa, and only thirty-seven years of age when he ascended the papal chair: he had been raised to it by his reputation for sanctity and learning. A worthy successor of Gregory VII, he elevated, like him, the sovereignty of the popes; but he seemed to labour for that purpose with a fanaticism more religious, and a pride less worldly: all his efforts tended much more to confirm the power of the church and of religion than his own. Like Alexander III he did not refuse to join the people in their efforts to obtain liberty. provided that liberty bowed with awe before the authority of the church, and admitted no private judgment in matters of faith. He founded the two mendicant orders of Franciscans and Dominicans; new champions of the church, who were charged to repress all activity of mind, to combat growing intelligence, and to extirpate heresy. He confided to the Dominicans the fearful powers of the inquisition, which he instituted: he charged them to discover and pursue to destruction the new reformers, who, under the name of *paterini*, multiplied rapidly in Italy. He roused the fanatics of France to exterminate, in the Albigenses, the same reformers; and to destroy not only heretics, but all who, in the population of Languedoc, had any wealth or independence. He addressed his orders to the kings of Europe with a haughtiness worthy of Gregory VII; but always fixing his attention much more on discipline and the maintenance of morality than on the augmentation of his temporal power. Finally, he gained a triumph over the eastern church, which he had not sought, but of which he knew how to profit, in subjecting to his authority, and attaching to the Latin church, the patriarch of Constantinople, till then his rival and antagonist.

In the beginning of his pontificate, 1198, a crusade had been preached in France by Fulk de Neuilly. The crusaders, having resolved to go by sea to the Holy Land, borrowed vessels of the republic of Venice; and finding themselves afterwards too poor to pay the freight on which they had agreed, they offered instead of it their military services. After having subdued Zara, which had revolted against the republic, they bore up to Constantinople in concert with old Andrea Dandolo, doge of Venice. On the 12th of April, 1204, they took by assault the capital of the Grecian empire. They named a Frenchman, Baldwin, count of Flanders, emperor of Constantinople, and elected under him a Latin patriarch. They gave the kingdom of Thessalonica to an Italian, the marquis of Montferrat; and they abandoned to the Venetians, for their share of the conquest, one fourth and a half of the Roman empire. The doge was named lord of this portion of the empire, but the conquests of the republic were in reality limited to the island of Candia, some other isles, Achaia, and the Morea. These possessions beyond the sea diverted for a long period the republic of Venice from any participation in the affairs of Italy.

While Innocent III caused his power to be felt in the remotest parts of Christendom, he suffered to be constituted at Rome, under his own eye, a republic, the liberty of which he respected, and over which he assumed no authority. The thirteen districts of Rome named each annually four representatives or *caporioni;* their meeting formed the senate of the republic, who, with the concurrence of the people, exercised the sovereignty, with the exception of the judicial power. This power belonged, as in other republics, to a foreign military chief, chosen for one year, and assisted by civil judges, dependent on him, but bearing the name of *senator*, instead of podesta. We have still extant the form of oath taken by the first of these senators, named in 1207. By it he engages to guarantee security and liberty to the pope as well as to his brothers the cardinals, but promises no submission to him for himself.

In the beginning of the pontificate of Innocent III, two German generals, to whom Henry VI had given the titles of duke of Spoleto, and marquis of Ancona, held in dependence and subjection the provinces nearest Rome. Innocent, to revive the spirit of liberty, sent thither two legates; and by their interference, the cities of these provinces, built for the most part in the mountains, and without any means of becoming either wealthy or populous, threw off the German yoke, and made alliance with those cities which from the preceding period had entered into the league of Lombardy: thus two Guelph leagues were formed, under the protection of the pope; one in the March, comprehending the cities of Ancona, Fermo, Osimo, Camerino, Fano, Jesi, Sinigallia, and Pesaro; the other in the duchy, comprehending those of Spoleto, Rieti, Assisa, Foligno, Nocera, Perugia, Agobbio, Todi, and Città di Castello. These leagues, however, in accustoming the cities of these two provinces to regard the pope as their protector, led them afterwards to submit without resistance to the sovereignty of the church.

Other legates had been about the same time sent into Tuscany by the pope: they convoked at St. Ginasio, a borough situated at the foot of the mountain of San Miniato, the diet of the towns of that country. These provincial diets were in the habit of assembling frequently, and had till then been presided over by an officer belonging to the emperor, in memory of whom the castle in which he resided is still called San Miniato al Tedesco. These diets settled the differences which arose between cities, and had succeeded in saving Tuscany from the civil wars between the Guelphs and Ghibelines. Pisa, which had been loaded with favours by the sovereigns of the house of Hohenstaufen, and which had obtained from them the dominion of sixty-four castles or fortified towns on the shores of Tuscany, and over the isles of Corsica, Elba, Capraia, and Pianosa, proclaimed its determination of remaining faithful to the Ghibeline party, and its consuls withdrew from the diet convoked at San Ginasio; but those of the cities of Florence, of Sienna, of Arezzo, of Pistoia and of Lucca, accepted the protection of the pope, offered by his two legates, and promised to coalesce in defence of their common liberty. Numerous noble families in these towns, both Guelphs and Ghibelines, had demanded the rights of citizenship. Hitherto the magistrates succeeded in maintaining peace, and one of the objects of the leagues was to preserve it; but, in 1215, a Guelph noble of the upper Vale of Arno, named Buondelmonte, who had been made citizen of Florence, demanded in marriage a young person of the Ghibeline house of Amidei, and was accepted. While the nuptials were in preparation, a noble lady of the family Donati stopped Buondelmonte as he passed her door, and, bringing him into the room where her women were at work, raised the veil of her daughter, whose beauty was exquisite. "Here," said she, "is the wife I had reserved for thee. Like thee, she is Guelph; whilst thou takest one from the enemies of thy church and race." Buondelmonte, dazzled and enamoured, instantly accepted the proffered hand. The Amidei looked upon his inconstancy as a deep affront. All the noble Ghibeline families of Florence, about twenty-four in number, met, and agreed that he should atone with his life for the offence. Buondelmonte was attacked on the morning of Easter Sunday, just as he had passed the Ponte Vecchio, on horseback, and killed at the foot of the statue of Mars, which still stood there. Forty-two families of the Guelph party met and swore to avenge him; and blood did indeed atone for blood. Every day some new murder, some new battle, alarmed Florence during the space of thirty-three years. These two parties stood opposed to each other within the walls of the same city; and although often reconciled, every little accident renewed their animosity, and they again flew to arms to avenge ancient wrongs.

The death of Innocent III, and, two years afterwards, of Otho IV, broke the unnatural alliance between a pope and the heir of a Ghibeline family. The Milanese, excommunicated by Innocent for having fought against Frederick II, did not the less persist in making war on his partisans; well convinced that the new pope, Honorius III, would soon thank them for it. They refused Frederick the iron crown of Lombardy, preserved at Monza, and contracted an alliance with the count Thomas of Savoy, and with the cities of Crema, Placentia, Lodi, Vercelli, Novara, Tortona, Como, and Alexandria, to drive the Ghibelines from Lombardy. The Ghibelines defeated them on the 6th of June, 1218, in a great battle fought against the militias of Cremona, Parma, Reggio, and Modena, before Ghibello. This reverse of fortune calmed for some time their military ardour. The citizens of every town accused the nobles of having led them into war from family enmities and interests foreign to the city: at Milan, Placentia, Cremona, and Modena, there were battles between the nobles and the people. Laws were proposed, to divide the public magistracy in due proportions between them; finally the Milanese, in the year 1221, expelled all the nobles from their city.

The young Frederick re-entered Italy; and, after some differences with Honorius III, received from him, on the 22d of November, 1220, the crown of the empire. He afterwards occupied himself in establishing order in his kingdom of the Two Sicilies, where, during his minority, the popes had encouraged an universal insubordination. Born in the march of Ancona, at Jesi, in December, 1194, he was Italian as well by language as by affection and character. The Italian language, spoken at his court, first rose above the *patois* in common use throughout Italy, regarded only as a corruption of Latin: he expressed himself with elegance in this language, which, from his time, was designated by the name of *lingua cortigiana;* he encouraged the first poets, who employed it at his court, and he himself made verses; he loved literature and encouraged learning; he founded schools and universities; he promoted distinguished men; he spoke with equal facility Latin, Italian, German, French, Greek, and Arabic; he had the intellectual suppleness and finesse peculiar to the men of the south, the art of pleasing, a taste for philosophy, and great independence of opinion, with a leaning to infidelity; hence he is accused of having written a book against the three revelations of Moses, Jesus, and Mahomet, entitled "De Tribus Impostoribus," which no one has ever seen, and which perhaps never existed. His want of faith in the sacred character of the Roman church, and the sanctity of popes, is less doubtful; he was suspicious of them, and he employed all his address to defend himself against their enterprises. Honorius III, desirous of engaging him to recover the Holy Land from the Saracens, made him, in 1225, marry Yolanda de Lusignan, heiress of the kingdom of Jerusalem; after which, Honorius and his successor Gregory IX pressed him to pass into Palestine. A malady stopped him, in 1227, just as he was about to depart: the pope, to punish him for this delay, excommunicated him. He still pursued him with his anathema when he went to the Holy Land the year following, and haughtily testified his indignation, because Frederick, in the year 1229, recovered Jerusalem from the hands of the sultan by treaty, rather than exterminate the infidels with the sword.

Meanwhile the Guelph party again raised their standard in Lombardy, the republics of Milan, Bologna, Placentia, Verona, Brescia, Faenza, Mantua, Vercelli, Lodi, Bergamo, Turin, Alexandria, Vicenza, Padua, and Treviso, assembled their consuls in council at San Zenone in the Mantuan territory, on the 2d of March, 1226. They renewed the ancient league of Lombardy for twenty-five years; and engaged to defend in concert, their own liberty and the independence of the court of Rome. Three years afterwards, they sent succour to

Gregory IX, when he was attacked by Frederick II on his return from the Holy Land; and they were included in the treaty of peace between the pope and the emperor in 1230.

The pope, however, though defended by the arms of the Lombards, made them pay dearly for the favour which he showed in naming them to the emperor as his allies. He consented to protect their civil liberty only so far as they sacrificed to him their liberty of conscience. The same spirit of reformation which animated the Albigenses had spread throughout Europe: many Christians, disgusted with the corruption and vices of the clergy, or whose minds revolted against the violence on their reason exercised by the church, devoted themselves to a contemplative life, renounced all ambition and the pleasures of the world, and sought a new road to salvation in the alliance of faith with reason. They called themselves *cathari*, or the purified; *paterini*, or the resigned. The free towns had, till then, refused permission to the tribunals of the inquisition, instituted by Innocent III, to proceed against them within their walls; but Gregory IX declared the impossibility of acknowledging as allies of the holy see republicans so indulgent to the enemies of the faith: at the same time, he sent among them the most eloquent of the Dominicans, to rouse their fanaticism. Leo dà Perego, whom he afterwards made archbishop of Milan, had only a too fatal success in that city, where he caused a great number of *paterini* to be burnt. Saint Peter Martyr, and the monk Roland of Cremona, obtained an equal triumph in the other cities of Lombardy. The monk John of Vicenza had the cities of the March assigned to him as a province, where the heretics were in still greater numbers than in Lombardy, and included in their ranks some of the most powerful nobles in the country; among others, Eccelino II of Romano. The monk John announced himself the minister of peace, not of persecution. After having preached successively in every town, he assembled, on the plain of Paquara, the 28th of August, 1233, almost the whole population

of the towns of the March: he exhorted them to peace
in a manner so irresistible, that the greatest enemies,
setting aside their animosities, pardoned and embraced
each other; and all, with tears of joy, celebrated the
warm charity of this man of God. This man of God,
however, celebrated the festival of this reconciliation
by judging and condemning to the flames sixty cathari
in the single town of Verona, whose sufferings he witnessed in the public square; and afterwards obtained
full power from the towns of Vicenza and Padua to act
there in the like manner.

It was only a short period after the peace of Paquara
that Frederick II, believing he had sufficiently re-
established his power in southern Italy, began to turn
his attention towards Lombardy; he had no intention
of disputing the rights guaranteed by his grandfather
at the peace of Constance; but it was his will that the
cities should remain, what they ought to be by the
treaty, members of the empire, and not enemies of the
emperor. He had raised an army, over which he feared
neither the influence of the monks nor the pope. He
had transported from the mountains of Sicily, into the
city of Luceria, in the capitanate, and into that of
Nocera, in the principato, two strong colonies of Saracens, which could supply him with 30,000 mussulman
soldiers, strangers, by their language and religion, to
all the intrigues of the court of Rome. There was in the
Veronese march a man endowed with great military
talents, ambitious, intrepid, and entirely devoted to the
emperor—Eccelino III, of Romano, already powerful
by the great fiefs he held in the mountains, and the
number of his soldiers, whom Frederick made still more
so, by placing him at the head of the Ghibeline party
in all the cities. Eccelino, born on the 4th of April, 1194,
was precisely of the same age as the emperor. The
pope had summoned him to arrest his father, and deliver him to the tribunal of the inquisition as a paterino:
but though Eccelino knew neither virtue, pity, nor remorse, he was not sufficiently depraved for such a
crime.

As Frederick was on the point of attacking the
Guelphs of Lombardy on the south with the Saracens,
while Eccelino advanced on the east, he learnt that his
son Henry, whom he had in the year 1220 crowned
king of Germany, in spite of his extreme youth, seduced by the Guelphs and the agents of the pope, had
revolted against him. The Milanese, in 1234, sent deputies to offer him the iron crown, which they had refused
to his father. The latter hastened into Germany, and
ordered his son to meet him at Worms, where he threw
himself at the feet of his father, and entreated forgive-
ness. Frederick deprived him of the crown, and sent
him to Apulia, where he died a few years afterwards.
The emperor was obliged to employ two years in restoring order in Germany: he after that returned into
Italy by the valley of Trento, and arrived, on the 16th
of August, 1236, at Verona with 3000 German cavalry.
A senate of eighty members, nobles and Ghibelines,
then governed that republic: Frederick, by his address
in managing men, engaged them to name Eccelino captain of the people: this committed to him at the same
time the command of the militia and the judicial power;
and, in the state of excitement in which the parties
were, much more occupied with the triumph of their
faction than with the security of their liberty, gave him
almost sovereign power. Frederick, obliged to return
to Germany, left under the command of Eccelino a
body of German soldiers, and another of Saracens, with
which this able captain made himself, the same year,
master of Vicenza, which he barbarously pillaged, and
the following year of Padua. This last was the most
powerful city of the province, that in which the form
of government was the most democratic, and in which
the Guelphs had always exercised the most influence.
Eccelino judged it necessary to secure obedience by
taking hostages from the richest and most powerful
families; he employed his spies to discover the malcontents, whom he punished with torture, and redoubled
his cruelty in proportion to the hatred which he excited.
The same year, 1237, Frederick approached Mantua;

and thus giving courage to the Ghibeline party, made them triumph over the Guelphs, who had, till then, the ascendant in that city: he was joined there by 10,000 Saracens, whom he summoned from Apulia, and afterwards advanced into the Cremonese territory to attack the confederate army of the Guelphs, commanded by the consuls of Milan, who knew no other art of war but the bravery evinced in battle. Frederick was a more able captain: by manœuvring between Brescia and Cremona, he drew the Milanese beyond the Oglio, and finally succeeded, as they believed the campaign finished, in placing himself between them and their country at Cortenuova near Crema. The Guelphs, although thus cut off from retreat, boldly accepted battle on the 27th of November, 1237, and long disputed the victory. Their defeat was only the more bloody: it cost them 10,000 men killed or taken prisoners, with the loss of the *carroccio*. The fugitives followed during the night the course of the Oglio to enter the Bergamasque mountains; they would all, however, have fallen into the hands of the Ghibelines, if Pagan della Torre, the lord of Valsassina, and a Guelph noble, had not hastened to their assistance, opened the defiles covered by his fortresses, and brought them thus safely to Milan. The citizens of this town never forgot so important a service; and they contracted with the house of della Torre an alliance which subsequently proved dangerous to their freedom.

The defeat of the Guelphs at Cortenuova alarmed the towns of Lombardy, the greater number of which detached themselves from Milan. Frederick, entering Piedmont the following year, gave preponderance to the Ghibeline party in the cities of Turin, Asti, Novara, Alexandria, and several others. The constitution was not changed when the power in council passed from one party to another; but the emperor generally reckoned his partisans among the nobility, while the people were devoted to the church: accordingly, the triumph of the aristocracy generally accompanied that of the Ghibeline party. Four cities only, Milan, Brescia, Pla-

centia, and Bologna, remained at the end of the year
opposed to the imperial power. Frederick began his attack on them by laying siege to Brescia, but the Brescians dared to face the storm: they supported, during
sixty-eight days, the repeated attacks of the emperor,
rendered all his efforts fruitless, and forced him at last
to raise the siege with an army weakened and discouraged.

In the mean time, Gregory IX redoubled his efforts
to save the Guelph party from ruin. He saw, with alarm,
an emperor, master of the Two Sicilies and of Germany, on the point of vanquishing all resistance in
Upper Italy. He anticipated that this monarch, whose
mussulman soldiers were constantly passing through
the states of Rome, would escape the influence of the
church, and soon evince no respect whatever for a
religion which he was accused of not believing. Gregory had recourse to the two maritime republics of
Venice and Genoa, which, in general occupied with
their conquests and commerce in the East, seldom took
any part in the politics of Italy. He represented to
them, that they would be soon deprived of the freedom of the seas, if they did not make some effort to
save the champions of liberty and of the church in
Lombardy. He at length obtained their agreement to
contract an alliance with the four only surviving cities
of the league of Lombardy; and finally, towards the
beginning of the year 1239, he fulminated another sentence of excommunication against Frederick. This had
a greater effect than Gregory ventured to hope. A considerable number of nobles of Guelph origin, seduced
by court favours, had been won over to the imperial
party. They perceived that after the anathema of the
pope, the emperor distrusted them. The marquis d'Este
and the count di San Bonifacio were even warned that
their heads were in danger, and they made their escape from the imperial camp: all the other Guelph
nobles followed their example; and the Guelph cities
gained captains habituated to arms and familiarised
with higher ideas of politics.

Gregory began to think he should give still greater weight to the anathemas which he launched against the emperor, if they were sanctioned by a council. In the year 1241 he convoked at Rome all the prelates of Christendom. Frederick, who had been established at Pisa since the autumn of the year 1239, exerted himself to prevent the meeting of a council which he dreaded. While the two other maritime republics had declared for the Guelphs, Pisa was entirely of the Ghibeline party. The people were enthusiastically attached to the emperor, and among the nobles, a few only, proprietors of fiefs in Sardinia, headed by the Visconti of Gallura, had forsaken him for the Guelphs. The Pisans, further excited by their jealousy of the Genoese, promised Frederick that they would brave for him all the thunders of the church, and assured him they knew well how to hinder the meeting of the council. A considerable number of French prelates had embarked at Nice for Ostia, on board Genoese galleys. Ugolino Buzzacherino de Sismondi, admiral of the Pisans, lay in wait with a powerful fleet before Meloria, attacked them on the 3d of May, 1241, sunk three vessels, took nineteen, and made prisoners all the French prelates who were to join the council at Pisa. The republic loaded them with chains, but they were chains made of silver, and imprisoned them in the chapter house of the cathedral. Gregory, alarmed at this reverse of fortune, survived only a few months: he died the 21st of August, 1241; and the college of cardinals, reduced to a very small number, passed nearly two years before they could agree on a new choice. At last, on the 24th of June, 1243, Sinibald de' Fieschi, of Genoa, who took the name of Innocent IV was elected to the chair of St. Peter. His family, powerful in Genoa and in the Ligurian mountains, was also allied to many noble families, who possessed castles on the northern side of the Apennines; and this position gave him great influence in the neighbouring cities of Placentia, Parma, Reggio, and Modena. The elevation of a Fieschi to the pontifi-

cate gave courage to the Guelph party in all these
cities.

Frederick had recourse in vain to the new pope to
be reconciled to the church; Innocent IV was determined to see in him only an enemy of religion, and of
the pontifical power, and a chief of barbarians, who in
turns summoned his Germans and his Saracens to tyr-
annise over Italy. He drew closer his alliance with the
cities of the league of Lombardy, and promised them
to cause the emperor to be condemned and deposed
by an *œcumenical* council, as his predecessor would
have done; but instead of convoking the council in
Italy, he fixed for that purpose on the city of Lyons,
one half of which belonged to the empire, and the
other to the kingdom of France. He determined on
placing himself with the prelates whom he had summoned under the protection of St. Louis, who then
reigned in France. He went from Rome to Genoa by
sea, escaping the Pisan fleet which watched to inter-
cept his passage: he excited by his exhortations the
enthusiasm of the Guelphs of Genoa, and of the cities
of Lombardy and Piedmont, which he visited on his
passage; and arriving at Lyons, he opened, on the 28th
of June, 1245, in the convent of St. Just, the council
of the universal church. He found the bishops of
France, England, and Germany eager to adopt his passions; so that he obtained from them at their third
sitting, on the 17th of July, a sentence of condemnation
against Frederick II. The council declared, that for his
crimes and iniquities God had rejected him, and would
no longer suffer him to be either emperor or king. In
consequence, the pope and the council released his
subjects from their oath of allegiance; forbade them
under pain of excommunication to obey him under any
title whatever; and invited the electors of the empire
to proceed to the election of another emperor, while
the pope reserved to himself the nomination of another
king of the Two Sicilies.

Frederick at first opposed all his strength of soul
against the sentence of excommunication pronounced

by the council on him. Causing his jewels to be brought him, and placing the golden crown of the empire on his head, he declared before a numerous assembly that he would still wear it, and knew how to defend it; but, notwithstanding the enthusiasm of the Ghibeline party, the devotion of his friends, and the progress of philosophical opinions, which he had himself encouraged, the man whom the church had condemned was in constant danger of being abandoned or betrayed. The mendicant monks every where excited conspiracies against him. They took advantage of the terrors inspired by sickness and age, to make sinners return, as they said, to the ways of salvation, and desired them to make amends for their past transgressions, by delivering the church of God from its most dangerous enemy. Insurrections frequently broke forth in one or other of the Two Sicilies; still oftener the emperor discovered amongst his courtiers plots to destroy him, either by the dagger or poison; even his private secretary, his intimate friend, Pietro delle Vigne, whom he had raised from abject poverty, to whom he had intrusted his most important affairs, gave ear to the counsel of the monks, and promised to poison his master. Frederick, on his part, became suspicious and cruel: his distrust fell on his most faithful friends; and the executions which he ordered sometimes preceded the proofs of guilt. He had confided Germany to his son Conrad, and the exclusive government of the Veronese marches to Eccelino. The hatred which this ferocious man excited by his crimes fell on the emperor. Eccelino imprisoned in the most loathsome dungeons those whom he considered his enemies, and frequently put them to death by torture, or suffered them to perish by hunger: he was well aware that the relatives of these victims must also be his enemies: they were, in their turn, arrested; and the more he sacrificed to his barbarity, the more he was called upon to strike. The citizens of Milan, Mantua, Bergamo, and Brescia every day heard of new and horrible crimes committed by the governor of the marches; they conceived the greater detestation of the

Ghibeline party, and entertained the firmer determination to repel Frederick. He, on the contrary, had no
thoughts of attacking them: he established himself during the council of Lyons at Turin, and thence entered
into a negotiation with St. Louis, to obtain by his mediation a reconciliation with the church, to which he made,
in token of his submission, the offer to accompany
Louis to the Holy Land.

The revolt of Parma, on the 16th of June, 1247,
obliged Frederick to resume his arms at a moment when
he was least disposed. The friends and relatives of
pope Innocent IV, the Guelph nobles of the houses of
Corregio, Lupi, and Rossi, re-entering Parma, whence
they had been exiled, triumphed over their adversaries,
and in their turn expelled them from the city. Frederick was determined at any price to recover Parma. He
sent for a numerous band of Saracens from Apulia,
commanded by one of his natural sons, named Frederick, to whom he gave the title of king of Antioch. He
assembled the Lombard Ghibelines, under the command of another of his illegitimate sons, named Hans
or Hensius, called by him king of Sardinia, and whom
he had made imperial vicar in Lombardy. Eccelino arrived too at his camp from the Veronese march, with
the militias of Padua, Vicenza, and Verona; and the
soldiers whom he had raised in his hereditary fiefs. On
the other side, the Guelphs of Lombardy hastened to
send succour to a city which had just sacrificed itself
for them. The Milanese set the example; the militias
of Mantua, Placentia, and Ferrara followed it; and the
Guelphs, who had been exiled from Reggio, Modena,
and other Ghibeline cities, thinking they served their
country in fighting for their faction, arrived in great
numbers to shut themselves up in Parma. Frederick
was prevented from hanging the hostages given previous to the revolt, before the walls of the city, by the
militia of Pavia; who declared it was with the sword
of Ghibeline soldiers only, and not with that of the
executioner, that they would secure the throne of the
emperor. The siege made little progress; the winter had

begun, but Frederick persisted in his attempt. He proclaimed his determination to rase Parma to the ground,
and to transfer those of the inhabitants who should be
spared into his fortified camp, of which he would make
a new town, called Vittoria. This camp, which he
quitted on a hawking party, on the 8th of February,
1248, was in his absence surprised by a sortie of a
Guelph army from Parma, taken, and pillaged, his soldiers were dispersed, and the emperor had the humiliation of being forced to raise the siege.

Before this event, he had sent his son, the king of
Antioch, into Tuscany with 1600 German cavalry, to
secure Florence to his party; where, since the death of
Buondelmonte, the Guelphs and Ghibelines, always in
opposition, had not ceased fighting. There was seldom
an assembly, a festival, a public ceremony, without
some offence given, either by one or other of the
parties. Both flew to arms; chains were thrown across
the streets; barricades were immediately formed, and
in every quarter, round every noble family; the more
contiguous, who had the most frequent causes of quarrel, fought at the same time in ten different places.
Nevertheless the republic was supposed to lean towards
the Guelph party; and the Florentine Ghibelines, in
their relations with other people, had never sought to
separate from their fellow-countrymen, or to place
themselves in opposition to their magistrates. Frederick,
fearing to lose Florence, wrote to the Uberti, the chiefs
of the Ghibeline faction, to assemble secretly in their
palace all their party, to attack afterwards in concert
and at once all the posts of the Guelphs; whilst his son,
the king of Antioch, should present himself at the gates,
and thus expel their adversaries from the city. This
plan was executed on the night of Candlemas, 1248:
the barricades of the Guelphs were forced in every
quarter, because they defended themselves in small
bands against the whole of the opposite party. The
Ghibelines, masters of the town, ordered all the
Guelphs to quit it. They afterwards demolished thirty-
six palaces belonging to the same number of the most

illustrious families of that party; and intimidating the other cities of Tuscany, they constrained them to follow their example, and declare for the emperor.

Frederick II, after the check experienced by him at Parma, returned to his kingdom of the Two Sicilies, and left to his son Hensius, who established himself at Modena, the direction of the war in Lombardy. The pope, however, had sent a legate, the cardinal Octavian degli Ubaldini, to the Guelph cities, to engage them to pursue their victory, and punish the imperial party for what he called their revolt against the church. The powerful city of Bologna, already celebrated for its university, and superior to the neighbouring ones by its wealth, its population, and the zeal which a democratic government excites, undertook to make the Guelph party triumph throughout the Cispadane region. Bologna first attacked Romagna, and forced the towns of Imola, Faenza, Forli, and Cervia to expel the Ghibelines, and declare for the church. The Bolognese next turned their arms against Modena. The Modenese cavalry, entering Bologna one day by surprise, carried off from a public fountain a bucket, which henceforth was preserved in the tower of Modena as a glorious trophy. The war which followed furnished Tassoni with the subject of his mock-heroic poem, entitled "La Secchia Rapita." The vengeance of the Bolognese was, however, any thing but burlesque; after several bloody battles, the two armies finally met at Fossalta on the 26th of May, 1249. Philip Ugoni of Brescia, who was this year podesta of Bologna, commanded the Guelph army, in which was united a detachment from the militias of all the cities of the league of Lombardy. The Ghibelines were led by king Hensius: each army consisted of from fifteen to twenty thousand combatants. The battle was long and bloody, but ended with the complete defeat of the Ghibeline party; king Hensius himself fell into the hands of the conquerors: he was immediately taken to Bologna, and confined in the palace of the podesta. The senate of that city rejected all offers of ransom, all intercession in his favour. He was entertained in a splendid manner, but kept a prisoner during the rest of his life, which lasted for twenty-two years.

This last check overwhelmed Frederick. He had now during thirty years combated the church and the Guelph party: his bodily as well as mental energy was worn out in this long contest. His life was embittered by the treason of those whom he believed his friends, by the disasters of his partisans, and by the misfortunes which had pursued him even in his own family. He saw his power in Italy decline; while the crown of Germany was disputed with his son Conrad, by competitors favoured by the church. He appeared to be at length himself disturbed by the excommunications of the pope, and the fear of that hell with which he had been so incessantly menaced. He implored anew the assistance and mediation of St. Louis of France, who was then in the isle of Cyprus. He provided magnificently for the wants of the crusade army, which this king commanded: he solicited leave to join it. He offered to engage never to return from the Holy Land, and to submit to the most humiliating expiations which the church could impose. He succeeded in inspiring St. Louis with interest and gratitude. Frederick, while waiting the effect of St. Louis's good offices, seemed occupied solely in the affairs of his kingdom of the Two Sicilies, where he restored order, and established a prosperity not to be seen elsewhere in Europe. On the 13th of December, 1250, he was seized with a dysentery, of which he died, in the fifty-sixth year of his age, at his castle of Florentino, in the capitanate where he had fixed his residence.

CHAPTER IV

THE Italian cities, which for the most part date the
commencement of their liberty from the conflicts between the sovereigns of Italy and Germany, or the
invasion of Otho the Great, in 951, had already, at the
death of Frederick II, enjoyed for three centuries the
protection and progressive improvement of their municipal constitutions. These three centuries, with reference
to the rest of Europe, are utterly barbarous. Their
history is every where obscure and imperfectly known.
It records only some great revolution, or the victories
and calamities of princes; the people are always left in
the shade: a writer would have thought it beneath him
to occupy himself about the fate of plebeians; they
were not supposed to be worthy of history. The towns
of Italy, so prodigiously superior to all others in wealth,
intelligence, energy, and independence, were equally
regardless of preserving any record of past times. Some
grave chroniclers preserved the memory of an important crisis, but in general the cities passed whole centuries without leaving any written memorial; thinking
it perhaps good policy not to attract notice, and to
envelope themselves in obscurity. They, however, of
necessity departed from this system in the last century,
owing to the two conflicts, in both of which they remained victorious. From 1150 to 1183, they had fought
to obtain the peace of Constance, which they regarded
as their constitutional charter. From 1183 to 1250, they
preserved the full exercise of the privileges which they
had so gloriously acquired: but while they continually
advanced in opulence, while intelligence and the arts
became more and more developed, they were led by
two passions, equally honourable, to range themselves

under two opposite banners. One party, listening only
to their faith, their attachment, and their gratitude to
a family which had given them many great sovereigns,
were ready to venture their all for the cause of the
Ghibelines; the other, alarmed for the independence of
the church, and the liberty of Italy, by the always increasing grandeur of the house of Hohenstaufen, were
not less resolute in their endeavours to wrest from it
the sceptre which menaced them. The cities of the
Lombard league had reached the summit of their power
at the period of this second conflict. During the interregnum which lasted from the death of Frederick II
to the entrance into Italy of Henry VII in 1310, the
Lombard republics, a prey to the spirit of faction,
and more intent on the triumph of either the Guelph
or Ghibeline parties, than on securing their own constitutions, all submitted themselves to the military
power of some nobles to whom they had intrusted the
command of their militias, and thus all lost their liberty.

On the death of Frederick II, his son, Conrad IV,
king of Germany, did not feel himself sufficiently
strong to appear in Italy, and place on his head, in succession, the iron crown at Monza, and the golden crown
at Rome. He wished first of all to secure that of the
Two Sicilies; and embarked at some port in Istria for
Naples, in a Pisan vessel, during the month of October,
1251. The remainder of his short life was passed in
combating and vanquishing the Neapolitan Guelphs.
He died suddenly at Lavello, on the 21st of May, 1254.
His natural brother, Manfred, a young hero, hardly
twenty years of age, succeeded by his activity and
courage in recovering the kingdom which Innocent IV
had already invaded, with the intention of subduing it
to the temporal power of the holy see. But Manfred,
beloved by the Saracens of Luceria, who were the first
to defend him, and admired by the Ghibelines of the
Two Sicilies, was for a long time detained there by the
attacks of the Guelphs, before he could in his turn
pursue them through the rest of Italy. Conrad had left
in Germany a son, still an infant, afterwards known

under the name of Conradin; he was acknowledged king of Germany, under the name of Conrad V, by a small party only. The electors left the empire without a head; and when they afterwards proceeded to elect one, in the year 1257, their suffrages were divided between two princes, strangers to Germany, where they had never set foot; one, an Englishman, Richard earl of Cornwall; the other, a Spaniard, Alphonso X of Castile.*

Innocent IV was still in France, when he learnt the death of Frederick II; he returned thence in the beginning of the spring of 1251; wrote to all the towns to celebrate the deliverance of the church; gave boundless expression to his joy; and made his entry into Milan, and the principal cities of Lombardy, with all the pomp of a triumph. He supposed that the republicans of Italy had fought only for him, and that he alone would henceforth be obeyed by them; of this he soon made them but too sensible. He treated the Milanese with arrogance, and threatened to excommunicate them for not having respected some ecclesiastical immunity. It was the moment in which the republic, like a warrior reposing himself after battle, began to feel its wounds. It had made immense sacrifices for the Guelph party; it had emptied the treasury, obtained patriotic gifts from every citizen who had any thing to spare; pledged its revenues, and loaded itself with debt to the extent of its credit. For the discharge of their debts, the citizens resigned themselves to the necessity of giving to their podestà, Beno de' Gozzadini of Bologna, unlimited power to create new imposts, and to raise money under every form he found possible. The ingratitude of the pope, at a moment of universal suffering, deeply offended the Milanese; and the influence of the Ghibelines in a city, where, till then, they had been treated as enemies, might be dated from that period.

Innocent IV pursued his journey towards Rome; but

* Until the end of the year 1256, William, count of Holland, one of the competitors whom the Guelph party had given to Frederick II, bore the title of King of the Romans.

found the capital of Christendom still less disposed than
the first city of Lombardy to obey him. The Romans,
in 1253, called another Bolognese noble, named Brancaleone d'Andolo, to the government of their republic;
and gave him, with the title of senator, almost unlimited authority. The citizens, continually alarmed by the
quarrels and battles of the Roman nobles, who had
converted the Colisæum, the tombs of Adrian, Augustus, and Cæcilia Metella, the arches of triumph, and
other monuments of ancient Rome, into so many
fortresses, whence issued banditti, whom they kept in
pay, to pillage passengers, and peaceable merchants,
demanded of the government, above all things, vigour
and severity. They forgot the guarantee due to the accused, in their attention to those only which were required by the public peace. The senator Brancaleone,
at the head of the Roman militia, successively attacked these monuments, become the retreat of robbers and assassins; he levelled to the ground the towers
which surmounted them; he hanged the adventurers
who defended them, with their commanders the nobles,
at the palace windows of the latter; and thus established, by terror, security in the streets of Rome. He
hardly showed more respect to Innocent than to the
Roman nobility. The pope, in order to be at a distance
from him, had transferred his court to Assisi. Brancaleone sent him word, that it was not decorous in a
pope to be wandering like a vagabond from city to city;
and that, if he did not immediately return to the capital
of Christendom, of which he was the bishop, the Romans, with their senator at their head, would march
to Assisi, and send him out of it by setting fire to the
town.

Thus, although the power of kings had given way to
that of the people, liberty was in general ill understood
and insecure. The passions were impetuous; a certain
point of honour was attached to violence; the nobles
believed they gave proof of independence by rapine
and outrage; and the friends of order believed they
had attained the highest purpose of government, when

they made such audacious disturbers tremble. The turbulence and number of the noble criminals, the support
which their crimes found in a false point of honour,
form an excuse for the judicial institutions of the Italian republics, which were all more calculated to strike
terror into criminals too daring to conceal themselves,
than to protect the accused against the unjust suspicion of secret crimes. Order could be maintained only
by an iron hand; but this iron hand soon crushed liberty. Nevertheless, among the Italian cities there was
one which, above all others, seemed to think of justice
more than of peace, and of the security of the citizen
more than of the punishment of the guilty. It was
Florence: its judicial institutions are, indeed, far from
meriting to be held up as models; but they were the
first in Italy which offered any guarantee to the citizen;
because Florence was the city where the love of liberty
was the most general and the most constant in every
class; where the cultivation of the understanding was
carried farthest; and where enlightenment of mind
soonest appeared in the improvement of the laws.

The Ghibeline nobles had taken possession of the
sovereignty of Florence, with the help of the king of
Antioch, two years before the death of his father,
Frederick II; but their power soon became insupportable to the free and proud citizens of that republic, who
had already become wealthy by commerce, and who
reckoned amongst them some distinguished literary
men, such as Brunetto Latini, and Guido Cavalcante,
without having lost their simplicity of manners, their
sobriety of habits, or their bodily vigour. Frederick II
still lived, when, by an unanimous insurrection, on
the 20th of October, 1250, they set themselves free. All
the citizens assembled at the same moment in the
square of Santa Croce; they divided themselves into
fifty groups, of which each group chose a captain, and
thus formed companies of militia: a council of these
officers was the first-born authority of this newly-revived
republic. The podestà, by his severity and partiality,
had rendered himself universally detested: they de-

posed him, and supplied his place by another judge, under the name of captain of the people, but soon afterwards decreed that the podestà and the captain should each have an independent tribunal, in order that they should exercise upon each other a mutual control; at the same time, they determined that both should be subordinate to the supreme magistracy of the republic, which was charged with the administration, but divested of the judicial power. They decreed that this magistracy, which they called the *signoria*, should be always present, always assembled in the palace of the republic, ever ready to control the podestà or the captain, to whom they had been obliged to delegate so much power. The town was divided into six parts, each *sestier*, as it was called, named two *anziani*. These twelve magistrates ate together, slept at the public palace, and could never go out but together; their function lasted only two months. Twelve others, elected by the people, succeeded them; and the republic was so rich in good citizens, and in men worthy of its confidence, that this rapid succession of *anziani* did not exhaust their number. The Florentine militia, at the same time, attacked and demolished all the towers which served as a refuge to the nobles, in order that all should henceforth be forced to submit to the common law.

The new *signoria* was hardly informed of the death of Frederick, when, by a decree of the 7th of January, 1251, they recalled all the Guelph exiles to Florence. They henceforth laboured to give that party the preponderance throughout Tuscany. They declared war against the neighbouring cities of Pistoia, Pisa, Sienna, and Volterra; not to subjugate them, or to impose hard conditions, but to force them to rally round the party which they considered that of the church and of liberty. The year 1254, when the Florentines were commanded by their podestà, Guiscardo Pietra Santa, a Milanese, is distinguished in their history by the name of the "year of Victories." They took the two cities of Pistoia and Volterra; they forced those of Pisa and Sienna to sign a peace favourable to the Guelph party;

they refused to profit by a treason which had given them possession of the citadel of Arezzo, and they restored it to the Aretini; lastly, they built in the Lunigiana, beyond the territory of Lucca, a fortress destined to shut the entry of Tuscany on the Ligurian side, which, in memory of their podesta, bears to this day the name of Pietra Santa. The signoria showed themselves also worthy to be the governors of a city renowned for commerce, the arts, and liberty. The whole monetary system of Europe was at this period abandoned to the depredations of sovereigns who continually varied the title and weight of coins—sometimes to defraud their creditors, at other times to force their debtors to pay more than they had received, or the taxpayers more than was due. During 150 years more, the kings of France violated their faith with the public, making annually, with the utmost effrontery, some important change in the coins. But the republic of Florence, in the year 1252, coined its golden florin, of 24 carats fine, and of the weight of one drachm. It placed the value under the guarantee of publicity, and of commercial good faith; and that coin remained unaltered, as the standard for all other values, as long as the republic itself endured.

A conspiracy of Ghibelines to recover their power in Florence, and to concentrate it in the aristocratic faction, forced the republic, in the year 1258, to exile the most illustrious chiefs of that party. It was then directed by Farinata degli Uberti, who was looked upon as the most eloquent orator and the ablest warrior in Tuscany. All the Florentine Ghibelines were favourably received at Sienna, although the two republics had mutually engaged in their last treaty not to give refuge to the rebels of either city. Farinata afterwards joined Manfred, whom he found firmly established on the throne of the Two Sicilies; and represented to him that, to guard his kingdom from all attack, he ought to secure Tuscany, and give supremacy to the Ghibeline party. He obtained from him a considerable body of German cavalry, which he led to Sienna. Hostilities between the

two republics had already begun: the colours of Manfred had been dragged with contempt through the
streets by the Florentines. Farinata resolved to take
advantage of the irritation of the Germans, in order to
bring the two parties to a general battle. He knew that
some ignorant artisans had found their way into the
signoria of Florence, and he tried to profit by their
presumption. He flattered them with the hope that he
would open to them one of the gates of Sienna, if they
ordered their army to present itself under the walls of
that city. At the same time, his emissaries undertook to
excite the ill will of the plebeians against the nobles of
the Guelph party, who, being more clear-sighted, might
discover his intrigues. Notwithstanding the opposition
of the nobles in council, the *signoria* resolved to march
a Guelph army through the territory of Sienna. They
demanded, for this purpose, succour from Bologna,
Pistoia, Prato, San Miniato, San Gemignano, Volterra,
and Colle. They appointed a meeting with the militias
of Arezzo and of Orvieto at Monte Aperto, five miles
from Sienna, on the other side of the Arbia. The whole
power of the Guelph party in Tuscany, amounting to
30,000 infantry and 3000 cavalry, was collected there.
The Guelphs were only anxious how they should draw
their enemies from within the walls of Sienna. They
were themselves in a state of perfect security, when,
on the 4th of September, 1260, they were unexpectedly attacked by Farinata degli Uberti, and by the
generals of Manfred. The Ghibelines had not more than
13,000 men, reckoning the emigrants of Florence, the
militias of Sienna and of Pisa, and the Germans; but
they relied on a treacherous understanding in the
Guelph camp. Bocca degli Abbati, placing himself at
the head of the traitors, and suddenly seizing the great
standard of the republic, threw it to the ground. The
whole army was panic-struck when they saw the colours fall: they learned that the enemy was master of
the head-quarters, without knowing their numbers. The
Guelphs fled on all sides; but, unrelentingly pursued,

left 10,000 dead on the field of battle, and a great number of prisoners in the hands of the enemy.

The Florentine Guelphs found themselves too much weakened by the defeat of Arbia to maintain themselves in Florence. The circumference of the walls was too vast, and the population too much discouraged by the enormous loss which they had experienced, to admit of defending the city. All those, accordingly, who had exercised any authority in the republic—all those whose names were sufficiently known to discover their party—left Florence for Lucca together, on horseback. The Guelphs of Prato, Pistoia, Volterra, and San Gemignano could not hope to maintain their ground, when those of Florence failed. All abandoned their dwellings, and joined the Florentines at Lucca. That city granted to the illustrious fugitives the church and portico of San Friano, and the surrounding quarter, where they pitched their tents. The Ghibelines entered Florence on the 27th of September; immediately abolished the popular government; and formed a new magistracy, composed entirely of nobles, who took the oath of fidelity to Manfred, king of the Two Sicilies.

At a diet of the Ghibeline cities, assembled at Empoli, the ambassadors of Pisa and Sienna strongly represented, that whilst Florence existed, the preponderance of the Ghibeline party in Tuscany could never be secure. They affirmed, that the population of that proud and warlike city was entirely devoted to the Guelph party; that there was no hope of mitigating their hatred of the nobles and of the family of the last emperor; that democratic habits were become a sort of second nature to every one of the inhabitants; they concluded with demanding that the walls of Florence should be rased to the ground, and the people dispersed among the neighbouring towns. All the Ghibelines of Tuscany, all the deputies of the cities jealous of Florence, received the proposition favourably. It was about to be adopted, when Farinata degli Uberti rose, and repelled with indignation this abuse of the victory which he had just gained. He protested that he loved his country far better than his party; and declared that he would, with those same companions in arms whose bravery they had witnessed at the battle of Arbia, join the Guelphs, and fight for them, sooner than consent to the ruin of what was in the world most dear to him. The enemies of Florence dared not answer him; and the diet of Empoli contented itself with decreeing that the league of Tuscany should take into pay 1000 of the soldiers of Manfred, to support in that province the preponderance of the Guelph party. Dante has immortalised Farinata as the saviour of Florence, and Bocca degli Abbati as the traitor who placed it on the brink of destruction. His poem is filled with allusions to this memorable epoch.

While the Ghibelines thus acquired the preponderance in Tuscany, the tyrant fell who at the head of that party had caused so much blood to flow in the Trevisan march. Eccelino was hereditary lord of Bassano and Pedemonte: he succeeded in making himself named captain of the people by the republics of Verona, Vicenza, Padua, Feltre, and Belluno. By this title he united the judicial with the military power; he was subject only to councils which he might assemble or not at his pleasure. It does not appear that there was any permanent magistracy, like the *signoria* of Florence, to repress his abuse of power. Accordingly, he soon changed the authority which he derived from the people into a frightful tyranny: fixing his suspicions upon all who rose to any distinction, who in any way attracted the attention of their fellow-citizens, he did not wait for any expression of discontent, or symptom of resistance, in the nobles, merchants, priests, or lawyers, who by their eminence alone became suspected, to throw them into prison, and there, by the most excruciating torture, extract confessions of crimes that might justify his suspicions. The names which escaped their lips in the agony of torture were carefully registered, in order to supply fresh victims to the tyrant. In the single town of Padua there were eight prisons always full, notwithstanding the incessant toil of the executioner to empty them; two of these contained each 300 prisoners. A brother of Eccelino, named Alberic, governed Treviso with less ferocity, but with a power not less absolute. Cremona was in like manner subject to a Ghibeline chief; Milan no longer evinced any repugnance to that party. In that city, as well as in Brescia, the factions of nobles and plebeians disputed for power.

Alexander IV, to destroy the monster that held in terror the Trevisan march, caused a crusade to be preached in that country. He promised those who combatted the ferocious Eccelino all the indulgences usually reserved for the deliverers of the Holy Land. The marquis d'Este, the count di San Bonifazio, with the cities of Ferrara, Mantua, and Bologna, assembled their troops under the standard of the church; they were joined by a horde of ignorant fanatics from the lowest class, anxious to obtain indulgences, but unsusceptible of discipline, and incapable of a single act of valour. Their number, however, so frightened Eccelino's lieutenant at Padua, that he defended but feebly the passage of the Bacchiglione, and the town. The legate Philip, elected archbishop of Ravenna, entered Padua at the head of the crusaders, on the 18th of June, 1256; but he either would not or could not restrain the fanatic and rapacious rabble, which he had summoned to the support of his soldiers: for seven days the city was inhumanly pillaged, by those whom it had received as its deliverers. As soon as Eccelino was informed of the loss he had sustained, he hastened to separate and disarm the 11,000 Paduans belonging to his army; he confined them in prisons, where all, with the exception of 200, met a violent or lingering death. During the two following years, the Guelphs experienced nothing but disasters: the legate, whom the pope had placed at their head, proved incompetent to command them; and the crowd of crusaders whom he called to his ranks served only to compromise them, by want of courage and discipline. The Ghibeline nobles of Brescia even delivered their country into the hands of Eccelino after he had put the legate's army to flight, in the year 1258. The following year, this tyrant, unequalled in Italy for bravery and military talent, always an enemy to luxury, and proof against the seductions of women, making the boldest tremble with a look, and preserving in his diminutive person, at the age of sixty-five, all the vigour of a soldier, advanced into the centre of Lombardy, in the hope that the nobles of Milan, with whom he had already opened a correspondence, would surrender this great city to him. He passed the Oglio, and afterwards the Adda, with the most brilliant army he had ever yet commanded: but the marquis Palavicino, Buoso da Doara, the Cremonese chieftain, and other Ghibelines, his ancient associates, disgusted with his crimes, had secretly made an alliance with the Guelphs, for his destruction. When they saw him advance so far from his home, they rushed upon him from all sides. On the 16th of September, 1259, whilst he was preparing to retire, he found himself stopped at the bridge of Cassano. The Brescians, no longer obedient to his command, began their movement to abandon him; all the points of retreat were cut off by the Milanese, Cremonese, Ferrarians, and Mantuans: repulsed, pursued as far as Vimercato, and at last wounded in the foot, he was made prisoner, and taken to Soncino: there, he refused to speak, rejected all the aid of medicine; tore off all the bandages from his wounds, and finally expired, on the eleventh day of his captivity. His brother with all his family were massacred in the following year.

The defeat of Eccelino, and the destruction of the family of Romano, may be regarded as the last great effort of the Lombards against the establishment of tyranny in their country. About this time, the cities began to be accustomed to absolute power in a single person. In each republic, the nobles, always divided by hereditary feuds, regarded it as disgraceful to submit to the laws, rather than do themselves justice by force of arms: their quarrels, broils, and brigandage carried troubles and disorder into every street and public place. The merchants were continually on the watch to shut their shops on the first cry of alarm; for the satellites of the nobles were most commonly banditti, to whom they gave shelter in their palaces, and who took advantage of the tumult to plunder the shops. At the same time that the nobles irritated the plebeians by their arrogance, they ridiculed their incapacity, and endeavoured to exclude them from all the public offices. The people often, in their indignation, took arms; the streets were barricaded, and the nobles, besieged in their town houses, were driven to take refuge in their castles; but if the militias of the towns afterwards presumed to pursue in the plains of Lombardy the nobles whom they forced to emigrate, they soon found themselves sadly inferior. In the course of this century, the nobles had acquired the habit of fighting on horseback, with a lance, and covered with heavy armour. Continual exercise could alone render them expert in the manœuvres of cavalry, and accustom them to the enormous weight of the cuirass and helmet; on the other hand, this armour rendered them almost invulnerable. When they charged with couched lance, and with all the impetuosity of their war-horses, they overthrew and annihilated the ill-armed infantry opposed to them, without experiencing themselves any damage. The cities soon felt the necessity of opposing cavalry to cavalry, and of taking into their pay either those nobles who made common cause with the people, or foreigners and adventurers, who about this time began to exchange their valour for hire. As the custom was prevalent of giving the command of the militia to the first officer of justice, in order to give him authority either to direct the public force against rebels or disturbers of order, or to discipline the soldier by the fear of punishment, no commander could be found who would undertake the military service of a town, without at the same time possessing the power of the judicial sword—such power as was intrusted to the podestà or captain of the people. It became necessary then to deliver into his charge what was named the *signoria;* and the more considerable this corps of cavalry, thus placed for a certain number of years at the service of the republic, the more this *signoria*, to which was attached the power of adjudging life or death in the tribunals, became dangerous to liberty.

Among the first feudal lords who embraced the cause of the people, and undertook the service of a town, with a body of cavalry raised among their vassals, or among the poor nobles, their adherents, was Pagan della Torre, the lord of Valsassina. He had endeared himself to the Milanese by saving their army from the pursuit of Frederick II after the battle of Cortenuova. He was attached by hereditary affection to the Guelph party; and although himself of illustrious birth, he seemed to partake the resentment of the plebeians of Milan against the nobility who oppressed them. When he died, his brother Martino, after him Raymond, then Philip, lastly, Napoleon della Torre, succeeded each other as captains of the people, commanders of a body of cavalry which they had raised and placed at the service of the city; they were the acknowledged superiors of the podestà and the tribunals. These five lords succeeded each other in less than twenty years; and even the shortness of their lives accustomed the people to regard their election as the confirmation of a dynasty become hereditary. Other Guelph cities of Lombardy were induced to choose the same captain and governor as Milan, because they believed him a true Guelph, and a real lover of the people. These towns found the advantage of drawing closer their alliance with the city which directed their party; of placing themselves under a more powerful protection; and of supporting their tribunals with a firmer hand. Martin della Torre had been elected podestà of Milan in 1256; three years later, he obtained the title of elder, and lord of the people. At the same time, Lodi also named him lord. In 1263, the city of Novara conferred the same honour on him. Philip, who succeeded him in 1264, was named lord by Milan, Como, Vercelli, and Bergamo. Thus began to be formed among the Lombard republics, without their suspecting that they divested themselves of their liberty, the powerful state which a century and

a half later became the duchy of Milan. But the pope,
jealous of the house of Della Torre, appointed archbishop of Milan Otho Visconti, whose family, powerful on the borders of the Lago Maggiore, then shared
the exile of the nobles and Ghibelines. This prelate
placed himself at the head of their faction; and henceforward the rivalry between the families of Della Torre
and Visconti made that between the people and the nobles almost forgotten.

The bitter enmity between the two parties of the
Guelphs and Ghibelines was fatal to the cause of liberty. With the former, the question was religion, the
independence of the church and of Italy, menaced by
the Germans and Saracens, to whom Manfred granted
not less confidence than Frederick II; with the latter,
honour and good faith towards an illustrious family,
and the support of the aristocracy as well as of royalty;
but both were more intent on avenging offences a
thousand times repeated, and guarding against exile,
and the confiscation of property, which never failed to
follow the triumph of the opposite party. These party
feelings deeply moved men who gloried in the sacrifices which they or their ancestors had made to either
party; while they regarded as entirely secondary the
support of the laws, the impartiality of the tribunals, or
the equal participation of the citizens in the sovereignty. Every town of Lombardy forgot itself, to make
its faction triumph; and it looked for success in giving
more unity and force to power. The cities of Mantua
and Ferrara, where the Guelphs were far the more
numerous, trusted for their defence, the one to the
count di San Bonifazio, the other to the marquis d'Este,
with so much constancy, that these nobles, under the
name of captains of the people, had become almost
sovereigns. In the republic of Verona, the Ghibelines,
on the contrary, predominated; and as they feared their
faction might sink at the death of Eccelino, they called
to the command of their militia, and the presidency of
their tribunals, Mastino della Scala, lord of the castle
of that name in the Veronese territory; whose power

became hereditary in his family. The marquis Pela-
vicino, the most renowned Ghibeline in the whole valley of the Po; whose strongest castle was San Donnino,
between Parma and Placentia, and who had formed
and disciplined a superb body of cavalry, was named,
alternately with his friend, Buoso da Doara, lord of the
city of Cremona. Pavia and Placentia also chose him
almost always their captain; and this honour was at the
same time conferred on him by Milan, Brescia, Tortona, and Alexandria. The Ghibeline party had, since
the offence given by Innocent IV to the Guelphs of
Milan, obtained the ascendency in Lombardy. The
house of Della Torre seemed even to lean towards it;
and it was all powerful in Tuscany. The city of Lucca
had been the last to accede to that party in 1263; and
the Tuscan Guelphs, obliged to leave their country, had
formed a body of soldiers, which placed itself in the
pay of the few cities of Lombardy still faithful to the
Guelph party.

The court of Rome saw, with great uneasiness, this
growing power of the Ghibeline party, firmly established in the Two Sicilies, under the sceptre of Manfred. Feared even in Rome and the neighbouring
provinces, master in Tuscany, and making daily progress in Lombardy, Manfred seemed on the point of
making the whole peninsula a single monarchy. It was
no longer with the arms of the Italians that the pope
could expect to subdue him. The Germans afforded
no support. Divided between Richard of Cornwall and
Alphonso of Castile, they seemed desirous of delivering
themselves from the imperial authority, by dividing
between foreigners an empty title; while each state
sought to establish a separate independence at home,
and abandon the supremacy of the empire over Italy.
It was accordingly necessary to have recourse to other
barbarians to prevent the formation of an Italian monarchy fatal to the power of the pontiff. Alexander IV
died on the 25th of May, 1261: three months afterwards, a Frenchman, who took the name of Urban IV,

was elected his successor; and he did not hesitate to arm the French against Manfred.

His predecessor had already opened some negotiations, for the purpose of giving the crown of Sicily to Edmund, son of Henry III king of England. Urban put an end to them by having recourse to a prince nearer, braver, and more powerful. He addressed himself to Charles count of Anjou, the brother of St. Louis, sovereign in right of his wife of the county of Provence. Charles had already signalised himself in war; he was, like his brother, a faithful believer, and still more fanatical and bitter towards the enemies of the church, against whom he abandoned himself without restraint to his harsh and pitiless character. His religious zeal, however, did not interfere with his policy; his interest set limits to his subjection to the church; he knew how to manage those whom he wished to gain; and he could flatter, at his need, the public passions, restrain his anger, and preserve in his language a moderation which was not in his heart. Avarice appeared his ruling passion; but it was only the means of serving his ambition, which was unbounded. He accepted the offer of the pope. His wife Beatrice, ambitious of the title of queen, borne by her three sisters, pawned all her jewels to aid in levying an army of 30,000 men, which she led herself through Lombardy. He had preceded her. Having gone by sea to Rome, with 1000 knights, he made his entry into that city on the 24th of May, 1265. A new pope, like his predecessor a Frenchman, named Clement IV, had succeeded Urban, and was not less favourable to Charles of Anjou. He caused him to be elected senator by the Roman republic, and invested him with the kingdom of Sicily, which he charged him to conquer; under the condition, however, that the crown should never be united to that of the empire, or to the sovereignty of Lombardy and Tuscany. A tribute of 8000 ounces of gold, and a white palfrey, was, by this investiture, assigned to St. Peter.

The French army, headed by Beatrice, did not pass through Italy till towards the end of the summer of

1265; and in the month of February of the following year, Charles entered, at its head, the kingdom of Naples. He met Manfred, who awaited him in the plain of Grandella, near Benevento, on the 26th of February. The battle was bloody. The Germans and Saracens were true to their ancient valour; but the Apulians fled like cowards, and the brave son of Frederick II, abandoned by them on the field of battle, perished. The kingdom of the Two Sicilies was the price of this victory. Resistance ceased, but not massacre. Charles gave up the pillage of Benevento to his soldiers; and they cruelly put to death all the inhabitants. The Italians, who believed they had experienced from the Germans and Saracens of Frederick and Manfred all that could be feared from the most barbarous enemies, now found that there was a degree of ferocity still greater than that to which they had been accustomed from the house of Hohenstaufen. The French seemed always ready to give as to receive death. The two strong colonies of Saracens at Luceria and Nocera were soon exterminated, and in a few years there remained not in the Two Sicilies a single individual of that nation or religion, nor one German who had been in the pay of Manfred. Charles willingly consented to acknowledge the Apulians and Sicilians his subjects; but he oppressed them, as their conqueror, with intolerable burdens. While he distributed amongst his followers all the great fiefs of the kingdom, he so secured, with a hand of iron, his detested dominion, that two years afterwards, when Conradin, the son of Conrad, and the nephew of Manfred, arrived from Germany to dispute the crown, few malcontents in the Two Sicilies had the courage to declare for him.

The victory of Charles of Anjou over Manfred restored the ascendant of the Guelph party in Italy. Philip della Torre, who for some time seemed to hesitate between the two factions, at last gave passage through the Milanese territory to the army of Beatrice. Buoso da Doara was accused of having received money not to oppose her on the Oglio. The count di San Bonifazio, the marquis d'Este, and afterwards the Bolognese, openly joined her party. After the battle of Grandella, the Florentines rose, and drove out, on the 11th of November, 1266, the German garrison, commanded by Guido Novello, the lieutenant of Manfred. They soon afterwards received about 800 French cavalry from Charles, to whom they intrusted, for ten years, the *signoria* of Florence; that is to say, they conferred on him the rights allowed by the peace of Constance to the emperors. At the same time they re-established, with full liberty, their internal constitution; they augmented the power of their numerous councils, from which they excluded the nobles and Ghibelines; and they gave to the corporations of trade, into which all the industrious part of the population was divided, a direct share in the government.

It was about the end of the year 1267 that the young Conradin, aged only sixteen years, arrived at Verona, with 10,000 cavalry, to claim the inheritance of which the popes had despoiled his family. All the Ghibelines and brave captains, who had distinguished themselves in the service of his grandfather and uncle, hastened to join him, and to aid him with their swords and counsel. The republics of Pisa and Sienna, always devoted to his family, but whose zeal was now redoubled by their jealousy of the Florentines, made immense sacrifices for him. The Romans, offended at the pope's having abandoned their city for Viterbo, as well as jealous of his pretensions in the republic, from the government of which he had excluded the nobles, opened their gates to Conradin, and promised him aid. But all these efforts, all this zeal, did not suffice to defend the heir of the house of Hohenstaufen against the valour of the French. Conradin entered the kingdom of his fathers by the Abruzzi; and met Charles of Anjou in the plain of Tagliacozzo, on the 23d of August, 1268. A desperate battle ensued: victory long remained doubtful. Two divisions of the army of Charles were already destroyed; and the Germans, who considered themselves the victors, were dispersed in pursuit of the enemy;

when the French prince, who, till then, had not appeared on the field, fell on them with his body of reserve, and completely routed them. Conradin, forced to fly, was arrested, forty-five miles from Tagliacozzo, as he was about to embark for Sicily. He was brought to Charles, who, without pity for his youth, esteem for his courage, or respect for his just right, exacted, from the iniquitous judges before whom he subjected him to the mockery of a trial, a sentence of death. Conradin was beheaded in the market-place at Naples, on the 26th of October, 1268. With him perished several of his most illustrious companions in arms—German princes, Ghibeline nobles, and citizens of Pisa; and, after the sacrifice of these first victims, an uninterrupted succession of executions long continued to fill the Two Sicilies with dismay.

The defeat and death of Conradin established the preponderance of the Guelph party throughout the peninsula. Charles placed himself at the head of it: the pope named him imperial vicar in Italy during the interregnum of the empire, and sought to annex to that title all the rights formerly exercised by the emperors in the free cities. Clement IV died on the 29th of November, 1268, one month after the execution of Conradin. The cardinals remained thirty-three months without being able to agree on the choice of a successor. During this interregnum—the longest the pontifical chair had ever experienced—Charles remained sole chief of the Guelph party, ruling over the whole of Italy, which had neither pope nor emperor. He convoked, in 1269, a diet of the Lombard cities at Cremona, in which the towns of Placentia, Cremona, Parma, Modena, Ferrara, and Reggio, consented to confer on him the *signoria:* Milan, Como, Vercelli, Novara, Alexandria, Tortona, Turin, Pavia, Bergamo, and Bologna, declared they should feel honoured by his alliance and friendship, but could not take him for master. Italy already felt the weight of the French yoke, which would have pressed still heavier if the crusade against Tunis to which Charles of Anjou was summoned by his brother, Saint Louis, had not diverted his projects of ambition.

The conclave assembled at Viterbo at length raised to the vacant chair Tebaldo Visconti, of Placentia, who was at that time in the Holy Land. On his return to Italy, in the year 1272, he took the name of Gregory X. This wise and moderate man soon discovered that the court of Rome had overreached itself: in crushing the house of Hohenstaufen, it had given itself a new master, not less dangerous than the preceding. Gregory, instead of seeking to annihilate the Ghibelines, like his predecessors, occupied himself only in endeavouring to restore an equilibrium and peace between them and the Guelphs. He persuaded the Florentines and Siennese to recall the exiled Ghibelines, for the purpose, as he announced, of uniting all Christendom in the defence of the Holy Land; and testified the strongest resentment against Charles, who threw obstacles in the way of this reconciliation. He relieved Pisa from the interdict that had been laid on it by the holy see. He showed favour to Venice and Genoa; both of which, offended by the arrogance and injustice of Charles, had made common cause with his enemies. He engaged the electors of Germany to take advantage of the death of Richard of Cornwall, which took place in 1271, and put an end to the interregnum by proceeding to a new election. The electors conferred the crown, in 1273, on Rodolph of Hapsburg, founder of the house of Austria. The death of Gregory X, in the beginning of January, 1276, deprived him of the opportunity to develop the projects which these first steps seem to indicate; but Nicolas III, who succeeded him in 1277, after three ephemeral popes, undertook more openly to humble Charles, and to support the Ghibeline party. He forced the king of Sicily to renounce the title of imperial vicar, to which Charles had no title except during the interregnum of the empire: he still further engaged him to resign the title of senator of Rome, and the dignity of the *signoria,* which had been conferred on him by the cities of Lombardy and Tuscany, by representing to him that his power over these provinces was contrary to the bull of investiture, which had put him in possession of the kingdom of Naples.

Rodolph of Hapsburg, who had never visited Italy, and was ignorant of the geography of that country, was, in his turn, persuaded by the pope to confirm the charters of Louis *le Débonnaire,* of Otho I, and of Henry VI, of which copies were sent to him. In these charters, whether true or false, taken from the chancery at Rome, the sovereignty of the whole of Emilia or Romagna, the Pentapolis, the march of Ancona, the patrimony of St. Peter, and the campagna of Rome, from Radicofani to Ceperano, were assigned to the church. The imperial chancery confirmed, without examination, a concession which had never been really made. The two Fredericks, as well as their predecessors, had always considered this whole extent of country as belonging to the empire, and always exercised there the imperial rights. A chancellor of Rodolph arrived in these provinces to demand homage and the oath of allegiance, which were yielded without difficulty; but Nicolas appealed against this homage, and called it a sacrilegious usurpation. Rodolph was obliged to acknowledge that it was in contradiction to his own diplomas, and resigned his pretensions. From that period, 1278, the republics, as well as the principalities situated in the whole extent of what is now called the States of the Church, held of the holy see, and not of the emperor.

A revolution, not long previous, in the principal cities of Lombardy, had secured the preponderance to the nobles and the Ghibeline party. These, having been for a considerable period exiled from Milan, experienced a continuation of disasters, and, instead of fear, excited compassion. While Napoleon della Torre, chief of the republic of Milan, was exasperating the plebeians and Guelphs with his arrogance and contempt of their freedom, he was informed that Otho Visconti, whom he had exiled, although archbishop of Milan, had assembled round him at Como many nobles and Ghib-

elines, with whom he intended making an attack on the
Milanese territory. Napoleon marched to meet him;
but, despising enemies whom he had so often vanquished, he carelessly suffered himself to be surprised
by the Ghibelines at Desio, in the night of the 21st of
January, 1277. Having been made prisoner, with five
of his relatives, he and they were placed in three iron
cages, in which the archbishop kept them confined.
This prelate was himself received with enthusiasm at
Milan, at Cremona, and Lodi. He formed anew the
councils of these republics, admitting only Ghibelines
and nobles; who, ruined by a long exile, and often supported by the liberality of the archbishop, were become
humble and obsequious: their deference degenerated
into submission; and the republic of Milan, henceforth
governed by the Visconti, became soon no more than a
principality.

Nicolas III, of the noble Roman family of the Orsini,
felt an hereditary affection for the Ghibelines, and
every where favoured them. A rivalry between two
illustrious families of Bologna, the Gieremei and the
Lambertazzi, terminated, in 1274, in the exile of the
latter, who were Ghibelines, with all their adherents.
The quarrel between the two families became, from
that period, a bloody war throughout Romagna. Guido
de Montefeltro, lord of the mountains in the neighbourhood of Urbino, who had never joined any republic,
received the Ghibelines into his country; and in commanding them gained the reputation of a great captain.
Nicolas III sent a legate to Romagna, to compel Bologna and all the Guelph republics to recall the Ghibelines, and establish peace throughout the province. He
succeeded in 1279. Another legate on a similar mission,
and with equal success, was sent to Florence and
Sienna. The balance seemed at last on the point of
being established in Italy, when Nicolas died, on the
19th of August, 1280.

Charles, who had submitted without opposition, and
without even manifesting any displeasure, to the de-
pression of a party on which were founded all his

hopes, and to a reconciliation which destroyed his influence in the Guelph republics, hastened to Viterbo as soon as he learned the death of the pope, fully resolved not to suffer another of his enemies to ascend the chair of St. Peter. He caused three cardinals, relatives of Nicolas, whom he regarded as being adverse to him, to be removed by force from the conclave; and, striking terror into the rest, he obtained, on the 22d of January, 1281, the election of a pope entirely devoted to him. This was a canon of Tours, who took the name of Martin IV. He seemed to have no higher mission than that of seconding the ambition of the king of the Two Sicilies, and serving him in his enmities. Far from thinking of forming any balance to his power, he laboured to give him the sovereignty of all Italy. He conferred on him the title of senator of Rome; he gave the government of all the provinces of the church to his French officers; he caused the Ghibelines to be exiled from all the cities; and he encouraged, with all his power, the new design of Charles to take possession of the Eastern empire. Constantinople had been taken from the Latins on the 25th of July, 1261; and the son of the last Latin emperor was son-in-law of Charles of Anjou. Martin IV excommunicated Michael Paleologus, the Greek emperor, who had vainly endeavoured to reconcile the two churches. The new armament, which Charles was about to lead into Greece, was in preparation at the same time in all the ports of the Two Sicilies. The king's agents collected the taxes with redoubled insolence, and levied money with greater severity. The judges endeavoured to smother resistance by striking terror. In the meanwhile, a noble of Salerno, named John da Procida, the friend, confidant, and physician of Frederick II, and of Manfred, visited in disguise the Two Sicilies, to reanimate the zeal of the ancient Ghibelines, and rouse their hatred of the French and of Charles. After having traversed Greece and Spain to excite new enemies against him, he obtained assurances that Michael Paleologus, and Constance, the daughter of Manfred and wife of don Pedro of Aragon, would not suffer the Sicilians to be destroyed, if these had the courage to rise against their oppressors. Their assistance was, in fact, promised—it was even prepared; but Sicily was destined to be delivered by a sudden and popular explosion, which took place at Palermo, on the 30th of March, 1282. It was excited by a French soldier, who treated rudely the person of a young bride as she was proceeding to the church of Montreal, with her betrothed husband, to receive the nuptial benediction. The indignation of her relations and friends was communicated with the rapidity of lightning to the whole population of Palermo. At that moment the bells of the churches were ringing for vespers: the people answered by the cry, "To arms—death to the French!" The French were attacked furiously on all sides. Those who attempted to defend themselves were soon overpowered; others, who endeavoured to pass for Italians, were known by their pronunciation of two words, which they were made to repeat—*ceci* and *ciceri,* and were, on their mispronunciation, immediately put to death. In a few hours, more than 4000 weltered in their blood. Every town in Sicily followed the example of Palermo. Thus the Sicilian vespers overthrew the tyranny of Charles of Anjou and of the Guelphs; separated the kingdom of Sicily from that of Naples; and transferred the crown of the former to don Pedro of Aragon, the son-in-law of Manfred, who was considered the heir to the house of Hohenstaufen.

CHAPTER V

ITALY NEGLECTED BY THE EMPERORS, ABANDONED BY THE POPES   COUNT UGOLINO   THE BIANCHI AND NERI AT FLORENCE   CLOSE OF THE GRAND COUNCIL AT VENICE   THE EMPEROR HENRY VII HIS EXPEDITION INTO ITALY

HITHERTO we have found the connecting chain of the events, of which we have undertaken the narrative, in a common interest felt throughout Italy. In seeking to trace the concurrent history of more than two hundred small states, we have found their frequent revolutions referable to the efforts made by the Italians to maintain the balance between the rights of the empire, of the church, and of each city. In the period on which we now enter, politics become complex, interests more widely spread; and it is much more difficult to seize and follow a dominant idea amidst the various revolutions to which Italy was a prey. This difference results chiefly from the fact, that no potentate existed in Italy at this time superior to the republics; such as the former kings of Naples, the emperors, and popes, who succeeded in acquiring the entire government of a faction, and in thus directing to one end the opposite efforts of all the people of the peninsula.

Charles of Anjou, the first French king of the Two Sicilies, survived the Sicilian vespers only three years. He died on the 7th of January, 1285, aged sixty-five years. At this period, his son, Charles II, was a prisoner in the hands of the Sicilians: he was set at liberty in 1288, in pursuance of a treaty, by which he acknowledged the separation and independence of the two crowns of Naples and Sicily. The first was assigned to the Guelphs and the house of Anjou; the second to the Ghibelines, and the house of Aragon: but Nicholas IV, by whose influence the treaty was made, broke it, released Charles from his oath, and authorised him to begin the war anew. This war, which lasted twenty-four years, occupied without lustre the whole reign of Charles II. This prince was milder than his father, but weaker also. He had neither the stern character of Charles of Anjou, which excited hatred; nor his talents, which commanded admiration or respect. He always called himself the protector of the Guelph party, but ceased to be its champion; and neither the court of Rome, nor the Guelph republics, any longer demanded counsel, direction, or support from the court of Naples. He died on the 5th of May, 1309; and was succeeded by his son Robert. The influence of the emperors, as protectors of the Ghibeline party, during this period was almost extinct in Italy. Rodolph of Hapsburg, who reigned with glory in Germany from 1273 to 1291, never passed the Alps to be acknowledged emperor and king of the Lombards; after him, Adolphus of Nassau, and his successor, Albert of Austria—the one assassinated in 1298, the other in 1308—remained alike strangers to Italy. The Ghibeline party was, accordingly, no longer supported or directed by the emperors, but it maintained itself by its own resources, by the attachment of the nobles to the imperial name, and still more by the self-interest of the captains; who, raised to the *signoria* either by the choice of the people or of their faction, created for themselves, in the name of the empire, a sovereignty to which the Italians unhesitatingly gave the name of tyranny.

Lastly, the third power, that of the pope, which till then had directed the politics of Italy, ceased about this time to follow a regular system, and consequently to give a powerful impulse to faction. Martin IV, whose life terminated two months after that of Charles I, had always acted as his creature, had seconded him in his enmities, in his thirst of vengeance against the Sicilians, and in his efforts to recover his dominion over Italy. But Honorius IV, who reigned after him, from 1285 to 1287, appeared to have no other thought than that of aggrandising the noble house of Savelli at Rome, of which he was himself a member: after him, Nicholas IV, from 1288 to 1292, was not less zealous in his efforts to do as much for that of Colonna. His predecessor, Nicolas III, had a few years previously set the example, by applying all his power as pope to the elevation of the Orsini. These are nearly the first examples of the nepotism of the popes, who had hardly yet begun to feel themselves sovereigns. They raised these three great Roman families above all their ancient rivals: almost all the castles in the patrimony of St. Peter, and in the Campagna of Rome, became their property. The houses of Colonna, Orsini, and Savelli, to support their nobility, soon began to traffic in their valour, by hiring themselves out with a body of cavalry to such as would employ them in war; whilst the peasants, their vassals, seduced by the spirit of adventure, and still more by the hope of plunder, abandoned agriculture to enlist in the troops of their liege lord. The effect of their disorderly lives was, that the two provinces nearest Rome soon became the worst cultivated and the least populous in all Italy, although the treasures of Europe poured into the capital of the Faithful. After Nicholas IV, a poor hermit, humble, timid, and ignorant, was raised, in 1294, to the chair of St. Peter, under the name of Celestine V. His election was the effect of a sudden burst of religious enthusiasm, which seized the college of cardinals; although this holy senate had never before shown themselves more ready to consult religion than policy. Celestine V maintained himself only a few months on the throne; all his sanctity could not serve as an excuse for his incapacity; and the cardinal Benedict Caietan, who persuaded him to abdicate, was elected pope in his place, under the name of Boniface VIII. Boniface, able, expert, intriguing, and unscrupulous, would have restored the authority of the holy see, which during the latter pontificates had been continually sinking, if the violence of his character, his ungovernable pride, and his transports of passion, had not continually thwarted his policy. He endeavoured at first to augment the power of the Guelphs by the aid of France; he afterwards engaged in a violent quarrel with the family of Colonna, whom he would willingly have exterminated; and, finally, taking offence against Philip le Bel, he treated him with as much haughtiness as if he had been the lowest of his vassals. Insulted, and even arrested, by the French prince, in his palace of Anagni, on the 7th of September, 1303, Boniface died a few weeks afterwards of rage and humiliation.

While the power of the kings of Naples, of the emperors, and of the popes, was as it were suspended in Italy, innumerable small states, which had risen to almost absolute independence, experienced frequent revolutions, for the most part proceeding from internal and independent causes. We can, at most, only indicate shortly those of the republics, the most distinguished and the most influential in Italy: but, before thus entering within the walls of the principal cities, it is right to give a sketch of the general aspect of the country, particularly as the violent commotions which it experienced might give a false idea of its real state. This aspect was one of a prodigious prosperity, which contrasted so much the more with the rest of Europe that nothing but poverty and barbarism were to be found elsewhere. The open country, designated by the name of *contado*, appertaining to each city, was cultivated by an active and industrious race of peasants, enriched by their labour, and not fearing to display their wealth in their dress, their cattle, and their instruments of husbandry. The proprietors, inhabitants of towns, advanced them capital, shared the harvests, and alone paid the land-tax: they undertook the immense labour which has given so much fertility to the Italian soil—that of making dikes to preserve the plains from the inundation of the rivers, and of deriving from those rivers innumerable canals of irrigation. The *naviglio grande* of Milan, which spreads the clear waters of the Ticino over the finest part of Lombardy, was begun in 1179, resumed in 1257, and terminated a few years afterwards. Men who meditated, and who applied to the arts the fruits of their study, practised already that scientific agriculture of Lombardy and Tuscany which became a model to other nations; and at this day, after five centuries, the districts formerly free, and always cultivated with intelligence, are easily distinguished from those half-wild districts which had remained subject to the feudal lords.

The cities, surrounded with thick walls, terraced, and guarded by towers, were, for the most part, paved with broad flag-stones; while the inhabitants of Paris could not stir out of their houses without plunging into the mud. Stone bridges of an elegant and bold architecture were thrown over rivers; aqueducts carried pure water to the fountains. The palace of the podestas and *signorie* united strength with majesty. The most admirable of those of Florence, the *Palazzo-Vecchio,* was built in 1298. The Loggia in the same city, the church of Santa Croce, that of Santa Maria del Fiore, with its dome, so admired by Michael Angelo, were begun by the architect Arnolfo, scholar of Nicolas di Pisa, between the years 1284 and 1300. The prodigies of this first-born of the fine arts multiplied in Italy: a pure taste, boldness, and grandeur struck the eye in all the public monuments, and finally reached even private dwellings; while the princes of France, England, and Germany, in building their castles, seemed to think only of shelter and defence. Sculpture in marble and bronze soon followed the progress of architecture: in 1300, Andrea di Pisa, son of the architect Nicolas, cast the admirable bronze gates of the Baptistery at Florence; about the same time, Cimabue and Giotto revived the art of painting, Casella music, and Dante gave to Italy his divine poem, unequalled in succeeding generations. History was written honestly, with scrupulous research, and with a graceful simplicity, by Giovanni Villani, and his school; the study of morals and philosophy began; and Italy, ennobled by freedom, enlightened nations, till then sunk in darkness.

The arts of necessity and of luxury had been cultivated with not less success than the fine arts: in every street, warehouses and shops displayed the wealth that Italy and Flanders only knew how to produce. It excited the astonishment and cupidity of the French or German adventurer, who came to find employment in Italy, and who had no other exchange to make than his blood against the rich stuffs and brilliant arms which he coveted. The Tuscan and Lombard merchants, however, trafficked in the barbarous regions of the west, to carry there the produce of their industry. Attracted by the franchises of the fairs of Champagne and of Lyons, they went thither, as well to barter their goods as to lend their capital at interest to the nobles, habitually loaded with debt; though at the risk of finding themselves suddenly arrested, their wealth confiscated, by order of the king of France, and their lives, too, sometimes endangered by sanctioned robbers, under the pretext of repressing usury. Industry, the employment of a superabundant capital, the application of mechanism and science to the production of wealth, secured the Italians a sort of monopoly through Europe: they alone offered for sale what all the rich desired to buy; and, notwithstanding the various oppressions of the barbarian kings, notwithstanding the losses occasioned by their own often-repeated revolutions, their wealth was rapidly renewed. The wages of workmen, the interest of capital, and the profit of trade, rose simultaneously, while every one gained much and spent little; manners were still simple, luxury was unknown, and the future was not forestalled by accumulated debt.

The republic of Pisa was one of the first to make known to the world the riches and power which a small state might acquire by the aid of commerce and liberty. Pisa had astonished the shores of the Mediterranean by the number of vessels and galleys that sailed under her flag, by the succour she had given the crusaders, by the fear she had inspired at Constantinople, and by the conquest of Sardinia and the Balearic Isles. Pisa was the first to introduce into Tuscany the arts that ennoble wealth: her dome, her baptistery, her leaning tower, and her Campo Santo, which the traveller's eye embraces at one glance, but does not weary of beholding, had been successively built from the year 1063 to the end of the twelfth century. These *chefs-d'œuvre* had animated the genius of the Pisans: the great architects of the thirteenth century were, for the most part, pupils of Nicolas di Pisa. But the moment was come in which the ruin of this glorious republic was at hand; a deep-rooted jealousy, to be dated from the conquest of Sardinia, had frequently, during the last two centuries, armed against each other the republics of Genoa and Pisa: a new war between them broke out in 1282. It is difficult to comprehend how two simple cities could put to sea such prodigious fleets as those of Pisa and Genoa.

In 1282, Ginicel Sismondi commanded thirty Pisan galleys, of which he lost the half in a tempest, on the 9th of September; the following year, Rosso Sismondi commanded sixty-four; in 1284, Guido Jacia commanded twenty-four, and was vanquished. The Pisans had recourse the same year to a Venetian admiral, Alberto Morosini, to whom they intrusted 103 galleys: but, whatever efforts they made, the Genoese constantly opposed a superior fleet. This year, however, all the male population of the two republics seemed assembled on their vessels: they met on the 6th of August, 1284, once more before the Isle of Meloria, rendered famous forty-three years before by the victory of the Pisans over the same enemies. Valour was still the same, but fortune had changed sides; and a terrible disaster effaced the memory of an ancient victory. While the two fleets, almost equal in number, were engaged, a reinforcement of thirty Genoese galleys, driven impetuously by the wind, struck the Pisan fleet in flank: seven of their vessels were instantly sunk, twenty-eight taken. 5000 citizens perished in the battle, and 11,000 who were taken prisoners to Genoa preferred death in captivity rather than their republic should ransom them, by giving up Sardinia to the Genoese. This prodigious loss ruined the maritime power of Pisa; the same nautical knowledge, the same spirit of enterprise, were not transmitted to the next generation. All the fishermen of the coast quitted the Pisan galleys for those of Genoa. The vessels diminished in number, with the means of manning them; and Pisa could no longer pretend to be more than the third maritime power in Italy.

While the republic was thus exhausted by this great reverse of fortune, it was attacked by the league of the Tuscan Guelphs; and a powerful citizen, to whom it had intrusted itself, betrayed his country to enslave it. Ugolino was count of the Gherardesca, a mountainous country situated along the coast, between Leghorn and Piombino: he was of Ghibeline origin, but had married his sister to Giovan di Gallura, chief of the Guelphs of Pisa and of Sardinia. From that time he artfully op-

posed the Guelphs to the Ghibelines; and though several accused him of having decided the issue of the
battle of Meloria, others regarded him as the person
most able, most powerful by his alliance, and most
proper, to reconcile Pisa with the Guelph league. The
Pisans, amidst the dangers of the republic, felt the
necessity of a dictator. They named Ugolino captain-
general for ten years: and the new commander did,
indeed, obtain peace with the Guelph league; but not
till he had caused all the fortresses of the Pisan territory
to be opened by his creatures to the Lucchese and
Florentines—a condition of his treaty with them which
he dared not publicly avow. From that time he sought
only to strengthen his own despotism, by depriving all
the magistrates of power, and by intimidating the archbishop Roger degli Ubaldini, who held jointly with him
the highest rank in the city. The nephew of Ubaldini,
having opposed him with some haughtiness, was killed
by him on the spot with his own hand. His violence,
and the number of executions which he ordered, soon
rendered him equally odious to the two parties: but he
had the art, in his frequent changes from one to the
other, to make the opposite party believe him powerfully supported by that with which he at the moment
sided. In the summer of 1282 the Guelphs were exiled:
but finding in the Ghibeline chiefs, the Gualandi Sismondi and Lanfranchi, a haughtiness which he thought
he had subdued, he charged his son to introduce anew
the Guelphs into the city. His project was discovered
and prevented; the Ghibelines called the people on all
sides to arms and liberty. On the 1st of July, 1288, Ugolino was besieged in the palace of the *signoria:* the
insurgents, unable to vanquish the obstinate resistance
opposed to them by himself, his sons, and his adherents,
set fire to the palace; and, having entered it amidst the
flames, dragged forth Ugolino, two of his sons, and two
of his grandsons, and threw them into the tower of the
Sette Vie. The key was given to the archbishop; from
whom was expected the vigilance of an enemy, but the
charity of a priest. That charity, however was soon ex-

hausted: the key after a few months was thrown into the river; and the wretched count perished in those agonies of hunger, and of paternal and filial love, upon which poetry,* sculpture, and painting have conferred celebrity.

The victory over count Ugolino, achieved by the most ardent of the Ghibelines, redoubled the enthusiasm and audacity of that party; and soon determined them to renew the war with the Guelphs of Tuscany. Notwithstanding the danger into which the republic was thrown by the ambition of the last captain-general, it continued to believe, when engaged in a hazardous war, that the authority of a single person over the military, the finances, and the tribunals was necessary to its protection; and it trusted that the terrible chastisement just inflicted on the tyrant would hinder any other from following his example. Accordingly Guido de Montefeltro was named captain. He had acquired a high reputation in defending Forli against the French forces of Charles of Anjou; and the republic had not to repent of its choice. He recovered by force of arms all the fortresses which Ugolino had given up to the Lucchese and Florentines. The Pisan militia, whom Montefeltro armed with cross-bows, which he had trained them to use with precision, became the terror of Tuscany. The Guelphs of Florence and Lucca were glad to make peace in 1293.

While the Pisans became habituated to trusting the government to a single person, the Florentines became still more attached to the most democratic forms of liberty. In 1282 they removed the *anziani,* whom they had at first set at the head of their government, to make room for the *priori delle arti,* whose name and office was preserved not only to the end of the republic, but even to our day. The corporation of trades, which they called the *arti,* were distinguished by the titles of major and minor. At first only three, afterwards six, major *arti* were admitted into the government. The college, con-

* Dante.

sisting of six *priori delle arti,* always assembled, and living together, during two months, in the public palace, formed the *signoria,* which represented the republic. Ten years later, the Florentines completed this *signoria* by placing at its head the gonfaloner of justice, elected also for two months, from among the representatives of the arts, manufactures, and commerce. When he displayed the gonfalon, or standard of the state, the citizens were obliged to rise and assist in the execution of the law. The arrogance of the nobles, their quarrels, and the disturbance of the public peace by their frequent battles in the streets, had, in 1292, irritated the whole population against them. Giano della Bella, himself a noble, but sympathising in the passions and resentment of the people, proposed to bring them to order by summary justice, and to confide the execution of it to the gonfaloner whom he caused to be elected. The Guelphs had been so long at the head of the republic, that their noble families, whose wealth had immensely increased, placed themselves above all law. Giano determined that their nobility itself should be a title of exclusion, and a commencement of punishment; a rigorous edict, bearing the title of "ordinance of justice," first designated thirty-seven Guelph families of Florence, whom it declared noble and great, and on this account excluded for ever from the *signoria;* refusing them at the same time the privilege of renouncing their nobility, in order to place themselves on a footing with the other citizens. When these families troubled the public peace by battle or assassination, a summary information, or even common report, was sufficient to induce the gonfaloner to attack them at the head of the militia, rase their houses to the ground, and deliver their persons to the podestà, to be punished according to their crimes. If other families committed the same disorders, if they troubled the state by their private feuds and outrages, the *signoria* was authorised to ennoble them, as a punishment of their crimes, in order to subject them to the same summary justice. A similar organisation, under different names, was made at

Sienna, Pistoia, and Lucca. In all the republics of Tuscany, and in the greater number of those of Lombardy, the nobility by its turbulence was excluded from all the magistracies; and in more than one, a register of nobles was opened, as at Florence, on which to inscribe, by way of punishment, the names of those who violated the public peace.

However rigorous these precautions were, they did not suffice to retain in subjection to the laws an order of men who believed themselves formed to rule, and who despised the citizens with whom they were associated. These very nobles, to whom was denied all participation in the government of the republic, and almost the protection and equality of the law, were no sooner entered into their mountain castles, than they became sovereigns, and exercised despotic power over their vassals. The most cultivated and wooded part of the Apennines belonged to the republic of Pistoia. It was a considerable district, bordering on the Lucchese, Modenese, Bolognese, and Florentine territory, and was emphatically designated by the name of the *Mountain.* It was covered with castles belonging either to the Cancellieri, or Panciatichi, the two families most powerful in arms and wealth in all Italy: the first was Guelph, the second Ghibeline; and as the party of the former then ruled in Tuscany, they had obtained the exile of the Panciatichi from Pistoia. The Cancellieri took advantage of this exile to increase their power by the purchase of land, by conquest, and by alliance; in their family alone they reckoned one hundred men at arms. This family was divided into two branches, of distant relationship and which were distinguished by the names of *Bianchi* and *Neri* (whites and blacks); a quarrel arose between them, and was maintained with all the perfidy and ferocity of which the Pistoiese nobility were then accused. Mutilations, assassinations, and desperate battles, from 1296 to 1300, followed each other with a frequency which at last alarmed all Tuscany. The Florentines, desirous of pacifying Pistoia, engaged that city to banish from its bosom all the Cancellieri, but at the same time opened their own gates to them, in the hope of being able to accomplish a reconciliation. This powerful family, allied to all the Guelph nobility of Italy, instead of forgetting their reciprocal injuries, drew their hosts into their quarrel: there were, it is true, already other causes of excitement in Florence. Corso Donati, a Guelph, possessed great influence over the ancient families who had from the beginning directed that party. Vieri de Cerchi, a Guelph also, was the chief of those who, like himself, had recently risen to wealth and power; he reproached the former for not forgetting the ancient enmity between the Guelphs and Ghibelines; for still troubling the republic with factions, when there was no longer any motive; and proposed to substitute equal laws, for superannuated proscriptions. The Cancellieri of the Neri party sided with Corso Donati, the ancient nobles, and the most violent of the Guelphs. Those of the Bianchi, on the contrary, took part with Vieri de Cerchi, the moderate Guelphs, and subsequently with the Ghibelines and the Panciatichi. In this last party enlisted Dante, the historian Dino Compagni, the father of Petrarch, and all those who began about this time at Florence to distinguish themselves in literature.

Boniface VIII endeavoured to reconcile the two parties who, under the names of Bianchi and Neri, began to divide all Tuscany; but, violent and choleric, he was ill calculated to make peace between men as intemperate as himself. He soon espoused with zeal the party of the Neri, the aristocracy, and the most zealous Guelphs. He had called Charles de Valois, the brother of Philip le Bel, to Italy, to place him at the head of an expedition which he meditated against Sicily. He charged him to pacify Tuscany in his way; and gave him to understand that it would be easy, in states so rich, to repay himself for his trouble. The republic of Florence dared not refuse the mediation of Charles: it was accustomed to regard the house of France as the protector of the church and of the Guelph party. It, however, limited, in precise terms, the authority allowed him, before receiving him, and the 800 cavalry which he commanded, within the city. But the French princes, at this period, neither respected nor comprehended the liberty of the citizen: they were incapable of forming any idea of the reciprocal rights which they had to maintain. Charles, making no account of the engagements which he had taken, formed an intimate alliance with the Neri, whom he soon discovered to be the more aristocratic, and more virulent in their enmities. Having agreed on his share of the booty, he gave, from the 5th to the 11th of November, 1301, a loose rein to their passions. He permitted them to pillage and burn the houses of their enemies; to kill those who were the most odious to them; to carry off the heiresses of rich families, and marry them to their sons; to cause sentences of exile and confiscation to be pronounced against all the most illustrious families of the Bianchi party by the podestà, a creature of Charles de Valois, whom he had brought there. The French cavalry, and the Guelphs of Romagna, whom Charles had also introduced into the city, assisted in all these outrages. It was then that Dante, and Petracco dell'Ancisa, the father of Petrarch, were exiled from their country, with many hundred others. Charles at last quitted Florence, on the 4th of April, 1302, carrying off immense wealth. His cavalry were loaded with gold and precious stuffs; but he carried with him also the curse of the Florentines, which seemed to follow him in his unsuccessful expedition against Sicily. Benedict XI, the successor of Boniface, vainly endeavoured, during his short pontificate, to reconcile the Bianchi and Neri in the cities of Tuscany, and to recall the latter from exile. He died of poison, on the 4th of July, 1304. Some accuse Philip le Bel of the crime; he at least reaped all the benefit. This king succeeded by fraud in getting a Frenchman elected pope, under the name of Clement V, whom, to keep him more subservient to his will, he always retained in France; drawing thither, also, the college of cardinals, who were recruited in that country, so that the successors of Clement might also be Frenchmen.

It was the beginning of the long retirement, or, as the Italians call it, exile of the popes, at Avignon, which terminated in 1377, and soon after began anew with the great western schism. This exile was favourable to the independence of Rome, and of the other cities of the pontifical states; and at the same time rendered the holy see almost indifferent to the Guelph party, which it had often indecently seconded.

While the nobles of the Italian cities had, by their turbulence, excited the resentment of all classes of the people—while, by their disobedience to the laws, contempt of the tribunals and of public peace, they had drawn on themselves the exclusion not only from the magistracies, but from the common rights, the most precious to the citizens of a free state, the nobility of Venice rose in importance, and took possession of the government. Submissive to the laws, but shaping them for their own use, forgetting individuals and families, to occupy themselves only about their corporate interests, they arrived, by insensible usurpations, to the sovereignty of this ancient republic. This nobility of Venice, which appeared so docile to the laws, so patient, so skilful, was the oldest in Europe. It inherited the honours of the Roman empire; and alone preserved, from the fifth to the eleventh century, the family names, according to the Roman custom, which had been abandoned by the rest of Europe. Like the nobles in the other cities of Italy, they were in turn sovereigns in their fiefs, and subjects in the city. After the conquest of the Greek empire, the Venetians distributed among their nobles several islands in the Archipelago, of which they preserved the sovereignty, with the titles of dukes or counts, even after the Greeks had recovered Constantinople; but they had not, and could not have, any fortresses in the vast plains that surround Venice. They had no devoted vassals, always ready to espouse their quarrels; nor retreats, into which to withdraw from the power of the law. They acknowledged and submitted to the authority of the tribunals; they conducted themselves as citizens, and thus soon became masters of the state.

It was by slow and artfully disguised encroachments that the nobility of Venice succeeded in substituting itself for the civic power, and investing itself with the sovereignty of the republic. During the earlier period, the doge was an elective prince, the limit of whose power was vested in assemblies of the people. It was not till 1032 that he was obliged to consult only a council, formed from amongst the most illustrious citizens, whom he designated. Thence came the name given them of *pregadi* (invited). The grand council was not formed till 1172, 140 years later, and was, from that time, the real sovereign of the republic. It was composed of 480 members, named annually on the last day of September, by twelve tribunes, or grand electors, of whom two were chosen by each of the six sections of the republic. No more than four members from one family could be named. The same counsellors might be re-elected each year. As it is in the spirit of a corporation to tend always towards an aristocracy, the same persons were habitually re-elected; and when they died, their children took their places. The grand council, neither assuming to itself nor granting to the doge the judicial power, gave the first example of the creation of a body of judges, numerous, independent, and irremovable; such, nearly, as was afterwards the parliament of Paris. In 1179, it created the criminal *quarantia;* called, also, the *vecchia quarantia,* to distinguish it from two other bodies of forty judges, created in 1229. The grand council gave a more complete organisation to the government formed from among its members. It was composed of a doge; of six counsellors of the red robe, who remained only eight months in office, and who, with the doge, formed the *signoria;* and of the council of pregadi, composed of sixty members, renewed each year. The doge was obliged, on entering office, to take a rigorously detailed oath, which guaranteed all the public liberties. At his death, a commission of enquiry was formed, to examine whether he had not exceeded his powers; and in case he had, his heirs were responsible. In 1249, the sovereign council renounced the election of the doge, and entrusted it to a commission drawn by lot from among the whole council. This commission named another; which, reduced by lot to one fourth, named a third; and by these alternate operations of lot and election, at length formed the last commission of forty-one members, who could elect the doge only by a majority of twenty-five suffrages. It was not till towards the end of the thirteenth century that the people began to discover that they were no more than a cipher in the republic, and the doge no more than a servant of the grand council —surrounded, indeed, with pomp, but without any real power. In 1289, the people attempted themselves to elect the doge; but the grand council obliged him whom the popular suffrages had designated to leave Venice, and substituted in his place Pietro Gradenigo, the chief of the aristocratic party. Gradenigo undertook to exclude the people from any part in the election of the grand council, as they were already debarred from any participation in the election of a doge. He represented it to the grand council as notorious, that for more than a century the same persons, or families, were invariably re-elected; that the twelve tribunes charged with the annual election contented themselves with examining only whether any of the ancient members merited exclusion from the sovereign council, and confirming all the others; that since the election was reduced only to the condemnation of some individuals, it was more expedient to confide that judgment to the equity of the same tribunal to which the citizens intrusted their honour and their lives, than to the arbitrary will of twelve individuals, most frequently nominated by intrigue. He proposed, accordingly, instead of election, the purification of the grand council by the forty criminal judges. The decree which he proposed and carried on the 28th of February, 1297, is famous in the history of Venice, under the name of *serrata del maggior consiglio* (shutting of the grand council). He legally founded that hereditary aristocracy—so prudent, so jealous, so ambitious—which Europe regarded with astonishment; immovable in principle, unshaken in power; uniting some of the most odious practices of despotism with the name of liberty; suspicious and perfidious in politics; sanguinary in revenge; indulgent to the subject; sumptuous in the public service, economical in the administration of the finances; equitable and impartial in the administration of justice; knowing well how to give prosperity to the arts, agriculture, and commerce; beloved by the people who obeyed it, whilst it made the nobles who partook its power tremble. The Venetian aristocracy completed its constitution, in 1311, by the creation of the Council of Ten, which, notwithstanding its name, was composed of sixteen members and the doge. Ten counsellors of the black robe were annually elected by the great council, in the months of August and September; and of the six counsellors of the red robe, composing a part of the signoria, three entered office every four months. The Council of Ten, charged to guard the security of the state with a power higher than the law, had an especial commission to watch over the nobles, and to punish their crimes against the republic. In this they were restrained by no rule: they were, with respect to the nobility, the depositaries of the power of the great council, or rather of a power unlimited, which no people should entrust to any government. Some other decrees completed the system of the *serrata del maggior consiglio*. It was forbidden to the quarantia to introduce any *new man* into power. In 1315, a register was opened, called the Golden Book, in which were inscribed the names of all those who had sat in the great council. In 1319, all limitation of number was suppressed; and, from that period, it sufficed to prove that a person was the descendant of a counsellor, and twenty-five years of age, to be by right a member of the grand council of Venice.

On the 25th of November, 1308, the diet of Germany named Henry VII of Luxembourg as successor to Albert of Austria; and this election suddenly brought

Italy back to the same struggle for her independence
which she had so heroically supported against the two
Fredericks. From the death of the second Frederick,
fifty-eight years had passed since she had seen an emperor. Rodolph of Hapsburg, Adolphus of Nassau, and
Albert of Austria, had too much to do in Germany, to
occupy themselves with this constantly agitated country, where they could demand obedience only with
arms in their hands. Henry VII was a brave, wise, and
just prince; but he was neither rich nor powerful. He
secured to his son, by marriage, the crown of Bohemia,
which had excited some jealousy among the Germans;
and he believed it would be expedient, in order to
avoid all quarrel in the empire, to quit it for some time.
To flatter the national vanity, he determined on an expedition to Italy.

Henry, himself a Belgian, had no power but in Bel-
gium and the provinces adjoining France. From Luxembourg he went through the county of Burgundy to
Lausanne. Here he received, in the summer of 1310,
the ambassadors of the Italian states, who came to do
him homage. He entered Piedmont, by Mont Cenis,
towards the end of September, accompanied by only
two thousand cavalry, the greater part of whom were
Belgians, Franc-Comtois, or Savoyards. This force would
have been wholly insufficient to subdue Italy; but
Henry VII presented himself there as the supporter of
just rights, of order, and, to a certain degree, of liberty.
The result of the violence of faction, and of the ex-
haustion of the citizens, had been, to subject almost
all Lombardy to petty tyrants. Every city had its lord,
sometimes chief of the Guelph, sometimes of the Ghibeline faction, whom his partisans had, for their own
interests, invested with dictatorial power. Sometimes he
was a neighbouring noble, who, seconded by a band
of his vassals, had inspired terror, and whom the people
respected, because he forced to obedience turbulent
nobles who had never submitted to any law; and sometimes too he was a captain of foreign cavalry, called
to the service of the republic by the council, with the

title of lord assigned at the same time. The name of liberty, and the cry of *"Popolo! Popolo!"* were everywhere frequently heard; but it was only to overthrow the existing power, and substitute another quite as arbitrary. These despotisms, it is true, were of short duration; but yet hardly one city enjoyed true liberty. The desire of tranquillity, resulting from the outrages committed by the nobles or by factions, was so great, that the citizens demanded, above all, of the lords and magistrates strength to make themselves feared—to punish rapidly and severely whoever troubled the public peace. Every city submitted to a form of summary justice, preferring that to anarchy, although the sovereign lord often made an ill use of it, either to gratify his brutal passions, or to accumulate wealth which should be his resource in exile; an evil always to be expected.

The lords of all Lombardy and Piedmont came to present themselves to Henry; some at Turin, others at Asti. He received them with kindness, but declared his determination to establish legal order, such as had been settled by the peace of Constance, in all the cities of the empire; and to name in each an imperial vicar, who should govern in concert with the municipal magistrates. Philippone di Langusco, at Pavia; Simon da Colobiano, at Vercelli; William Brusato, at Novara; Antonio Fisiraga, at Lodi; in obedience to this intimation, laid down the sovereign power. At the same time, Henry every where recalled the exiles, without distinction of party: at Como and Mantua, the Ghibelines; at Brescia and Placentia, the Guelphs; leaving out, however, the exiles of Verona, a powerful city, which he did not visit, and which was governed by Can' Grande della Scala, the most able Ghibeline captain in Italy, the best soldier, the best politician, and the person whose services and attachment the emperor most valued. The rich and populous city of Milan required also to be treated with address and consideration. The archbishop, Otho Visconti, had retained the principal authority in his hands to a very advanced age. But long previously to his death, which took place in 1295, he had transferred to his nephew, Matteo Visconti, the title of captain of the people, and had accustomed the Milanese to consider him as his lieutenant and successor. Matteo did, in fact, govern after him, and with almost despotic power, from 1295 to 1302. He was also named lord of several other cities of Lombardy; at the same time he strengthened his family by many rich alliances. But Visconti had not the art to conciliate either the remains of national pride, or the love of liberty which still subsisted among his subjects, or the jealousy of the other princes of Lombardy. A league to give the preponderance to the Guelph party in this province was formed by Alberto Scotto, lord of Placentia, and by Ghiberto da Correggio, lord of Parma: they forced the Viscontis to quit Milan, in 1302, and installed in their place Guido della Torre and his family, who had been exiles twenty-five years. When Henry VII presented himself before Milan, he found it governed by Guido della Torre and the Guelphs. Matteo Visconti and the Ghibelines were exiled. Henry exacted their recall; he was crowned in the church of St. Ambrose, on the 6th of January, 1311, and afterwards asked of the city a gratuity for his army of one hundred thousand florins. Till then, the Italians had seen in the monarch only a just and impartial pacificator; but when he demanded money, the different parties united against him. A violent sedition broke forth at Milan. The Della Torres and the Guelphs were forced to leave that city. Matteo Visconti and the Ghibelines were recalled, and the former restored to absolute power. The Guelphs, too, in the rest of Lombardy, rose, and took arms against the emperor. Crema, Cremona, Lodi, Brescia, and Como revolted at the same time. Henry consumed the greater part of the summer in besieging Brescia, which at last, towards the end of September, 1311, he forced to capitulate. He granted to that town equitable conditions, impatient as he was to enter Tuscany; but, although Lombardy seemed subdued to his power, he left more germs of discontent and discord in it than he had found about a year before.

Henry VII arrived with his little army at Genoa, on the 21st of October, 1311. That powerful republic now maintained at St. Jean d'Acre, at Pera opposite to Constantinople, and at Caffa in the Black Sea, military and mercantile colonies, which made themselves respected for their valour, at the same time that they carried on the richest commerce of the Mediterranean. Several islands in the Archipelago, amongst others, that of Chios, had passed in sovereignty to Genoese families. The palaces of Genoa, already called the "superb," were the admiration of travellers. Its sanguinary rivalry with Pisa had terminated by securing to the former the empire of the Tyrrhene Sea. From that time, Genoa had no other rival than Venice. An accidental rencounter of the fleets of these two cities in the sea of Cyprus lighted up between them, in 1293, a terrible war, which for seven years stained the Mediterranean with blood, and consumed immense wealth. In 1298, the Genoese admiral, Lamba Doria, meeting the Venetian commander, Andrea Dandolo, at Corzuola or Corcyra the Black, at the extremity of the Adriatic Gulf, burnt sixty-six of his galleys, and took eighteen, which he brought into the port of Genoa, with 7000 prisoners; suffering only twelve vessels to escape. The humbled Venetians, in the next year, asked and obtained peace. The Genoese, vanquishers in turn of the Pisans and Venetians, passed for the bravest, the most enterprising, and the most fortunate mariners of all Italy. The government of their city was entirely democratic; but the two chains of mountains which extend from Genoa, the one towards Provence, and the other towards Tuscany (called by the Italians *Le Riviere di Genoa,* because the foot of these mountains forms the shore of the sea), were covered with the castles of the Ligurian nobles; the peasantry were all dependent on them, and were always ready to make war for their liege lords. Four families were pre-eminent for their power and wealth —the Doria and the Spinola, Ghibelines; the Grimaldi and the Fieschi, Guelphs. These nobles, incensed against each other by hereditary enmity, had disturbed the state by so many outrages, that the people adopted, with respect to them, the same policy as that of the Tuscan republics, and had entirely excluded them from the magistracy. On the other hand, they had rendered such eminent and frequent services to the republic; above all, they had produced such great naval commanders, that the people, whenever the state was in danger, had always recourse to them for the choice of an admiral. Seduced by the glory of these chiefs, the people often afterwards shed their blood in their private quarrels; but often, also, wearied by the continual disturbances which the nobles excited, they had recourse to foreigners to subdue them to the common law. The people were in this state of irritation against the Ligurian nobles, when Henry VII arrived at Genoa, in 1311; and to oblige them to maintain a peace, which they were continually breaking, the Genoese conferred on that monarch absolute authority over the republic for twenty years. But when the emperor suppressed the podestà, and then the abbate or defender of the people, and afterwards demanded of the city a gift of 60,000 florins, the Genoese perceived that they needed a government not only to suppress civil discord, but also to protect rights not less precious than peace; an internal fermentation of increasing danger manifested itself; and Henry was happy to quit Genoa in safety, on the 16th of February, 1312, on board a Pisan fleet, which transported him with about 1500 cavalry to Tuscany.

Henry VII, when he entered Italy, was impartial between the Guelphs and Ghibelines. He owed his election to the influence of the popes, and he was accompanied by cardinal legates, who were to crown him at Rome. He had no distrust either of Robert, then king of Naples, the son of Charles II, or of the Guelph cities. He had no hereditary affection for the Ghibelines, the zealous partisans of a family long extinct. He endeavoured, accordingly, to hold the balance fairly between the two parties, and to reconcile them wherever he was allowed; but experience had already taught him

that the very name of elected emperor had a magic influence on the Italians, either to excite the devoted affection of the Ghibelines, or the terror and hatred of
the Guelphs. It was with the latter that resistance to
him had begun in the preceding year in Lombardy;
and that revolt had burst forth on all sides since his
departure. Robert, king of Naples, who assumed the
part of champion of the Guelph party, already testified
an open distrust of him; and Florence, which by its prudence, ability, wealth, and courage, was the real director of that party, took arms to resist him, refused audience to his ambassadors, raised all the Guelphs of Italy
against him, and finally constrained him to place that
city under the ban of the empire. The republic of Pisa,
on the other hand, whose affection for the Ghibeline
party was connected with its hopes, as well as its recollections, served him with a devotion, zeal, and prodigality, which he had not met elsewhere. The Pisans
had sent him, when at Lausanne, a present of 60,000
florins, to aid him on his passage to Italy. They paid his
debts at Genoa, and they gave him another present
when he entered their city; finally, they placed at his
disposal thirty galleys and 600 cross-bowmen, who accompanied him to Rome, where he received the golden
crown of the empire from the hands of the pope's legate, in the church of St. John de Lateran, on the 29th of
June, 1312. The Romans, who had taken arms against
him, and had received within their walls a Neapolitan
garrison, kept their gates shut during the ceremony, and
would not suffer one of his soldiers to enter the city.

The coronation of the emperor at Rome was the term
of service of the Germans: they took no interest afterwards in what was passing, or might be done, in that
country. They were anxious to depart; and Henry found
himself at Tivoli, where he passed the summer, almost
entirely abandoned by his transalpine soldiers. Had the
Neapolitan king Robert been bolder, Henry would have
been in great danger. In the autumn, however, the
Ghibelines and Bianchi of central Italy rallied round
him, and formed a formidable army, with which he

marched to attack Florence, on the 19th of September, 1312. The Florentines, accustomed to leave their defence to mercenaries, whose valour was always ready for pay, made small account of a military courage which they saw so common among men whom they despised; but no people carried civil courage and firmness in misfortune farther. Their army was soon infinitely superior in numbers to that of Henry; they carried on with perfect calmness their commerce and negotiations, as if their enemies had already departed for Germany, but they would not drive them out of their territory by giving battle; they preferred bearing patiently their depredations, and waiting till they had worn out their enthusiasm, exhausted their finances, and should depart of themselves, which they did on the 6th of January, 1313, finding they could obtain no advantage. Henry, after having given some months of repose to his army, took the command of the militia of Pisa, and made war at their head against Lucca; at the same time, he solicited from his brother, the archbishop of Treves, a German reinforcement, which he obtained in the following month of July. On the 5th of August, 1313, Henry VII departed from Pisa, commanding 2500 ultramontane and 1500 Italian cavalry, with a proportionate number of infantry. He began his march towards Rome, having been informed that Robert, called by the Florentines to their aid, advanced with all the forces of the Guelph party to oppose him. The declining military reputation of the Neapolitans inspired the Germans with little fear, and Robert had but a small number of French cavalry to give courage to his army; but the priests and monks, animated with zeal in defence of the ancient Guelph party and the independence of the church, seconded him with their prayers, and the report soon spread that they had seconded him in another manner and in their own way. The emperor took the road of San Miniato to Castel Fiorentino; arrived at Buon Convento, twelve miles beyond Sienna; and stopped there to celebrate the festival of St. Bartholomew. On the 24th of August, 1313, he received the communion from the hands of a Dominican monk, and expired a few hours afterwards. It was said the monk had mixed the juice of Napel in the consecrated cup. It was said, also, that Henry was already attacked by a malady which he concealed. A carbuncle had manifested itself below the knee; and a cold bath, which he took to calm the burning irritation, perhaps occasioned his sudden and unexpected death.

CHAPTER VI

THE POWER AND GREATNESS OF SOME OF THE GHIBELINE
     CHIEFS   DISORGANISATION OF THAT PARTY, THROUGH
THE INCONSISTENCY AND PERFIDY OF THE EMPEROR
LOUIS OF BAVARIA   EFFORT OF THE FLORENTINES
TO MAINTAIN AN EQUILIBRIUM BETWEEN THE DIFFER-
ENT POWERS OF ITALY   THE TYRANNY AND EXPUL-
SION OF THE DUKE OF ATHENS

THE electors of the empire were not convoked at Frankfort to name a successor to Henry VII till ten months after his death. Ten, instead of seven, princes presented themselves; two pretenders disputed the electoral rights in each of the houses of Saxony, Bohemia, and Brandenburg. The electors, divided into two colleges, named simultaneously, on the 19th of October, 1314, two emperors: the one, Louis IV of Bavaria; the other, Frederick III of Austria. Their rights appeared equal; their adherents in Germany were also of nearly equal strength; the sword only could decide; and war was accordingly declared, and carried on till the 28th of September, 1322; when Frederick was vanquished and made prisoner at Muhldorf.

The church abstained, while the civil war lasted, from pronouncing between the two pretenders to the empire. Clement V did not witness their double election; he died on the 20th of April, 1314. It was necessary, two years afterwards, to use fraud and violence, to confine the cardinals in conclave at Lyons, for the

purpose of naming his successor. They at last elected
the bishop of Avignon. He was a native of Cahors, the
devoted creature of king Robert of Naples; and took
the name of John XXII. He was the first who made
Avignon, which was his episcopal town, the residence
of the Roman court, exiled from Italy. He was an intriguer, notoriously profligate, scandalously avaricious:
he fancied himself, however, a philosopher, and took a
part in the quarrel between the realists and nominalists;
he made himself violent enemies in the schools, on the
members of which he sometimes inflicted the punishment of death. While he used such violence towards
his adversaries as heretics, he shook the credit of the
court of Rome, by being himself accused of heresy.
His great object was to raise to high temporal power
the cardinal Bertrand de Poiet, whom he called his
nephew, and who was believed to be his son. For that
purpose, he availed himself of the war between the
two pretenders to the empire, regarded by him as a
prolongation of the interregnum, during which he asserted all the rights of the emperors devolved on the
holy see. He charged cardinal Bertrand to exercise those
rights as legate in Lombardy, crush the Ghibelines, support the Guelphs; but above all, subdue both to the
authority of the church and its legate.

The cardinal Bertrand de Poiet launched his excommunications, and employed the soldiers, whom his
father had raised for him in Provence, particularly
against Matteo Visconti, lord of Milan, one of the most
able and powerful of the Ghibeline chiefs. Visconti
made himself beloved by the Milanese, whom he had
always treated with consideration. Without being virtuous, he had preserved his reputation unstained by
crime. His mind was enlightened. To a perfect knowledge of mankind, he added quick-sightedness, prompt
decision, and a certain military glory, heightened by
that of four sons, his faithful lieutenants, who were all
distinguished among the brave. The Italians gave him
the surname of Great, at a period when, it is true, they
were prodigal of that epithet. Matteo Visconti, in his

war with the Lombard Guelphs, took possession of
Pavia, Tortona, and Alexandria. He besieged, in concert with the Genoese Ghibelines, Robert king of Naples, who had shut himself up in Genoa, desirous of
making that city the fortress of the Guelphs of Lombardy. Visconti compelled the retreat of Philip de
Valois, who, before he was king, had entered Italy at
the solicitation of the pope, in 1320. The following year
he vanquished Raymond de Cardona, a Catalonian, and
one of the pope's generals; he persuaded Frederick of
Austria, who had sent his brother to aid the pope, to
recall his Germans, making him sensible it could suit
neither of the pretenders to the empire to weaken the
Ghibelines, who defended in Italy the interests of whoever of the two remained conqueror. But, after having
made war against the church party twenty years, without ever suspecting that he betrayed his faith, for he
was religious without bigotry, age awakened in him the
terrors of superstition; he began to fear that the excommunications of the legate would deprive him of
salvation; he abdicated in favour of his eldest son,
Galeazzo; and died a few weeks afterwards, on the 22d
of June, 1322. The remorse and scruples of Matteo
Visconti had carried trouble and disorder into his own
party, and gave boldness to that of his adversaries. A
violent fermentation at Milan at length burst forth;
Galeazzo was obliged to fly, and the republic was proclaimed anew: but virtue and patriotism, without which
it could not subsist, were extinguished; and, after a few
weeks, Galeazzo was recalled, and reinvested with the
lordship of Milan.

The two parties of the Guelphs and Ghibelines, since
the death of Henry VII, no longer nearly balanced
each other in virtue, talents, and patriotism. In the beginning of their struggle, there were almost as many
republics on one side as the other; and sentiments as
pure, and a devotion as generous, equally animated the
partisans of the empire and of the church. But, in the
fourteenth century, the faction of the Ghibelines had
become that of tyranny—of the Guelphs that of liberty.

The former displayed those great military and political talents which personal ambition usually develops. In the second were to be found, almost exclusively, patriotism, and the heroism which sacrifices to it every personal interest. The republic of Pisa alone, in Italy, united the love of liberty with the sentiments of the Ghibeline party. This republic had been thunderstruck by the death of Henry VII at a moment when a career of glory and prosperity seemed to open on him. Pisa, exhausted by the prodigious efforts which she had made to serve him, was true to herself, when all the Guelphs of Tuscany rose at once, on the death of Henry, to avenge on her the terror which that monarch had inspired. She gave the command of her militia to Uguccione dà Faggiuola, a noble of the mountainous part of Romagna, which, with the March, produced the best soldiers in Italy. The Pisans, under the command of Faggiuola, obtained two signal advantages over the Guelphs. They took Lucca, on the 14th of June, 1314, while the Lucchese Guelphs and Ghibelines were engaged in battle in the streets of that city; and, on the 29th of August of the same year, they defeated, at Montecatino, the Florentines, commanded by two princes of the house of Naples, and seconded by all the Guelphs of Tuscany and Romagna. But the Pisans soon perceived that they were fighting, not for themselves, but for the captain whom they had chosen. Almost immediately after his victory, he began to exercise an insupportable tyranny over Pisa and Lucca. Fearing much more the citizens of these republics than the enemies of the state, he, on the slightest suspicion, employed the utmost severity against all the most illustrious families. At Lucca, he threw into a dungeon Castruccio Castracani, the most distinguished of the Ghibeline nobles, who had recently returned to that city with a brilliant reputation, acquired in the wars of France and Lombardy. A simultaneous insurrection at Lucca and Pisa, on the 10th of April, 1316, delivered these cities from Uguccione dà Faggiuola, and his son, while, at the head of their cavalry, they were departing to join each other. This revolution re-established the republic of Pisa; but left it exhausted and ruined by long hostilities, and discontented with the Ghibelines and with its own nobility, who, by a blind spirit of party, had drawn it into continual war. In the month of May, 1322, fifteen chiefs of noble Ghibeline families, defeated in an obstinate battle, were exiled from Pisa; and, in less than a year afterwards, all the Pisans established in Sardinia were massacred on the same day, in consequence of a plot, formed by a Pisan rebel, to deliver Sardinia to Alphonso, the son of James II of Aragon. The war with the Aragonese, to defend the island, completed the ruin of the republic; and hostilities terminated with the abandonment of this important possession, on the 10th of June, 1326.

The revolution of Lucca, which had deprived Uguccione dà Faggiuola of power, conferred it on his prisoner, Castruccio Castracani, who still bore the fetters on his feet when the insurgents delivered him from his dungeon to be proclaimed lord of Lucca. Castruccio was of the ancient family of the Interminelli, so long exiled, with all the Ghibelines, from that city, that it might well have been believed that they had lost all influence; but the emigrants of the Italian republics frequently acquired, during their exile, new wealth and consideration. Want frequently forced them to labour with redoubled diligence—to devote themselves to commerce, or to military studies. Lucca had been esteemed the citadel of the Guelph party in Tuscany during the latter part of the thirteenth century: since its rich Ghibeline exiles had been recalled, it was become entirely of the latter party. The family of Castruccio had acquired its wealth in England; he had himself learned the art of war there, and in France and Lombardy. He had seen displayed, in these countries, the bravery of the soldier; but he owed to his own intellect and studies the art of leading and disposing armies, which in Italy only began to deserve the name of military science. Signally brave himself, he had the art of communicating to the soldier his courage and enthusiasm. No one had so quick and sure an eye on the field of battle. He was a no less able politician than warrior; and whether he took part with the Ghibeline chiefs of Lombardy, or the emperor Louis of Bavaria, he became always the sole director of those who admitted him into their council. To such talents and acquirements was added hardly one virtue: without fidelity in his engagements, without pity for the people, without gratitude to those who had served him, he put to death, by various cruel executions, all those who at Lucca excited in him the slightest suspicion; and, amongst others, the Quartigiani and the Poggi, to whom he owed his elevation. Castruccio was thirty-two years of age when he obtained the sovereignty of his country. He was tall, with an agreeable countenance; and his face, thin and surrounded with long fair hair, was remarkable for its paleness.

The republic of Florence found itself called upon to make head against Castruccio, and defend, against his ambition, the independence of Tuscany. Florence was the Athens of Italy. The genius displayed by some of its citizens, the talent and intelligence in business to be found even in the mass of the people, the generosity which seemed the national character, whenever it was necessary to protect the oppressed or defend the cause of liberty—raised this city above every other. Sienna, Perugia, and Bologna were at this period, like Florence, attached to the Guelph party; and these four republics, with some weaker towns, formed the Guelph league of Lombardy. The democratic spirit of the Florentines, which imparted so much energy, had also its dangers. These republicans, jealous of all distinction, and passionately attached to equality, demanded it not only in obedience, but in command. They insisted that the greatest possible number of citizens should, in turn, arrive at the office of *priori*, which, for two months, represented the sovereignty. It, however, did not proceed from base cupidity: this office, as well as every other of the magistracy, was gratuitous. The republic provided the table of the *priori* only when they were in the palace. In the month of October, 1323, the Florentines introduced drawing by lot into the nomination of their first magistrates. They ordained that a general list of all the eligible citizens, Guelphs, and at least thirty years of age, should be formed by a majority of five independent magistracies, of which each represented a national interest: the *priori*, that of the government; the gonfaloner, that of the militia; the captains of the party,* that of the Guelphs; the judges of commerce represented the merchants; and the consuls of the arts, industry. Each of these had a right to point out the most eligible citizen. The list which they prepared was submitted to the revision of a *balia* (a word signifying power), composed of the magistrates in office, and in the thirty-six deputies chosen by the six divisions of the town. The balia effaced from the list the names of all those whom it considered incapable; and classed the others according as they appeared suitable to the different magistracies, to which they were finally to be raised by lot. Lastly, it divided the list of names by series; so that the destined purse from which to draw the signoria contained twenty-one tickets, on each of which was inscribed a gonfaloner and six priori; similar purses were prepared, from which to draw by lot the names of the twelve *buon' uomini*, the nineteen gonfaloniers of the companies, and all the other magistrates of the republic. All this arrangement was to last only three years and a half, after which a new balia recommenced. Still, in our day, the municipal magistrates of Tuscany are drawn by lot, in the same manner. The activity, wisdom, and extensive views of the Florentine republic, while its supreme magistrates were changed by lot every two months, proves, at the same time, how much intelligence and patriotism there was in the people, and how worthily the *priori* appreciated statesmen, who, without having ostensible offices, directed the republic by their counsel.

This movable signoria, however, could not meet in

---

* The Capitani di Parte were the elective heads of the Guelph party, three in number.

war on equal terms with Castruccio, who united to high
talents an energetic character, promptitude, secrecy,
and unity of design. He began the war by taking from
the Florentines Pistoia, where an abbot, by the little
artifices of a monk, had obtained possession of the sovereignty. The abbot, on the 5th of May, 1325, sold his
country to Castruccio. Florence took into its service Don
Raymond de Cardona, a Catalonian general, whom the
cardinal Bertrand de Poiet had introduced into Italy.
But all who served the Florentines speculated on their
wealth: Cardona remarked, that in the brilliant army
which the republic had placed under his command,
there were many rich merchants, who bore impatiently
the fatigues and privations of the service: in order to
sell them leave of absence at a higher price, he resolved
to complete their disgust. He led them in the middle
of summer round the marshes of Bientina, where he
long detained them. Many merchants obtained leave of
absence by rich presents; but many more died or fell
sick. With his army thus weakened by his own fault,
he engaged Castruccio at Alto Pascio, and was defeated, on the 23d of September, 1325. Raymond was
taken prisoner; the carroccio fell into the hands of the
enemy; and these trophies of victory ornamented the
triumphal pomp with which Castruccio returned to
Lucca at the head of his army. A signal defeat of the
Bolognese, at Monteveglio, on the 15th of November,
1325, completed the discouragement of the Guelph
party. Bologna sought a protector in the cardinal de
Poiet, on whom was conferred the signoria. The Florentines had recourse to the king of Naples, who agreed
to aid them only on condition that they would confer
the signoria on his son, the duke of Calabria. Intelligence that Castruccio had engaged the emperor Louis
of Bavaria to enter Tuscany, induced them, though with
the utmost repugnance, to adopt this measure.

Louis of Bavaria had treated his prisoner Frederick
of Austria with magnanimity. He not only set him at
liberty, but associated him in his government. Louis
passed in Germany for a loyal and generous prince;

perhaps, only because violent and cruel actions inspired
there little horror; public opinion was not yet awakened; and no one rendered an account to the people
of the motives of princes, or of their sudden changes
from one party to another: but when the emperor arrived in a civilised country, where free and virtuous
men had a share in the government, and brought to
light the actions of princes, his conduct, for the most
part, seemed stained with cowardice and perfidy—the
more so, that he deceived without remorse men whom
he called deceivers, only because they were more
clever than himself. Louis of Bavaria gave a meeting
at Trento, in the month of February, 1327, to the principal chiefs of the Ghibeline party; they advanced him
150,000 florins, to pay the expenses of his expedition
to Italy: three months afterwards he entered that country with a suite of not more than 600 horsemen; but
the lords of Milan, Mantua, Verona, and Ferrara met
him, with their men at arms, for the most part German
mercenaries, who thus formed for him a fine army. He
received the iron crown at Milan, on the 30th of May;
Galeazzo Visconti, the richest and most powerful of the
Lombard lords, entertained him hospitably: but at the
same time that he excited the jealousy of the other
Ghibeline chiefs, his fine German cavalry and his treasure awakened the cupidity of Louis. Having secured
the obedience of these mercenaries, and feigning to
lend an ear to the reports made against Galeazzo by
the other Ghibeline lords, he arrested Visconti, together
with his sons and his two brothers, in his palace at
Milan, on the 6th of July, 1327; and threatened to put
them to the torture if they did not deliver to him their
fortresses and their treasure. He detained them eight
months in dungeons, without trial, and without assigning any reason for this severity. After eight months he
liberated them, at the intercession of Castruccio. He
then offered to sell them the sovereignty, of which he
had himself deprived them: but they were not rich
enough; for he had deprived them of the means by
which they could profit by his offer. In the month of

September, Louis passed into Tuscany, at the head of
the army which he had seduced from the Visconti. The
Pisans, exhausted with the war against Lucca and Sardinia, and desirous of preserving the peace which they
had concluded with the Guelphs, sent to offer the emperor 60,000 florins, on that condition. Louis arrested
their ambassadors, and threatened to put them to death
by torture, if their country did not implicitly obey his
will; after one month of hesitation, Pisa acknowledged
him sovereign, and was forced to advance him 150,000
florins.

From the moment Louis of Bavaria was joined by
Castruccio, he listened to no other counsel; and under
the direction of this able politician, he showed a vigour
and intelligence that promised to give him the dominion over all Italy, in spite of the excommunications
which the pope poured on him with redoubled irritation, upon seeing him defeat all the intrigues of his
favourite, Bertrand de Poiet. Castruccio persuaded
Louis of the importance of confirming his right to the
empire by his coronation at Rome; he delayed, therefore, the war on Florence, near which the duke of
Calabria had assembled a numerous army, till his return. It is not improbable that Castruccio meant to reserve for himself the conquest of that city. Louis had
named him duke of Lucca, Pistoia, Volterra, and the
Lunigiana, on the 11th of November, 1327; and he
flattered himself with the hope of uniting all Tuscany
to this dukedom, after the departure of the emperor.
Castruccio accompanied Louis to Rome; he was made
senator of that city, and count palatine of St. John de
Lateran. He carried the imperial sword at the coronation, which took place on the 17th of January, 1328,
at the Vatican: the ceremony was performed by schismatic bishops, and in contempt of the excommunications of John XXII. Louis in his anger commenced a
process in law to depose the pope and appoint a successor; but at this moment he was deprived of the counsel of Castruccio, who had been recalled to Tuscany
by news of the taking of Pistoia by the Florentines, on

the 28th of January, 1328. On his return he took Pisa by surprise; besieged Pistoia, and made himself master of it on the 3d of August of the same year; but not till after such fatigue as to occasion an illness, of which he died, on the 3d of September following. The death of this formidable and ambitious captain saved Florence from the greatest danger which she had yet incurred; and, to complete her good fortune, the sovereign she had chosen to oppose Castruccio, the duke of Calabria, died also about the same time. He had distinguished himself only by his vices, his want of foresight, and his depredations. Louis of Bavaria, too, ceased to be formidable: he completed his discredit by his perfidy towards those who had been the most devoted to him. Salvestro de' Gatti, lord of Viterbo, had been the first Ghibeline chief to open a fortress to him, in the states of the church; Louis arrested him, and put him to the torture, to force him to reveal the place where he had concealed his treasure. The emperor had rendered himself odious and ridiculous at Rome, by the puerility of his proceedings against John XXII, and his vain efforts to create a schism in the church. Having returned to Tuscany, he deprived the children of Castruccio of the sovereignty of Lucca, on the 16th of March, 1329, and sold it to one of their relatives, who, a month afterwards, was driven out by a troop of German mercenaries, which had abandoned the emperor to make war on their own account, that is to say, to live by plunder. Louis passed the summer of 1329 in Lombardy. Towards the end of the autumn he returned to Germany, carrying with him the contempt and detestation of the Italians. He had betrayed all who had trusted in him; and completely disorganised the Ghibeline party, which had relied on his support.

That party had just lost another of their most distinguished chiefs, Can' Grande della Scala. He was the grandson of the first Mastino, whom the republic of Verona had chosen for master after the death of Eccelino, in 1260. Can' Grande reigned in that city from 1312 to 1329, with a splendour which no other prince

in Italy equalled. Brave and fortunate in war, and wise
in council, he gained a reputation for generosity, and
even probity, to which few captains could pretend.
Among the Lombard princes, he was the first protector
of literature and the arts. The best poets, painters, and
sculptors of Italy, Dante, to whom he offered an asylum, as well as Uguccione dà Faggiuola, and many
other exiles illustrious in war or politics, were assembled at his court. He aspired to subdue the Veronese
and Trevisan marches, or what has since been called
the Terra Firma of Venice. He took possession of Vicenza; and afterwards maintained a long war against
the republic of Padua, the most powerful in the district,
and that which had shown the most attachment to the
Guelph party and to liberty. But Padua gave way to
all the excesses of democracy: the people evinced such
jealousy of all distinction, such inconstancy in their
choice, such presumption, that the imprudence of the
chiefs as well as of the mob drew down the greatest
disasters on the republic. The Paduans, repeatedly defeated by Can' Grande della Scala from 1314 to 1318,
sought protection by vesting the power in a single person; and fixed for that purpose on the noble house of
Carrara, which had long given leaders to the Guelph
party. The power vested in a single person soon extinguished all the courage and virtue that remained;
and on the 10th of September, 1328, Padua submitted
to Can' Grande della Scala. The year following he attacked and took Treviso, which surrendered on the 6th
of July, 1329. He possessed himself of Feltre and Civi-
dale soon after. The whole province seemed subjugated
to his power; but the conqueror also was subdued. Attacked in his camp with a mortal disease, he gave orders on entering Treviso, that his couch should be
carried into the great church, in which, four days afterwards, on the 22d of July, 1329, he expired. He was
not more than forty-one years of age: Castruccio was
forty-seven at his death. Galeazzo Visconti died nearly
about the same age, less than a year before. The Ghibeline party, which had produced such great captains,

thus saw them all disappear at once in the middle of their career. Passerino de' Bonacossi, tyrant of Mantua, who belonged to the same party, had been assassinated on the 14th of August, 1328, by the Gonzagas, who thus avenged an affront offered to the wife of one of them. They took possession of the sovereignty of Mantua, and kept it in their family till the eighteenth century. Of all the princes who had well received Louis of Bavaria in Italy, the marquis d'Este was the only one who preserved his power. He was lord of Ferrara; and even this prince, though Guelph by birth, was forced by the intrigues of the pope's legate to join the Ghibelines.

The Ghibeline party, which had been rendered so formidable by the ability of its captains, was now completely disorganised. The Lombards placed no confidence in those who remained; they had forgotten liberty, and dared no longer aspire to it; but they longed for a prince capable of defending them, and who, by his moderation and good faith, could give them hopes of peace. They saw none such in Italy: Germany unexpectedly offered one. John, king of Bohemia, the son of Henry VII, arrived at Trent towards the end of the year 1330. The memory of his father was rendered dearer to the Italians by the comparison of his conduct with that of his successor; and John was calculated to heighten this predilection. He could not submit to the barbarism of Bohemia; and inhabited, in preference, the county of Luxemburg, or Paris, and having acquired a spirit of heroism, by his constant reading, or listening to the French romances of chivalry, he aspired to the glory of being a complete knight. All that could at first sight seduce the people was united in him; beauty, valour, dexterity in all corporeal exercises, eloquence, an engaging manner. His conduct in France and Germany, where he had been, by turns, warrior and pacificator, was noble. He never sought any thing for himself; he seemed to be actuated only by the love of the general good or glory. The Italians, justly disgusted with their own princes, eagerly offered to throw

themselves into his arms; the city of Brescia sent deputies to Trent, to offer him the sovereignty of their republic. He arrived there, to take possession of it, on the
31st of December, 1330. Almost immediately after,
Bergamo, Cremona, Pavia, Vercelli, and Novara followed the example of Brescia. Azzo Visconti himself,
son of Galeazzo, who, in 1328, had repurchased Milan
from Louis of Bavaria, could not withstand the enthusiasm of his subjects; he nominally ceded the government to John, taking henceforth the title of his vicar
only. Parma, Modena, Reggio, and, lastly, Lucca also,
soon gave themselves to John of Bohemia. John, in all
these cities, recalled indiscriminately the Guelph and
Ghibeline exiles, restored peace, and made them, at
last, taste the first-fruits of good government.

But the Florentines, attached to liberty, and satisfied
with their constitution, who saw a foreign prince, a
Ghibeline, and the son of Henry VII, whom they had
always resisted, arrive on their frontier, could not participate in this infatuation. They knew that, whatever
might be the virtue and talents of an absolute prince,
his government always degenerated into tyranny; that,
if he was not himself corrupted by power, his successors
never failed of being so. Numerous examples in Italy,
in their own time, sufficiently demonstrated the rapid
degeneracy of the race of princes, and the profound
pity merited by a people governed by the son of a great
man. They were well aware that it was the municipal,
democratic, independent constitutions of the cities of
Italy, and the constant emulation between them, that
had given them such an immense superiority over the
rest of Europe. They easily perceived that Italy, in
spite of its division, had nothing to fear for its independence from its transalpine enemies; while it had
every thing to dread for its liberty, as well as for its
civilisation, from the immeasurable growth of an absolute principality formed within its bosom. The Florentines did not undertake to restore liberty to those
people who had no longer sufficient elevation of soul
to desire or energy to defend it; but they pursued for

themselves the noble policy of opposing all usurpation or conquest by any who pretended to domination in Italy; and if they could not preserve to each city its independence, at least of maintaining, through the changes which time necessarily brings, the balance between the different powers, in such a manner that respect for the rights of all should be guaranteed by the alliance of those who demanded only to be free themselves, and to preserve the liberty of others. This system of balancing the different powers in Italy, invented by the statesmen of Florence, was, during the fourteenth and the greater part of the fifteenth centuries, the fundamental rule of their conduct.

The Florentines did not find sufficient strength in the Guelph party to oppose the menacing greatness of the king of Bohemia. Robert of Naples was become old; he wanted energy, and his soldiers courage. The republic of Bologna, formerly so rich and powerful, had lost its vigour under the government of the legate, Bertrand de Poiet; those of Perugia and Sienna had within themselves few resources, and those few their jealousy of Florence prevented their liberally employing. There remained no more free cities in Lombardy; and all those, in the states of the church, which, during the preceding century, had shown so much spirit, had fallen under the yoke of some petty tyrant, who immediately declared for the Ghibeline party. The Florentines felt the necessity of silencing their hereditary enmities, and their ancient repugnances, and of making an alliance with the Lombard Ghibelines against John of Bohemia, with the condition that, in dividing his spoils, they should all agree to prevent the aggrandisement of any single power, and preserve between themselves an exact equilibrium, in order that Italy, after their conquests, should incur no danger of being subjugated by one of them. The treaty of alliance against the king of Bohemia, and the partition of the states which he had just acquired in Italy, was signed in the month of September, 1332. Cremona was to be given to Visconti; Parma to Mastino della Scala, the nephew and successor of Can' Grande; Reggio to Gonzaga; Modena to the marquis d'Este; and Lucca to the Florentines. John did not oppose to this league the resistance that was expected from his courage and talents. Of an inconstant character, becoming weary of every thing, always pursuing something new, thinking only of shining in courts and tournaments, he soon regarded all these little Italian principalities, of which he had already lost some, as too citizen-like and unlordly: he sold every town which had given itself to him, to whatever noble desired to rule over it; and he departed for Paris on the 15th of October, 1333, leaving Italy in still greater confusion than before. The Lombard Ghibelines, confederates of the Florentines, succeeded, before the end of the summer of 1335, in taking possession of the cities abandoned by the king of Bohemia. Lucca, which alone fell to the share of Florence, was defended by a band of German soldiers, who made it the centre of their depredations, and barbarously tyrannised over the Lucchese. Mastino della Scala offered to treat for the Florentines with the captains who then commanded at Lucca; and he succeeded in obtaining the surrender of the town to him, on the 20th of December, 1335. As soon as he became master of it, he began to flatter himself that it would afford him the means of subjugating the rest of Tuscany; and, instead of delivering it, as he had engaged, to the Florentines, he sought to renew against them a Ghibeline league jointly with the Pisans and all the independent nobles of the Apennines.

The Florentines, forced to defend themselves against their ally, who, after they had contributed to his elevation, betrayed them, sought the alliance of the Venetians, who also had reason to complain of Mastino. A treaty was signed between the two republics, on the 21st of June, 1336. The war to which Florence liberally contributed in money, was made only in Lombardy, and was successful. Padua was taken from Mastino on the 3d of August, 1337, and, as that town showed no ardent desire of liberty, it was given in sovereignty to the Guelph house of Carrara. The Venetians took possession of Treviso, Castel-Franco, and Ceneda. It was the first acquisition they had made beyond the Lagune, their first establishment on Terra Firma, which henceforward was to mingle their interests with those of the rest of Italy. But their ambition at this moment extended no farther. Satisfied themselves, and sacrificing their allies, they made peace with Mastino della Scala, on the 18th of December, 1338, without stipulating that the city of Lucca, the object of the war, should be given up to the Florentines, for which these had contracted a debt of 450,000 florins. The Florentines, successively betrayed by all their allies, saw the danger of their position augment daily; the Guelphs lost, one after the other, every supporter of their party: the vigour of the king of Naples, now seventy-five years of age, was gone. The pope, John XXII, had died at Avignon, on the 4th of December, 1334; and his successor, Benedict XII, like him a Frenchman, neither understood nor took any part in the affairs of Italy. A few months previous, on the 17th of March, 1334, the cardinal Bertrand de Poiet had been driven by the people from Bologna; and this ambitious legate, no longer supported by the pope his father, had disappeared from the political scene. But the Bolognese did not long preserve the liberty which they had recovered. One of their citizens, named Taddeo de Pepoli, the richest man in all Italy, had seduced the German guard which they held in pay, and by its aid took possession of the sovereignty of Bologna, on the 28th of August, 1337. He then made alliance with the Ghibelines. The number of the free cities, on the aid, or at least the sympathy, of which Florence could reckon, continually diminished. The Genoese, from the commencement of the century, had consumed their strength in internal wars between the great Guelph and Ghibeline families; as long as they were free, however, the Florentines, without any treaty of alliance, regarded them as friendly; but the long protracted civil wars had disgusted the people with the government: they rose on the 23d of September, 1339, and overthrew it, replacing the signoria by a single

chief, Boccanegra, on whom they conferred the title
of doge. It might have been feared they had only given
themselves a tyrant: but the first doge of Genoa was a
friend to liberty; and the Genoese people having imitated Venice, in giving themselves a first officer in the
state with that title, were not long before they carried
the imitation farther, by seeking to combine liberty
with power vested in a single person. In the mean while
Mastino della Scala suffered a Parmesan noble to take
from him the city of Parma. As from that time he had
no farther communication with Lucca, he offered to sell
it to the Florentines. The bargain was concluded in the
month of August, 1341; but it appeared to the Pisans
the signal of their own servitude, for it cut off all communication between them and the Ghibelines of Lombardy. They immediately advanced their militia into
the Lucchese states, to prevent the Florentines from
taking possession of the town; vanquished them in a
great battle, on the 2d of October, 1341, under the
walls of Lucca; and, on the 6th of July following, took
possession of that city for themselves.

The people of Florence attributed this train of disasters to the incapacity of their magistrates. The burden of the taxes, and of the debt with which the republic was loaded; and the jealousy entertained of the
rich merchants, who, in spite of the democratic form of
the constitution, in fact governed the state, excited a
discontent which soon took the darkest hue. The people
who in all Italy were regarded as by far the most republican, those who owed all their greatness to liberty,
for which they had made such immense sacrifices, the
people who carried their love of equality and their
jealousy of all distinction to excess, of a sudden appeared wearied of their own sovereignty; they demanded a master, in order to punish and humiliate
those who appeared too great to be reached by the
laws of a republic; they asked to submit to the authority of a single person. At this period, Gaultier de
Brienne, duke of Athens, a French noble, but born in
Greece, passed through Florence, on his way from Na-

ples to France. The duchy of Athens had remained in his family from the conquest of Constantinople till it was taken from his father in 1312. There remained to him only that of Lecce, in the kingdom of Naples. He had been the lieutenant of the duke of Calabria, at Florence, in 1326, and had then distinguished himself by his bravery and the acuteness of his understanding. It was for this man the Florentines, after their defeat at Lucca, took a sudden fancy. They protested they never should have experienced so many disasters if the duke of Athens had been at the head of their army. On the 1st of August, 1342, they obliged the signoria to confer on him the title of captain of justice, and give him the command of their militia.

The duke of Athens was of that degenerate race of Franks, established in the Levant, whom the people of the West designated by the name of *Pullani,* to indicate their small stature, their apparent weakness, and frequently their cowardice. To this physical conformation they joined the most unbridled love of pleasure, cunning, perfidy, habits of despotism, and contempt of human life; the vices, in short, which connection with the East necessarily communicates to barbarians, always more disposed to be corrupted than to improve. The duke of Athens was named president of the tribunals, and commander of the forces of the republic; offices of more power than ought to have been given to such a man, but not enough for his ambition: he aspired to be absolute sovereign, and to make a single duchy of Tuscany. He entered into negotiation with those cities which were subject to or allied with Florence, with a view to induce them to place themselves under his rule, and to shake off the yoke and alliance of the republic. With a rapidity of perception, and a talent for intrigue, which he had acquired in Greece, he, in a few days, unravelled all the secret designs, all the jealous passions, which divided the republic. He perceived that the first class of citizens, who had the greatest share in the government, had also the greatest share in the public hatred; they were objects of execration to the

ancient nobility, whom they had excluded from all the
offices of government; of jealousy to the second class of
citizens immediately under them; and of envy and anger to the populace, who declared themselves crushed
by the taxes. The duke of Athens sacrificed them to
these various passions; he beheaded many, and ruined
others by fines. He sent to France and Naples for a
troop of cavalry, better suited to intrigue than war. He
ordered them to mix among the people, seduce them
into taverns, and keep them in a constant state of in-
toxication, celebrating at the same time the valour and
liberality of the duke, and announcing to them that if
he was absolute master, he would make the poorest
people in Florence live in merriment and abundance.
Having thus excited the people to a ferment, he convoked them in parliament in the public square, on the
8th of September. The agitators directing the lowest
orders proclaimed him sovereign lord of Florence for
his life, forced the public palace, drove from it the
gonfalonier and the priori, and installed him there in
their place.

The liberty of Italy had been at an end, if the duke of
Athens had succeeded in establishing the despotism
of which he had just laid the foundation: all the other
republics seemed plunged in a deep lethargy. The desire of investing power in a single person had invaded
the proudest and most opulent cities, all those which
had before shown the greatest abhorrence of tyranny.
As the rest of Europe was not yet ready to profit by the
example and instruction of Italy, the slavery of Florence, the destruction of all liberty in the city which
gave impulse to the spirit of enquiry, to philosophy,
politics, eloquence, poetry, and the fine arts, would
have stopped, perhaps for centuries, the civilisation of
the world. Gaultier of Athens united all the qualities
that Machiavel, 160 years later, enumerated as necessary to a prince, the founder of a despotism. Courageous, dissembling, patient, clear-sighted, perfidious, he
knew neither respect nor pity; he was bound by no
affection and no principle: accordingly, he sought the

alliance of the Ghibeline tyrants of Romagna and Lombardy, whom he had till then combated as enemies to his sovereign the king of Naples. They on their side joyfully coalesced with a despot, who delivered them from an example which might prove contagious to their subjects in the liberty and happiness of Florence: he had no enemies abroad; and his executioners rapidly delivered him from the more dangerous of his enemies at home.

Happily, Florence was not ripe for slavery: ten months sufficed for the duke of Athens to draw from it 400,000 golden florins, which he sent either to France or Naples; but ten months sufficed also to undeceive all parties who had placed any confidence in him; to unite them all in one common hatred, and in a common determination to overthrow his tyranny. Three conspiracies, unconnected with each other, were secretly formed: they soon comprehended almost all the citizens of Florence. The duke, without discovering them, repeatedly defeated them, by the precautions, more rigorous each day, which he took for his security: his cruelty kept pace with his suspicions; he questioned with the torture all those on whom fell the slightest of his doubts; it was thus he was led to seize Baldinaccio degli Adimari, who, though the duke was unaware of it, was the chief of one of the conspiracies. The universal ferment which this arrest excited made him sensible that he was in the road to a discovery; he did not, however, betray his sentiments; he asked reinforcements from all his allies, and it was not till those were in motion that, on the 26th of July, he convoked three hundred of the most distinguished citizens, professedly to consult them on the affairs of the republic. Orders were given in the palace to put every one to death as soon as he entered; but the people also were ready. In each of the massive palaces of Florence, the citizens were silently assembling: they arrived one by one, without noise, and unperceived. The cavalry of the duke filled the street, where every body seemed occupied only with their own affairs; no agitation, no apparent confusion, announced any explosion, when suddenly the cry "To arms!" burst from the old market-place, and was re-echoed to the gates of St. Peter's. Instantly from every window, from the roofs of all the houses, fell a shower of stones and tiles, previously made ready, on the heads of the duke's cavalry; every palace opened and poured forth armed men, who threw chains across the streets, and made barricades: the cry of *"Popolo! Popolo! Libertà!"* resounded from one extremity of Florence to the other. The cavalry, surprised, dispersed, and overwhelmed with stones, were soon disarmed; the chains were then taken up, and troops of citizens united and marched to the Palazzo Vecchio, where the duke defended himself with 400 transalpine soldiers. Gaultier might have long held out in this massive fortress, if it had been sufficiently victualled; but hunger forced him to have recourse to the mediation of the bishop of Florence. He capitulated, on the 3d of August, 1343; the bishop concealed him till the 6th from the fury of the people, and sent him off secretly in the night with his cavalry, to whom the duke of Athens owed their pay; arrived at Venice, he stole away from his companions in misfortune, to avoid paying them, and escaped in a small vessel to Naples, whither he had previously sent his treasure.

CHAPTER VII

THE REVIVAL OF LETTERS   REVOLUTIONS ATTEMPTED BY TWO LEARNED MEN   ITALY RAVAGED BY THE PLAGUE, AND BY COMPANIES OF ADVENTURE   THE POWER OF THE HOUSE OF VISCONTI   WAR BETWEEN THE MARITIME REPUBLICS   THE DANGERS AND FIRMNESS OF THE REPUBLIC OF FLORENCE

THE oppression which weighed upon the rest of Europe contributed to the maintenance of barbarism, less by rendering difficult, and sometimes dangerous, the acquisition of knowledge, than by taking away all attraction from the exercise of the mind. Thought was a pain to those capable of judging the state of the human species—of studying the past; of comparing it with the present; and of thus foreseeing the future. Danger and suffering appeared on all sides. The men who, in France, Germany, England, and Spain, felt themselves endued with the power of generalising their ideas, either smothered them, not to aggravate the pain of thought, or directed them solely to speculations the farthest from real life—towards that scholastic philosophy which so vigorously exercised the understanding, without bringing it to any conclusion. In Italy, on the contrary, liberty secured the full enjoyment of intellectual existence. Every one endeavoured to develop the powers which he felt within him, because each was conscious that the more his mind opened the greater was his enjoyment; every one directed his powers to a useful and practical purpose, because each felt himself placed in a state of society in which he might attain some influence, either for his own benefit or that of his fellow-creatures. The first want which towns had experienced was that of their defence. Accordingly, military architecture had taken precedence in the arts. From its exercise the transition was easy to that of religious architecture, at a time when religion was indispensable to every heart, to civil architecture, then encouraged by a government in which every thing was for all. The study and pursuit of the beautiful in this first of the fine arts had paved the way to all the others. From the pleasures of the imagination through the eye, men ascended to those derived from the soul; and hence the birth of poetry.

In the sciences, also, the Italians had begun with the personal protection of man. The consideration of his health presented itself; and the earliest school of medicine was founded at Salerno, in the neighbourhood of the three republics of Gaëta, Naples, and Amalfi. Then followed that of his private rights and property; and the university of Bologna acquired immense celebrity in the teaching of civil and canon law, before any other study was diligently pursued. The rights of all naturally rose out of the rights of each; and politics, as a science, yet existed only in Italy. Statesmen sought, in history, how governments made the happiness or misery of nations, and the study of antiquity was pursued with ardour; while the two Villani wrote history with as much judgment, elevation of soul, and philosophy as Polybius. At the same time, the thinking men in France, who, instead of brutifying themselves in order to suffer less from despotism, anarchy, and the invasion of the English, exercised their understandings, passionately embraced the study of the scholastic theology. They commented on, and developed with subtlety, principles of which they did not permit themselves to judge; and the faculty of the Sorbonne, in the university of Paris, was acknowledged to be the first theological school in Europe; it was that in which the most acuteness and depth of thought were united to the most implicit faith. In Italy, on the contrary, the mind, accustomed to examine the claims of authority, had already produced, since the time of Frederick II, and still more after the translation from the Arabic of the books of Averrhoes, thinkers whom the priests accused not only of heresy, but of incredulity and epicurism.

The popular form of government must have early accustomed the Italians to speak in public; but the example of their preachers was prejudicial to their eloquence: they made discourses, instead of speaking. They supposed that they ought always to begin with what they called *proposing;* that is, taking a text from some celebrated author, either sacred or profane. And this support which they sought in what was said by another, introduced the substitution of pedantry for reason. Accordingly, the fourteenth century, in Italy so fruitful in great men, has left us no model of political eloquence. The Italians were accustomed to express in verse all that strongly moved them. Poetry was for them the language of truth and of persuasion, as much as of the imagination. Lyric poetry, above all, took the place of eloquence: it shone forth with great brilliancy in the fourteenth century. Some of the canzoni of Petrarch express the elevated sentiments of a great soul. A crowd of poets at this epoch obeyed the same inspiration. The name of Petrarch, born in 1304, and that of Boccaccio, in 1313, both Florentines, are the most universally known. The second owes his celebrity to the light, elegant, and easy prose of his novels, more than to his poetry. Both have descended to posterity with their Italian writings alone, which they regarded only as relaxations from their labour, and not with their Latin works, upon which they depended for their glory.

The Italians, in the fourteenth century, discovered, as it were, anew the ancient world: they felt an affinity of thoughts, hopes, and tastes with the best Latin writers, which inspired them with the highest admiration. Petrarch, and particularly Boccaccio, passed from this study to that of Grecian antiquity; and, on his solicitation, the republic of Florence, in 1360, founded a chair of Grecian literature, the first in the West. A passion for erudition spread from one end of Italy to the other, with an ardour proportionable to the dark ignorance of the preceding centuries. It was imagined that all knowledge consisted in knowing and imitating the ancient masters. The highest glory was attached to classical learning; and Petrarch and Boccaccio attained a degree of celebrity, credit, and power, unequalled by any other men in the middle ages; not by reason of those merits which we feel at the present day, but as the pontiffs and interpreters of antiquity.

We owe to the learned of the fourteenth century, and to their school, a deep sentiment of gratitude. They discovered, and rendered intelligible to us, all the *chefs-d'œuvre* of antiquity. Fragments only of classic works remained, scattered throughout Europe, and on the point of being lost. Those learned men of Italy collected, collated, and explained them: without their antiquarian zeal, all the experience of past ages, all the models of taste, all the great works of genius, would never have reached us; and, probably, without such guides we should never have attained the point on which we now stand. But they injured their own age by their exclusive bias to erudition. The imagination was extinguished; genius disappeared; and even the language retrograded. It was abandoned, as too vulgar, for the Latin, by all those who attained any distinction for talents: the forms of thinking of the ancients were adopted with those of their language, and pedantry soon smothered all national originality.

Two of these men, learned in the Greek and Latin literature, friends of Petrarch, loving liberty, not like Italians of the middle ages, but like sons of ancient Rome, profited by their celebrity and by their power over their auditors to re-establish a republican government;—Cola di Rienzo, at Rome, in 1347, and Jacopo de' Bussolari, ten years later, at Pavia. The former, though of obscure birth, soon signalised himself by his progress in letters, by his familiarity with all the writers of antiquity, by his knowledge of the manners and laws of the Romans, and of the monuments and inscriptions which still ornamented the capital of the world. No one possessed like him the art of explaining them, and of striking out in his explanations those traits of grandeur and glory which distinguish the ancient republic. Born at Rome, he was a more ardent Roman than republican; seeking rather to restore the sovereignty of the ancient city than the liberty of mankind. He rejected with deep indignation the usurpations of two barbarians; the one a German, calling himself Roman emperor; the other a Frenchman, who called himself the pontiff of Rome. All those who rose to eminence by the study and example of the ancient Romans appeared to him bound to labour to bring back Italy and mankind under the dominion of Rome. Petrarch had also a religious respect for the name of Rome; but living by turns at the court of Avignon, or at those of the tyrants of Lombardy, he had much less elevation of soul and true enthusiasm than Cola di Rienzo. The latter was susceptible of all the emotion which the fine arts give; and he employed his own sensibility to act on a susceptible people. Sometimes at the foot of one of the most admirable

monuments of ancient architecture, he explained its
purpose to the crowd, by which he was always attended; he made them feel its beauty, and would take
occasion to recall the grandeur and freedom of ancient
Rome, which still spoke to her children from those colossal ruins. He would contrast it with the state of degradation and suffering to which Rome was then reduced. He sometimes interpreted in the public places
the inscriptions which he discovered; and would draw
forth proofs of the sovereignty which Rome exercised
over the whole world. Sometimes he displayed in the
capitol allegorical pictures which he had composed,
and, in explaining them, would call upon the Roman
people to quit their state of servitude, and recover what
he emphatically called the *good state*. The pope had
never exercised any sovereign power in Rome; but the
absence of his court, in ruining the little commerce of
the tradesmen, had contributed to throw the city into
a desolate state of anarchy. The nobles had reduced
the government, composed of a senator and thirteen
caporioni to entire dependence on themselves; and the
nobility of Rome, as well as of the rest of Italy, believed it beneath their station to be submissive to the
law. The Colonna, Orsini, and Savelli families, always
at war with each other, garrisoned all the fortresses in
Rome with banditti, their satellites; and at their head
made daily attacks in the streets upon each other. Cola
di Rienzo had a classic hatred for these turbulent nobles; a hatred which he believed he had inherited from
the Gracchi. He felt anxious to be made tribune of the
people, in order to deliver them from the yoke of the
patricians; and on the 20th of May, 1347, while the
Colonnas had quitted Rome with a small body of troops,
he summoned the people to take possession of the government and of the guard of the city. The Romans appointed him, with the bishop of Orvieto, the pope's
vicar, or depository of his spiritual power, as tribunes.
They ascended the capitol together. At first the revolution seemed accomplished. The power of the name of
Rome; the joy of men of letters throughout Europe;

the hatred provoked by the Roman nobles; the indifference of the pope, and his distance from Rome, favoured this revolution. For some weeks it was approved and acknowledged by all Italy. But Cola di Rienzo, though eloquent, learned, and a poet, was neither a statesman nor a warrior: he knew not how to consolidate this *good state*, to which he pretended to have restored the Romans. He continued to occupy them with allegories, festivals, and processions, while they demanded of him something more positive. His head was turned by vanity; and he assumed a degree of pomp which excited ridicule. He had soon to support a war against the nobles whom he had exiled; and though several of the Colonnas perished in an ill-conducted attack on Rome, Cola in repelling them gave proofs of incapacity and cowardice. The pope sent a legate to Rome, to appease the civil war; and this legate, being a French noble, sided with the nobility. The latter having taken possession of a division of the town, the tocsin summoned the people to defend themselves, but it sounded in vain; and on the 15th of December, 1347, Cola di Rienzo, obliged to abandon the capitol, retreated to the castle of St. Angelo, and afterwards sought refuge with Charles IV, son of John, king of Bohemia, who gave him up to the pope in 1352.

The pope Innocent VI, having in the following year charged his legate, Egidio Albornoz, to recover the ecclesiastical states from the hands of the tyrants who in each city had seized the sovereignty, made Cola di Rienzo accompany him, in order to profit by the influence which the tribune might still have retained at Rome. The legate sent him there in the month of July, 1354; declaring at the same time that he made him Roman senator by the authority of the pope. Cola found again his friends at Rome, and for a short time succeeded in awakening the popular enthusiasm; but he was now only an instrument in the hand of the legate, and it did not depend on him to realise the hopes which he excited. A new sedition broke forth; and this time the people joined his enemies the Colonnas: his

palace was burnt down, he was arrested as he endeavoured to escape in disguise, dragged to the porphyry
lion at the foot of the capitol stairs, and there stabbed,
on the 8th of October, 1354.

The monk Jacopo de' Bussolari, who in the month of
March, 1356, had also restored a sort of ephemeral
liberty to Pavia, was, like Cola, a learned man, a poet,
and a friend of Petrarch; he was a man of ardent imagination, who had borrowed his love of liberty from
the ancients. He was a monk of St. Augustine, and was
sent to his birthplace, Pavia, to preach there during
Lent. This city had been governed, since the year 1313,
by the Ghibeline family of Beccaria, who were supported from abroad by the Viscontis, and the marquis
de Montferrat. A war having broken out between the
marquis and the lords of Milan, the Beccarias declared
against the Viscontis, who had till then regarded the
lords of Pavia almost as their lieutenants. The Viscontis
in their anger besieged Pavia; and the city would soon
have fallen, if Jacopo de' Bussolari had not, by his eloquent sermons, roused the energy of the Pavesans: he
preached the reform of morals, faith, liberty, and courage; he at the same time animated them by his example. On the 27th of May, 1356, in descending from the
pulpit, he placed himself at their head; marched out
of the town; attacked the redoubts of the Milanese,
took three, one after the other; and forced the Viscontis
to raise the siege. It was as important to deliver his
country from domestic tyranny as from a foreign yoke.
As he often preached against the vices and usurpations
of the Beccarias, they endeavoured to get him assassinated; the Pavesans, to protect him, supplied him with
a guard; there were several engagements between the
faithful troops of their pastor and the satellites of the
tyrants. At last Jacopo de' Bussolari issued an order to
the Beccarias, to leave the city: they obeyed, but, making an alliance with the Viscontis, renewed the war. In
1358, the monk caused the palaces of the Beccarias to
be rased to the ground; in 1359, the Viscontis again
besieged the city. An epidemical disease broke out in

it with virulence; all the allies which Jacopo de' Bussolari had procured the Pavesans successively abandoned them. The eloquent and courageous monk perceived that he must at last yield to fortune; and in the
month of October, 1359, offered to capitulate with the
Viscontis, and to deliver the city to them, on condition
that they should preserve all the municipal liberties,
that the exiles whom he had recalled should be allowed
to remain, and that an amnesty should be granted the
citizens, without a single exception: he stipulated nothing for himself; and the Viscontis employing his ecclesiastical superiors against him, he was confined in the
prison of his convent at Vercelli, where he died a miserable death. They afterwards annulled the capitulation of Pavia; declaring that, as they were imperial
vicars, they could not be held to execute any thing
which they promised, contrary to the rights of the
empire.

This empire had passed from Louis of Bavaria, who
died on the 10th of October, 1347, to Charles IV of
Bohemia. He had been set up as competitor with the
former by the pope, on the 10th of July, 1346, and
was called the king of the priests: he was, however,
soon after the death of Louis, acknowledged by the
whole empire. Desirous of obtaining the same acknowl-
edgment in Italy, he entered it on the 14th of October,
1354, but without an army; "appearing," says Villani,
"with his disarmed knights mounted on travelling pal-
freys, rather as a merchant going to a fair than an emperor." He was crowned at Milan, and afterwards at
Rome: and extracted from the republics, as he passed, a
ransom for their liberty; he caused, by his petty intrigues, much trouble and insurrection, but he at the
same time degraded, in the eyes of the Italians, the
imperial majesty, by his cupidity, and want of dignity
and energy. The popes who succeeded each other at
Avignon also lost the respect of the faithful by their
immoralities, intrigues, and ambition. To Benedict XII,
an honest but weak man, possessing a feeble understanding, had succeeded, in 1342, Clement VI, who

lighted the fire of civil war again in Germany, and signalised himself in his Italian politics by the most atrocious treachery. Towards the end of 1352, he was succeeded by Innocent VI. This pope formed the project of recovering the state belonging to the church; the sovereignty of which the imperial charters had abandoned to him. He made choice, for this purpose, of cardinal Albornoz, a Spaniard, who had already signalised himself in arms against the Moors; he gave the cardinal little money and few soldiers, but he reckoned, and with some reason, on the favour of the people. These last, in every city of Romagna and of the March, had suffered themselves to be enslaved by the boldest and richest of their fellow-citizens: all were wearied with the yoke of these petty tyrants, and, without any good reason to trust to the government of the church, they were glad of a change. Albornoz, who had still more ability in intrigue than he had military talent, succeeded in setting these tyrants at variance one with the other; in obtaining the assistance of the Guelphs of Tuscany; and, finally, in deposing and subduing them all: but before he terminated these conquests, Innocent VI died, on the 12th of September, 1362, and was succeeded by Urban V.

The kings of Naples, during this period, had sunk still lower in power and consideration. Robert died on the 19th of January, 1343, at the age of eighty. He had given his grand-daughter, Joan, in marriage to her cousin Andrew, the son of the king of Hungary. Andrew was son of the eldest son of Charles II; and had a better right than Robert himself to the crown of Naples. The latter, whom his nephew regarded as an usurper, had been desirous of confounding the rights of the two branches of his family, by marrying Joan to Andrew, and crowning them together; but these young people felt towards each other only jealousy and hatred. Andrew was brutal, Joan was elegant in her manners, but depraved. She consented to an assassination, which delivered her from her husband, on the 18th of September, 1345; and two years after, married her cousin,

Louis of Tarento, the instigator of the murder. The crown of Hungary had passed to the elder brother of Andrew—Louis, called the Great. To avenge his brother, he entered Italy, and conquered Naples in 1348. Joan, meanwhile, fled, with her husband, to Provence; and, to conciliate the favour of the pope, abandoned to him the sovereignty of Avignon. It was exactly at the period of the greatest calamity that ever befell mankind. The plague, brought from the East, made the circuit of Italy, and afterwards of all Europe; and in every place it reached carried off, in seven or eight months, one third of the population. It is known in history by the name of "the plague of Florence"; because, while it mowed down millions of obscure victims elsewhere, at Florence, where it carried off nearly a hundred thousand persons, an advanced civilisation rendered the loss more sensibly felt. Many distinguished men sank under this scourge; several philosophers studied it; and a great writer, Boccaccio, has left of it an admirable description. The terror and desolation, which an infliction so dreadful caused throughout Italy, superseded all political hatreds—all wars, however obstinate. Louis of Hungary, in the middle of his campaign and of his successes, was discouraged, upon seeing the most flourishing armies swept off by sickness. In 1351, he signed a peace with Joan, who returned with her husband to her kingdom of Naples, where both long continued their career of vice and voluptuousness; abandoning all care of administration, and of the national defence; permitting their provinces, in the bosom of peace, to be plundered and laid waste, in a manner hardly to be feared in the most disastrous wars.

The most immediate cause of the sufferings of the kingdom of Naples, and of all Italy, was the formation of what was called "companies of adventure." Wherever tyrants had succeeded to free governments, their first care had been to disarm the citizens, whose resistance was to be feared; and although a little industry might soon have supplied swords and lances, yet the danger of being denounced for using them soon made the subjects of these princes lose every military habit. Even the citizens of free towns no longer thought of defending themselves: their way of life had weakened their corporeal strength; and they felt an inferiority too discouraging when they had to oppose, without defensive armour, cuirassiers on horseback. The chief strength of armies henceforth was in the heavy-armed cavalry, composed of men who had all their lives followed the trade of war, and who hired themselves for pay. The emperors had successively brought into Italy many of their countrymen, who afterwards passed into the service of the tyrant princes. The Viscontis and Della Scalas had sent for many to Germany, believing that these men—who did not understand the language of the country, who were bound to it by no affection, and who were accessible to no political passion—would be their best defenders. They proved ready to execute the most barbarous orders, and for their recompense demanded only the enjoyments of an intemperate sensuality.

But the Lombard tyrants were deceived in believing the German soldier would never covet power for himself, and would continue to abuse the right of the stronger for the advantage of others only. These adventurers soon discovered that it would be better to make war and pillage the people for their own profit, without dividing the spoil with a master. Some men of high rank, who had served in Italy as *condottieri* (hired captains), proposed to their soldiers to follow them, make war on the whole world, and divide the booty among themselves. The first company, formed by an Italian noble at the moment that the Viscontis dismissed their soldiers, having made peace with their adversaries, made an attack suddenly on Milan, in the hope of plundering that great city; but was almost annihilated in a battle, fought at Parabiago, on the 20th of February, 1339. A German duke, known only by his Christian name of Werner, and the inscription he wore on his breast of "enemy of God, of pity, and of mercy," formed, in 1343, another association, which maintained itself for a long time, under the name of "the great company." It in turns entered the service of princes; and, when they made peace, carried on its ravages and plunderings for its own profit. The duke Werner and his successors—the count Lando, a German; and the friar Moriale, knight of St. John—devastated Italy from Montferrat to the extremity of the kingdom of Naples. They raised contributions, by threatening to burn houses and harvests, or by putting the prisoners whom they took to the most horrible tortures. The provinces of Apulia were, above all, abandoned to their devastations; and the king and queen of Naples made not a single effort to protect their people.

There now remained no more than six independent princes in Lombardy. The Viscontis, lords of Milan, had usurped all the central part of that province; the western part was held by the marquis of Montferrat, and the eastern by the Della Scala, lords of Verona, Carrara of Padua, Este of Ferrara, and Gonzaga of Mantua. These weaker princes felt themselves in danger, and made a league against the Viscontis, taking into their service the great company; but, deceived and pillaged by it, they suffered greater evils than they inflicted on their enemies. When at last the money of the league was exhausted, and it could no longer pay the company, this band of robbers entered into the service of the republic of Sienna, to be let loose on that of Perugia, of which the Siennese had conceived a deep jealousy. But the Florentines would not consent to their entering Tuscany, where their depredations had been already felt. They shut all the passes of the Apennines; they armed the mountaineers; they made these adventurers experience a first defeat at the passage of Scalella, on the 24th of July, 1358, and obliged them to fall back on Romagna. The legate Albornoz, to deliver himself from such guests, made them enter Perugia the year following. Never had the company been so brilliant and so formidable: it levied contributions on Sienna, as well as Perugia; but vengeance and cupidity alike excited them against the Florentines. They determined on pillaging those rich merchants, whom they considered far from warlike, or forcing them to ransom themselves.

The Marquis de Montferrat, desirous of taking the company into his service, pressed the republic of Florence, by his ambassadors to do what the greatest potentates had always done—pay the banditti to be rid of them. He offered himself for mediator and guarantee, and promised a prompt and cheap deliverance; but the Florentine republic protested it would not submit to any thing so base; it assembled an army purely Italian, placing it under the command of an Italian captain, who was ordered to advance to the frontier, and offer battle to the company. The robbers gave way in proportion to the firmness of the republic: they made the tour of the Florentine frontier by Sienna, Pisa, and Lucca, always threatening, yet never daring to violate it. On the 12th of July, 1359, they sent the Florentine commander a challenge to battle, and afterwards failed to keep the rendezvous which they had given. They escaped at last from Tuscany, without having fought, and divided themselves in the service of different princes, humbled indeed, but too much accustomed to this disorderly life not to be anxious to begin it anew.

The republic of Florence was continually occupied, since the expulsion of the duke of Athens, in guarding against the ambition of the Viscontis, which threatened the subjugation of all Italy. Azzo Visconti, the son of that Galeazzo who had been so treacherously used by Louis of Bavaria, had, in 1328, purchased the city of Milan from that emperor, and soon afterwards found himself master of ten other cities of Lombardy; but he died suddenly, in the height of his prosperity, the 16th of August, 1339. As he left no children, his uncle Luchino succeeded him in the sovereignty. Luchino was false and ferocious, but clever, and possessed in war the hereditary talent of the Viscontis. He was called a lover of justice, probably because he punished criminals with an excess of cruelty, and maintained by terror a perfect police in his states. He died, poisoned by his wife, on the 23d of January, 1349. His brother John, archbishop of Milan, succeeded him in power. The latter found himself master of sixteen of the largest cities in Lombardy; cities which, in the preceding century, had been so many free and flourishing republics. His ambition continually aspired to more extensive conquests; and, on the 16th of October, 1350, he engaged the brothers Pepoli to cede to him Bologna. These nobles, who had usurped the sovereignty of their country, were at this time engaged in a quarrel with the legate, Giles Albornoz, who asserted that Bologna belonged to the holy see. The archbishop was already treated by the pope as an enemy; and preferred exciting still further his wrath, to the renunciation of so important an acquisition. When Clement VI summoned him to come, and justify himself at the court of Avignon, he answered, that he would present himself there at the head of 12,000 cavalry and 6000 infantry. The pope, in his alarm, ceded to him the fief of Bologna, on the 5th of May, 1352, on condition of receiving from him an annual tribute of 12,000 florins. Florence saw, with terror, this city, which had so long been her most powerful and faithful ally, the Guelph city of letters, commerce, and liberty, thus pass under the yoke of a tyrant, who had designs upon her liberty also; who laid snares around her; who formed alliances against her with all the petty tyrants of Romagna, and all the Ghibeline lords of the Apennines. She was at peace with him, it was true; but she well knew that the Viscontis neither believed themselves bound by any treaty, nor kept any pledge.

The number of free cities continually diminished. Pisa was still free, but had, from attachment to the Ghibeline party, made alliance with the Viscontis. Sienna and Perugia were free also, but weak and jealous; they were incessantly disturbed by internal dissensions. The Florentines could not reckon on them. The archbishop of Milan suddenly ordered, towards the end of the summer, 1351, John Visconti da' Oleggio, his lieutenant at Bologna, to push into Tuscany at the head of a formidable army, without any declaration of war. The republic had no ally, and but slight reliance on the mercenaries in its service; but the Florentines, who showed little bravery in the open field, defended themselves obstinately behind walls; and the great village of Scarperia, in the Mugello, although so ill fortified that the walls of many of the houses served instead of a surrounding wall, and having a garrison of only 200 cuirassiers and 300 infantry, stopped the Milanese general sixty-one days. He was at last obliged, on the 16th of October, to retire to Bologna.

The republics of Venice and Genoa were, it might have been thought, the natural allies to whom the Florentines should have had recourse for their common defence. Their interests were the same; and the Viscontis had resolved not to suffer any free state to subsist in Italy, lest their subjects should learn that there was a better government than their own. Unhappily, these two republics, irritated by commercial quarrels in the East, were then engaged in an obstinate war with each other. The Genoese had fortified Pera, a suburb of Constantinople, of which they had rendered themselves masters, as well as of Caffa in the Crimea; and these two colonies almost equalled the metropolis in wealth and magnificence. These republicans engaged in a quarrel with the emperor Cantacuzene, besieged his capital, and burnt his fleet. Two years later, they quarrelled also with the Crimean Tartars at Caffa, and attempted to interdict the Latins from carrying on any commerce with them at Tana, now Taganrok. This attempt produced a quarrel with the Venetians, and a war between these two states was the consequence. The Venetians formed an alliance with the Greek emperor, and with Peter IV of Aragon; formidable fleets, commanded the one by the Genoese admiral, Paganino Doria, the other by the Venetian, Nicolo Pisani, displayed a courage and ability to resist at once man and the elements, which no maritime people have ever since surpassed. On the 13th of February, 1352, Paganino Doria, with sixty-four galleys, attacked, in the straits of the Bosphorus, the Venetians, Catalonians, and Greeks, who had collected, at least, seventy-eight vessels. A violent tempest assailed, in those narrow seas, the two fleets in the midst of their combat: they were over-taken by a dark night; whilst the violence of the winds and tide mixed their vessels, and drove them one against the other. The loss on both sides was prodigious; but the morning discovered to Pisani that he was no longer in a state to continue the combat: he retired to Candia, and the Greeks made peace with the Geno-ese. A battle, not less bloody, took place in the following year, on the 29th of August, off the coast of Loiera, in Sardinia. Paganino Doria no longer commanded the Genoese; they were defeated with immense loss: in their distress and discouragement, they gave themselves up, on the 10th of October, 1353, to John Visconti, lord of Milan. This tyrant, the richest in Italy, helped them to re-establish their fleet; the command was given anew to Paganino Doria, who attacked and destroyed the Venetian fleet in the Gulf of Sapienza, in the Morea, on the 3d of November, 1354. The Venetians, ex-hausted by such great exertions, made peace in the month of May following.

Genoa had sacrificed her liberty to her thirst of vengeance; for although the republic had not conferred the signoria on the archbishop Visconti without im-posing conditions, it soon experienced that oaths are not binding on a prelate and a tyrant. The freedom of Venice also was in the utmost danger from the conse-quences of the same war. It was only a few months after the peace was signed, that Marino Faliero was elected successor to Andrea Dandolo, in the ducal chair, on the 11th of September, 1354. The disorders and calamities of war had relaxed every social tie; the merchants, and the workmen employed in the construc-tion of vessels, were discontented; the nobles conducted themselves with increasing insolence; and the laws were ill observed. Marino Faliero, who was old, and furiously jealous of a young and beautiful wife, was insulted, under a mask, during the carnival, by the president of the quarantia. He believed the offender in love with his wife. The offence he received was not punished with the severity which he demanded. He lent an ear to the complaints of the plebeians, many of whom had experienced in their domestic life mortal injuries from the young nobility; and excited a conspiracy, of which he consented to be the chief. But just as he was on the point of wreaking his vengeance on the government of his country, and on the whole order of nobles, some of his accomplices were denounced to the Council of Ten: they were seized, and put to the torture, on the night of the 15th of April, 1355. Their disclosures implicated the doge, who was also arrested, and on the day after was beheaded.

Though the war of the maritime republics might have deprived Florence of the aid of Venice or Genoa, it had at least diverted the attention of John Visconti; made him direct his exertions elsewhere; and procured some repose to Tuscany. He died on the 5th of October, 1354, before he could renew his attacks; and his three nephews, the sons of his brother Stephen, agreed to succeed him in common. The eldest, who showed less talent for government, and more sensuality and vice, than his brothers, was poisoned by them the year following. The two survivors, Barnabas and Galeazzo, divided Lombardy between them; preserving an equal right on Milan, and in the government. Their relative, Visconti da' Oleggio, who was their lieutenant at Bologna, made himself independent in that city nearly about the same time that the Genoese, indignant at seeing all their conventions violated, rose in insurrection on the 15th of November, 1356, drove out the Milanese garrison, and again set themselves free.

The entry of Charles IV into Tuscany formed also a favourable diversion, by suspending the projects of the Viscontis against the Florentines; but it cost them 100,000 florins, which they agreed to pay Charles by treaty on the 12th of March, 1355, to purchase his rights on their city, and to obtain his engagement that he should nowhere enter the Florentine territory. The republics of Pisa and Sienna, who received him within their walls, paid still dearer for the hospitality which they granted him. The emperor encouraged the malcontents in both cities; he aided them to overthrow the existing governments; he hoped by so doing to make these republics little principalities, which he intended to bestow as an apanage on his brother, the patriarch of Aquileia: but after having caused the ruin of his partisans; after having ordered or permitted the execution of the former magistrates, who were innocent of any crime, insurrections of the people forced him to quit both cities, without retaining the smallest influence in either. After he had quitted Italy, the Viscontis were engaged in the war to which we have already alluded, against the marquises of Este, of Montferrat, della Scala, Gonzaga, and Carrara. The siege of Pavia, and the ravages of the great company exhausted their resources, but did not make them abandon their projects on Tuscany. The influence which they retained in the republic of Pisa, as chiefs of the Ghibeline party, seemed to facilitate their schemes.

Pisa, in losing its maritime power and its possessions in Sardinia, had not lost its warlike character; it was still the state in Italy where the citizens were best exercised in the use of arms, and evinced the most bravery. It had given proofs of it in conquering, under the eye of the Florentines, the city of Lucca, which it still retained. Nevertheless, since the peace made by the duke of Athens on the 14th of October, 1342, commercial interests had reconciled the two republics. The Florentines had obtained a complete enfranchisement from all imposts in the port of Pisa; they had established there their counting-houses, and attracted thither a rich trade. From that time the democratic party predominated in the Pisan republic; at its head was a rich merchant, named Francesco Gambacorta, who attached himself to the Florentines, and to the maintenance of peace. His party was called that of the Bergolini; while that of the great Ghibeline families attached to the counts of la Gherardesca, who despised com-

merce and excited war, was called the Raspanti party.
The Viscontis sought the alliance of the latter; the moment did not appear to them yet arrived in which they
could assume to themselves the dominion over all Tuscany. It was sufficient for their present views to exhaust
the Florentine republic by a war, which would disturb
its commerce; to weaken the spirit of liberty and energy
in the Pisans, by subduing them to the power of the
aristocracy, in the hope, that when once they had
ceased to be free, and had submitted to a domestic
tyrant, they would soon prefer a great to a little prince,
and throw themselves into his arms. The revolution,
which in 1355 had favoured the emperor in restoring
power to the Raspanti, facilitated this project.

In pursuance of this view, the party of the Raspanti,
at the suggestion of the Viscontis, in 1357 began to
disturb the Florentines in the enjoyment of the franchises secured to them at Pisa by the treaty of peace.
The Florentines, guessing the project of the Lombard
tyrant, instead of defending their right by arms, resolved on braving an unwholesome climate, and sub-
mitting to the inconvenience of longer and worse roads,
transported all their counting-houses to Telamone, a
port in the maremma of Sienna. They persisted till 1361
in despising all the insults of the Pisans, as well as in
rejecting all their offers of reconciliation: at length,
animosity increasing on both sides, the war broke out,
in 1362. The Viscontis supplied the Pisans with soldiers.
France during this period had been laid waste by the
war with the English; and as the sovereigns were rarely
in a state to pay their troops, there had been formed,
as in Italy, companies of adventurers, English, Gascon,
and French, who lived at the cost of the country, plundering it with the utmost barbarity. The peace of
Bretigny permitted several of these companies to pass
into Italy: they carried with them the plague, which
made not less ravages in 1361 than it had done in 1348.
The English company commanded by John Hawkwood,
an adventurer, who rendered himself celebrated in
Italy, was sent to the Pisans by Barnabas Visconti. After

various successes, the two republics, at last exhausted
by the plague, and by the rapacity, and want of discipline of the adventurers whom they had taken into
pay, made peace on the 17th of August, 1364. But the
purpose of the Viscontis was not the less attained. The
Pisans having exhausted their resources, were at a loss
to make the last payment of 30,000 florins to their
army; they were reduced to accept the offer made them
by Giovanni Agnello, one of their fellow-citizens, of
advancing that sum, on condition of being named doge
of Pisa. The money had for this purpose been secretly
advanced by Barnabas Visconti, to whom Agnello had
pledged his word never to consider himself more than
his lieutenant at Pisa. Thus the field fertilised by liberty
became continually more circumscribed; and Florence,
always threatened by the tyrants of Lombardy, saw
around her those only who had alienated their liberty,
and who had no longer any sentiment in common with
the republic.

CHAPTER VIII

THE FLORENTINES SUMMON THE CITIES BELONGING TO
THE STATES OF THE CHURCH TO RECOVER THEIR
LIBERTY   GREAT   WESTERN   SCHISM   WAR   OF
CHIOZZA   INSURRECTIONS   OF   THE   POPULACE
AGAINST   THE   CITIZENS   CONQUESTS   OF   GIAN
GALEAZZO VISCONTI, DUKE OF MILAN   HIS DEATH

THE chief magistrates of the Florentine republic could
not conceal from themselves the danger which now
menaced the liberty of Italy. They found themselves
closed in—blockaded, as it were—by the tyrants, who
daily made some new progress. The two brothers Visconti, masters of Lombardy, had at their disposal immense wealth and numerous armies; and their ambition
was insatiable. They were allied, by marriage, to the
two houses of France and England: their intrigues extended throughout Italy, and every tyrant was under

their protection. At the same time, their own subjects trembled under frightful cruelties. They shamelessly published an edict, by which the execution of state criminals was prolonged to the period of forty days. In it the particular tortures to be inflicted, day by day, were detailed, and the members to be mutilated designated, before death was reached. On the other hand, their finances were in good order; they liberally recompensed their partisans, and won over traitors in every state inimical to them. They pensioned the captain of every company of adventurers, on condition that he engaged to return to their service whenever called upon. Meanwhile, these captains, with their soldiers, over-ran, plundered, and exhausted Italy, during the intervals of peace; reducing the country to such a state as to be incapable of resisting any new attack. All the Ghibelines, all the nobles who had preserved their independence in the Apennines, were allied to the Viscontis. The march of these usurpers was slow, but it seemed sure. The moment was foreseen to approach when Tuscany would be theirs, as well as Lombardy; particularly as Florence had no aid to expect either from Genoa or Venice. These two maritime republics appeared to have withdrawn themselves from Italy, and to place their whole existence in distant regions explored by their commerce.

For a moment, the few Italian states still free were led to believe that the succour, now so necessary, to enable them to resist the Viscontis, would arrive both from France and Germany. The pope and the emperor announced their determination to deliver the country, over which they assumed a supreme right, from every other yoke. Urban V, moved by the complaints of the Christian world, declared that his duty, as bishop of Rome, was to return and live there; and Charles IV protested that he would deliver his Roman empire from the devastations of the adventurers, and from the usurpations of the Lombard tyrants. In 1367, Urban returned to Italy; and the same year formed a league with the emperor, the king of Hungary, the lords of

Padua, Ferrara, and Mantua, and with the queen of
Naples—against the Viscontis. But when Charles entered Italy, on the 5th of May, 1368, he thought only
of profiting by the terror with which he inspired the
Viscontis, to obtain from them large sums of money; in
return for which he granted them peace. He afterwards
continued his march through the peninsula, with no
other object than that of collecting money. His presence, however, caused some changes favourable to liberty. A festival was prepared for him at Lucca, on the
7th of September; on which day he intended confirming, by his investiture, the sovereignty of the doge Gian
Agnello over Pisa and Lucca. But the stage on which
Agnello had mounted gave way, and in the fall he
broke his leg. The Pisans profited by this accident to
recover their freedom, and the emperor kept Lucca for
himself. At Sienna, he favoured a revolution which
overthrew the ruling aristocracy; intending, on his return to that city, after a devotional visit to Rome, to
take advantage of the disturbance, and get himself appointed to the signoria: but a sedition against him broke
forth on the 18th of January, 1369. Barricades were
raised on all sides; his guards were separated from him,
and disarmed; his palace was broken into. No attempt,
indeed, was made on his person; but he was left alone
several hours in the public square, addressing himself
in turn to the armed troops which closed the entrance
of every street, and which, immovable and silent, remained insensible to all his entreaties. It was not till
he began to suffer from hunger, that his equipages
were restored to him, and he was permitted to leave
the town. He returned to Lucca, where he had already
lived, in the time of his father, as prince royal of Bohemia. The Lucchese were attached to him, and placed
in him their last hope to be delivered from a foreign
yoke, which had weighed upon them since the year
1314. They declared themselves ready to make the
greatest sacrifices for the recovery of their freedom;
and they, at the same time, testified to him so much
confidence and affection as to touch his heart. By a

diploma, on the 6th of April, 1369, Charles restored
them to liberty, and granted them various privileges;
but, on quitting their city, he left in it a German garrison, with orders not to evacuate that town till the Lucchese had paid the price of their liberty. It was not till
the month of April, 1370, and not without the aid of
Florence and their other allies, that they could acquit
the enormous sum of 300,000 florins, the price of the
re-establishment of their republic. The Guelph exiles
were then immediately recalled; a close alliance was
contracted with Florence; and the signoria, composed
of a gonfalonier and ten anziani, to be changed every
two months, was reconstituted.

Urban V, on his arrival in Italy, endeavoured also to
oppose the usurpations of the Viscontis, who had just
taken possession of San Miniato, in Tuscany, and who,
even in the states of the church, were rendering themselves more powerful than the pope himself. Of the two
brothers, Barnabas Visconti was more troublesome to
him, by his intrigues. Urban had recourse to a bull of
excommunication, and sent two legates to bear it to
him; but Barnabas forced these two legates to eat, in
his presence, the parchment on which the bull was
written, together with the leaden seals and silken
strings. The pope, frightened at the thought of combating men who seemed to hold religion in no respect,
and wearied, moreover, with his ill successes, was glad
to return to the repose of Avignon, where he arrived in
the month of September, 1370; and died the November
following.

Gregory XI, who succeeded him, was ambitious, cov-
etous, and false. He joined the Florentines in their war
against the Viscontis; but the legates, to whom he had
entrusted the government of the ecclesiastical states,
and who had rendered themselves odious by their rapacity and immorality, formed the project of seizing
for themselves Tuscany, which they had engaged to
defend. All the troops of the Florentines had been
placed at their disposal, for the purpose of carrying
the war into Lombardy. The cardinal legate, who com-

manded the combined army, resided at Bologna; the
church having rescued that city from the grasp of Visconti da' Oleggio, on the 31st of March, 1360. He
signed a truce with Barnabas Visconti, in the month
of June, 1375; and, before the Florentines could recall
their soldiers, sent John Hawkwood with a formidable
army to surprise Florence. The Florentines, indignant
at such a shameless want of good faith on the part of
the church, whose most faithful allies they had always
been, vowed vengeance on the see of Rome. They determined to rouse the spirit of liberty in every city belonging to it, and drive out the French legates—more
odious and perfidious than the most abhorred of the
Italian tyrants. They, in the month of June, 1375, without placing any confidence in Barnabas Visconti, made
an alliance with him against the priests, who had just
deceived them under the faith of the most solemn
oaths. They admitted the republics of Sienna, Lucca,
and Pisa into this league; they formed a commission of
eight persons, to direct the military department, called
"the eight of war"; they assembled a numerous army,
and gave it colours, on which was inscribed, in golden
letters, the word "LIBERTY." This army entered the
states of the church, proclaiming that the Florentines
demanded nothing for themselves—that not only would
they make no conquests, but would accept dominion
over no people who might offer themselves: they were
desirous only of universal liberty—and would assist the
oppressed with all their power, solicitous for the recovery of their freedom.

The army of liberty carried revolution into all the
states of the church with an inconceivable rapidity:
eighty cities and towns, in ten days, threw off the yoke
of the legates. The greater number constituted themselves republics; a few recalled the ancient families of
princes, who had been exiled by Egidio Albornoz, and
to whom they were attached by hereditary affection.
Bologna did not accomplish her revolution before the
20th of March, 1376. This ancient republic, in recovering its liberty, vowed fidelity to the Florentines, to

whom it owed the restoration of its freedom. The legates, beside themselves with rage, endeavoured to restrain the people by terror. John Hawkwood, on the
29th of March, 1376, delivered up Faenza to a frightful
military execution: 4000 persons were put to death,
property pillaged, and women violated. The pope, not
satisfied with such rigour, sent Robert of Geneva, another cardinal legate, into Italy, with a Breton company
of adventurers, considered as the most ferocious of all
those trained to plunder by the wars of France. The
new legate treated Cesena, on the 1st of February,
1377, with still greater barbarity. He was heard to call
out, during the massacre, "I will have more blood!—
kill all!—blood, blood!" Gregory XI at last felt the necessity of returning to Italy, to appease the universal
revolt. He entered Rome on the 17th of January, 1377;
although the Florentines, who had sent the standard
of liberty to the senators and bannerets of Rome, and
had made alliance with the Romans, expostulated on
the danger they incurred, if they admitted the pontiff
within their walls.

The two parties, however, began to be equally weary
of the war. Some of the cities enfranchised by the Florentines were already detached from the league. The
Bolognese had made, on the 21st of August, 1377, a
separate peace with the pope, who had agreed to acknowledge their republic. Barnabas Visconti carried on
with the holy see secret negotiations, in which he offered to sacrifice to the church his ally, the republic of
Florence. This republic was then pressed for its consent
to the opening of a congress for restoring peace to Italy,
to be held at Sarzana, in the beginning of the year
1378: the presidency of the congress was given to Barnabas Visconti. The conference had scarcely opened
when the Florentines perceived, with more indignation
than surprise, that the Lombard tyrant, who had fought
in concert with them, intended that they should pay to
him and to the pope the whole expenses of the war.
The negotiations took the most alarming turn, when the
unexpected news arrived of the death of Gregory XI,

on the 27th of March, 1378; and the congress separated, without coming to any decision. The year which now opened was destined to bring with it the most important revolutions throughout Italy. Amidst those convulsions, the peace of Florence with the court of Rome, weakened by the great western schism, was not difficult to accomplish.

The pontifical chair had been transferred to France since the year 1305. Its exile from Italy lasted seventy-three years. The Christian world, France excepted, had considered it a scandal; but the French kings hoped by it to retain the popes in their dependence; and the French cardinals, who formed more than three fourths of the sacred college, seemed determined to preserve the pontifical power in their nation. They were, however, thwarted in this intention by the death of Gregory XI at Rome—for the conclave must always assemble where the last pontiff dies. The clamour of the Romans, and the manifestation of opinion throughout Christendom, were not without influence on the conclave. On the 8th of April, 1378, it elected—not, indeed, a Roman, whom the people demanded; but an Italian—Bartolomeo Prignani; who, having lived long in France, seemed formed to conciliate the prejudices of both parties. He was considered learned and pious. The cardinals had not, however, calculated on the development of the passions which a sudden elevation sometimes gives; or on the degree of impatience, arrogance, and irritability of which man is capable, in his unexpected capacity of master, though in an inferior situation he had appeared gentle and modest. The new pope, who took the name of Urban VI, became so violent and despotic, so confident in himself, and so contemptuous of others, that he soon quarrelled with all his cardinals. They left him; assembled again at Fondi; and, on the 9th of August, declared the holy see vacant; asserting that their previous election was null, having been forced by their terror of the Romans. Consequently, on the 20th of September, they elected another pope. Their choice, no better than the former, fell on Robert,

cardinal of Geneva, who had presided at the massacre
of Cesena: he took the name of Clement VII. He was
protected by queen Joan, with whom Urban had already quarrelled. Clement established his court at Naples; but an insurrection of the people made him quit
it the year following, and determined him on returning,
with his cardinals, to Avignon. Urban VI, meanwhile,
deposed, as schismatics, all the cardinals who had
elected Clement, and replaced them by a new and more
numerous college; but he agreed no better with these
than with their predecessors. He accused them of a
conspiracy against him; he caused many to be put to
the torture in his presence, and while he recited his
breviary; he ordered others to be thrown into the sea
in sacks, and drowned; he quarrelled with the Romans,
and the new sovereign of Naples, whom he had himself
named; he paraded his incapacity and rage through all
Italy; and finally took refuge at Genoa, where he died,
on the 9th of November, 1389. The cardinals who acknowledged him named a successor on his death, as the
French cardinals did afterwards on the death of Clement VII, which took place on the 16th of September,
1394. The church thus found itself divided between
two popes and two colleges of cardinals, who recipro-
cally anathematised each other. Whilst the catholic
faith was thus shaken, the temporal sovereignty of the
pope, founded by the conquests of the cardinal Albornoz, was overthrown. Several of the cities enfranchised
by the Florentines in the war of liberty, preserved their
republican government; but the greater number, particularly in Romagna, fell again under the yoke of petty
tyrants.

The part which Joan of Naples had taken in the
schism, by protecting what the orthodox called the revolt of Robert of Geneva and the cardinals, awakened
the resentment which Louis of Hungary still entertained for the murder of her first husband; she had
since successively married three others, without having
a child: her natural heir was the last prince of the race
of Charles of Anjou, named Charles da Durazzo, the

grandson of king Robert's brother, and cousin to the king of Hungary, at whose court he had been brought up. The aged Louis, learning that Urban VI had excommunicated and deposed Joan, charged Charles da Durazzo to execute the sentence. He entrusted him with an army, with which the young prince traversed Italy, without meeting any resistance; he entered Naples on the 16th of July, 1381, and proclaimed himself king, under the name of Charles III. The queen, who could not arm a single person in her defence, was constrained to surrender to him five weeks afterwards. After detaining her nine months in prison, he caused her to be smothered under a feather bed. Louis of Hungary did not long survive this revolution: he died on the 11th of September, 1382, leaving heiress to his dominions a daughter, with whom Charles da Durazzo soon disputed the crown of Hungary. The emperor Charles IV had died before Louis, at Prague, on the 29th of November, 1378, and had been succeeded by his son, the debauched Wenceslaus. About the same period (1380) the crown of France had passed to a minor, Charles VI, who afterwards became mad. Italy had little to fear from abroad; the danger sprang up in her own bosom.

The republics of Venice and Genoa, on every occasion mutually opposed, regarded each other as rivals. The Genoese carried on a considerable commerce in Cyprus, but had excited there the resentment of the people, who in 1372 rose, and at a public festival massacred all the Genoese on whom they could lay hands. The republic avenged this outrage committed on its citizens; and in 1373 conquered the isle of Cyprus: but, using its victory with moderation, restored the island in fief to the house of Lusignan. The Venetians, notwithstanding, offered their alliance to the Cypriots, and in 1378 they, in concert, besieged the Genoese at Famagosta. In the many quarrels of the Venetians with Louis of Hungary, and with Francesco da Carrara, lord of Padua, they had always found the Genoese siding with their adversaries. The two republics finally attached themselves to the two opposite factions which disputed the remains of the empire of Constantinople, now arrived at its last term. Mutual animosity went on continually increasing. At last the Venetian and Genoese fleets met before Antium, in the month of July, 1378. They attacked each other in the height of a tempest; and the Genoese were vanquished. It was the first battle of a fearful war: Lucian Doria was charged, in the month of May, 1379, to avenge the Genoese. Having entered the Adriatic, on the 29th of that month he met the Venetian fleet, commanded by Vittor Pisani, before Pola. Lucian was killed early in the engagement; but that only served to redouble the animosity of the Genoese; and the Venetian fleet was almost annihilated. The senate threw Vittor Pisani, the greatest admiral the republic ever had, into prison, to punish him for a disaster which would have been avoided had his counsel been taken; for he had given battle by the express order of the senate, contrary to his own judgment. Pietro Doria, who succeeded Lucian in the command of the Genoese fleet, arrived on the 6th of August, to attack the canal or port of Chiozza, twenty-five miles south of Venice. It is one of the numerous openings which cut the *Aggere*, or long bank formed by nature between the *Lagune* and the sea. Francesco da Carrara sent at the same time a flotilla of Paduan boats, to attack in rear the Venetians, who defended this opening. The port of Chiozza was forced, and the town taken, on the 16th of August. Chiozza, like Venice, is in the bosom of the *Lagune*. The Genoese fleet, having arrived thus far, could pass up to the canals of Venice. Never had the republic been in such imminent danger; never had she offered to purchase peace by greater or more humiliating sacrifices. But the Genoese, the king of Hungary, and the lord of Padua, rejected all advances: Pietro Doria declared that he would not make peace, before he had bridled, with his own hand, the bronze horses in the square of St. Mark (the same which have since been seen in the Place du Carrousel at Paris). The Venetians, driven to the last extremity, redoubled their patriotic exertions: they drew Vittor Pisani from his dungeon, to place him in the command of a new fleet; they shut their canals with stockades; they recalled their many vessels dispersed in the Levant, and gave the command of them to Carlo Zeno, another of their greatest citizens. The defence of Venice was, notwithstanding, so far doubtful, that the signoria had made preparations to remove to Candia on the first reverse of fortune.

On the 1st of January, 1380, Carlo Zeno arrived with the fleet which he had collected in the eastern seas; the Venetians, instead of waiting to be besieged, proposed blockading the Genoese fleet in the *Lagune* of Chiozza, into which it had so victoriously entered. They succeeded in first shutting the canal of Chiozza, and afterwards all the other ports or canals which cut the *Aggere:* each of these advantages was, however, purchased by an obstinate battle. Forty-eight galleys, and 14,000 Genoese mariners or soldiers, were shut in at Chiozza; but they were not abandoned by their country: it sent a new fleet into the Adriatic for their deliverance, while the lord of Padua made the utmost exertions to open a communication with them. The Venetians, always investing the besieged still closer, succeeded in avoiding the battle continually offered them. The Genoese at last perceived that there was no possibility of saving their galleys; they constructed boats, in which they intended to escape, and gain the fleet which awaited them in the high seas. The moment these boats were transported to the sea-shore, they were attacked and burnt by the Venetians. Deprived of all resource, and pressed by famine, the Genoese at last surrendered at discretion, on the 21st of June, 1380. Notwithstanding this great reverse of fortune, Genoa was not cast down. The Venetians, hard pressed by land, were obliged to abandon Treviso, and shut themselves up anew in their *Lagune.* But the two republics, equally exhausted by the war, were glad to sign, on the 8th of August, 1381, a treaty of peace, which reestablished their former relations, nearly as they stood before it commenced. The treaty of peace with the king of Hungary was more disadvantageous to the Venetians: they ceded to him the whole of Dalmatia; but as he died the year following, they took advantage of the embarrassment into which his daughter was thrown, to recover their possessions in that province.

The discord which had so long fermented in Florence between the higher citizens who administered the government, and the lower orders, who demanded a more complete equality, broke out in 1378; a year fruitful in events to Italy. The form of the Florentine constitution was entirely democratic, the only sovereign was the people; the nobles and the Ghibelines were excluded from all participation in the government; but a perfect equality appeared to exist in the rest of the nation, which was rendered more complete by the citizens being called by lot to the highest dignities in the state. Nevertheless, if government is instituted for the good of all, to invest all indiscriminately with power, would be very far from obtaining that good, the object of the common effort. Education, and the leisure which gives time for reflection, are two conditions equally necessary to man, in order to attain the complete development of his understanding, and the knowledge, if ever he should arrive at the administration of public affairs, of what would constitute the happiness of all. Those who have not learnt to think, those to whom manual labour leaves no time for meditation, ought not to undertake the guidance of their fellow-citizens, by entering the difficult career of government. There was at Florence, as there is every where, a distinction to be made between families whose fortune gives them the means of intellectual improvement, and those who, to live, are obliged to devote themselves to mere labour, so much calculated to render the faculties of the mind obtuse. This distinction was marked by the division of citizens into twenty-one corporations of arts and trades; the seven higher arts were distinguished by the name of *arti maggiori*. In those alone the magistrates were always chosen; and they comprehended families some-

times so enriched by commerce as to rival princes in
magnificence: they were designated by the new ap-
pellation of *nobili popolani*, nobles of the people, and
produced men distinguished in the government of the
republic for as much virtue as talent.

There was, however, a want of union among these
great families; they had been divided between the two
parties, which were at first headed by the Albizzi and
Ricci: the Albizzi were among the number of those
families which the same revolution that drove out the
Ghibelines had, for more than a century, placed at the
head of the republic. They made it a part of their religion to maintain the Guelph party in all its purity, and
they caused the law of admonition, which excluded
from the magistracy every descendant of the ancient
Ghibelines, and under that pretext every *new man*, to
be executed in all its rigour. Their faction, then, was
essentially aristocratic. The Ricci, and with them the
Scali, Strozzi, Alberti, and the Medici, had attained
later their immense opulence. The name of Medici was
never pronounced before the middle of this century:
their adversaries profited by the obscurity of their origin, to pretend that their ancestors were Ghibelines.
The interest of new families led them to support democratic opinions, and to demand that the distinction between Guelph and Ghibeline, which no longer related
to any thing real, should be annihilated. The commission of eight, for the department of war, which had
directed, with such courage and ability, the attack on
the holy see, were all of the Ricci faction. In arming
the republic against the church, it appeared as if they
had made it adopt all the principles of the Ghibelines;
but when the citizens, impatient of the weight of taxes,
began to sigh for peace, the Albizzi took advantage of
their discontent, to revive against their adversaries the
accusation of Ghibelinism. They even intended, under
this pretext, to exclude them from their country. The
increasing ill-will between the two factions made it ob-
vious that the quarrel must soon break out. When Salvestro de' Medici was, in the month of June, 1378, made

by lot gonfaloner, he proposed a law to suspend the proceedings called *admonition,* which the Albizzi directed against his party. The college or little council of the signoria rejected it, as too favourable to the Ghibelines. Salvestro appealed, on the 18th of June, to a council of the people, and afterwards to the people themselves. Violent indignation was immediately manifested against this small oligarchy, which, under pretext of maintaining the ancient Guelph party in all its purity, had branded so many honourable names with exclusion, had encouraged divisions in a republic to which union was necessary, and had thrown doubts on the civic rights of half Florence. The law proposed by Salvestro de' Medici passed by an immense majority.

But this first victory awakened more violent disputes upon the rights and equality of the citizens; on the privileges of the *nobili popolani;* on the artifices by which they reserved among themselves the nomination to the magistracies; on the prerogatives of the major in opposition to the minor arts; and upon the dependent condition of the numerous artificers who must range under the banner of the major arts, without being permitted to form themselves into a corporation, or to enjoy any of the advantages attached to these associations. The law which the Medici had just carried, provided only that no new family should be excluded from the magistracies under the pretext that their ancestors were Ghibelines. The people soon demanded that those who had previously been excluded by the admonition should be reinstated in all their rights; that the minor arts should be admitted to furnish members for the magistracies in the same proportion as the major arts; finally, that three new corporations should be formed, to include workmen, dyers, weavers, fullers, and others employed in the woollen trade. These men, belonging to the *woollen art,* having no participation in the government, regarded themselves as excluded from every political right. They formed a numerous portion of the population at Florence, called in derision by the name of *ciompi.* The signoria, so far from yielding to these demands, reckoned on restraining the people by terror; on the 20th of July they caused one of the chiefs of the ciompi to be put to the torture, as having been found guilty of a plot against the state; but this only proved a signal for explosion. The ciompi, and all the poorer classes of artisans, flew to arms. The signoria called the urban guard to their aid; but those dared not assemble. On the 22d of July the ciompi laid siege to the palace of the podestà, and took it on the 23d; they attacked and made themselves masters also of the palace of the signoria: at that moment a carder of wool, named Michele Lando, in a short waistcoat and bare-footed, marched at the head of the people, carrying in his hand the gonfalon of the state, which he had seized in the palace of the podestà: an acclamation suddenly resounded from the crowd who followed him, proclaiming him gonfaloner. During the three preceding days, the populace, masters of the city, had committed many crimes and disorders; but they had no sooner given a new chief to the state, than the chief thus chosen laboured, with admirable courage and capacity, to restore order and peace. He ordained that for the future the supreme magistracy should be composed of three members of the major arts, three of the minor, and three of the ciompi. He put an immediate end to pillaging, burning, and every other disorder. He restored authority to the tribunals, security to the citizens; and exhibited by his own example how much a free government spreads sound sense and elevated sentiments among even the lowest classes of society. The ciompi, it is true, did not long submit to a government which they had themselves created. They rose anew; but Michele Lando vigorously attacked and vanquished them: a vast number were exiled from the city.

The popular party, however, is near its defeat when the moderate chiefs are forced to subdue the spirit of the more ardent. Frightened at some blamable excesses committed by their partisans, they deprive themselves of all vigour in order to suppress them; they disarm those by whose strength they have conquered; they distrust their friends, and confide in their enemies. A man of the lower order had vanquished the anarchists whom no other than himself could have subdued: but immediately afterwards, Florence blushed to have entrusted so much power to a man of his class; and on the next drawing of lot for the magistracy, the three ciompi drawn for the priori were not permitted to sit in the signoria. Giorgio Scali, Salvestro de' Medici, and Benedetto Alberti were placed at the head of the republic: although belonging themselves to the aristocracy, they were the enemies of that order. On discovering a plot of the Albizzi, their ancient rivals, to effect a revolution, with the aid of the troops of Charles III king of Naples, which then traversed Tuscany, they caused men who had so long administered the republic with glory to die on the scaffold. The public, notwithstanding the confession of the accused, were not convinced that they were really guilty, or justly punished. But division soon sprang up in the new administration: some, no longer fearing any rival, insolently abused their power. Giorgio Scali, learning that one of his creatures, accused of bearing false witness, was in the prison of the captain of the people, who prosecuted him, forced the palace of that judge, on the 13th of January, 1382, at the head of a troop of armed men; gave it up to pillage; and set its prisoner free. Benedetto Alberti, who had always acted honestly, and in the principles of an austere republican, was indignant at the conduct of his ancient associate. He summoned the people to avenge the insulted honour of the tribunals: for that purpose, he made advances to the major arts and the party of the Albizzi. Giorgio Scali was placed at the bar, and received sentence of death, which was immediately executed. The aristocracy felt, meanwhile, that it had recovered power. On the 21st of January, the city rose at the cry of "Long live the Guelph party!" The nobles, the rich merchants, and the higher citizens comprehended in the major arts, took possession of the public places, created a *balia*, or supreme commission, to reform the state; abolished all the laws which had arisen from the revolution, or the tumult of the ciompi; exiled Michele Lando, Benedetto Alberti, and all those who had in any way signalised themselves in the insurrection; and, finally, reconstituted the aristocracy of the nobili popolani more firmly than it had ever yet stood.

Similar revolutions broke out at the same time in the other Italian republics: in every one the same progress was to be distinguished. The party which in all had risen to power, as democratic, no sooner felt themselves in possession of it than they turned towards aristocracy. The leaders of the rising generation presented themselves as hereditary tribunes of the people, at the same time that they impugned hereditary rights. At Genoa, men of new families completely usurped from the ancient houses of Doria, Spinola, Grimaldi, and Fieschi, all power in the government; and ranged themselves, soon after the middle of the century, under the standard of two plebeian families—the one named Adorni, and Guelphs; the other Fregosi, and Ghibelines. While they proclaimed their hatred of the aristocracy, and their determination not to allow the doge to be taken from a noble family, they combated for the Adorni and Fregosi, with the same enthusiasm and spirit of clientelage with which their ancestors had fought for a Doria or a Fiesco. The ruinous civil wars into which the republic was precipitated by the rivalry between these two families, and the fear that the Viscontis might profit by these troubles to enslave it, at last determined Antoniotto Adorni, the doge, in 1396, to confer, on the 25th of October, the signoria on Charles VI king of France, in the hope that a distant monarch might lend the support of his name to the government, without having either the power or the inclination materially to injure the liberty of the republic.

At Sienna, after the nobles had been excluded from the magistracies, several plebeian aristocracies succeeded each other. The signoria, composed of nine members, renewed every two months, had found means of reserving to themselves the nomination of those by whom they were to be replaced. From that time, the

election ran among not more than ninety families of
rich merchants, who, from 1283 to 1355, remained the
real rulers of the republic. This first burgher aristocracy
was called "the order," or "monte," of "nine." The jealousy it excited in the rank next below it caused the
revolution, which Charles IV encouraged, in the hope
of becoming master of Sienna, on his first passage
through that city. The Nine, like the nobles, were excluded from all participation in the government. It was
agreed to replace them by a popular magistracy of
twelve members, chosen from the burghership; but
these men were no sooner in power, than, affecting to
observe an exact medium between the aristocracy just
excluded and the democracy whose invasion they
feared, they created an order or monte of twelve, out
of those burgher families who aspired only to a respectable mediocrity. This order, once in possession of the
magistracy, became not less exclusive than its predecessors, and consequently not less odious. When Charles
returned in 1368, for the second time, to Sienna, the
twelve were deprived of power; and a third order was
created, named "the reformers," taken from among the
classes inferior in wealth and education to the monte of
nine and of twelve. This order did not, at first, usurp all
the power of the republic—it demanded only an equal
partition with the other two; but soon betrayed irritation, because, being by far the most numerous, it had
not the most influence. Its pretensions often occasioned
commotions, and changes in the constitution. When the
ciompi seized the government at Florence, the reformers, who regarded themselves as holding the same rank
in life, made alliance with them; but, frequently giving
way to sudden bursts of passion, they were accused of
failing in good faith as well as prudence. They were at
length driven out of Sienna, on the 24th of March,
1385, after an obstinate battle between them and the
other orders of citizens. Four thousand were exiled;
and Sienna remained, from that time, weakened and
shaken in her principles of liberty.

The terror in which the house of Visconti had held

Florence and the other Italian republics began somewhat to subside. Barnabas, grown old, had divided the
cities of his dominions amongst his numerous children.
His brother, Galeazzo, had died on the 4th of August,
1378; and been replaced by his son, Gian Galeazzo,
called count de Virtus, from a county in Champagne,
given him by Charles V, whose sister he had married.
Barnabas would willingly have deprived his nephew of
his paternal inheritance, to divide it among his children.
Gian Galeazzo, who had already discovered several
plots directed against him, uttered no complaint, but
shut himself up in his castle of Pavia, where he had
fixed his residence. He doubled his guard, and took
pains to display his belief that he was surrounded by
assassins. He affected, at the same time, the highest
devotion: he was always at prayers, a rosary in his
hand, and surrounded with monks; he talked only of
pilgrimages and expiatory ceremonies. His uncle regarded him as pusillanimous, and unworthy of reigning.
In the beginning of May, 1385, Gian Galeazzo sent to
Barnabas to say, that he had made a vow of pilgrimage
to our Lady of Varese, near the Lago Maggiore; and
that he should be glad to see him on his passage. Barnabas agreed to meet him at a short distance from
Milan, accompanied by his two sons. Gian Galeazzo
arrived, surrounded, as was his custom, by a numerous
guard. He affected to be alarmed at every sudden motion made near him. On meeting his uncle, however,
on the 6th of May, he hastily dismounted, and respectfully embraced him; but, while he held him in his arms,
he said, in German, to his guards, "strike!" The Germans, seizing Barnabas, disarmed and dragged him,
with his two sons, to some distance from his nephew.
Gian Galeazzo made several vain attempts to poison
his uncle in the prison into which he had thrown him;
but Barnabas, suspicious of all the nourishment offered
him, was on his guard, and did not sink under these
repeated efforts till the 18th of December of the same
year.

All Lombardy submitted, without difficulty, to Gian

Galeazzo. His uncle had never inspired one human being with either esteem or affection. The nephew had no better title to these sentiments. False and pitiless, he joined to immeasurable ambition a genius for enterprise, and to immovable constancy a personal timidity which he did not endeavour to conceal. The least unexpected motion near him threw him into a paroxysm of nervous terror. No prince employed so many soldiers to guard his palace, or took such multiplied precautions of distrust. He seemed to acknowledge himself the enemy of the whole world. But the vices of tyranny had not weakened his ability. He employed his immense wealth, without prodigality; his finances were always flourishing; his cities well garrisoned and victualled; his army well paid; all the captains of adventure scattered throughout Italy received pensions from him, and were ready to return to his service whenever called upon. He encouraged the warriors of the new Italian school: he well knew how to distinguish, reward, and win their attachment. Many young Italians, in order to train themselves to arms, had, from about the middle of this century, engaged in the German, English, and French troops, which inundated Italy; and they soon proved, that Italian valour, directed by the reflection and intelligence of a highly civilised nation, who carried their arms as well as tactics to perfection, had greatly the advantage over the brute courage of barbarians. Alberic, count of Barbiano, a Romagnole noble, and an ancestor of the princes Belgiojoso, of Milan, formed a company, under the name of St. George, into which he admitted Italians only, and which, in 1378, he placed in the service of Urban VI. This company defeated, at Ponte Molle, that of the Bretons, attached to Clement VII, and regarded as the most formidable of the foreign troops. From that time, the company of St. George was the true school of military science in Italy. Young men of courage, talent, or ambition flocked into it from all parts; and all the captains who, twenty years later, attained such high renown, gloried in having served in that company.

Gian Galeazzo was no sooner firmly established on the throne of Milan, than he resumed his project of subjugating the rest of Italy: the two principalities of the Della Scala at Verona, and of the Carrara at Padua, were the first to tempt his ambition. The house of La Scala had produced, in the beginning of the century, some great captains and able politicians; but their successors had been effeminate and vicious—princes, who hardly ever attained power without getting rid of their brothers by poison or the dagger. The house of Carrara, on the contrary, which gloried in being attached to the Guelph party, produced princes who might have passed for virtuous, in comparison with the other tyrants of Italy. Francesco da Carrara, who then reigned, his son and grandson, were men of courage, endued with great capacities, and who knew how to gain the affection of their subjects. The republic of Venice never pardoned Carrara his having made alliance against her, with the Genoese and the king of Hungary. After the death of the last named, Venice engaged Antonio della Scala to attack Padua, offering him subsidies to aid him in the conquest of that state. Carrara did all in his power to be reconciled to the prince, his neighbour, whom, in 1386, he repeatedly vanquished; as well as with the republic—always ready to repair the losses sustained by the lord of Verona. Unable to obtain peace, he was at last reduced to accept the proffered alliance of Gian Galeazzo Visconti, who took Verona on the 18th of October, 1387. Instead of restoring to Carrara the city of Vicenza, as he had promised, he immediately offered his assistance to the Venetians against Padua: that republic was imprudent enough to accept the offer. Padua, long besieged, was given up to Visconti, on the 23d of November, 1388. A few days afterwards, Treviso was surrendered to him; so that the frontiers of the lord of Milan's dominions extended even to the edge of the *Lagune*. He had no sooner planted his standard there, than he menaced Venice, which had so unwisely facilitated his conquests.

All the rest of Lombardy was dependent on the lord

of Milan. The marquis of Montferrat was brought up
at the court of Galeazzo, who governed his states as
guardian of this young prince. Albert, marquis d'Este,
had, on the 26th of March, 1388, succeeded his brother
in the sovereignty of Ferrara, to the prejudice of his
nephew Obizzo, whom he caused to be beheaded with
his mother. He put to death by various revolting executions almost all his relations, at the suggestion of
Gian Galeazzo, whose object was, by rendering him
thus odious to the people, to make the lord of Ferrara
feel that he had no other support than in him. According to the same infernal policy, Gian Galeazzo accused
the wife of the lord of Mantua, daughter of Barnabas,
and his own cousin and sister-in-law, of a criminal intercourse with her husband's secretary. He forged letters by which he made her appear guilty, concealed
them in her apartment, and afterwards pointed out
where they were to be found to Francesco da Gonzaga, who, in a paroxysm of rage, caused her to be beheaded, and the secretary to be tortured, and afterwards
put to death in 1390: it was not till after many years
that he discovered the truth. Thus all the princes of
Lombardy were either subdued or in discredit for the
crimes which Visconti had made them commit, and by
which he held them in his dependence; he then began
to turn his attention towards Tuscany. In the years 1388
and 1389, the Florentines were repeatedly alarmed
by his attempts to take possession of Sienna, Pisa,
Bologna, San Miniato, Cortona, and Perugia: not one
attempt had yet succeeded; but Florence saw her
growing danger, and was well aware that the tyrant
had not yet attacked her, only because he reserved her
for his last conquest.

The arrival at Florence of Francis II of Carrara,
who came to offer his services and his hatred of Gian
Galeazzo to the republic, determined the Florentines to
have recourse to arms. The lord of Milan, in receiving
the capitulation of Padua, had promised to give in
compensation some other sovereignty to the house of
Carrara; but he had either poisoned Francis I, or suf-

fered him to perish in prison. Several attempts had
been made to assassinate Francis II in the province of
Asti, whither he had been exiled. In spite of many
dangers, he at last escaped, and fled into Tuscany,
taking his wife, then indisposed, with him. He left her
there, and passed into Germany, in the hopes of exciting new enemies against Gian Galeazzo; while the
Florentines made alliance with the Bolognese against
the lord of Milan, and placed their army under the
command of John Hawkwood, who ever afterwards
remained in their service. Carrara, seconded by the
duke of Bavaria, the son-in-law of Barnabas, whose
death the duke was desirous of avenging, re-entered
Padua on the 14th of June, 1390, by the bed of the
Brenta, and was received with enthusiasm by the inhabitants, who regarded him more as a fellow-citizen
than a master. He recovered possession of the whole
inheritance of his ancestors.

The extensive commerce of the Florentines had accustomed them to include all Europe in their negotiations; and, as they liberally applied their wealth to the
defence of their liberty, they easily found allies abroad.
After having called the duke of Bavaria from Germany,
in 1390, they in the year following sent to France for
the count d'Armagnac with a formidable army; but the
Germans as well as the French found, with astonishment, that they could no longer cope with the new
Italian militia, which had substituted military science
for the routine of the transalpine soldier. Armagnac
was vanquished and taken prisoner, on the 25th of July,
1391, by Giacomo del Verme; and died a few days
afterwards. John Hawkwood, who, in the hope of joining him, had advanced far into Lombardy with the
Florentine army, had great difficulty in leading it back
in safety through plains inundated by the Adige. After
this campaign, the republic, feeling the want of repose,
made peace with Galeazzo, on the 28th of January,
1392; well knowing that it could place no trust in him,
and that this treaty was no security against his intrigues and treachery.

These expectations were not belied; for one plot followed another in rapid succession. The Florentines about this time reckoned on the friendship of the Pisans, who had placed at the head of their republic Pietro Gambacorta, a rich merchant, formerly an exile at Florence, and warmly attached to peace and liberty: but he was old, and had for his secretary Jacopo Appiano, the friend of his childhood, who was nearly of his own age. Yet Galeazzo found means to seduce the secretary: he instigated him to the assassination of Gambacorta and his children, on the 21st of October, 1392. Appiano, seconded by the satellites furnished him by the duke of Milan, made himself master of Pisa: but, after his death, his son, who could with difficulty maintain himself there, sold the city to Gian Galeazzo, in the month of February, 1399; reserving only the principality of Piombino, which he transmitted to his descendants. At Perugia, Pandolpho Baglione, chief of the noble and Ghibeline party, had, in 1390, put himself under the protection of Gian Galeazzo, who aided him in changing the limited authority conferred on him into a tyranny: but three years afterwards he was assassinated; and the republic of Perugia, distracted by the convulsions of opposing factions, was compelled to yield itself up to Gian Galeazzo, on the 21st of January, 1400.

The Germans observed with jealousy the continually increasing greatness of Visconti; which appeared to them to annihilate the rights of the empire, and dry up the sources of tribute, on a partition of which they always reckoned. They pressed Wenceslaus to make war on Gian Galeazzo. But that indolent and sensual monarch, after some threats, gave it to be understood that for money he would willingly sanction the usurpations of Gian Galeazzo: and, in fact, on the 1st of May, 1395, he granted him, for the sum of 100,000 florins, a diploma which installed him duke of Milan and count of Pavia; comprehending in this investiture twenty-six cities and their territory, as far as the *Lagune* of Venice. These were the same cities which, more than three centuries before, had signed the glorious league of Lombardy. The duchy of Milan, according to the imperial bull, was to pass solely to the legitimate male heir of Gian Galeazzo. This concession of Wenceslaus caused great discontent in Germany: it was one of the grievances for which the diet of the empire, on the 20th of August, 1400, deposed the emperor, and appointed Robert elector palatine in his stead. Robert concluded a treaty of subsidy with the Florentines, or rather entered into their pay, to oppose Gian Galeazzo: but when, on the 21st of October, 1401, he met the Milanese troops, commanded by Jacopo del Verme, not far from Brescia, he experienced, to his surprise and discomfiture, how much the German cavalry were inferior to the Italian. He was saved from a complete defeat only by Jacopo da Carrara, who led a body of Italian cavalry to his aid. Robert found it necessary to retreat, with disgrace, into Germany, after having received from the Florentines an immense sum of money.

Gian Galeazzo Visconti continued his course of usurpation. In 1397, he attacked, at the same time, Francesco da Gonzaga at Mantua, and the Florentines, without any previous declaration of war. After having ravaged Tuscany and the Mantuan territory, he consented, on the 11th of May, 1398, to sign, under the guarantee of Venice, a truce of ten years, during which period he was to undertake nothing against Tuscany. That, however, did not prevent him, in 1399, from taking under his protection the counts of Poppi and Ubertini, in the Apennines; or from engaging the republic of Sienna to surrender itself to him, on the 11th of November in the same year.

The plague broke out anew in Tuscany, and deprived the free states of all their remaining vigour. The magistrates, on whose prudence and courage they relied, in a few days sank under the contagion, and left free scope to the poorest intriguer. This happened at Lucca to the Guelph house of Guinigi, which had produced many distinguished citizens, all employed in the first magistracies. They perished under this disease nearly about the same time. A young man of their family, named Paulo Guinigi, undistinguished either for talent or character, profited by this calamity, on the 14th of October, 1400, to usurp the sovereignty. He immediately abjured the Guelph party, in which he had been brought up, and placed himself under the protection of Gian Galeazzo. At Bologna, also, the chief magistrates of the republic were, in like manner, swept away by the plague. Giovanni Bentivoglio, descended from a natural son of that king Hensius so long prisoner at Bologna, took advantage of the state of languor into which the republic had fallen, to get himself proclaimed sovereign lord, on the 27th of February, 1401. He at first thought of putting himself under the protection of the duke of Milan; but Gian Galeazzo, coveting the possession of Bologna, instead of amicably receiving, attacked him the year following. Bentivoglio was defeated at Casalecchio, on the 26th of June, 1402. His capital was taken the next day by the Milanese general, he himself made prisoner, and two days afterwards put to death. Another general of Galeazzo, in May, 1400, took possession of Assisa: the liberty of Genoa, Perugia, Sienna, Pisa, Lucca, and Bologna had, one after the other, fallen a sacrifice to the usurper. The Cancellieri, in the mountains of Pistoia, the Ubaldini, in those of the Mugello, had given themselves up to the duke of Milan. The Florentines, having no longer communications with the sea, across the territories of Sienna, Pisa, Lucca, and Bologna, saw the sources of their wealth and commerce dry up. Never had the republic been in more imminent danger; when the plague, which had so powerfully augmented its calamities, came to its aid. Gian Galeazzo Visconti was seized with it at his castle of Marignano, in which he had shut himself up, to be, as he hoped, secure from all communication with man. He was carried off by the pestilence, on the 3d of September, 1402.

CHAPTER IX

ANARCHY IN THE DUCHY OF MILAN — THE VENETIANS
MAKE THE CONQUEST OF PADUA AND VERONA — THE
FLORENTINES OF PISA — FLORENCE, MENACED IN
TURN BY LADISLAUS KING OF NAPLES AND FILIPPO
MARIA VISCONTI, MAINTAINS AGAINST THEM THE BAL-
ANCE OF ITALY

THE regeneration of liberty in Italy was signalised still
more, if it were possible, by the development of the
moral than by that of the intellectual character of the
Italians. The sympathy existing among fellow-citizens,
from the habit of living for each other and by each
other, of connecting every thing with the good of all,
produced in republics virtues which despotic states cannot even imagine. Man must have a country, before
he can conceive the duty of sacrificing himself for it.
The arts of intrigue and flattery are recommendations
to a master; his favour is gained by encouraging his
vices: and, in his turn, he recompenses those who serve
him at the expense of morality, by dividing with them
his power. But to please the people, to rise by the people, virtues must be exhibited to them, not vices: the
sympathy of all is gained only by that which is most
honourable in each. A popular assembly is swayed only
by an appeal to its virtues: even in its errors, some
frankness, probity, and generosity, by which men
sympathise together, are always to be found; while, if
a dark deed be but conceived, it is a secret carefully
kept, with conscious shame, from every eye—it would
be easier to execute than to announce or recommend
it to the public. Tyrants act on men by terror, corruption, venality, *espionnage*, envy. Free governments can
lead the people only by exciting their more honourable
passions. Eloquence, to move men in masses, must
make its appeals to honour, pity, justice, and courage.
Accordingly, how rich in virtues was Italy in the twelfth
century, when covered with republics, and when ev-

ery city simultaneously fought for liberty! These virtues, the most precious of all treasures, diminished with
the progress of time, and in exact proportion with the
diminution of free states. From the moment a man
entered one of those republics, he might reckon with
certainty on finding good faith in treaties and negotiations; zeal for the common advantage in all alliances;
courage and fortitude in adversity; an unbounded
liberality from the rich to the poor; in all great calamities, an eagerness, in every one who had property, to
devote it to the salvation of all; finally, an energy in
the people to resist, by common exertion, every act of
injustice or violence. Even their excesses arose most
commonly from some virtuous indignation. From the
moment, on the contrary, that a man entered the states
of one of the tyrants of Lombardy or Romagna, he
found a government hostile to public opinion, supporting itself only by perfidy and crime. Spies watched and
denounced every expression of generous feeling; they
insinuated themselves into families to betray them;
they abused the sacred ties of kindred, home, and
neighbourhood, to convert them into snares; they made
all feel that the wisdom of the subject consisted in dis-
trusting every one, and not meddling in the affairs of
another. Assassination and poison were common means
of government. Every Italian tyrant was stained with
the blood of his kindred; paid murderers despatched
the objects of his suspicions; he outraged public virtue, and could maintain order only by fear. Death itself at length failing to inspire terror, he combined
with capital punishment protracted tortures, the ex-
hibition of which only rendered men more hardened
and fierce.

But the field of virtue in Italy contracted from age
to age, while that of crime enlarged itself. The inhabitants of the kingdom of Naples, from its foundation
in the twelfth century—from the subjugation of the
three republics of Naples, Gaëta, and Amalfi—had been
dead to every feeling of association, sympathy, or patriotism: they had since that time been governed by a

corrupt court and nobility, which offered examples only of vices. In the thirteenth century, Lombardy also had been detached from the domain of liberty. During the convulsions occasioned either by the violence of the Guelph and Ghibeline factions, or by the contempt of the nobles for all law, every republic, in its turn, fell repeatedly under the yoke of some tyrant; and, however short his reign, it sufficed to familiarise the mind with violence instead of justice, and with the success of crime. At the same time, the devotion of factions to their chiefs, the reference of patriotism to party, and not to the common weal, perverted morality, and confounded the rules of right and wrong.

In the fourteenth century it was still worse: power in Lombardy had passed to those who made of it the uses most destructive of public virtue. Men rose to be princes by crime: their perfidy towards their neighbours, and their domestic treachery, marked the commencement and duration of every reign. Tyrants were so numerous, so constantly under the observation of every citizen, that their example was always operating to corrupt the people. No father of a family could hide from his children the fact, that the prince they must obey had attained power only by betraying his friends or his fellow-citizens, by poisoning or poniarding his uncle or his brother. The states of the church exhibited not fewer examples of the success of crime: every city of Romagna, of the March, of the patrimony of St. Peter, had its tyrant; and every tyrant reigned only to tread under foot every moral duty. Nay, more: Barnabas and Gian Galeazzo Visconti had, in some sort, kept a school of treachery for Tuscany and the states of the church. They had always encouraged every usurpation; and promised beforehand their alliance to whoever could smother the voice of a free people, and seduce them from the sway of morality to that of crime.

These causes of immorality, all which in Italy conspired against public virtue, operated in the beginning of the 15th century with redoubled force. When Gian Galeazzo unexpectedly died of the plague, in the height

of his successful career, he divided his estates between
his two sons—Gian Maria, then thirteen years of age,
whom he declared duke of Milan; and Filippo Maria,
twelve years old, whom he left count of Pavia. But, as
these princes were too young to reign, he recommended
them to the condottieri in his service, whom he introduced into the council as part of the regency: these
were the captains of that new militia which had so well
served him in the accomplishment of his projects, and
in whom he placed the greatest confidence. The school
of Alberic Barbiano, which had formed such brave soldiers and able generals, could not, in like manner, produce good citizens and virtuous men; and Gian
Galeazzo, for the protection of his children, needed
counsellors guided by principles that would have stood
in his way as long as these men were his servants.
Jacopo del Verme, Pandolpho Malatesta, Facino Cane,
Ottobon Terzo, and the other captains in whom he
trusted, were soldiers of fortune, who made of their
valour a trade of carnage and plunder; who, indifferent to what was just or unjust, were ready to fight for
whoever would pay them, and to betray those for any
other who would pay them more. They did not long
remain faithful guardians to the trust which their master had reposed in them. They shared it with Catherine, widow of Gian Galeazzo, and with Francesco
Barbavara, supposed to be her lover, and known to
have commenced his career as valet-de-chambre to the
duke. Warriors disdained to obey a woman and her
valet; the chiefs, too, of the ancient parties in the cities
which Visconti had subdued, rose with their partisans
to recover the sovereignty of their fathers. The condottieri resisted them, but resisted them for themselves:
Facino Cane made himself tyrant at Alexandria; Ottobon Terzo at Parma; Pandolpho Malatesta at Brescia.
Amidst this anarchy, the duchess Catherine believed
herself energetic in proportion as she was violent and
cruel. She caused several Milanese nobles to be beheaded without trial; she gave up many cities to be
sacked by the soldiers; and thus only redoubled the

hatred which she excited: she was thrown into prison, where she died by poison on the 16th of October, 1404; and Francesco Barbavara was obliged to fly. The rest of the duchy of Milan was divided into as many principalities as there were cities. In some, it was the ancient chiefs of the Guelph or Ghibeline party who recovered power; in others, the captain of adventure who happened to be in garrison there: in several it was some daring villain, such as Giovanni da Vignate at Lodi, or Gabrino Fondolo at Cremona, who, profiting by the friendship and confidence of some other usurper, assassinated him, and took his place. Never, even in that country so fertile in tyrants, was power stained with so many crimes.

Gian Maria Visconti, who had seen almost all the cities subdued by his father detached from his dominion, still continued to bear the title of duke of Milan; while his power, even in that city, passed from one ambitious chief to another, and was at last assumed by Facino Cane, one of the best generals of his father. All that Gian Maria Visconti preserved of sovereign power was an unbounded indulgence in every vice. His libertinism would hardly have been remarked; he was chiefly signalised by the frightful pleasure which he sought in the practice of cruelty. He was passionately devoted to the chace; but such sports soon failed to quench his thirst for cruelty. The tortures inflicted on mute animals, not finding expression by speech, did not come up to his ferocious ideas of enjoyment. He therefore resolved to substitute men for brute animals; and caused all the criminals condemned by the tribunals to be given up to him as objects of this inhuman sport. He had his hounds fed with human flesh, in order to render them more ferocious in tearing the victims; and, when ordinary convicts were scarce, he denounced to the tribunals even the crimes in which he had participated, to obtain the condemnation of his accomplices: after which he delivered them to his huntsman, Squarcia Giramo, charged with providing for the ducal chace. He was at last, on the 16th of May, 1412, assassinated by some Milanese nobles.

The virtue and elevation of soul which had done such honour to the Italian nation became obscured even in the republics of Genoa, Lucca, Pisa, Sienna, Perugia, and Bologna. These republics, in the course of the fourteenth century, had all more than once fallen under the power of some tyrant: accordingly, the examples of cruelty, perfidy, and the success of those usurpers to whom they had been forced to submit, had had a corrupting influence on their citizens. Neither had Venice preserved the true Italian virtue: its citizens often gave proofs of an unbounded devotion to their country, of an unreserved submission to its most severe ordinances; but it was a narrow-minded and jealous aristocracy, which, according to the spirit of that government, substituted national selfishness for patriotism. The Venetians took not into the least consideration any other people: they fancied they gave proofs of heroism, when the advantage of their republic was in question, in suppressing every human sentiment, in silencing every moral duty. Venice was governed by secret councils, where the voice of the people was never heard: its foreign policy was administered by the Council of Ten; which, in its mysterious meetings, took interest only for a guide. The decemvirs dared unblushingly propose to their colleagues deliberating under the sanction of an oath, and animated with the same spirit as themselves, the sacrifice of what was honest and just to what was useful. Italian virtue had taken refuge at Florence: it was there only that the people deliberated; that they associated together either for peace or war, or negotiation, as well as for the common administration of the government. Nothing was proposed to the public, nothing could obtain the assent of all, except what all felt to be just, honourable, and generous. The republic of Florence was always ready to risk its repose and wealth for the equilibrium and independence of Italy; for the common liberty; and for the progress of intelligence and

civilisation. During two centuries, it was always seen
eager to put itself forward as the champion of all that
was good and noble. Italy might justly glory in the
fact, that wherever she was free, she was always found
constant in the road to virtue: she is not answerable
for the crimes with which she was sullied by her tyrants. Several thousand citizens had always contributed, by their vote, to all that Florence did that was
grand and noble; while about fifty princes, distributed
in as many palaces, with the few wretches which it
belongs to tyrannical governments always to bring forward, sufficed to commit, in spite of a whole population, all the crimes which affrighted Italy.

At the moment in which the death of Gian Galeazzo
annihilated, at least for a time, the threatening power
of the dukes of Milan, the two republics in Italy which
alone had survived his intrigues, and which he had in
vain menaced, profited by the anarchy into which Lombardy had fallen, to recover their power, and aggrandise themselves by conquest. Venice, which had shut
itself up in its *Lagune,* issued forth to extend its frontiers to the Lake of Garda; and Florence, to which
Gian Galeazzo had interdicted all approach to the sea,
conquered Pisa, whose ports were necessary to its
commerce, and almost to its existence.

Francesco da Carrara, re-established in the sovereignty of Padua in the year 1390, had from that period remained faithful to the Guelph party and to
Florence: he hoped to profit by the confusion in which
the death of Gian Galeazzo had left all Lombardy; and
he invited Gulielmo della Scala to join him, and recover together the sovereignties of Verona and Vicenza. Gulielmo was the son of that Antonio della
Scala who, by his alliance with the Venetians fifteen
years before, had caused the ruin of Carrara and his
own; but a community of misfortune had reconciled
them. On the 7th of April, 1404, they, in conjunction,
took Verona. On the 21st of the same month Della
Scala died; and the report was spread that Carrara
had poisoned him. Be that as it may, Carrara, on the

17th of May following, arrested the two sons of Della Scala, and took possession of the city and fortress of Verona. Vicenza, in the mean time, yielded to the Venetians. The latter had hitherto sought their grandeur only in commerce, in their navy, and in their possessions beyond sea; but the confusion into which Lombardy was thrown gave birth in them to a new ambition: they resolved on extending their dominion in a country which seemed to offer itself for their conquest.

They entered into treaty with the duchess Catherine Visconti, who renounced all right which her son might have on Verona and Padua; and they set on foot an army of 9000 cavalry. Their immense wealth permitted them to choose the most distinguished captains and the best soldiers in Italy. The republic, in taking them into pay, made it one rule, never to confide the command of its armies to one of its own citizens, that they might have nothing to fear from his power or glory; and another, not to allow the soldiers to enter the city of Venice, the defence of which needed no more than its *Lagune*, galleys, and sailors. Two senators, distinguished by the title of procurators of St. Mark, were charged to attend in the camp, and watch over the foreign general whom the signoria had chosen.

War between Venice and the lord of Padua was declared on the 23d of June, 1404. Francesco da Carrara carried it on with the utmost valour; but opposed, without allies, to forces infinitely superior to his own, he saw successively forced the passage of several canals which intersected his territory, and behind which he had raised fortifications. The whole of the Paduan territory was ravaged by the Venetian army, and almost all its fortresses taken before the end of the campaign of 1404. A division of the army arrived to besiege Carrara in his capital, on the 12th of June, 1405; at the same time that another division besieged his second son, Jacopo da Carrara, in Verona, and forced him to capitulate, on the 23d of June. The whole rural population had taken refuge in Padua; and the privations and sufferings experienced in consequence occasioned a

contagious malady, which carried off 40,000 persons.
Carrara and his son continued to fight at the head of
the survivors with determined bravery, till the Venetians made themselves masters of the first entrench-
ment. On the 19th of November, 1405, a capitulation
became necessary. Carrara always flattered himself that
the Venetians would grant him some remuneration for
the principality which they wrested from him. He repaired to Venice, with his eldest son, on the faith of
the general with whom he had capitulated. On their
arrival, they were thrown into prison; where they
found Jacopo da Carrara, who had been taken prisoner
at Verona. The Council of Ten, putting in practice the
advice given later by Machiavelli, of annihilating the
whole race of dethroned tyrants, in order to destroy
with them the zeal, hopes, and plots of their partisans,
caused Francesco da Carrara and his two sons to be
strangled in prison, on the 16th of January, 1406. They,
at the same time, set a price on the head of the young-
est princes, who had escaped from them, and on those
of all the survivors of the house of Della Scala: not one
fell under the dagger of the assassin, notwithstanding
the great recompense shamelessly promised by the Venetians; but, on the other hand, not one ever recovered
the states of his fathers.

The Florentines regarded Francesco da Carrara as
one of the firmest champions of the Guelph party in
Lombardy: they valued his alliance; but they did not
think themselves obliged to plunge into war for him,
whom they accused of having provoked it by his unjust
aggression on Verona. All their efforts, also, were then
directed against Pisa: they regarded the conquest of
that city as a necessary condition of their existence,
ever since the blockade which Gian Galeazzo had
made them experience, by subjugating all the states
that opened to them any communication with the sea.
Gian Galeazzo had left the lordship of Pisa to his natural son, Gabriel Maria, who had, with his mother,
taken possession of that city. That of Sienna had recovered its freedom in the month of March, 1404, and

had renewed its alliance with Florence. Perugia and
Bologna had also, in the preceding month of September, thrown off the yoke of the Viscontis, and voluntarily submitted to the church; which had left them
their republican form of government. The Cancellieri,
the counts Guidi and Ubertini, and the other feudal
nobles of the Apennines, who had placed themselves
under the protection of Gian Galeazzo, had been punished for it by the Florentine republic, which had again
subdued them to its power. Lucca remained subject
to Paulo Guinigi, who governed that ancient republic
with moderation, and desired only to be forgotten by
his neighbours. Pisa alone, in Tuscany, remained the
enemy of Florence. As Gabriel was sensible that his
brothers, the Viscontis, were then in no state to defend him, he purchased the protection of the marshal
Boucicault, the representative of the king of France
at Genoa. Boucicault exercised only the limited authority assigned by the constitution to the doge. The
Genoese were far more zealous than the marshal in
the support of the independence of Pisa. They feared
the competition of the Florentines in their maritime
commerce, if once they were masters of Pisa, Leghorn,
and Porto Pisano. Boucicault, on the contrary, after
having taken Gabriel Maria under his protection, soon
thought of making them an article of trade. He offered
to sell Pisa to the Florentines, in the month of June,
1405, for the sum of 400,000 florins; which he agreed
to divide with Gabriel Maria. The Pisans, informed of
this negotiation, rose on the 21st of July; disarmed the
garrison of their tyrants; made themselves masters of
the gates of the city; but failed in their attack on the
citadel. Boucicault, informed of these matters, moder-
ated his demand; and asked the Florentines no more
than 206,000 florins for the Pisan citadel, and the
castles which he still held in the territory of Pisa.
The Florentines paid him that sum: he was engaged
to divide it with Gabriel Maria; but, to rid himself of
this claim, he accused Gabriel of a plot against the king
of France, and caused him to be beheaded.

The Florentines hoped to induce the Pisans to submit to them by negotiations; and they offered the most advantageous conditions: but the Pisans, who proudly regarded themselves as the most ancient and illustrious of the Tuscan republics, and as having preserved, more than any other, their warlike courage, vigorously besieged their citadel, and retook it on the 6th of September. They afterwards demanded peace of the Florentines, offering to reimburse them the money they had paid: to facilitate the negotiation, they recalled from exile Giovanni Gambacorta, whose family had been always favoured by Florence, and named him captain of the people. But their offers were all rejected; and the Pisans, forced to have recourse to arms, not only fought valiantly themselves, but eagerly sacrificed their whole fortune to purchase the services of the condottieri, whom they called to their aid from all parts of Italy. The war continued for more than a year: the Pisans successively lost all their fortresses and territory: their city was blockaded during the campaign of 1406; and they courageously supported privations, maladies, and, finally, famine. But the chief whom they had elected did not show a like heroism: Giovanni Gambacorta secretly treated with the Florentines; and obtained the gift of 50,000 florins, and the county of Bagno, to open to them the gates of Pisa; which was done in the night of the 8th and 9th of November, 1406. The Florentines did all in their power to reconcile the Pisans to the yoke which they forced on them: their army was preceded into the famished towns by wagon-loads of bread, which the soldiers distributed themselves to all that demanded it. Gino Capponi, the commissioner of Florence, promised, not only the strictest attention to justice, but privileges, and even friendship, to the conquered people. These advances were all in vain; the Pisans were too haughty to submit to rivals whom they had so long combated. The most ancient and opulent families removed to Lucca, Sardinia, and Sicily. The young men almost all engaged in the companies of adventure, to find in the camp an independence which they could no longer hope for in their own country: and Pisa, in losing its liberty, lost its commerce, population, and every remnant of prosperity.

The Florentines endeavoured to relieve Pisa from its state of poverty, by filling it with foreigners: they offered it to the church for the meeting of the council which was to terminate the great western schism. This schism had lasted since the year 1378. Pietro di Luna, an Aragonese, one of the cardinals who had given rise to it, had succeeded Clement VII, who died at Avignon in 1394. The succession of popes in the other division of the church had been more rapid. Boniface IX, who had succeeded the turbulent Urban VI, in 1389, was a better warrior than churchman; he reconquered successively all the states which his predecessor had lost: he entered Rome, and consolidated his power by executions. Innocent VII, who succeeded him, in 1404, was a gentle and moderate man; but as he abandoned the exercise of power to his brother, who governed only by terror, the number of executions drove the Romans to revolt. The pope was anew driven from his capital; but, returning in 1406, he died a few months afterwards, and Gregory XII, a Venetian, was named his successor.

In both divisions of the church, the prolongation of the schism was considered dishonourable and calamitous to Christendom: in both the sovereigns were zealous to suppress it; but on both sides the popes opposed an obstinate resistance. They had been each elected by the two colleges of cardinals, under the express condition that each would be ready to cede his rights, and abdicate at the same time with his competitor. They either refused, or by a thousand artifices delayed, to do so. Benedict XIII was besieged in his palace at Avignon by the troops of the king of France, in order to constrain him to yield: but, after he had declared himself ready to abdicate, his adversary, Gregory XII, refused. Benedict, however, advanced as far as La Spezzia, and Gregory as far as Lucca, to meet in con-

ference with their two colleges; but both persisted in
not taking the last step. Towards the end of 1408,
their cardinals, losing all patience, left them, and assembled at Leghorn; whence they issued a summons
to convoke the oecumenical council at Pisa, in the
month of March following. This council, in which were
assembled almost all the prelates of Christendom, after
long discussion, condemned and deposed the two
popes, on the 5th of June, 1409; and, on the 7th of
July, the assembled cardinals of the two "obediences"
named in their place a third, Alexander V. The deposed popes would not submit to the sentence of the
council: both preserved a small flock of the faithful—
the one in Aragon, the other at Rimini and Naples.
Gregory had retired to the first-mentioned town; so
that, instead of two, there were three popes in the
western church. To terminate the schism, it became
necessary to assemble a second general council; which,
sitting at Constance, on the 1st of November, 1414,
forced two of the popes to abdicate, and deposed the
third. The church, at the same time, implored a reform;
to accomplish which, a third council was assembled at
Basle, on the 23d July, 1431, and this laid the foundation of a new schism.

While two or three pretenders to the pontifical chair
were thus obliged to defend themselves against each
other, as well as against their own cardinals and against
all Christendom, the king of Naples profited by the
confusion to take possession of nearly all the states
of the church. That king was Ladislaus, son of Charles
III da Durazzo, whom he had succeeded in 1386,
being at that time only ten years old. Louis II of Anjou,
a minor, like Ladislaus, disputed the throne with him.
The queen, Joan, when pressed by the Hungarians,
had adopted Louis I, duke of Anjou, the brother of
Charles V; who had entered the kingdom of Naples in
1382, and died there in 1384. He left one son, Louis
II, then under age, to whom his mother and her partisans gave the title of king of Sicily. The war between
these two children, directed by their mothers, ruined

the kingdom of Naples during the latter part of the fourteenth century, and destroyed its influence over the rest of Italy. It was not till 1399 that Ladislaus succeeded in driving out the princes of Anjou, and subduing the kingdom. He had grown up amidst civil war, receiving the hardening education of privation and danger, alternately seconded or obstructed by intrigue and treachery. He was brave, and had studied the art of war; but was still more expert in dissimulation and perfidy. His ambition was unbounded, and his passions unrestrained by any one moral principle. After short attempts to preserve Provence, and to acquire the crown of Hungary, to which his birth gave him a title, he judged it more advantageous to direct all his efforts against the states which bounded his dominions in Italy. In April, 1408, he took possession of Rome; and soon afterwards of Perugia. He conquered almost all the cities of the March, and of the duchy of Spoleto; from thence he entered Tuscany, ravaged the territories of Arezzo and of Sienna, and took possession of Cortona.

The Florentines, when they saw themselves thus attacked, without any subject of quarrel, by this ambitious and faithless prince, resolved on opposing to him Louis II of Anjou. They recalled Louis from France, in 1409; and offered a subsidy to aid him in recovering the crown of Naples. At the same time, they formed a closer connection with one of the two generals who then attracted the attention of all Italy. Among the numerous captains who had been formed in the school of Alberic da Barbiano, there were two regarded as infinitely superior to all others, from the progress which they had made in the art of war. Braccio da Montone, a noble of Perugia, had studied how to render his army manageable, by augmenting the number of officers, and by accustoming it to fight in detached bodies, which dispersed and rallied at will. The other was Sforza Attendolo, a peasant of Cotignola, in Romagna, who at first distinguished for prodigious strength of body and undaunted bravery, soon became equally distinguished in military tactics; but, instead of adopting the new

method of Braccio, he applied himself to bringing the
ancient system to perfection. He continued to move
his army in large masses; which no one conducted
with such unison and steadiness. Braccio distinguished
himself by impetuous valour, by prompt and decisive
action, and sometimes by trusting to chance: Sforza,
by prudent, steady, and cool conduct. All the soldiers
of fortune in Italy soon attached themselves to one or
other of these two captains; who, nearly of the same
age, and having made their first campaigns together,
now found themselves opposed to each other in a
rivalry of interest and glory. The name of the Bracceschi school was given to the band of soldiers of the
one, and Sforzeschi to the other; and, when a state
called one of these into its service, it was nearly sure
of having the other opposed to it.

The Florentines formed a close connection with Braccio: they placed him at the head of their army; and
they settled on him a considerable pension, which was
to continue even when out of their service, provided he
always returned to it when called upon. Louis of Anjou
rendered them but little service: he was engaged in a
war on their account in the states of Rome, when he
received news that the Genoese had, on the 6th of
September, 1409, risen against the French, and driven
them out of Genoa. Apprehending that his communication with France might be interrupted, he hastily returned to Provence. After his departure, Braccio carried
on the war successfully against the Neapolitans. With
the Florentine army he made himself master of Rome,
on the 2d of January, 1410. Florence, however, had no
sooner gained a signal advantage over Ladislaus, than
it offered him peace, which he eagerly accepted: he
bound himself by treaties in terms the most precise,
and confirmed them by oaths the most solemn; which
were no sooner taken than unblushingly violated by
him. The war was interrupted only for the time necessary for the repose of the troops; each year forced them
to a new campaign. Louis of Anjou was twice called
into Italy by the Florentines: he gained over Ladislaus,

at Roccasecca, on the 19th of May, 1411, a great victory, of which he knew not how to take advantage. He again retired, and left Ladislaus to finish the conquest of the ecclesiastical states; while John XXIII, successor of Alexander V, only struggled to prevent the convocation of the council of Constance, which deposed him. Ladislaus, who owed his success chiefly to the talents and bravery of Sforza, then in his pay, made every year some fresh conquest in Tuscany. The Florentine republic, attacked by him on all sides, and, exhausted by continual exertion, found no longer any resource by which to resist him, and began to lose all hope; when the king of Naples was seized in his camp with a violent and painful malady, attributed to his debaucheries. He was conveyed in a litter to Naples; and died on arriving there, on the 6th of August, 1414. His sister, Joan II, widow of the son of the duke of Austria, succeeded him. She was forty years of age; and, like her brother, abandoned to the most unrestrained libertinism. She left the government of her kingdom to her lovers, who disputed power by arms: they called into her service, or into that of her second husband, or of the rival princes whom she in turn adopted, the two armies of Sforza and Braccio. The consequence was the ruin of the kingdom of Naples; which ceased to menace the rest of Italy.

The moment Ladislaus disappeared, a new enemy arose to disturb the Florentines—Filippo Maria Visconti, the brother of Gian Maria, and third duke of Milan. He was received in that capital on the 16th of June, 1412, four days after the murder of his brother. Filippo immediately married the widow of Facino Cane, the powerful condottiere, who had retained Gian Maria in his dependence; and who died the same day that Gian Maria was assassinated. By this sudden marriage he secured the army of Facino Cane—which was, in fact, master of the greater part of the Milanese: with its aid he undertook, without delay, to recover the rest of his states from the hands of those tyrants who had divided amongst them the dominions of his father. Filippo Maria, like him, united immeasurable ambition with extreme timidity. During the first year of his reign, which was to decide his existence as prince or subject, he fought with determined courage; but from that time, though he continually made war, he never showed himself to his armies. Even in his palace and garden, he shrank from the eye of man: he never consented to an interview with the emperor Sigismond, who had gone to Milan to exert himself for the extinction of the schism. It is asserted that Filippo Maria was so sensible of his extreme ugliness, that he could not support the humiliation of being looked at. He had the art of discovering great talents, and of attaching the best captains of Italy, in as great a degree as his father; but placed less confidence in those worthy of obtaining it, and possessed less elevation and constancy in his projects. Always as timid as he was ambitious, he became discouraged on the smallest reverse of fortune in the attacks which he continually made on his neighbours: versatile in politics, he no sooner made peace than he renewed war, or contracted an alliance than he broke it. He seemed no less alarmed at the success of his own generals, than at that of his enemies. He was always the first to stop their progress, and to prevent them from profiting by their success; so that his tortuous conduct daily produced some unexpected thwarting result. Without pity for his subjects, he exposed them both to the vexations of his own soldiers and those of the enemy. He would have ruined Lombardy, if the fertility of that rich province had not exceeded his power of mischief.

In the battle of Monza, by which he acquired his brother's inheritance, and the only battle in which he was ever present, he remarked the brilliant courage of Francesco Carmagnola, a Piedmontese soldier of fortune, and immediately gave him a command. Carmagnola soon justified the duke's choice by the most distinguished talents for war, the most brilliant victories, and the most noble character. Francesco Carmagnola was, after a few years, placed at the head of the duke's

armies; and, from the year 1412 to that of 1422, successively attacked all the tyrants who had divided the
heritage of Gian Galeazzo, and brought those small
states again under the dominion of the duke of Milan.
Even the republic of Genoa submitted to him, in 1421,
on the same conditions as those on which it had before
submitted to the king of France—reserving all its liberties; and granting the duke's lieutenant, who was Carmagnola himself, only those prerogatives which the
constitution yielded to the doge.

As soon as Filippo Maria had accomplished the conquest of Lombardy, he resumed the projects of his
father against Romagna and Tuscany. He confirmed the
treaties of alliance which Gian Galeazzo had contracted
with all the Ghibeline tyrants of the first-named province; renewed his intrigues against the republic of
Florence, and combined them with those which he at
the same time carried on in the kingdom of Naples.
Joan, who had sent back to France her second husband,
Jaques, count de la Marche, and who had no children,
was persuaded, in 1420, by one of her lovers, to adopt
Alphonso the Magnanimous, king of Aragon and Sicily,
to whom she entrusted some of the fortresses of Naples.
She revoked this adoption in 1423; and substituted in
his place Louis III of Anjou, son of Louis II. The former
put himself at the head of the ancient party of Durazzo;
the latter, of that of Anjou. The consequence was a
civil war, in which the two great captains, Sforza and
Braccio, were opposed to each other, and acquired new
titles to glory. The duke of Milan made alliance with
Joan II and Louis III of Anjou: Sforza, named great
constable of the kingdom, was their general. The Florentines remained constant to Braccio, whom Alphonso
had made governor of the Abruzzi; and who had seized,
at the same time, the signoria of Perugia, his native
city. He found a warlike disposition in the Perugians,
associated them in his glory, and made them sharers
in the wealth which his arms had procured him. He
subdued several of the small neighbouring states, and
seemed to be forming a military principality; which

Florence accepted as an ally, to defend, in concert, the independence of Tuscany. But Sforza and Braccio both perished, as Italy awaited with anxiety the result of the struggle about to be commenced. Sforza was drowned at the passage of the Pescara, on the 4th of January, 1424; Braccio was mortally wounded at the battle of Aquila, on the 2d of June of the same year. Francesco, son of the former, succeeded to his father's name and the command of his army, both of which he was destined to render still more illustrious. The son of Braccio, on the contrary, lost the sovereignty of Perugia, which resumed its freedom on the 29th of July of the same year; and the remnant of the army formed by this great captain elected for its chief his most able lieutenant, Nicolo Piccinino.

This was the moment which Filippo Maria chose to push on his army to Romagna, and vigorously attack the Florentines, after he had acknowledged their right to defend that province. The Florentines, having no tried general at the head of their troops, experienced, from the 6th of September, 1423, to the 17th of October, 1425, not less than six successive defeats, either in Liguria or Romagna. Undismayed by defeat, they reassembled their army for the seventh time: the patriotism of their rich merchants made up for the penury of their exhausted treasury. They, at the same time, sent their most distinguished statesmen as ambassadors to Venice, to represent to that republic, that if it did not join them while they still stood, the liberty of Italy was lost for ever. Lorenzo Ridolfi, one of the ten commissioners of war, had been sent on this mission to the signoria of Venice: finding great difficulty in persuading it to take part in the war, he exclaimed, "I acknowledge we have been wrong in not opposing Filippo Maria in time; for, by our slowness, we have made him duke of Milan and master of Genoa: but you, by sacrificing us, render him king of Italy. We, in our turn, if we must submit to him, will make him emperor." An illustrious fugitive, Francesco Carmagnola, who arrived about this time at Venice, accomplished what Florence had nearly failed in, by discovering to the Venetians the project of the duke of Milan to subjugate them. Francesco Carmagnola had, by the victories he had gained, the glory he had acquired, and the influence he obtained over the soldiers, excited the jealousy, instead of the gratitude, of Filippo Maria; who disgraced him, and deprived him of his employment, without assigning any reason. Carmagnola returned to court, but could not even obtain an interview with his master. He retired to his native country, Piedmont: his wife and children were arrested, and his goods confiscated. He arrived at last, by Germany, at Venice; soon afterwards some emissaries of the duke of Milan were arrested for an attempt to poison him. The doge, Francesco Foscari, wishing to give lustre to his reign by conquest, persuaded the senate of Venice to oppose the increasing ambition of the duke of Milan. A league, formed between Florence and Venice, was successively joined by the marquis of Ferrara, the lord of Mantua, the Siennese, the duke Amedeus VIII of Savoy, and the king Alphonso of Naples, who jointly declared war against Filippo Maria Visconti, on the 27th of January, 1426. Carmagnola was charged to raise an army of 16,000 cuirassiers and 8000 infantry in the states of Mantua.

The good fortune of Carmagnola in war still attended him in the campaign of 1426. He was as successful against the duke of Milan as he had been for him: he took from him the city and whole province of Brescia. The duke ceded this conquest to the Venetians by treaty on the 30th of December: but he employed the winter in assembling his forces; and in the beginning of spring renewed the war. He equipped a considerable fleet on the Po, in order to take possession of the states of Mantua and Ferrara, the allies of the two republics. This fleet was attacked by the Venetians, and, after an obstinate battle, burnt, near Cremona, on the 21st of May, 1427. The duke of Milan had given the command of his army to Nicolo Piccinino, the pupil of Braccio, who had brought with him the flower of the Bracceschi army. Nicolo attacked Carmagnola on the

12th of July, at Casalsecco; but the heat was so intense, and the dust rose in such clouds from under the horses' feet, that the two armies, enveloped in nearly the darkness of night, could no longer distinguish each other, or discern the signals: they separated without claiming advantage on either side. A third battle took place, on the 11th of October, 1427, in a marsh near Macalo: Carmagnola here completely defeated the Milanese army, commanded by Carlo Malatesta, in which were united Francesco Sforza, Nicolo Piccinino, and all the most illustrious captains of Italy. By an imprudent generosity, Carmagnola released these important prisoners; and thus provoked the resentment of the procurators of St. Mark, who accompanied him. A new peace, signed on the 18th of April, 1428, again suspended hostilities without reconciling parties, or inspiring either of the belligerents with any confidence. The Florentines took advantage of this interval of repose to attack Paulo Guinigi, lord of Lucca; whose alliance with the duke of Milan had irritated them, although he had afterwards been abandoned by Filippo Maria. The Lucchese, profiting by this last circumstance, revolted against their lord in the month of September, deposed him, and sent him prisoner to Milan. The Florentines were afterwards driven out of the states of Lucca by Nicolo Piccinino, who defeated them on the borders of the Serchio, on the 2d of December, 1430; and the general war recommenced.

In this last campaign, fortune abandoned Carmagnola. On the 17th of May, 1431, he suffered himself to be surprised at Soncino, which he had reached with his advanced guard, by Francesco Sforza, who took prisoners 1600 of his cavalry: he, however, escaped, and rejoined his still brilliant army. On the 23d of May he approached the Po, to second the Venetian fleet in an attack on Cremona: but the fleet, pushed by that of the Milanese on the opposite shore, was destroyed in his presence, without the possibility of his rendering it any aid. However great his desire to repair these checks, he could not meet the enemy again during the remainder of the summer. A deadly distemper broke out among the horses throughout Italy; his troops were dismounted: and, as the fate of battle depended almost entirely on the cavalry, this calamity reduced him to complete inaction.

The senate of Venice, which made it a rule never to defend the republic but by foreign arms—never to enlist its citizens under its banners either as generals or soldiers—further observed that of governing with extreme rigour those foreign adventurers of whom its armies were composed, and of never believing in the virtue of men who trafficked in their own blood. The Venetians distrusted them: they supposed them ever disposed to treachery; and if they were unfortunate, though only from imprudence, they rendered them responsible. The condottieri were made fully to understand that they were not to lose the armies of the republic without answering for the event with their lives. The senate joined to this rigour the perfidy and mystery which characterise an aristocracy. Having decided on punishing Carmagnola for the late disasters, it began by deceiving him. He was loaded with marks of deference and confidence: he was invited to come to Venice in the month of April, 1432, to fix with the signoria the plan of the ensuing campaign. The most distinguished senators went to meet him, and conduct him in pomp to the palace of the doge. Carmagnola, introduced into the senate, was placed in the chair of honour: he was pressed to speak; and his discourse applauded. The day began to close: lights were not yet called for; and the general could no longer distinguish the faces of those who surrounded him; when suddenly the *sbirri,* or soldiers of police, threw themselves on him, loaded him with chains, and dragged him to the prison of the palace. He was next day put to the torture—rendered still more painful by the wounds which he had received in the service of this ungrateful republic. Both the accusations made against him, and his answers to the questions, are buried in the profound secrecy with which the Venetian senate covered all its acts. On the 5th of May, 1432, Francesco Carmagnola, twenty days after his arrest, was led out—his mouth gagged to prevent any protestation of innocence—and placed between the two columns on the square of St. Mark: he was there beheaded, amidst a trembling people, whom the senate of Venice was resolved to govern only by terror.

CHAPTER X

COSMO DE' MEDICI, CHIEF OF THE REPUBLIC OF FLORENCE
    DEATH OF THE LAST VISCONTI   EFFORTS OF THE
    MILANESE TO RECOVER THEIR LIBERTY   THEY ARE
    ENSLAVED BY FRANCESCO SFORZA   CONSPIRACY OF
    STEFANO PORCARI AT ROME

THE fermentation which had manifested itself at Florence among the lower orders of the people, in the momentary triumph of the Ciompi, began to subside. Manufacturers, artisans, men who to live needed their daily labour, themselves renounced the first offices of the republic. They felt that political equality did not exclude a certain degree of subordination: they acknowledged the power of capital, by which they lived; of knowledge, which discovered outlets for the productions of their industry; and they were disposed to obey the rich merchants who employed them. Accustomed by the habits of private life to trust to the intelligence of their superiors for their most important interests, for those which most constantly occupied their minds, they regarded them as still more proper to decide on political questions, which sometimes excite the passions of the people, but seldom lead them to prudent counsel. It is from time to time only that society, even in the freest states, is universally agitated by some abstract question, which makes the deeper impression the less it is understood: experience comes afterwards to disabuse people of an exaggerated or unreasonable expectation. Thus, false ideas of equality made the Florentines first demand that every citizen should have an equal share in the government: after they had experienced the violences and depredations caused by the anarchy of the Ciompi, they unhappily forgot the advantages of true equality. They did not sufficiently seek to procure to all equal protection and equal justice, to awaken in all that interest in public affairs which should excite the development of their faculties. The flame which burnt too fiercely in 1378 had consumed the materials which should have nourished it; and, fifty years later, the Florentine people no longer evinced any jealousy of those who, by their position, seemed naturally destined to rule them.

General ideas exercise a durable influence only on minds capable of comprehending them. Let liberty exist for all; but let power remain with those who comprehend its objects—with those who can distinguish the means by which to attain them—with those who are too proud to acknowledge masters, and too generous to desire subjects—with those who, anxious for the intellectual progress and for the material well-being of their kind, would give up all their time and attention to obtain both—with those who, enjoying the advantages of a liberal education, have minds neither irritated by jealousy, narrowed by prejudice, nor disturbed by chimerical apprehensions. Let all, however, have some share in political power; such a share as may be necessary to preserve them from oppression—to raise their minds and feelings in emergency above material interests—to divest them of selfishness, that they may, when called upon, comprehend the great questions of morality: but let them participate in this political power as citizens, not as magistrates.

The number of republics had so much diminished in Italy, that the lower orders ran a far greater risk of being corrupted by the example of servility, than by that of the excesses of democracy. In the kingdom of Naples, in Romagna, and Lombardy, those orders remained without protection, exposed to the outrages of the soldier and the oppression of the fiscal officer. Nev-

ertheless, with the exception of the calamities inflicted
by the passage of companies of adventure, the burden
imposed on them was subject to rules of equal distribution: they were unacquainted with the personal
vexations, the domestic oppression, which the nobles
inflicted on the plebeians in the west of Europe. Accordingly, in spite of frequent calamities, and of a great
diminution of productive energy, Italy, which had
ceased to be free, had not ceased to be prosperous. In
Lombardy, especially, agriculture and husbandry being
well understood, the natural fertility of the soil was
turned to the most profitable account; while innumerable manufactures and extensive commerce animated
and enriched the towns.

After the kingdom of Naples and the duchy of Milan,
the republic of Venice was, in power, the third state of
Italy. The people of Venice were deprived, almost as
much as those of Milan, of all participation in political
power. Their suffrages were never demanded, their
voice was never heard; they never thought even of
questioning the wisdom of their government. But the
senate, far wiser in its administration than the tyrants
of Lombardy, never allowed their subjects to bear any
other burdens than those imposed by itself; and those
were always moderate, always equally distributed, in a
spirit of justice. All that the Venetians paid the state
was employed scrupulously, and with economy, either
for the common defence, or for the ornament of their
country. The government cost the people nothing. The
people, themselves, looked with pride upon the employment of their money in the public works. The provinces
of the Terra Firma were carefully secured from the
vexations of the soldier, and as much as possible from
the invasion of the enemy. The city of Venice from the
period of its foundation had never been invaded—had
never seen the Rialto soiled by the feet of foreign
armies—had never suffered even the temporary domination of a tyrant. The riches of commerce and industry,
fostered by such constant security, had grown beyond
all precedent. The provinces of the Terra Firma, for-

getting all pretension to independence, found themselves happy by comparison with their neighbours. The
peasantry, in particular, were ready to give their lives
for St. Mark:—it was thus they always designated the
state. The only possessions of the republic that had
reason to complain were those of the Levant: there the
Venetian merchants sacrificed their industry to the narrow spirit of monopoly.

The republic of Florence was the fourth state of Italy
in wealth and importance. More generous than Venice,
it had more frequently endangered itself by wars, which
exposed it often to invasion. Less prudent in its internal
administration, it had more than once experienced the
convulsions of contending factions, and sometimes even
those of temporary tyranny. On the other side, the
Florentines owed to the nature of their government a
degree of energy, activity, and intelligence which put
them in a state to repair their losses much more rapidly.
They had in their city manufactures renowned through
the western world, particularly that of woollen stuffs,
which occupied more hands than any other, and those
of silk and gold brocade. Their merchants were the
greatest capitalists of Europe; their counting-houses
were scattered throughout the commercial parts of the
world; and their funds were often lent to princes at
enormous interest. The territory of the Florentines was
enriched by the most industrious agriculture. In it was
concentrated, on a given space, the most labour and the
largest capital. The citizens submitted of their own
accord to heavy imposts; but the peasantry were
treated with more consideration. A moderate and equa-
ble partition of the taxes was sought to be maintained;
and it was in this view that the Florentines, in 1429,
invented the *catasto*—an enumeration and description
of property of every kind, with an estimate of its value,
to serve as a basis to taxes always imposed in due proportion. The subjects of Florence must have found
themselves at least as happy as those of Venice: but
the memory of liberty and independence was more
recent; and Pisa, Pistoia, Arezzo, Volterra, and even

less important towns, made repeated efforts to recover their liberty. Not one town could yet resign itself to be subject to the Florentines. Within the circle of Tuscany, too, Lucca, which did not lose its liberty from the time of Paulo Guinigi until our day, and Sienna, which preserved hers till 1555, seemed to invite these cities to govern themselves as independent republics. In the two above mentioned, however, the democratic fermentation which had agitated all free states during the latter half of the fourteenth century began to subside, and the government had returned to the hands of those who were fitted for it by their education and talents.

The democratic party at Florence, directed by the Alberti, Ricci, and Medici, were deprived of power in 1381, in consequence of the abuse which their associates, the Ciompi, had made of their victory. From that time their rivals, the Albizzi, directed the republic for the space of fifty-three years, from 1381 to 1434, with a happiness and glory till then unexampled. No triumph of an aristocratic faction ever merited a more brilliant place in history. The one in question maintained itself by the ascendency of its talents and virtues, without ever interfering with the rights of the other citizens, or abusing a preponderance which was all in opinion. It was the most prosperous epoch of the republic—that during which its opulence acquired the greatest development—that in which the arts, sciences, and literature adopted Florence as their native country—that in which were born and formed all those great men, of whom the Medici, their contemporaries, have reaped the glory, without having had any share in producing them—that, finally, in which the republic most constantly followed the noblest policy: considering itself as the guardian of the liberty of Italy, it in turns set limits to the ambition of Gian Galeazzo Visconti; of Ladislaus, king of Naples; and of Filippo Maria, duke of Milan. Tomaso degli Albizzi, and after him Nicolo da Uzzano, had been the chiefs of the aristocracy at this period of glory and wisdom. To those succeeded Rinaldo, son of Tomaso degli Albizzi; who forgot, a little more than his predecessors, that he was only a simple citizen. Impetuous, arrogant, jealous, impatient of all opposition, he lost the pre-eminence which his family had so long maintained.

Rinaldo degli Albizzi saw, with uneasiness, a rival present himself in Cosmo, son of Giovanni de' Medici, who revived a party formerly the vanquishers of his ancestors. This man enjoyed an hereditary popularity at Florence; because he was descended from one of the demagogues who, in 1378, had undertaken the defence of the minor arts against the aristocracy: he, at the same time, excited the jealousy of the latter by his immense wealth, which equalled that of the greatest princes of Italy. Although the Albizzi saw with distrust the family of their rivals attain the supreme magistracy, they could not exclude from it Giovanni de' Medici, who was gonfalonier in 1421. His son Cosmo, born in 1389, was priore in 1416: he was the head of a commercial establishment which had counting-houses in all the great cities of Europe, and in the Levant: he, at the same time, cultivated literature with ardour. His palace, one of the most sumptuous in Florence, was the resort of artists, poets, and learned men; of those, among others, who about this time introduced the Platonic philosophy into Italy. The opulence of Cosmo de' Medici was always at the service of his friends. There were very few poor citizens at Florence to whom his purse was not open.

Cosmo de' Medici had no thought of reviving the doctrine of his ancestors, respecting the right of the lowest order of citizens to enter the magistracy. He expressed no democratic opinions, although he severely criticised the government and its measures, whilst under the direction of Rinaldo degli Albizzi. He wished to have seen adopted other alliances and another policy. He asserted that, since the death of Nicolo da Uzzano, in 1427, the security of the state had been endangered by imprudent wars, and the finances dilapidated by the robbery of the commissaries, particularly in the expedition against Lucca. Constant opposition and accusation at last so provoked Rinaldo, whose character was impetuous and violent, that he determined on proceeding against Cosmo as a state criminal. In the month of September, 1433, a signoria, drawn by lot, was found to be composed of the most devoted creatures of the Albizzi. Bernardo Guadagni presided at it as gonfalonier. On the 7th of September, he summoned Cosmo de' Medici to present himself at the palace, and render an account of his conduct; and, on his arrival there, committed him prisoner to the tower of the clock. The people were immediately called to a parliament by the tolling of the great bell. The Florentines had preserved, from the first period of their republic, the custom of these parliaments, in which the whole population assembled in the public square. Without its being necessary to make those present prove that they were citizens, and without securing any guarantee to the feeble against the powerful, they voted by acclamation on what was proposed by the signoria. In consequence of the sovereignty of the people, the parliament was regarded as superior to all law, to the constitution itself, and even to justice; when warned of some great national danger which justified revolutionary measures, it was supposed to be invested with the whole power of the state, to be raised above all rule: but experience proved that the parliament always sanctioned every revolution, and that the sovereignty of the people lent its name to every act of tyranny. As such a parliament could not deliberate, it was required to transmit its power to a *balia*, or commission, which it invested with all the rights possessed by the Florentine people themselves. Rinaldo degli Albizzi presented a list of the names of those of whom he wished the balia to be composed; about two hundred in number. The balia obtained the purses from which were to be drawn the names of the magistrates. They excluded whom they pleased; they entered new names; they condemned to exile Cosmo de' Medici and his friends. Albizzi had reckoned on Cosmo's being executed: he accused Bernardo Guadagni of having received money from his enemy to spare him; and regarded as a defeat the incomplete vengeance which he had just wreaked.

The event justified his fears. Precisely a year afterwards, in the month of September, 1434, a new signoria was drawn, with Nicolo Donati president, and entirely favourable to Cosmo de' Medici. The balia, notwithstanding its partiality, had not dared to exclude from the magistracy all the eminent men attached to that great citizen. Donati, in his turn, summoned to the palace, Rinaldo degli Albizzi and his friends; who, instead of obeying, endeavoured to defend themselves: but the same people who had voted for them in the last parliament, so far from taking arms at their call, appeared at a new one convoked by Donati, where they showed the same docility, where they approved in the same manner by their acclamation another balia presented by the gonfalonier: and this was no sooner constituted, than Cosmo de' Medici, with all his friends, were recalled; and Rinaldo Albizzi, with all his party exiled.

Albizzi sought an asylum with Filippo Maria, duke of Milan, on whom, as long as he had directed the republic, he had always made war. Forgetting the danger which he had often foretold to liberty in the aggrandisement of the Visconti, and believing, like all exiles, that his country could never submit to be without him, but would rise in his favour on his approach, he pressed Filippo to make war on Florence. The war actually broke out in the same year. Nicolo Piccinino, the successor of Braccio, whom the duke of Milan had placed at the head of his armies, repeatedly penetrated into Tuscany: but the presence of Albizzi, who accompanied him, produced no effect. Francesco Sforza was opposed, on the side of the Florentines, to Piccinino. Sforza had formed an intimate friendship with Cosmo de' Medici; he had often in his need had recourse to the purse of the rich banker; and he already laboured to rise from the rank of condottiere to that of sovereign. In 1443, he had made the pope, Eugenius IV, cede to him the March of Ancona, in recompense for his services against the pope's subjects; and he purposed, in making himself feared by Filippo Maria, to obtain in marriage his only but illegitimate daughter, who would bring him in dower at least some fragments of the duchy of Milan.

During the remainder of the reign of Filippo Maria, he was habitually at war with the two republics of Venice and Florence. He was desirous of recovering from the former the Brescian and Bergamasque territory, which he had been forced to cede to the Venetians; and he resumed against the Florentines the project of his ancestors, to extend the dominion of the Viscontis over Tuscany. Francesco Sforza and Bartolomeo Coleoni gave many proofs of their great talents in the service of the two republics. Nicolo Piccinino and his two sons, Francesco and Jacomo, showed not less ability in the service of the duke of Milan. The last named, however, almost always lost ground by his distrust of his own generals, his versatility, his taste for contradictory intrigues, his eagerness to sign peace every year, and to recommence hostilities a few weeks afterwards. The history of this war is rendered so confused by the secret practices of Filippo Maria, which most commonly seemed in opposition to his own interest, that we do not attempt to fix it in the memory. The duke of Milan, in making peace with the two republics, on the 21st of October, 1441, granted their general, Francesco Sforza, his daughter Bianca in marriage, ceding with her in dower the lordships of Cremona and Pontremoli. It seemed to be his purpose thus definitively to reconcile himself with Sforza: but it was impossible for this prince to remain firm in one resolution, or to preserve his confidence in those whom he had rendered powerful. He soon entered into the most complicated intrigues to deprive his son-in-law of all his lordships. The war was renewed between him and the two republics; and Sforza was again the general whom the republics put at the head of their combined army. He was still their commander in 1447, when Filippo Maria, pressed by the Venetians, menaced even in the country around Milan, and fearing to lose his sovereignty, implored the aid of his son-in-law, promising him a sincere reconciliation. Francesco Sforza, who had just lost the March of Ancona by the secret practices of the duke of Milan, yet accepted these last offers. He renounced his ancient alliance with the Florentines and Venetians; and, on the 9th of August, he set forward with his army from Romagna, where he then was, to the succour of his father-in-law. Arrived at Cotignola, the village of his family—the village in which his father, after having thrown his pickaxe into the branches of an oak, to be decided either by its ominous fall, or by its remaining fixed, had seized the sword to engage in a company of adventure—he there learned the death of the duke of Milan, which had taken place at his capital, on the 13th of August, 1447.

The war of Lombardy was complicated by its connection with another war which at the same time ravaged the kingdom of Naples. The queen, Joan II, had died there, on the 2d of February, 1345; three months after the death of her adopted son, Louis III of Anjou: by her will she had substituted for that prince his brother René, duke of Lorraine. But Alphonso, king of Aragon and Sicily, whom she had primarily adopted, and who had advanced as far as Ischia, the more effectually to observe the events which might occur at Naples, claimed the succession, on the ground of this first adoption, as well as of the ancient rights of Manfred, to whom he had succeeded in the female line. The kingdom of Naples was divided between the parties of Aragon and Anjou. The Genoese, who had voluntarily ranged themselves under the protection of the duke of Milan, offered their assistance to the duke of Anjou; their ancient enmity to the Catalonians and Aragonese being further quickened by commercial jealousies. On the 5th of August, 1435, their fleet met that of Alphonso, before the island of Ponza. They defeated it in a great battle; in which Alphonso had been made prisoner, with his brother, and all the first nobles of his kingdom. These prisoners were conducted to Milan, and there in a little time set at liberty, by an unexpected generosity of Filippo Maria; whom Alphonso had made sensible how much the subjection of the kingdom of Naples to the French would endanger the independence of the duchy of Milan, as well as of all Italy. Visconti contracted not only a close alliance with his prisoner, whom he liberated, but promised to aid him in ascending the throne of Naples. This alliance, however, cost him the lordship of Genoa; for the Genoese, indignant at seeing the fruits of their victory carried off by the prince whom they had chosen, rose on the 27th of December, 1435, drove out the Milanese garrison, and recovered their freedom. Alphonso, seconded by the duke of Milan, recommenced the war against René of Anjou with greater advantage. On the 2d of June, 1442, he took from him the city of Naples: from that time peace was re-established in that kingdom, and Alphonso signalised himself by a liberality which gained for him the surname of "the Magnanimous." No monarch ever showed more zeal in literature, or granted a more constant and more enlightened protection to men of letters. He proved, by many noble actions, that he had profited by the lessons of antiquity which he admired and studied with so much ardour. He established himself amidst a people which he had conquered, but whose hearts he gained; and returned no more either to Sicily or Aragon. He died at Naples, on the 27th of June, 1458.

Filippo Maria Visconti, at his death, left no legitimate successor: the distant relatives who bore his name were not descended from the princes his ancestors, who had usurped the seigniory of Milan; and they had not been even thought of in the imperial bull which had instituted the Milanese duchy in favour of Gian Galeazzo. This bull had expressly excluded women from the succession; who had, besides, never inherited any Italian seigniory. Accordingly, Valentina Visconti, sister to the last duke, and married to the duke of Orleans, and Bianca Visconti, the natural daughter of Filippo Maria, married to Francesco Sforza, had neither of them any right to succeed to the last duke. Upon the extinction of the male line of Visconti, on whom the republic of Milan had conferred the seigniory, the sovereignty legitimately returned to the republic itself, which claimed its restoration. Four illustrious citizens, Antonio Trivulzio, Teodoro Bossi, Giorgio Lampugnani, and Innocenzio Cotta, on the 14th of August, 1447, excited the people to insurrection; and, with their support, reconstituted the Milanese republic. They, at the same time, engaged all the captains of adventure and men at arms who had been in the service of the duke of Milan to declare for them. The most illustrious among these were the two brothers Piccinino, sons of Nicolo, who had died on the 15th of October, 1444; the three brothers San Severino, natural children of a princely house at Naples; but, above all, Francesco Sforza, who, with his brilliant army, entered the service of the republic, upon condition that the republic should confirm the cession of Cremona, which his wife had brought to him in dower, and add to it the seigniories of Brescia and Verona, if Sforza succeeded in taking either or both those towns from the Venetians.

An excellent opportunity then presented itself of restoring to Italy liberty and independence. In the country most exposed to the invasion of the transalpine nations there were three rich and powerful republics —Milan, Venice, and Florence—supported on one side by the warlike republics of Switzerland; on the other, by the more feeble ones of Genoa, Lucca, Sienna, and Bologna. An equitable alliance between them would have sufficed to secure Italy for ever from the barbarians who menaced it on the side of France and Germany. The opulence of these three republics, their numerous population, and the devotion with which the citizens of free states always concur, with their whole power, in the defence of their country, would have been sufficient to render vain every foreign attack. Unhappily, the two men at the head of the republics of Florence and Venice considered only a present and sordid advantage; they had not the elevation of soul to prefer the future liberty of Italy; and they refused to admit the republic of Milan into a confraternity so desirable for the three states.

Francesco Foscari, who was doge of Venice from 1423 to 1457, had communicated to the republic, of which he was the chief, his own warlike ambition. He had made it achieve the conquest of the Brescian and Bergamasque territory. He judged the opportunity favourable to detach new provinces from the duchy of Milan, or perhaps to subjugate the whole; and he rejected all the advances of the Milanese republic, which ardently desired peace. Cosmo de' Medici, at Florence, also, so far from having, like the preceding chiefs of that republic, a true love of liberty, began to aspire to become the prince of a country in which he had risen as head of the democratic party. He was so superior to his former associates, in wealth, in the number of dependants, in the deference shown him by foreign powers; he was likewise so elated by the flattery of all the most distinguished men of letters; that he believed himself formed to govern without opposition, and without a rival. Almost all the Italian republics had successively submitted to the influence of some family, which had raised itself above every other. The turn of Florence seemed at last come; Cosmo was determined the Medici should take the same rank there which the Bentivogli held at Bologna. He had himself contributed to retain that republic, the ally of Florence, under the domineering power of an usurping family. When Annibal Bentivoglio fell, on the 24th of June, 1445, by the hand of assassins, armed by the pope and the duke of Milan, Cosmo de' Medici supplied the Bolognese with another Bentivoglio, by disclosing an affair of gallantry which one of that name had with a Florentine lady of burgher family. The fruit of that intrigue was a son, named Santi Cascese, whom Cosmo de' Medici caused to be received as the head of the Bolognese republic. The moment was, in fact, come when the credit of the Medici was to prevail over the legal power of the Florentine signoria; and in which they might, like the

Bentivogli, transmit their usurped power, not only to their legitimate children, but to their spurious descendants. Cosmo felt no kind of sympathy for the newly forming republic at Milan, which vainly endeavoured to awaken in Italy the ancient enthusiasm for liberty: he was jealous, too, of the republic of Venice, which appeared to him to aspire to the dominion of the whole peninsula. By way of counterpoise, he promised Francesco Sforza his support to mount the throne which had been filled by the duke of Milan.

Francesco Sforza, who had evinced talents for war superior to those of the most distinguished captains of the age, possessed, at the same time, the frankness and the liberality which military habits produce. He was considered a man eminently true and generous; his friends felt devotion to him, his soldiers enthusiasm. But it is not in the trade of captains of adventure that men can be formed to true honour. Francesco Sforza showed himself, more than once, perfidious even to his own lieutenants; some of whom he put to death with great cruelty, for having only excited his suspicion. But what, above all, revealed his character, and, at the same time, his cleverness, was the address with which he, in turn, deceived the two republics which trusted him; rendering their subsidies and soldiers subservient to his own elevation, and betraying them, one after the other, when he had gained his object. It was thus he won at once the admiration of his friend and disciple, Louis XI, and lost the esteem of all honourable men.

The duke of Orleans, in the name of his mother, Valentina Visconti, advanced pretensions to the duchy of Milan; and caused it to be attacked by French troops on the side of Asti. Sforza, not to commit himself with France, left the care of repelling them to Bartolomeo Coleoni, who served the Milanese, but not under the command of Sforza. Sforza, himself, in the mean while, on the 16th of November, 1447, took by assault Placentia, then the second city of Lombardy, and pillaged it with a barbarity from which it never recovered. He also employed himself in exasperating

the dissension which began to manifest itself in the
Milanese council. Trivulzio was a Guelph, Bossi and
Lampugnani were Ghibelines; and the hereditary hatred between their families envenomed their mutual
jealousy. Trivulzio engaged the Venetians to offer peace
to the republic of Milan, on condition of ceding to
them Crema and the Ghiara d'Adda. The Ghibelines,
excited by Sforza, refused to accede to the treaty, and
caused it to be rejected by the council of 800: he, at
the same time, strengthened their confidence by his
victories. In the month of May, 1448, he took from the
Venetians all they had conquered on the right of the
Adda. On the 17th of July, he burnt their fleet on the
Po, near Casal Maggiore; and, on the 15th of September, he gained a great and last victory over them at
Caravaggio, where he made nearly their whole army
prisoners of war.

Sforza, after these victories, thought the Venetians
sufficiently subdued to prevent them from attempting
to conquer a state which offered such vigorous resistance. He feared likewise that the Milanese might be
too much elated to submit to him. He therefore released
all the Venetian prisoners taken by him at Caravaggio;
and on the 18th of October, 1448, signed a treaty
with the Venetians, by which he guaranteed to them
Brescia and Bergamo, and ceded Crema and the Ghiara
d'Adda, on condition that they should aid him in making the conquest of the duchy of Milan, with all the
territory attached to it under Filippo Maria. The Milanese, indignant at this treachery, soon perceived the
extremity of their danger. Several of the condottieri
in their pay, imagining they might derive greater advantages from an ambitious usurper than from a republic, preferred following the fortune of a captain so
able and so fortunate as Sforza. Among the subject
cities, also, there were many that, despairing of setting
themselves free, desired, at least, that Milan, of which
they were jealous, should, like them, be subject to a
master. Placentia was the first to yield to Sforza;
Abbiate-Grasso, Varese, Tortona, Alexandria, soon after

successively opened their gates to him. Pavia had submitted to him in the preceding year, while he was still
in the service of the Milanese. In the month of February, 1449, he took possession of Parma; in the September following, of Lodi and Crema. The Milanese, however, though so hardly pressed, were not wanting to
themselves. They obtained some succour from the duke
of Savoy; and the richest citizens placing their whole
fortunes at the service of the state, it was enabled to
supply its militia with firelocks, then a recent invention,
and a costly arm, but inspiring the cavalry with great
terror.

The republic of Venice perceived at last, but too late,
that its own interests, and the independence of Italy,
equally demanded of them to save the republic of
Milan. On the 27th of September, 1449, they signed a
treaty with the Milanese, by which they acknowledged
the new republic, and assigned as limits to it the Adda,
the Tessin, the Po, and the Swiss Alps: at the same
time, they abandoned to Sforza seven of the largest
cities of Lombardy, with their fertile provinces. Sforza
believed himself too near attaining his object to renounce it: he, however, sent his brother to Venice to
declare his acceptance of the treaty; and, in conformity
with the orders which he had received, he removed his
army from Milan. The events occurred in the sowing
season; and he was desirous of inspiring the Milanese
with confidence, to finish the sowing of their land, and
thus consume the greater part of their grain. As soon
as this operation was over, he hastily recalled his army;
he stopped the supplies of provisions, which the Milanese sent for in every direction; and he renewed hostilities. The Venetians attempted to succour Milan; but
he defeated them, on the 28th of December. The
famine which he produced soon became extreme: the
people, incapable of supporting it, rose on the 25th of
February, 1450; and, on the 26th, they opened the
gates to Francesco Sforza, proclaiming him duke of
Milan. The Venetians still attempted, for some years
after, to dispute his newly acquired greatness: in this

view, they made alliance with Alphonso, king of Naples, and the duke of Savoy. But Cosmo de' Medici, who became daily more powerful at Florence, and who substituted private affection for the generous and ancient love of liberty, drew closer his alliance with Sforza, and sent him aid. Meanwhile, the taking of Constantinople by the Turks, on the 29th of May, 1453, spread terror throughout Christendom. The Italians began to feel the necessity of re-establishing peace among themselves, for the sake of their common defence against barbarians: and a treaty was accordingly signed at Lodi, on the 9th of April, 1454. Bergamo and Brescia, with the territory thereunto belonging, fell to the Venetians; but to Francesco Sforza was secured the duchy of Milan, in which Crema and the Ghiara d'Adda were comprehended.

The consent of the emperor was wanting to legitimatise the title of duke of Milan to Francesco Sforza. But Frederick III of Austria, who reigned since the 2d of February, 1440, positively refused to acknowledge him. The new duke, however, felt not the least uneasiness: he despised Frederick as a weak and indolent prince, incapable either of defending Germany or his hereditary states; and who thought of Italy only as a fair, in which to sell at auction titles, dignities, and investitures to the vanity of the great. In 1432, Sigismond had sold the title of marquis of Mantua to Giovanni Francesco da Gonzaga, for 12,000 florins; on the 15th of May, 1452, Frederick III sold, at a higher price, the title of duke of Modena and Reggio to Borso d'Este. This family did not obtain from pope Paul II till nineteen years later the title of duchy for the seigniory of Ferrara, which they held from the church. Sigismond, and after him Frederick, sold, with the utmost effrontery, the titles of counts, barons, knights, imperial notaries, and the legitimatising of bastards, to all who would purchase them; and Francesco Sforza, believing himself sure of obtaining a vain diploma whenever he asked for one, did not esteem it worth the price.

Almost at the same time that the last attempt of
the Lombards to recover their liberty failed at Milan,
the last attempt of a Roman citizen to restore liberty
to Rome was punished with death by pope Nicholas
V. The liberties of Rome, as well as those of all the
states of the church, had been lost, without the possibility of marking the exact moment of their destruction. The senator and caporioni, or bannerets of Rome,
had long administered the government of the republic,
without having the limits of their authority, and of
that of the pope, the first citizen of the state, properly
defined. The former, in the oaths taken on entering
office, instead of swearing obedience to the pope,
promised him protection: they swore not to allow any
one to touch his life or limb, or to infringe his liberty.
These magistrates, as well as those of the other states
of the church, were always elected by the people. The
church was regarded as the protector of popular liberty; and, when a city returned under its sovereignty,
it always considered that it had recovered freedom.
The pope, however, often made the people transfer to
him the right of naming the senator of Rome, or the
rectors of the other cities of the church. During the long
residence of the popes at Avignon, the court of Rome
had forgotten its ancient principles of liberty: its legates had assumed absolute power. The anarchy of
Rome, the outrages committed by the nobles, the tyranny of several usurpers, had accustomed the people
to the loss of liberty. They had frequently sought
refuge, from a tyranny more cruel, in the absolute
power of the prelates. Perugia, Bologna, and other
cities, had often conferred the signoria on the legate,
or the Roman people on the pope, with the suspension
of all the rights of the citizen. The great western
schism again shook the power of the pontiffs in the
states of the church, a few years after they had been
conquered by the cardinal Albornoz. The popes, un-
acknowledged by one half of the church, impoverished,
and endangered, lived, nearly the whole duration of
the schism, exiled from Rome, and most frequently

dependent on the sovereign lord of Rimini. Martin V, who was elected at the conclusion of the schism by the council of Constance, did not immediately recover the obedience of the Roman states: he passed the greatest part of his pontificate at Florence. Eugenius IV, who succeeded him on the 3d of May, 1431, again lost, in consequence of his turbulent, ambitious, and despotic character, several of the states that Martin V had recovered. His prime minister, the patriarch Vitelleschi, stained his reign with numerous acts of cruelty and perfidy: not one of the liberties of Rome, or of the states of the church, were any longer respected.

Nicholas V, who succeeded Eugenius IV on the 6th of May, 1447, was known at Florence under the name of Tomaso da Sarzana. He had been preceptor to Rinaldo degli Albizzi, and afterwards the daily guest of Cosmo de' Medici. His knowledge in ancient literature, in the fine arts, and philosophy, caused him to be ranked among the most distinguished members of the society that assembled at the house of that illustrious citizen. But the studies of Tomaso da Sarzana had not destroyed the servile habits of his mind and education. Grammarians, poets, and rhetoricians were, in this century, too much accustomed to regard themselves as clients or dependants on the rich and great; to live by their bounty, and at their table; to receive from their mouths the word of command for their opinions and sentiments. Tomaso da Sarzana could not learn, in the palace of Cosmo de' Medici, to love or respect a liberty which his patron was secretly undermining, and of which he was labouring to deprive his country. After he had obtained the pontificate, he showed the same zeal for the progress of ancient learning, for collections of manuscripts, for translations of Greek works, for the restoration of the monuments of antiquity, and for the encouragement of contemporary artists, that had distinguished him in a more humble career. But Nicholas V rejected impatiently all opposition, all control of his will: he determined on seeing in the Romans only submissive subjects, to whom he denied all participation in the government. Stefano Porcari, a Roman noble, willing to profit by the interregnum which preceded the nomination of Nicholas V, to make the Roman citizens demand the renewal and confirmation of their ancient rights and privileges, was denounced to the new pope as a dangerous person; and, so far from obtaining what he had hoped, he had the grief to see the citizens always more strictly excluded from any participation in public affairs. Those were entrusted only to prelates, who, being prepared for it neither by their studies nor sentiments, suffered the administration to fall into the most shameful disorder.

In an insurrection of the people in the Piazza Navona, arising from a quarrel which began at a bullfight, Stefano Porcari endeavoured to direct their attention to a more noble object, and turn this tumult to the advantage of liberty. The pope hastily indulged all the fancies of the people, with respect to their games or amusements; but firmly rejected all their serious demands, and exiled Porcari to Bologna. The latter hoped to obtain by conspiracy what he had failed to accomplish by insurrection. There were not less than 400 exiled Roman citizens: he persuaded them all to join him, and appointed them a rendezvous at Rome, for the 5th of January, 1453, in the house of his brother-in-law. Having escaped the vigilance of the legate of Bologna, he proceeded there himself, accompanied by 300 soldiers, whom he had enlisted in his service. The whole band was assembled on the night of the appointed 5th of January; and Stefano Porcari was haranguing them, to prepare them for the attack of the capitol—in which he reckoned on re-establishing the senate of the Roman republic—when, his secret having been betrayed, the house was surrounded with troops, the doors suddenly forced, and the conspirators overcome by numbers before their arms had been distributed. Next morning, the body of Stefano Porcari, with those of nine of his associates, were seen hanging from the battlements of the castle of St. Angelo. In spite of their ardent entreaties, they had been denied confession and the sacrament. Eight days later, the executions, after a mockery of law proceedings, were renewed, and continued in great numbers. The pope succeeded in causing those who had taken refuge in neighbouring states to be delivered up to him; and thus the last spark of Roman liberty was extinguished in blood.

CHAPTER XI

ITALY LOSES THE GREAT MEN WHO GAVE LUSTRE TO THE
    PRECEDING PERIOD   THE REPUBLIC OF FLORENCE
    ENSLAVED BY THE MEDICI   WAR OF THE VENETIANS
    AGAINST THE TURKS   CONQUEST OF CYPRUS

THE generation which witnessed the taking of Constantinople by the Turks, was absorbed by the danger with which this terrible calamity menaced Italy. That country saw on its confines the dominion of the Turks: the banner of the crescent floated over the whole eastern coast of the Adriatic; from the extremity of the Morea to the rugged mountains of Bosnia. Italy was alarmed every year by the conquest and destruction of some Christian kingdom, or by the taking and sacking of some flourishing city. It became filled with emigrants, from the palaces or convents of the whole eastern world. These emigrants were still full of the recollections of a civilisation not inferior to that of Italy herself. They felt the same ardour for ancient literature and science; they were equally habituated to the luxuries and charms of life; while, at the same time, they had escaped from scenes of desolation, massacre, and martyrdom, which their imagination vividly retraced as being about to be repeated in the country which gave them hospitality. On this plea, they implored pity and aid from those to whom they exposed their wretchedness; and their benefactors themselves felt that the hour of Italy was near when the knell of Greece had tolled.

The Turks arrived in Europe with an organisation wholly military, that seemed to ensure them a continuation of new conquests. Still intoxicated with the religious fanaticism of their prophet, which had been revived by communicating it to a new nation and monarchy, they believed that they secured their salvation by the destruction of infidels. Always aggressors, they marched to battle to gain heaven rather than the riches of the earth. The Turkish horseman was unequalled in the use of his scimitar, and in the precision with which he managed his horse; which, running at full speed, stopped, turned, and returned, with a docility which the Latin cavalry could never attain. The new militia of the janissaries was, at the same time, the best infantry in Europe; the most steady and the most intrepid; the only disciplined force at a period when there were no troops of the line in the west. Finally, the artillery of the Turks was more numerous, and better served, than that of the western nations. Industry was not annihilated in the countries which they had conquered: they knew how to profit by the arts which had been carried to perfection in those countries; and thus united the knowledge of civilised people with the courage of barbarians. The report soon spread at Rome, that the same Mahomet who had conquered Constantinople, had vowed to enter also as conqueror the ancient capital of the world, in order to destroy there what he called the idolatry of the Christians.

The fears of Italy were augmented by the consciousness of the want of great leaders. During the first quarter of the century after the taking of Constantinople, all those who had directed with so much glory the powerful states of that country had disappeared, one after the other, without being any where replaced by successors worthy of them. No great name any longer inspired confidence; no great character undertook the direction of government; no generous sentiment animated the people, who passed alternately from fear to languor; and the country, which had till then presented a scene glowing with so much life, exhibits a continual conflict of selfish interests, to the entire exclusion of every nobler passion.

The first among the eminent men who quitted the scene in Italy was the old doge, Francesco Foscari. He had directed the republic of Venice for the space of thirty-four years; and, by communicating his ambition to his fellow-citizens, had excited them to the conquest of a part of Lombardy. The council of ten did not, it appears, pardon Foscari an influence and glory which had changed the spirit of the republic, and had drawn it into the whirlpool of Italian politics, of which till then it had kept clear. The jealous aristocracy of Venice could not endure that the chief of the state should acquire the respect and affection of the people; he was made to expiate by domestic grief the lustre attached to his name. Jacopo Foscari, the son of the doge, was accused, in 1445, of having received money from the duke of Milan. The informer was a Florentine exile of bad repute: nevertheless, as it was the rule of Venice to act upon every suspicion, however slight, in matters concerning the safety of the state, the son of the doge was put to the torture. His sufferings forced from him an avowal; and he was condemned to exile. A confession thus extorted leaves the guilt of the accused uncertain, while the barbarous means by which such evidence is obtained places beyond doubt the criminality of the judges. Jacopo Foscari was, probably, as guiltless on this occasion as he was five years later, when he was again tortured and condemned. One of the judges who presided at his first trial was assassinated in 1450, and it was suspected that the murderer was an emissary of Jacopo. Jacopo was accordingly declared guilty, and the period of his exile prolonged. His innocence, however, was soon afterwards proved, the assassination having been acknowledged by another person, who declared that Jacopo had no share in the murder. On receiving the news of this disclosure, the son of the doge, in exile at Canea, entreated his judges to allow him to return to Venice. He preserved for a country, where he had twice been put to the torture, and twice branded with infamy, the passionate attachment so characteristic of the Venetians. He had only one wish, one hope—that of carrying back to Venice his bones broken by the executioner, and dying beside his aged father, his mother, his wife, and children, on the spot which had given him birth. Unable to soften his judges, he wrote to beg the duke of Milan to intercede for him: the letter was intercepted, and transferred to the council of ten. He declared, that this was what he expected; that he wished to awaken fresh suspicion, as the only means of being restored to home. He was brought back to Venice, as he desired. His third criminal prosecution began, like the two others, with torture; and it was at this terrible price that he purchased the happiness of once more embracing his parents, wife, and children. He was again sent back to die at Canea. Fifteen months afterwards, on the 23d of October, 1457, his father was deposed from his functions of doge, on the ground of incapacity from extreme age. The old man died while listening to the tolling of the bell for the inauguration of his successor. No one who succeeded to the ducal throne ever ventured, from that time, to provoke the jealousy of the aristocracy.

The next great man whom Italy lost, after the doge Foscari, was Alphonso of Aragon, king of Naples: he died on the 27th of June, 1458, in the sixty-fourth year of his age. He had constantly inhabited Italy, or the adjoining isles, since the year 1420, when he was adopted by queen Joan II, and became completely Italian. He proved it by his zeal for reviving literature; by the protection which he granted to men of letters; by his admiration of the ancients. He deserved the title of Magnanimous, which had been given him by his people. No sovereign of Naples had been so much beloved, or had done so much good to that fine country. Alphonso left to his brother John, king of Navarre, his kingdoms of Aragon, Valencia, Catalonia, Sardinia, the Balearic Isles, and Sicily. But he regarded the kingdom of Naples, which he had conquered, as belonging immediately to himself; and he left it to Ferdinand, the offspring of his love. The queen, wife of Alphonso, believed that this son was born of Marguerite de Hijar; and put her to death by smothering. The victim was said to have sacrificed her reputation to save that of a more illustrious person. Alphonso never forgave his wife this atrocity; he did not punish her, but he bade her an eternal adieu. He sent her back to Spain, whither he vowed never to return. He legitimatised Ferdinand; and caused him to be acknowledged his successor by the three orders of the Neapolitan nation assembled in parliament, and by the pope, lord paramount of the kingdom. Ferdinand had scarcely mounted the throne before he showed he in no ways merited the predilection of his father. He was avaricious, cruel, and perfidious. He soon alienated all the Neapolitan barons; and his long reign was passed in repressing the conspiracies of his vassals. These last called to their aid John, duke of Calabria, the son of René of Anjou, who had been formerly the competitor of Alphonso. The duke of Calabria, in his enterprise to place his father on the throne of Naples, believed that he should be assisted both by Francesco Sforza—who, before he was duke of Milan, had long fought, as his father had done before him, for the party of Anjou—and by the Florentine republic, which had always been devoted to France. But Sforza judged that the security and independence of Italy could be maintained only so long as the kingdom of Naples did not fall into the hands of France. The French were already masters of Genoa and the gates of Italy: they would traverse in every direction, and hold in fear or subjection every state in the peninsula, if they should acquire the sovereignty of Naples. For these reasons Sforza resisted all his friends, dependants, and even his wife, who vehemently solicited him for the house of Anjou: he also brought Cosmo de' Medici over to his opinion; and thus prevented the republic of Florence from seconding a party towards which it found itself strongly inclined. The duke of Calabria, who had entered Naples in 1459, had begun successfully; but, receiving no assistance from abroad, he soon wearied and exhausted the people, who alone had to furnish him with supplies. He lost, one after the other, all the provinces which had declared for him; and was finally, in 1464, constrained to abandon the kingdom.

Ferdinand, to strengthen himself, kept in dungeons, or put to death, all the feudatories who had shown any favour to his rival: above all, he resolved to be rid of the greatest captain that still remained in Italy, Jacopo Piccinino, the son of Nicolo, and head of what was still called the militia, or school of Braccio. He sent to Milan, whither Piccinino, who had served the party of Anjou, had retired, and where he had married a daughter of Sforza, to invite him to enter his service, promising him the highest dignities in his kingdom. He gave the most formal engagements for his safety to Sforza, as well as to Jacopo himself. He received him with honours, such as he would not have lavished on the greatest sovereign. After having entertained him twenty-seven days in one perpetual festival, he found means to separate him from his most trusty officers, caused him to be arrested in his own palace, and to be immediately strangled. This happened on the 24th of June, 1465.

A few months after the duke of Calabria had quitted the kingdom of Naples, the great citizen, Cosmo de' Medici, who governed Florence, died, in his seventy-fifth year, on the 1st of August, 1464. It was then thirty years since he had been recalled to his country, by the same revolution that had banished the Albizzi. By his authority during that long space of time, he had completely allayed the fermentation which formerly agitated that republic. The constitution had not apparently changed: the executive power was still entrusted to a gonfalonier and eight priori; who, during the two months they were in office, did not quit the public palace. The judicial power was still exercised by two or three rectors, aliens to the state, who, under the titles of Captain of the people, of Podestà, and of Bargello, were invested with unlimited power over the lives of the citizens. They were chosen each year from some friendly city; they arrived with their judges, serjeants, and all their officers of justice; they received a munificent salary: but, on leaving office, they were obliged to render an account of their administration before a syndicate charged with the examination of their conduct. Finally, the laws could not be executed without the triple sanction of the college, of the council of the people, and of the common council. But the Florentines had in vain preserved all this outward scaffolding of popular power. Inequality took birth from the immeasurable progress of wealth; and the citizens felt the distance between individuals among them too enormous to retain the sentiment of equality even in their political rights. The revenues of many Florentine citizens surpassed those of the greatest monarchical princes. Their palaces, which are to this day the object of our admiration, already displayed all the prodigies of art; at the same time that they presented, with the crowd of servants who filled them, the aspect of fortresses, within which public justice dared not penetrate. Artisans no longer claimed any participation in political power; and even citizens of easy fortune no longer felt themselves independent. They knew that the credit and protection of their richer fellow-citizens had become necessary to the prosperity of their industry.

It was in consequence of this great inequality that a close aristocracy possessed itself of the whole direction of the state. It acknowledged as chiefs Cosmo de' Medici, the richest of the Italians, and Neri Capponi, the ablest statesman of Florence. The former made the most liberal use of his fortune: he built palaces, churches, and hospitals on all sides. He was profuse of gifts, loans, and his credit to the poorest of the citizens. He granted pensions to the learned, and to artists. He collected manuscripts from the Levant and all parts of Europe, and had them copied. Men celebrated his taste and acquirements. Without having written any thing himself, he passed for a man of letters; and the revival of the Platonic philosophy was attributed to him, in consequence of the translations made by his direction. While Cosmo de' Medici thus fixed the public attention by his private life, Neri Capponi gained the suffrages of the people by his public conduct. Charged, as ambassador, with every difficult negotiation—in war, with every hazardous enterprise—he participated in all the brilliant successes of the Florentines, as well during the domination of the Albizzi as during that of the Medici. From the year 1434 to 1455, in which Neri Capponi died, these two chiefs of the republic had six times assembled the parliament to make a balia; and, availing themselves of its authority, which was above the law, they obtained the exile of all their enemies, and filled the balloting purses of the magistracy with the names of their own partisans, to the exclusion of all others. It appears that all the efforts of their administration were directed towards calming the passions of the public, and maintaining peace without, as well as repose within, the state. They had, in fact, succeeded in preventing Florence from being troubled with new factions, or engaged in new wars; but they drew on the republic all the evils attending an aristocratic government. Medici and Capponi had not been able to find men who would sacrifice the liberties of their country without allowing them to gratify their baser passions. These two heads of the republic, therefore, suffered their subordinate agents to divide among themselves all the little governments of the subject cities, and every lucrative employment; and these men, not satisfied with this first injustice, made unequal partitions of the taxes, increasing them on the poor, lowering them on the rich, and exempting themselves. At last they began to sell their protection, as well with respect to the tribunals as the councils: favour silenced justice; and, in the midst of peace and apparent prosperity, the Florentines felt their republic, undermined by secret corruption, hastening to ruin.

When Neri Capponi died the council refused to call a new parliament to replace the balia, whose power expired on the 1st of July, 1455. It was the aristocracy

itself, comprehending all the creatures of Cosmo de'
Medici, that, from jealousy of his domination, wished
to return to the dominion of the laws. The whole republic was rejoiced, as if liberty had been regained.
The election of the signoria was again made fairly by
lot, the catasto was revised, the contributions were
again equitably apportioned, the tribunals ceased to
listen to the recommendations of those who, till then,
had made a traffic of distributive justice. The aristocracy, seeing that clients no longer flocked to their
houses with hands full, began to perceive that their
jealousy of Cosmo de' Medici had only injured themselves. Cosmo, with his immense fortune, was just as
much respected as before: the people were intoxicated
with joy to find themselves again free; but the aristocracy felt themselves weak and abandoned. They endeavoured to convoke a parliament without Cosmo; but
he baffled their efforts, the longer to enjoy their humiliation. He began to fear, however, that the Florentines might once more acquire a taste for liberty; and
when Lucas Pitti, rich, powerful, and bold, was named
gonfalonier, in July, 1458, he agreed with him to reim-
pose the yoke on the Florentines. Pitti assembled the
parliament; but not till he had filled all the avenues of
the public square with soldiers or armed peasants. The
people, menaced and trembling within this circle, consented to name a new balia, more violent and tyrannical than any of the preceding. It was composed of
352 persons, to whom was delegated all the power of
the republic. They exiled a great number of the citizens
who had shown the most attachment to liberty, and
they even put some to death.

Cosmo de' Medici was at this period sixty-nine years
of age; he reckoned that his two sons, now in the prime
of life, would support his declining years: but Pietro,
the eldest, was absolutely incapacitated by hereditary
gout. He could neither walk nor ride, but was carried
about in an armchair: he was, besides, undistinguished
by intellect or force of character. Giovanni, the second,
was endued with much more talent: it was on him

that Cosmo had placed the hopes of his house; but he died, in the month of November of the year 1463. Lucas Pitti, rising to the eminence from which they fell, looked on himself henceforth as the only chief of the state. It was about this time that he undertook the building of that magnificent palace which now forms the residence of the grand dukes. The republican equality was not only offended by the splendour of this regal dwelling; but the construction of it afforded Pitti an occasion for marking his contempt of liberty and the laws. He made of this building an asylum for all fugitives from justice, whom no public officer dared pursue when once he took part in the labour. At the same time individuals, as well as communities, who would obtain some favour from the republic, knew that the only means of being heard was to offer Lucas Pitti some precious wood or marble to be employed in the construction of his palace.

When Cosmo de' Medici died, at his country house of Careggi, on the 1st of August, 1464, Lucas Pitti felt himself released from the control imposed by the virtue and moderation of that great citizen; on whose tomb the signoria inscribed, in the following year, the title of "Father of his Country." His son, Pietro de' Medici, then forty-eight years of age, supposed that he should succeed to the administration of the republic, as he had succeeded to the wealth of his father, by hereditary right: but the state of his health did not admit of his attending regularly to business, or of his inspiring his rivals with much fear. To diminish the weight of affairs which oppressed him, he resolved on withdrawing a part of his immense fortune from commerce; recalling all his loans made in partnership with other merchants; and laying out this money in land. But this unexpected demand of considerable capital occasioned a fatal shock to the commerce of Florence; at the same time that it alienated all the debtors of the house of Medici, and deprived it of much of its popularity. The death of Sforza also, which took place on the 8th of March, 1466, deprived the Medicean party of its firmest support abroad. Francesco Sforza, whether as condottiere or duke of Milan, had always been the devoted friend of Cosmo. His son, Galeazzo Sforza, who succeeded him, declared his resolution of persisting in the same alliance; but the talents, the character, and, above all, the glory of his father, were not to be found in him. Galeazzo seemed to believe that the supreme power which he inherited brought him the right of indulging every pleasure—of abandoning himself to every vice without restraint. He dissipated by his ostentation the finances of the duchy of Milan; he stained by his libertinism the honour of almost all the noble families; and he alienated the people by his cruelty.

The friends of liberty at Florence soon perceived that Lucas Pitti and Pietro de' Medici no longer agreed together; and they recovered courage when the latter proposed to the council the calling of a parliament, in order to renew the balia, the power of which expired on the 1st of September, 1465: his proposition was rejected. The magistracy began again to be drawn by lot from among the members of the party victorious in 1434. This return of liberty, however, was but of short duration. Pitti and Medici were reconciled: they agreed to call a parliament, and to direct it in concert; to intimidate it, they surrounded it with foreign troops. But Medici, on the nomination of the balia, on the 2d of September, 1466, found means of admitting his own partisans only, and excluding all those of Lucas Pitti. The citizens who had shown any zeal for liberty were all exiled; several were subjected to enormous fines. Five commissioners, called accoppiatori, were charged to open, every two months, the purse from which the signoria were to be drawn, and choose from thence the names of the gonfalonier and eight priori, who were to enter office. These magistrates were so dependent on Pietro de' Medici, that the gonfalonier went frequently to his palace to take his orders; and afterwards published them as the result of his deliberations with his colleagues, whom he had not even consulted. Lucas

Pitti ruined himself in building his palace. His talents were judged to bear no proportion to his ambition: the friends of liberty, as well as those of Medici, equally detested him; and he remained deprived of all power in a city which he had so largely contributed to enslave.

Italy became filled with Florentine emigrants: every revolution, even every convocation of parliament, was followed by the exile of many citizens. The party of the Albizzi had been exiled in 1434; but the Alberti, who had vanquished it, were, in their turn, banished in 1466; and among the members of both parties were to be found almost all the historical names of Florence —those names which Europe had learned to respect, either for immense credit in commerce, or for the lustre which literature and the arts shed on all belonging to that renowned city. Italy was astonished at the exile of so many illustrious persons. At Florence, the citizens who escaped proscription trembled to see despotism established in their republic; but the lower orders were in general contented, and made no attempt to second Bartolomeo Coleoni, when he entered Tuscany, in 1467, at the head of the Florentine emigrants, who had taken him into their pay. Commerce prospered; manufactures were carried on with great activity; high wages supported in comfort all who lived by their labour; and the Medici entertained them with shows and festivals, keeping them in a sort of perpetual carnival, amidst which the people soon lost all thought of liberty.

Pietro de' Medici was always in too bad a state of health to exercise in person the sovereignty he had usurped over his country: he left it to five or six citizens, who reigned in his name. Tomaso Soderini, Andrea de' Pazzi, Luigi Guicciardini, Matteo Palmieri, and Pietro Minerbetti, were the real chiefs of the state. They not only transacted all business, but appropriated to themselves all the profit; they sold their influence and credit; they gratified their cupidity or their vengeance: but they took care not to act in their own names, or to pledge their own responsibility; they left that to the house of Medici. Pietro, during the latter months of

his life, perceived the disorder and corruption of his
agents. He was afflicted to see his memory thus stained,
and he addressed them the severest reprimands; he
even entered into correspondence with the emigrants,
whom he thought of recalling, when he died, on the
2d of December, 1469. His two sons, Lorenzo and
Giuliano, the elder of whom was not twenty-one years
of age, were presented by Tomaso Soderini to the
foreign ambassadors, to the magistrates, and to the first
citizens of the ruling faction; which last he warned,
that the only means of maintaining the influence of their
party was to preserve the respect of all for its chiefs.
But the two young Medici, given up to all the pleasures
of their age, had yet no ambition. The power of the
state remained in the hands of the five citizens who
had exercised it under Pietro.

While the republic of Florence thus lost its liberty,
that of Bologna fell equally under the domination of
the family of Bentivoglio. Its subjugation was still more
disgraceful. No lustre whatever was attached to the
name of Giovanni II (Bentivoglio), who governed that
state from 1462 to 1508. Having been left an infant by
his father Annibal, killed in 1445, he was brought up by
the illegitimate son of one of his relations, whom Cosmo
de' Medici had discovered at Florence; and received
from him, as a paternal inheritance, the sovereignty of
his country. The republics of Sienna and Lucca, taking
advantage of peace, had sunk into profound and obscure tranquillity: that of Genoa, wearied with internal
convulsions, which followed each other incessantly, had
lost all influence over the rest of Italy; continually oppressed by faction, it no longer preserved even the recollection of liberty. In 1458, it had submitted to the
king of France, then Charles VII; and John of Anjou,
duke of Calabria, had come to exercise the functions of
governor in the king's name. He made it, at the same
time, his fortress, from whence to attack the kingdom
of Naples. But this war had worn out the patience of
the Genoese: they rose against the French; and, on the

17th of July, 1461, destroyed the army sent to subdue
them by René of Anjou.

The Genoese had no sooner thrown off a foreign
yoke, than they became divided into two factions, the
Adorni and the Fregosi: both had, at different times,
and more than once, given them a doge. The more
violent and tyrannical of these factious magistrates was
Paolo Fregoso, also archbishop of Genoa, who had returned to his country, in 1462, as chief of banditti; and
left it again, two years afterwards, as chief of a band
of pirates. The Genoese, disgusted with their independence, which was disgraced by so many crimes and disturbances, had, on the 13th of April, 1464, yielded to
Francesco Sforza, duke of Milan; and afterwards remained subject to his son Galeazzo.

The Venetians alone, at this epoch, preserved in
honour the name of republic in Italy; but it was a republic without liberty. Their internal policy remains in
the shade: their efforts for the defence of Italy against
the Turks is all that is consigned to history. These efforts
would have been more glorious, if they had better
known how to govern their eastern subjects. Their possessions on the Illyrian coast, up to the extremity of
Greece, were so extensive—they comprehended countries the productions of which were so rich, the posi-
tions of which were so strong; of which one part of the
population were so brave, the other so industrious; that
if the Venetians had frankly put themselves at the head
of the Illyrian nation—if they had governed them only
with as much equity, with a protection as intelligent,
as that with which they governed their conquered
provinces in Lombardy, they would have founded an
imperishable empire, in which civilisation would not
have been lost: but the Venetians always regarded
these establishments beyond Italy as the Spaniards,
English, and Dutch, at a later period, have regarded
their possessions in the two Indies. They not only did
not allow the inhabitants the enjoyment of political
rights, but they denied them those of humanity: if they
allowed that they were men, they at least never per-

mitted them to forget that they were considered as an inferior race to the Italian. Instead of turning to account the superior intelligence and industry of the Greeks, they were determined to see in them no other qualities than those of cunning and perfidy; and they appropriated to themselves, at the expense of the natives, and in their own towns, the monopoly of commerce. The Albanians and Illyrians, very different from the Greeks, were impatient of control, and despised the restraints of regular industry; but they were energetic and brave. The republic would have found in them its best soldiers and sailors, if it had received them into its armies and navies on an equal footing; but it persisted in considering them only as savages, to whom it yielded no confidence, always restricting them to the lowest ranks in the army; and, when at last it consented to raise among them the light cavalry of the Stradiots, they were destined more to over-run and ravage than to defend the country.

The Venetians sent an ambassador to Mahomet II immediately after the taking of Constantinople, to redeem those of their countrymen who had been made captive in the capital of the Greek empire. On the 18th of April, 1454, this ambassador signed a treaty of peace and good neighbourhood with the sultan, by virtue of which the republic was to support at Constantinople, as in the time of the Greek empire, a *baile*, who was to be at the same time its ambassador there, and the judge of all the Venetian subjects in the Levant. Mahomet II took advantage of this peace to subdue successively the Illyrian or Greek princes whose independence had survived the fall of Constantinople. In 1458, he conquered the kingdoms of Rascia and of Servia; in the same year he over-ran the duchy of Athens, causing the last duke, Francesco Acciaiuolo, a Florentine, to be strangled. In 1460, he despoiled the two Paleologi, brothers of the last emperor, bearing the title of despots of the Morea. In 1462, he conquered Sinope, Cerasus, and Trebisond, little Greek states which maintained their independence on the borders of the Euxine sea. In 1463, he subdued Wallachia and Moldavia, afterwards the kingdom of Bosnia, and the bannat of Sclavonia. During the same year, the war again broke out in the Morea, between the Venetians and Turks. The former had possessed, for a long period, several strong places in the peninsula, Coron, Modon, Argos, and Napoli di Malvagia. The commandant of Coron had received within his fortress a slave, who had stolen the treasury chest of the Turkish commander at Athens, and had divided the money with him: he refused to surrender the culprit, under the pretence of his having turned Christian. The Turks immediately commenced hostilities. Luigi Loredano, captain general of the Venetians, excited to revolt the Greeks of the Peloponnesus, and undertook jointly with them to defend the isthmus of Corinth; but he suffered himself to be driven out of it the following year. He abandoned the Greeks who had joined him: they were all massacred, while he returned to seek refuge in his fortresses.

The Venetians, notwithstanding this check, used their endeavours to form a powerful league against the Mussulmans. On the 12th of September, 1463, they concluded an alliance with Matthias Corvinus the liberator of Hungary: they reckoned on the powerful assistance of a crusade which the duke of Burgundy had promised to lead against the infidels, and which the pope Pius II had caused to be preached in all the Latin countries. But when the pope visited the army, which he had ordered to assemble at Ancona, he found only a disorderly and cowardly troop, greedy of gain, clamorous for money and arms, on receiving which they immediately deserted. Pius II himself, worn down by illness, expired at Ancona, on the 14th of August, 1464. The few remaining crusaders immediately dispersed; the pope had engaged the valiant George Castriot, surnamed Scanderbeg, on the occasion of this crusade, to break the treaty of peace which he had made with the Turks, after twenty years of victories gained over them, from 1442 to 1462. Abandoned alone to those enemies whom he had so long braved, he lost, in 1465, nearly the whole of Epirus, which he had excited to insurrection against the Turks: he himself died on the 17th of January, 1466, in the Venetian town of Alessio, to which he had been driven to take refuge. Matthias Corvinus alone remained to the Venetians: by combating the Turks in Hungary, he prevented them from concentrating their forces against the republic; but the pope, Paul II, who had succeeded Pius II, feared the reformers of Bohemia still more than the Mussulmans. He engaged Matthias Corvinus to turn his arms against the king of Bohemia, and depose him for having tolerated the Hussites. The Turks took advantage of the absence of this formidable antagonist to invade Croatia, in 1469, and to massacre almost all the inhabitants. The year following they, for the first time, equipped a fleet, with which they drove that of the Venetians out of the Grecian seas; attacked Eubœa, which belonged to the republic; took Negropont by assault, on the 12th of July, 1470, and put all the inhabitants to the sword.

The Venetians, whose commerce extended through the known world, now attempted to find allies against Mahomet in the distant regions of Asia, situated to the east of Turkey. Their ambassadors, on this occasion, have written relations of their travels, which have been handed down to us; and they, for the first time, revealed the eastern world to the Latins. Hassan Beg, or Hussun Cassan, who had conquered Persia from the descendants of Timour, in the year 1468, then threatened the Turkish empire. He had married a Greek princess of Trebisond: the Venetians sent to him as ambassador a relation of that princess, named Catterino Zeno, who, on his way to him, traversed with infinite danger Caramania, the little Armenia, and the country of the Curds. This route was soon shut by the Turks against other Venetians disposed to follow him: and Josaphat Barbaro, Ambrosio Contarini, and others whom the republic successively sent to Hussun Cassan, attempted alternately either to join the caravans of the Mamelukes in Egypt, and traverse with them Syria up to the Persian Gulf; or to arrive by Germany and

Poland at the Black Sea, and from thence enter Persia by Georgia and Mingrelia. When Contarini wanted to return to Europe, he was cut off from both these routes by the Turks, and obliged to venture along the whole length of the Caspian Sea, to pass the gates of Derbend, and reach Poland by Astracan and Muscovy. But these travels, wonderful for the fifteenth century, and giving a great impulse to geography, were of little advantage in the war: the communications were too slow and uncertain to admit the possibility of any concert in action between the Persians and Venetians. Their efforts to meet had no other effect than the ruin and pillage of several Greek cities of Asia. In 1472, Pietro Mocenigo laid waste Caria and the Isle of Cos; he pillaged Satalia, Pamphylia, Smyrna, and Ionia. The following year he burnt Myra in Lycia, every where seeking news of Hussun Cassan, of whose defeat, near Trebisond, he at last heard. These two campaigns were stained with atrocious cruelties inflicted on the Greek Christians, subjects of the Turks, whom the Venetians pretended to deliver.

At this period the Venetian admiral was diverted from the war against the Turks, by the part which he took in the civil wars that for twelve years desolated the island of Cyprus. James III de Lusignan, king of Cyprus, at his death in 1458, left only one legitimate child—a daughter—who, in the following year, married Louis, the second son of the duke of Savoy: he had also a natural son named James, who, with the aid of the soudan of Egypt, whose vassal he acknowledged himself to be, seized the crown from his sister and the duke. James de Lusignan was repeatedly called upon to defend himself against his sister, to do which he stood in great need of money. A rich Venetian merchant gave him his daughter Caterina Cornaro in marriage, with a dower of 100,000 ducats. To render this simple citizen's daughter worthy a royal alliance, the republic adopted Caterina Cornaro, and pronounced her daughter of Saint Mark. The marriage was celebrated in 1471; and on the 6th of June, 1473, James

de Lusignan died, leaving his wife pregnant. The republic hastened to proclaim itself guardian of its
adopted daughter, and of the child she might bear.
This child died in a year after its birth; and the republic again proclaimed that Caterina Cornaro inherited
from her son, and that the republic, in its turn, should
inherit from its daughter: regarding itself as eternal,
it was sure of surviving Caterina, but it was not equally
certain that she might not marry again, and have other
children. To secure their guardianship, the Venetians
had garrisoned all the cities of the island, since the
year 1473; but this precarious possession did not satisfy them. In 1489, they engaged the queen Caterina
Cornaro to abdicate, and to retire to Asolo in the
Trevisan. It was thus the Venetian republic gained the
kingdom of Cyprus, the crown of which it united with
those of Candia and the Morea. The isle of Cyprus,
rich in wine, corn, oil, and copper, was the most important of the three.

The Turks vainly besieged Scutari in the year 1474,
and Lepanto the year following; but in the same year
(1475) Mahomet II took and ruined the city of Caffa,
the flourishing colony of the Genoese, in the Crimea.
The Turks, afterwards masters of Bosnia, began, in
1477 and 1478, to threaten the states of the Terra
Firma of the Venetians. They passed the Isonzo, and
even the Tagliamento; they laid waste the fertile countries of the patriarchate of Aquilea and of Friuli; they
massacred the people, or led them away captive; and
thus began to make the Italians experience the horrors
of those wars of barbarians which depopulated before
they enslaved the Eastern Empire. On the 15th of
June, 1478, they took Croia, which had been the
capital of Scanderbeg, and massacred the inhabitants,
in contempt of a capitulation. They afterwards renewed
the siege of Scutari. The republic of Venice, abandoned by all Christendom, exhausted by long exertions,
and fearing soon to see the Turkish armies enter Lombardy, accounted itself fortunate in purchasing peace
by giving up to the Mussulmans Scutari, together with

several fortresses which it possessed in Illyria and the Morea. Such were the conditions on which peace was signed between the sultan and the republic, on the 26th of January, 1479.

CHAPTER XII

FREQUENCY OF CONSPIRACIES   THE LAST RESOURCE
    OF THE ITALIAN PATRIOTS   THEIR ILL SUCCESS
    CONSPIRACY OF THE PAZZI   THE ADMINISTRATION
    OF LORENZO DE' MEDICI   HIS DEATH

ITALY had reached the fatal period at which liberty can no longer be saved by a noble resistance, or recovered by open force. There remained only the dangerous and, most commonly, the fatal resource of conspiracy. So long as habits of liberty are preserved amongst a whole people; so long as every class has an equal horror of slavery; a sudden explosion of the sentiment which fills every heart suffices to accomplish a revolution—to render vain the efforts of usurpers, or to overthrow a recent tyranny, though at the moment it may have succeeded in establishing itself. The despot, even when he has silenced by terror the people whom he has oppressed and disarmed, always feels at war with them; he has too much to fear from every class, to hope, with any chance of success, to attach any of them to his cause. But when absolute power has been established long enough for the violence of its first origin to be forgotten; when the majority of the men in the prime of life have been born under its yoke, and have never known a better state; the usurper finds himself supported by the inert part of the nation—by those who, incapable of thinking, or of investigating for themselves, must be contented with borrowed ideas, and with blindly assenting to every doctrine which the government may promulge. With the loss of liberty is lost also that free and animated intercourse which warms the soul, and diffuses noble sentiments even among classes unenlightened by the knowledge of the past, or by the experience of foreign nations. In slavish countries, the prince alone speaks, amidst universal silence: he dictates the proclamations of authorities, the sentences of the tribunals; he even inspires the language to be uttered from the pulpit or the confessional: because the disposal of the revenue is at his will, he appears as a dispensing providence; and makes the people believe he gives all that he does not take from them. The indigent are grateful to him for the public charities; the labourer, for the justice and police which protect his property. The populace of towns applaud the rigour which falls on the higher classes. The national pride takes offence at the foreigner who expresses his pity for an unhappy and ill-governed people; and the vanity of the vulgar is interested in the support of what exists. If any memory of the period of liberty is preserved amongst the ignorant classes, it only refers to unhappiness and pain. They have heard of the efforts, the sacrifices, made by their fathers in defence of the people's rights; but they see only the evils of the struggle, while the result, because it is not of a material nature, escapes their imagination. They conclude that bread was as dear, and labour as painful, in the days of liberty as in their times; and to the privations they endure were then added dangers and violent catastrophes, of which fathers transmitted to their children some terrible details. Slavery, it is said, so debases man as to make him love it; and experience confirms the maxim. Nations every where appear attached each to its government in proportion to its imperfections; what is most vicious in institutions is every where most liked; and the most obstinate resistance is that which the people oppose to their moral advancement.

Such, in particular, was the state of Italy towards the end of the fifteenth century. The lower orders in the cities of Lombardy preserved no other memory of the period of liberty than that impressed on the imagination by some ruin, which their forefathers pointed out as monuments of ancient battles or of ancient violence. The peasantry, having never enjoyed any political rights, feared nothing but the scourge of war; and prized a government in proportion only to its pacific disposition. Galeazzo Sforza, the more to excite the attachment of the people, moved more by the senses than by reflection, surrounded himself with the magnificence of the richest monarch. The Milanese people were grateful to him for the spectacle, without considering that they paid for it themselves. The Medici, whose authority at Florence was more recent, endeavoured still more to render themselves popular, by keeping their fellow-citizens in a state of continual festivity; the expense of which, at least in part, was supplied from their own patrimony. The sovereigns of the other states of Italy, also, in various ways succeeded in gaining the affection of the peasantry and of the populace of towns. The protection against the law extended to the guilty was one of the great means of seduction. The law threatened criminals with the most terrible punishment: prosecutions began with torture, and ended with the wheel. Nevertheless every village festival produced a murder; and those who committed it were exactly the sort of determined men whom the tyrant most desired to have about him. By shielding them from justice, he obtained from them and their families a grateful attachment, proportioned to the cruelty of the punishment which they escaped. These men, the most dangerous leaders of a rabble, were therefore all devoted to the prince; and a call to the overthrow of his tyranny found no response either in the towns or in the country. On the other hand, all those who had any elevation of soul, who knew what their country had been, and what it had become, who could compare the servitude at home with the liberty abroad—all those whom philosophy enlightened on the increasing moral degradation of men subject to absolute power—could not resign themselves to the loss of liberty, which they knew would be followed by the loss of virtue. They would willingly have resisted; but sol-

diers, paid with their own money, shielded the tyrant
within walls which their fathers had raised to protect
their freedom. Social organisation, founded for the common good, was directed by an usurping hand for the
oppression of all. The right of the tribunals to punish,
and that of the prince to pardon, were exercised in
concert only to provide resolute assassins for the latter.
Alliances contracted in the name of the country established a mutual guarantee of the usurpers against the
people. No power existed which could be invoked by
the enlightened citizen: though he had been assured
that all endued with intelligence and virtue were on
his side—that the whole of the wealthy part of the
nation desired liberty—he knew that the tyrant could
arm against it the whole ignorant and brutal mass of
the people. It was resentment for the triumph of injustice and brutality—for the oppression exercised by
men governed only by the senses over all those actuated
by the nobler sentiments of the soul—that so frequently
in this century obliged the latter to resort to conspiracy.
The study of the works of the ancients, also, then
pursued with so much ardour, conciliated universal approbation, almost admiration, for conspirators. Harmo-
dius, Timoleon, Brutus, who with the dagger had restored liberty to Athens, Corinth, and Rome, were
pointed out to youthful pupils as the avengers of
abused law and justice—as the saviours of humanity;
murder, on the other hand, was so common, even men
of honour felt so little scrupulous respecting it, that
conspirators were never stopped by any repugnance to
shed blood: not only every prince and noble, but every
magistrate and citizen, throughout Europe, was ready
to kill, in order to defend the smallest right, to overcome
any obstacle, to inspire fear, to give proof of energy, or
to blot out an offence. Whoever kept servants, demanded above all that they should be brave, and that
they should wear arms for the execution of any sanguinary order in case of need. It was because murders
were generally committed by them, that domestic
service did not degrade. Persons well born placed their

children with nobles, as pages, footmen, and grooms, because they carried a sword, and their service was ennobled by the chance of spilling blood.

So far from experiencing the repugnance we now feel to assassination as a means of delivering our country, men of the fifteenth century perceived honour in a murder, virtue in the sacrifice, and historic grandeur in conspiracy. Danger alone stopped them; but that danger must be terrible. Tyrants, feeling themselves at war with the universe, were always on their guard; and as they owed their safety only to terror, the punishment which they inflicted, if victorious, was extreme in its atrocity. Yet these terrors did not discourage the enemies of the existing order, whether royalist or republican. Never had there been more frequent or more daring conspiracies than in this century. The ill success of some never deterred others from immediately treading in their steps.

The first plot was directed against the Medici. Bernardo Nardi, one of the Florentine citizens, who had been exiled from his country in the time of Pietro de' Medici, accompanied by about a hundred of his partisans, surprised the gate of Prato, on the 6th of April, 1470. He made himself master of the public palace, and arrested the Florentine podestà; he took possession of the citadel; and afterwards, traversing the streets, called the people to join him, and fight for liberty. He intended to make this small town the strong hold of the republican party, whence to begin his attack on the Medici. But although he had succeeded by surprise in making himself master of the town, the inhabitants remained deaf to his voice, and not one answered his call, not one detested tyranny sufficiently to combat it, at the peril of the last extremity of human suffering. The friends of the government, seeing that Nardi remained alone, at last took arms, attacked him on all sides, and soon overpowered him by numbers. Nardi was made prisoner, led to Florence, and there beheaded with six of his accomplices; twelve others were hanged at Prato.

The conspiracy, which broke out at Ferrara on the 1st of September, 1476, was directed by a monarchical party. The house of Este, sovereign of Ferrara, Modena, and Reggio, had successively for its chiefs two natural sons of Nicolas III;—Lionel, who reigned from 1441 to 1450; and Borso, who reigned from 1450 to 1470. It was not till after the death of the latter, that their brother, Hercules I, legitimately born in marriage, succeeded to an inheritance which had been strengthened and augmented under the reigns of the two bastards. It was Borso, in fact, who had caused an authority which his ancestors held from the people, to be sanctioned by the heads of the empire and the church. Frederick III had named him duke of Modena and Reggio, and Paul II duke of Ferrara. Borso had no children; but Lionel left a son, named Nicolo, who, when Hercules took possession of the sovereignty, sought refuge at Mantua. Of all the princes of the house of Este, Lionel and Borso had been the most beloved by their subjects. The gentleness of their dispositions, their generosity, talents, activity, and love of letters, had won every heart. Those who, for thirty years, had served these two princes, made it a point of duty to transmit their crown to the son of Lionel, and regarded the succession of Hercules as an usurpation. They plotted to establish the rights of one whom they considered the legitimate heir of the throne. On the 1st of September, 1476, they introduced Nicolo d'Este, with 600 infantry, into Ferrara, and, immediately dispersing themselves through the streets, called upon the people to take arms for the son of their benefactor. But the people were indifferent between their masters, and would not incur the risk of punishment by declaring for either in preference to the other: instead of flocking to their call, they fled, and shut themselves up in their houses. The satellites of Hercules, who, for a moment, had believed the revolution accomplished, recovered courage, and attacked and vanquished Nicolo, who, with one of his cousins, was immediately beheaded: twenty-five of his accomplices were hanged.

Girolamo Gentile, the same year, organised a conspiracy at Genoa to throw off the yoke of the duke of Milan: it failed in like manner, because the people hesitated to join him, though he had already made himself master of the gates. Notwithstanding these fatal examples, another conspiracy was formed the same year, at Milan, against Galeazzo Sforza, whose yoke became insupportable to all who had any elevation of soul. There was no crime of which that false and ferocious man was not believed to be capable. Among other crimes, he was accused of having poisoned his mother. It was remarked of him, that, enjoying the spectacle of astonishment and despair, he always preferred to strike the most suddenly and cruelly those whom he had given most reason to rely on his friendship. Not satisfied with making the most distinguished women of his states the victims of his seduction or his violence, he took pleasure in publishing their shame—in exposing it to their brothers or husbands. He not unfrequently gave them up to prostitution. His extravagant pomp exhausted his finances, which he afterwards recruited by the most cruel extortion on the people. He took pleasure in inventing new and most atrocious forms of capital punishment; even that of burying his victims alive was not the most cruel. At last, three young nobles, of families who had courageously resisted the usurpation of Francesco Sforza, and who had themselves experienced the injustice and outrages of his son, resolved to deliver their country from this monster; not doubting that, when he had fallen, the Milanese would joyfully unite in substituting a free government for a tyranny. Girolamo Olgiati, Carlo Visconti, and Andrea Lampugnani, resolved, in concert, to trust only to themselves, without admitting one other person into their secret. Their enthusiasm had been excited by the lessons of their literary instructor, Colas di Montano, who continually set before them the grandeur of the ancient republics, and the glory of those who had de-

livered them from tyranny. Determined on killing the
duke, they long exercised themselves in the handling
of the dagger, to be more sure of striking him, each in
the precise part of the tyrant's body assigned to him.
Animated with a religious zeal, not less ardent than
their republican enthusiasm, they prepared themselves
by prayer, by vows to St. Stephen, and by the assistance
of the mass, for the act which they were about to perform. They made choice of the 26th of December, 1476,
St. Stephen's day, on which they knew that the duke
Galeazzo would go in state to the church of the saint.
They waited for him in that church; and when they
saw him advance between the ambassadors of Ferrara
and Mantua, they respectfully approached him, their
caps in hand. Feigning to keep off the crowd, they
surrounded him, and struck him all at the same instant,
in the midst of his guards and courtiers. Galeazzo
Sforza fell dead under their weapons; and the crowd
which filled the church saw the tumult, and heard the
cries, without comprehending the cause.

The three conspirators endeavoured to escape from
the church, to call the people to arms and liberty; but
the first sentiments which they encountered were astonishment and terror. The guards of the duke drew
their swords only to avenge him. Lampugnani, in attempting to avoid them, got entangled in the trains of
the kneeling women, was thrown down, and killed by
an esquire of Galeazzo: a few steps from him, Visconti also was put to death by the guards. But Olgiati
had the misfortune to escape, in this first moment,
from all who pursued him; and, running through the
streets, called loudly to arms and liberty: not one person answered the call. He afterwards sought to conceal
himself; but was discovered, seized, and put to the
most excruciating torture. In the interval between that
infliction and his death, he wrote or dictated the narrative demanded of him, and which has been handed
down to us. It is composed in a strain of the noblest
enthusiasm, with a deep religious feeling, with an ardent love of liberty, and with the firm persuasion that

he had performed a good action. He was again de-livered to the executioner, to have his flesh torn with red-hot pincers. At the time of his martyrdom, he was only twenty-two years of age.

The conspiracy of the Pazzi at Florence speedily fol-lowed that of Olgiati at Milan. Andrea de' Pazzi, one of the five *accoppiatori,* who had exercised such great power under Pietro de' Medici, was dead; but had left three sons, and several grandsons. One of these last had married a sister of Lorenzo and Giuliano de' Medici. Their fortune was immense: it was engaged in commerce, which they carried on with great success. They considered that they had a right to be reckoned among those who held the first rank in their country; but Lorenzo and Giuliano de' Medici, on arriving at man's estate, endeavoured to recover all the authority which their father had suffered to escape from his hand: they, in particular, evinced an extreme jealousy of all those who, in his time, had administered the republic; and although the family of the Pazzi then reckoned nine citizens, who, by their age, rank, and talents, were formed to sit in the signoria, the Medici did not permit one of them to be called to it. One of the Pazzi had married the only daughter of Giovanni Borromeo, the richest citizen of Florence, to whose inheritance he was destined to succeed; but, at the moment of Bor-romeo's death, the Medici caused a law to be passed, by which the male issue in the collateral line were called to inherit, in preference to daughters; and they thus deprived Giovanni de' Pazzi of a fortune which he had looked upon as already his. Francesco de' Pazzi, his brother, whose temper was hot and impetuous, unable to endure such injustice, quitted Florence, to establish himself at Rome. There the pope, Sixtus IV, made him his banker, and soon gave him his whole confidence.

Sixtus IV was of the house of Rovere, a plebeian family of Savona, in the states of Genoa. His election to the holy see was tainted with simony; and he was charged with the most dissolute morals. He had four nephews, whom he had loaded with all the church had to give. He introduced two—Giuliano della Rovere, the son of his brother, and Pietro Riario, his sister's son—into the sacred college. He intended making princes of the two others, who were secular. He married Leonardo della Rovere to a natural daughter of Ferdinand: he made him prefect of Rome and duke of Sora. Girolamo Riario he married to a natural daughter of Galeazzo Sforza, duke of Milan; after which he purchased for him the city and principality of Imola, to which he purposed to add some principalities of Romagna. This dilapidation of the patrimony of the church, to aggrandise the nephews of the pope, was one of the most scandalous examples of what was afterwards called the nepotism of the court of Rome. But although Sixtus IV was a corrupt man, he was not destitute of talents, nor even of a certain elevation of sentiment. He had at heart the support of the independence of Italy; and he believed it could be maintained only by republican forms of government, and with the aid of liberty, the value of which he had learned to appreciate at Genoa. He found himself constantly thwarted in his politics by the Medici, whether pursuing no higher object than the elevation of his nephews, or following a nobler one, he endeavoured to engage all the states of Italy to join in a common league for its defence. This continual opposition soon engendered hatred; and Girolamo Riario and Francesco Pazzi laboured to render it more violent. Sixtus IV finally promised all the pontifical forces to second a conspiracy, the object of which was to restore liberty to Florence by killing the two brothers Medici. The approbation of the pope alone determined Jacopo de' Pazzi, the eldest of the family, and the uncle of Francesco, to take part in a plot so dangerous.

The Pazzi would not run the risk of being abandoned, as the conspirators of Milan had been, after the execution of the plot, because no one knew their intentions, or were prepared to second them. Accordingly, they admitted vast numbers into their secret:

amongst others, Francesco Salviati, whom the pope had named archbishop of Pisa; but the Medici had refused to let him take possession of his see. It was necessary for the success of the conspiracy, that the two Medici should be struck at the same moment; for if one survived, he would instantly be the avenger of the other. It was further advisable that some of the conspirators should occupy the public palace, and intimidate the signoria, while others called the people to liberty: four troops, to act simultaneously, were accordingly requisite. It was judged indispensable, also, that the two brothers should be in the same place, in order that the conspirators might stab them at the same moment. Raphael Riario, a son of the pope's nephew, a young man of eighteen years, whom the pope had just made a cardinal, and sent to Pisa, gave occasion, on his passage through Florence, to many entertainments; in one of which, it was hoped, the brothers might be found together. But Giuliano was neither at the fête given by Jacopo de' Pazzi to the young cardinal at Montughi, nor at that which Lorenzo de' Medici gave at Fiesole. The conspirators were, on both days, ready. The archbishop Salviati, with Jacopo, son of the historian Poggio Bracciolini, and a numerous troop of conspirators, were to make themselves masters of the palace, and force the signoria to approve the revolution; others, with Jacopo de' Pazzi, were to raise the people. Francesco Pazzi and Bernardo Bandini undertook to kill Giuliano, who, timid and suspicious, generally wore a cuirass under his robe; and Gian Battista da Montesecco, the captain of a troop of adventurers, was appointed to despatch Lorenzo. The absence of Giuliano on these two occasions obliged the conspirators to defer the execution of their project to a religious ceremony that was to take place in the cathedral, and at which the two brothers must indispensably be present. It was agreed that the assassins should strike them as they knelt, at the moment that the priest, in performing mass, raised the host, and they, with all present, bowed down their heads. But Gian Battista da Montesecco

declared, that though he had undertaken with pleasure
to kill Lorenzo at a festival—for he was accustomed to
murder—he could not offer the conspirators his assistance in a church, for he was not accustomed to sacri-
lege. All the others then refused to commit what
began to appear to them an irreligious act; so that they
were forced to have recourse to two priests, Antonio da
Volterra and Stefano di Bagnone, who, accustomed to
live in churches, and perform themselves all the offices,
felt neither respect nor fear for sacred things. This
caused the ruin of all.

Every one was at his post when the Medici entered
the temple, on the 26th of April, 1478: the brothers
took their places at some distance from each other. The
mass began: at the moment of the elevation of the host,
Antonio da Volterra put his hand on the left shoulder
of Lorenzo, the better to secure the blow he was to
strike on the right side. The touch, however, made
Lorenzo start up, and with his arm enveloped in his
cloak, he parried the blow; he drew his sword, as did
his two esquires, and the priests fled. At the same instant Giuliano had been killed by Bernardo Bandini.
Francesco de' Pazzi, intending also to strike him, deeply
wounded himself in the thigh; Bandini immediately ran
towards Lorenzo, who escaped from him, and shut
himself up in the sacristy. Seeing the people in a state
of tumult, and despairing of success, Bandini immediately left Florence, and did not think himself safe till
he had reached Constantinople. Salviati, meanwhile,
also failed at the palace of the signoria: he had concealed his followers near the entry, the door of which
shut with a spring lock, which his satellites were unable
to open, when they were to rejoin him. He afterwards
presented himself to the gonfalonier, but his troubled
look and embarrassed language so excited suspicion,
that, without listening to him, the gonfalonier sprang
to the door, seized by the hair Jacopo Bracciolini, who
was concealed behind it, delivered him to his sergeants,
and was soon master of the other conspirators in the
palace: he had them all instantly put to death, either

by the dagger, or by precipitating them alive from the windows; to the frames of which he hung archbishop Salviati, with two of his cousins and Jacopo Bracciolini. The two priests, who had failed in their attempt to kill Lorenzo, were pursued and cut to pieces by the friends of the Medici: lastly, Jacopo de' Pazzi, who had put himself at the head of the troop of conspirators, whose part it was to summon the people to liberty through the streets, lost all courage, seeing that no one answered his call. He left the city by the Romagna gate; but had not proceeded far before he was stopped by a party of peasants, and brought back. In the mean time the friends of the Medici had called the populace to vengeance; and to this cry, at least, they were not slow in answering: Francesco, Rinaldo, and Jacopo de' Pazzi were hung at the windows of the palace, beside the archbishop; all those who had any relation of blood or connection of friendship with them—all those who had shown any opposition to the government—were torn from their houses, dragged through the streets, and put to death. More than seventy citizens were torn to pieces by the mob, in these first days. Lorenzo de' Medici afterwards exerted all his activity to obtain the surrender of those who had sought refuge abroad: even Bernardo Bandini was sent back by Mahomet II from Constantinople. The executioner did not rest till 200 Florentines had perished in consequence of the conspiracy of the Pazzi.

The ill success of the conspiracy of the Pazzi strengthened, as always happens, the government against which it was directed. The Medici had been content till then to be the first citizens of Florence: from that time Lorenzo looked upon himself as the prince of the city; and his friends, in speaking of him, sometimes employed that title. In addressing him, the epithet of "most magnificent lord" was habitually employed. It was the mode of addressing the condottieri, and the petty princes who had no other title. Lorenzo affected in his habits of life an unbounded liberality, pomp, and splendour, which he believed necessary to make up for the real rank which he wanted. The Magnificent, his title of honour, is become, not without reason, his surname with posterity. On the failure of the conspiracy, he was menaced by all Italy at once. The pope fulminated a bull against him on the 1st of June, 1478, for having hanged an archbishop. He demanded that Lorenzo de' Medici, the gonfalonier, the priori, and the balia of eight, should be given up to him, to be punished according to the enormity of their crime. At the same time he published a league, which he had formed against them with Ferdinand of Naples and the republic of Sienna. He gave the command of the army of the league to Frederic da Montefeltro, duke of Urbino, and ordered him to advance into Tuscany. Lorenzo de' Medici, who was no soldier, did not join the army raised to defend him; he was obliged to confide the command of it to Hercules d'Este, duke of Ferrara, who entered the service of the Florentines, but who soon gave them room to think that there existed a secret understanding between him and the enemy. The duchess Bonne of Savoy, the widow of Galeazzo Sforza, regent of Milan, was the only ally on whom Lorenzo could reckon. But the king of Naples, to prevent her from sending troops into Tuscany, undertook to raise enemies against her at home. He began by offering aid to the Genoese, who, wearied of the yoke under which they had voluntarily placed themselves, rose and threw it off in the month of August, 1478. Having recovered their freedom, they restored the title of doge to Prosper Adorno, who had previously borne it.

Sixtus IV in the month of January, 1479, succeeded in engaging the Swiss of the canton of Uri, to declare war against the duchess of Milan. These formidable mountaineers obtained a victory, at Giornico, over the best Italian troops, to the astonishment, almost more than alarm, of the latter; who were made, for the first time, to appreciate the corporal strength and unconquerable courage of a race till then unknown to them. On the 7th of September, 1479, the Florentine army was defeated at Poggio Imperiale, by the duke of Calabria, who had there joined his forces with those of the duke of Urbino. Almost at the same time the brothers of Galeazzo Sforza, whom the duchess regent had exiled from Milan, re-entered at the head of their partisans, and accomplished a revolution in that city. They deprived the duchess of the regency; they punished her ministers and favourites with death, for having, as they said, abandoned the true interests of the state, and of the house of Sforza. They declared her son, Gian Galeazzo Sforza, of full age, though not more than twelve years old; and the eldest brother, Ludovico, surnamed the Moor, undertook the direction of affairs; from that time he was in fact the sovereign of Milan.

The situation of Lorenzo de' Medici became critical: he found himself, without allies, attacked by all the forces of Italy. His enemies had successively ravaged the provinces of the Florentine states, and were already masters of his strongest fortresses. Even his friends at Florence began to tire of a war which the pope and the king of Naples declared they made only against him. The people, whose attachment was founded on his prodigality and his public entertainments, showed, when his prosperity declined, that they were ready to abandon him. He felt the full extent of his danger when he was informed by the duke of Urbino, the general of the enemy's army, that, among his adversaries, the king of Naples and Ludovic the Moor were disposed to be reconciled to him. The dukes of Urbino and Calabria had not sufficient authority to make peace with him; but they strongly advised him to go in person to Naples, and they furnished him with a Neapolitan galley at Leghorn to convey him. It was not without fear that Lorenzo put himself into the hands of such an enemy as Ferdinand, who had so often shown himself cruel and perfidious. He departed, however, from Florence, on the 5th of December, 1479; and was received at Naples with more friendship and respect than he had ventured to hope. He frankly acknowledged to Ferdinand his danger; but he explained to him also his resources. Italy abandoned him; but he placed his hope in France. Louis XI and René II duke of Lorraine both pretended to inherit the right of the Angevins to the kingdom of Naples: they offered their alliance, and promised to send troops to Tuscany. Lorenzo endeavoured to convince Ferdinand of all the danger he incurred by the introduction of the French into Italy. He acknowledged that, for himself, he should derive no other advantage than that of injuring his enemies. He strongly represented how preferable it would be for both, to seek an arrangement between themselves, instead of opening their country to the incursion of barbarians; and, finally, he offered him an indemnity in the republic of Sienna, which the duke of Calabria, son of the king, already coveted. That state had made alliance with the pope and the king of Naples against Florence; had received, without distrust, the Neapolitan troops within its fortresses; and had repeatedly had recourse to the duke of Calabria to terminate, by his mediation, the continually renewed dissensions between the different orders of the republic. The duke of Calabria, instead of reconciling them, kept up their discord; and, by alternately granting succour to each party, was become the supreme arbitrator of Sienna. Lorenzo de' Medici promised to offer no obstacle to the transferring of that state in sovereignty to the duke of Calabria. On this condition, he signed his treaty with the king of Naples on the 6th of May, 1480. The republic of Sienna would have been lost, and the Neapolitans, masters of so important a place in Tuscany, would soon have subjugated the rest, when an unexpected event saved Lorenzo de' Medici from the consequences of his imprudent offer. Mahomet II charged his grand vizier, Achmet Giedik, to attempt a landing in Italy, which the latter effected, and made himself master of Otranto on the 28th of July, 1480. Ferdinand, struck with terror, immediately recalled the duke of Calabria, with his army, to defend his own states.

Lorenzo de' Medici, on his return from Naples to Florence, rendered still more oppressive the yoke which he had imposed on his country. He determined, above all, to efface from his authority the revolutionary, and consequently transitory, character which it still retained; at the same time to obliterate the memory of the sovereignty of the people, maintained by the periodical assembling of parliaments. He called one, however, on the 12th of April, 1480, which he purposed should be the last. He made that parliament create a balia; destined, likewise, to despoil itself for ever of a power which those extraordinary commissioners had, in fact, constantly abused. The balia transferred to a new council of seventy members the absolute power which had been delegated to them by the Florentine people. That council, henceforth, was to form a permanent part of the constituted authorities. It was charged to exercise a general scrutiny, and to choose only those among the Florentine citizens who were qualified for the magistracies. They were afterwards to distribute their names in the different elective purses of the signoria. They were to make a new division of the taxes; to re-establish an equilibrium in the finances, or rather, to employ the money of the state in acquitting the debts of the Medici, whose immense fortune was deranged, not only by the magnificence of Lorenzo, but by the profusion and disorder of his clerks, who carried on his commerce with the pomp and extravagance which they thought suitable to a prince.

It was not till the 3d of December, 1480, that the pope, Sixtus IV, reconciled the republic of Florence to the church. He yielded then only to the terror which the conquest of Otranto by the Turks had inspired. Although he had shown talent, and some elevated views for the defence of the independence of Italy, his absolute want of all principle, his impetuosity of character, and his blind partiality to his nephews, rendered him one of the worst popes that ever governed the church.

The Turks had no sooner been driven from Otranto, by Alphonso, the eldest son of the king of Naples, on the 10th of August, 1481, than Sixtus excited a new war in Italy. His object was to aggrandise his nephew, Girolamo Riario, for whom he was desirous of forming a great principality in Romagna. With that view, he proposed to the Venetians to divide with him the states of the duke of Ferrara; but a league was formed in 1482, by the king of Naples, the duke of Milan, and the Florentines, to defend the dukedom. The year following, Sixtus IV, fearing that he should not obtain for his nephew the best part of the spoils of the duke of Ferrara, changed sides, and excommunicated the Venetians, intending to take from them the provinces which he destined for Girolamo Riario. The new allies, without consulting him, soon afterwards made peace with the Venetians, at Bagnolo, on the 7th of August, 1484. This news threw him into a fit of gout, which, falling inward, destroyed him, on the 13th of August following. Innocent VIII, who succeeded him, was quite as corrupt as his predecessor; but endued with far less talent and energy. After having, in the beginning of his pontificate, made war without any reasonable motive against Ferdinand and the Florentines, he made peace with them on the 11th of August, 1486. He married his son, Franceschetto Cibo, to a daughter of Lorenzo de' Medici; and this alliance afterwards procured to his posterity the duchy of Massa-Carrara. In 1489, he gave a cardinal's hat to Giovanni, son of Lorenzo de' Medici, afterwards Leo X. By the venality of distributive justice, by monopoly, and by the ignorance and carelessness of the administration, he brought Rome into a state of poverty and spoliation hitherto unexampled. He died at last, on the 25th of July, 1492, the most despised, but not the most detested, of the popes who had yet filled the chair of St. Peter.

Lorenzo de' Medici, his friend and counsellor, has been ranked among the number of great men; and, in fact, he had some right to the gratitude of posterity, for the constant protection he afforded letters and the arts, and the impulse which he gave to them himself, as a poet and a man of taste. He gained the affection of the literary society which he assembled round him, as much by the charm of his character as by his liberality. But it is not as a statesman that he can pretend to glory. He was a bad citizen of Florence, as well as a bad Italian: he degraded the character of the Florentines, destroyed their energy, ravished from them their liberty, and soon further exposed them to the loss of their independence. Fearing the example and contagion of liberty in the rest of Italy, he preferred alliance with the sovereigns who were most odious—with Ferdinand king of Naples, with Galeazzo Sforza, with his widow, afterwards with Ludovic the Moor; and lastly, with pope Innocent VIII. At the same time he joined in every intrigue against the republics of Sienna, Lucca, and Genoa. He was suspected also of having favoured conspiracies against two petty princes of Romagna, his enemies. Girolamo Riario, whom Sixtus IV had made sovereign of Forli and Imola, and who had been the chief promoter of the Pazzi conspiracy, was stabbed in his own palace by three captains of his guard, on the 14th of April, 1488. Catherine Sforza, his widow, and the natural daughter of the duke Galeazzo, preserved, however, the principality for her son Octavian. She married, not long afterwards, Giovanni de' Medici, the grandfather of the first grand duke of Tuscany. It was she who gave her name, afterwards so sadly memorable, to her godchild Catherine de' Medici. Galeotto Manfredi, lord of Faenza, was stabbed by his wife on the 31st of May following, as he was about to sell his little principality to the Venetians, and Faenza remained to his son Astor de' Manfredi, under the protection of Lorenzo de' Medici.

The house of Medici had encouraged, at Florence, the taste for pleasure and luxury, as a means of confirming its power; but this corruption of morals began to produce a reaction. All the young men, who had abandoned themselves with enthusiasm to the study of the arts and of letters, who rendered a sort of worship to ancient literature, who studied the Grecian philosophy, and were accused of preferring even the religion of the ancient Romans to that of the church, were, at the same time, devotedly attached to the Medici. This feeling they shared with all the libertines, all those who thought only of sensual pleasure, and who sacrificed to it the liberty of their country: but those of graver morals, and of a deeper religious conviction—those who regarded the progress of corruption as certain to draw down the vengeance of Heaven on Florence—joined to compunctious penitence a love of ancient liberty, and a detestation of a tyranny founded on the triumph of vice. They were called *piagnoni* (the weepers). Girolamo Savonarola, a Dominican monk of Ferrara, and an eloquent orator, had preached to them a double reform, religious and political; for he had himself embraced with equal enthusiasm the cause of piety and that of liberty. He arrived on foot at Florence, in the year 1489, and lodged in the convent of St. Mark. He began immediately to preach there, with a profound conviction on his own part, and with a talent equal to his courage, against the scandalous abuses introduced into the church of Rome, and against the criminal usurpations in the state, which had deprived the citizen of his just rights. The partisans of the double reform soon reckoned in this flock the most respectable citizens of Florence.

In the beginning of the year 1492, Lorenzo de' Medici was attacked by a slow fever, joined to the gout, hereditary in his family: he retired to his country house of Careggi, where, being sensible of his danger, he sent for Girolamo Savonarola, who, till then, had refused to visit him, or to show him any deference; but it was from him that Lorenzo, struck with his reputation for sanctity and eloquence, desired, in dying, to receive absolution. Savonarola refused him neither his consolation nor his exhortations; but he declared that he could not absolve him from his sins till he proved his repentance by reparation, to the utmost of his power. He should forgive his enemies; restore all that he had usurped: lastly, give back to his country the liberty of which he had despoiled it. Lorenzo de' Medici would not consent to such a reparation; he accordingly did not obtain the absolution on which he set a high price, and died, still possessing the sovereignty he had usurped, on the 8th of April, 1492, in his forty-fourth year.

CHAPTER XIII

INVASION OF ITALY BY CHARLES VIII   PIETRO SON OF LORENZO DE' MEDICI DRIVEN FROM FLORENCE   RE- VOLT AND WAR OF PISA   THE POLITICAL AND RE- LIGIOUS REFORM OF SAVONAROLA AT FLORENCE   HIS DEATH

THE period was at length arrived, when Italy—which had restored intellectual light to Europe, reconciled civil order with liberty, recalled youth to the study of laws and of philosophy, created the taste for poetry and the fine arts, revived the science and literature of antiquity, given prosperity to commerce, manufactures, and agriculture—was destined to become the prey of those very barbarians whom she was leading to civilisa- tion. Her independence must necessarily perish with her liberty, which was hitherto the source of her gran- deur and power. In a country covered with republics three centuries before, there remained but four at the death of Lorenzo de' Medici; and in those, although the word "liberty" was still inscribed on their banners, that principle of life had disappeared from their in- stitutions. Florence, already governed for three genera- tions by the family of the Medici, corrupted by their licentiousness, and rendered venal by their wealth, had been taught by them to fear and to obey. Venice with its jealous aristocracy, Sienna and Lucca each gov- erned by a single caste of citizens, if still republics, had no longer popular governments or republican energy. Neither in those four cities, nor in Genoa, which had surrendered its liberty to the Sforzas, nor in Bologna, which yielded to the Bentivoglios, nor in any of the monarchical states, was there to be found throughout

Italy that power of a people whose every individual will tends to the public weal, whose efforts are all combined for the public benefit and the common safety. The princes of that country could appeal only to order and the obedience of the subject, not to the enthusiasm of the citizen, for the protection of Italian independence and of their own.

Immense wealth, coveted by the rest of Europe, was, it is true, always accumulating in absolute monarchies, as well as in republics; but if, on the one hand, it furnished the pay of powerful armies, on the other, it augmented the danger of Italy, by exciting the cupidity of its neighbours. The number of national soldiers was very considerable; their profession was that which led the most rapidly to distinction and fortune. Engaged only for the duration of hostilities, and at liberty to retire every month; instead of spending their lives in the indolence of garrisons or abandoning the freedom of their will, they passed rapidly from one service to another, seeking only war, and never becoming enervated by idleness. The horses and armour of the Italian men at arms were reckoned superior to those of the transalpine nations against which they had measured themselves in France, during "the war of the public weal." The Italian captains had made war a science, every branch of which they thoroughly knew. It was never suspected for a moment that the soldier should be wanting in courage; but the general mildness of manners, and the progress of civilisation, had accustomed the Italians to make war with sentiments of honour and humanity towards the vanquished. Ever ready to give quarter, they did not strike a fallen enemy. Often, after having taken from him his horse and armour, they set him free; at least, they never demanded a ransom so enormous as to ruin him. Horsemen who went to battle clad in steel, were rarely killed or wounded, so long as they kept their saddles. Once unhorsed, they surrendered. The battle, therefore, never became murderous. The courage of the Italian soldiers, which had accommodated itself to this milder warfare, suddenly gave way before the new dangers and ferocity of barbarian enemies. They became terror-struck when they perceived that the French caused dismounted horsemen to be put to death by their valets, or made prisoners only to extort from them, under the name of ransom, all they possessed. The Italian cavalry, equal in courage, and superior in military science, to the French, was for some time unable to make head against an enemy whose ferocity disturbed their imaginations.

While Italy had lost a part of the advantages which, in the preceding century, had constituted her security, the transalpine nations had suddenly acquired a power which destroyed the ancient equilibrium. Up to the close of the fifteenth century, wars were much fewer between nation and nation than between French, Germans, or Spaniards among themselves. Even the war between the English and the French, which desolated France for more than a century, sprang not from enmity between two rival nations, but from the circumstance that the kings of England were French princes, hereditary sovereigns of Normandy, Poitou, and Guienne. Charles VII at last forced the English back beyond [the] sea, and reunited to the monarchy provinces which had been detached from it for centuries. Louis XI vanquished the dukes and peers of France who had disputed his authority; he humbled the house of Burgundy, which had begun to have interests foreign to France. His young successor and son, Charles VIII, on coming of age, found himself the master of a vast kingdom in a state of complete obedience, a brilliant army, and large revenues; but was weak enough to think that there was no glory to be obtained unless in distant and chivalrous expeditions. The different monarchies of Spain, which had long been rivals, were united by the marriage of Ferdinand of Aragon with Isabella of Castile, and by the conquest which they jointly made of the Moorish kingdom of Granada. Spain, forming for the first time one great power began to exercise an influence which she had never till then claimed. The emperor Maximilian, after having united the Low Countries and the county of Burgundy, his wife's inheritance, to the states of Austria, which he inherited from his father, asserted his right to exercise over the whole of Germany the imperial authority which had escaped from the hands of his predecessors. Lastly, the Swiss, rendered illustrious by their victories over Charles the Bold, had begun, but since his death only, to make a traffic of their lives, and enter the service of foreign nations. At the same time, the empire of the Turks extended along the whole shore of the Adriatic, and menaced at once Venice and the kingdom of Naples. Italy was surrounded on all sides by powers which had suddenly become gigantic, and of which not one had, half a century before, given her uneasiness.

France was the first to carry abroad an activity un-employed at home, and to make Italy feel the change which had taken place in the politics of Europe. Its king, Charles VIII, claimed the inheritance of all the rights of the second house of Anjou on the kingdom of Naples. Those rights, founded on the adoption of Louis I of Anjou by Joan I, had never been acknowledged by the people, or confirmed by possession. For the space of a hundred and ten years, Louis I, II, and III, and René, the brother of the last, made frequent but un-successful attempts, to mount the throne of Naples. The brother and the daughter of René, Charles of Maine and Margaret of Anjou, at last either ceded or sold those rights to Louis XI. His son, Charles VIII, as soon as he was of age, determined on asserting them. Eager for glory, in proportion as his weak frame, and still weaker intellect, incapacitated him for acquiring it, he, at the age of twenty-four, resolved on treading in the footsteps of Charlemagne and his paladins; and undertook the conquest of Naples as the first exploit that was to lead to the conquest of Constantinople and the deliverance of the holy sepulchre.

Charles VIII entered Italy in the month of August, 1494, with 3600 men at arms or heavy cavalry; 20,000 infantry, Gascons, Bretons, and French; 8000 Swiss, and a formidable train of artillery. This last arm had received in France, during the wars of Charles VII, a degree of perfection yet unknown to the rest of Europe. The states of Upper Italy were favourable to the expedition of the French. The duchess of Savoy and the marchioness of Montferrat, regents for their sons, who were under age, opened the passages of the Alps to Charles VIII. Ludovic the Moor, regent of the duchy of Milan, recently alarmed at the demand made on him by the king of Naples, to give up the regency to his nephew Gian Galeazzo, then of full age, and married to a Neapolitan princess, had himself called the French into Italy; and, to facilitate their conquest of the kingdom of Naples, opened to them all the fortresses of Genoa which were dependent on him. The republic of Venice intended to remain neutral, reposing in its own strength, and made the duke of Ferrara and the marquis of Mantua, its neighbours, adopt the same policy; but southern Italy formed for its defence a league, comprehending the Tuscan republics, the states of the church, and the kingdom of Naples.

At Florence, Lorenzo de' Medici left three sons; of whom Pietro II, at the age of twenty-one, was named chief of the republic. His grandfather, Pietro I, son of Cosmo, oppressed with infirmities and premature old age, had shown little talent, and no capacity for the government of a state. Pietro II, on the contrary, was remarkable for his bodily vigour and address; but he thought only of shining at festivals, tilts, and tournaments. It was said that he had given proofs of talent in his literary studies, that he spoke with grace and dignity; but in his public career he proved himself arrogant, presumptuous, and passionate. He determined on governing the Florentines as a master, without disguising the yoke which he imposed on them: not deigning to trouble himself with business, he transmitted his orders by his secretary, or some one of his household, to the magistrates. Pietro de' Medici remained faithful to the treaty which his father had made with Ferdinand king of Naples, and engaged to refuse the French a free passage, if they attempted to enter southern Italy by Tuscany. The republics of Sienna and Lucca, too feeble to adopt an independent policy, promised to follow the impulse given by Medici. In the states of the church, Roderic Borgia had succeeded Innocent VIII, on the 11th of August, 1492, under the name of Alexander VI. He was the richest of the cardinals, and at the same time the most depraved in morals, and the most perfidious as a politician. The marriage of one of his sons (for he had several) with a natural daughter of Alphonso son of Ferdinand, had put the seal to his alliance with the reigning house of Naples. That house then appeared at the summit of prosperity. Ferdinand, though seventy years of age, was still vigorous: he was rich; he had triumphed over all his enemies; he passed for the most able politician in Italy. His two sons, Alphonso and Frederick, and his grandson, Ferdinand, were reputed skilful warriors: they had an army and a numerous fleet under their orders. However, Ferdinand dreaded a war with France, and he had just opened negotiations to avoid it when he died suddenly, on the 25th of January, 1494. His son, Alphonso II, succeeded him; while Frederick took the command of the fleet, and the young Ferdinand that of the army, destined to defend Romagna against the French.

It was by Pontremoli and the Lunigiana that Charles VIII, according to the advice of Ludovic the Moor, resolved to conduct his army into southern Italy. This road, traversing the Apennines from Parma to Pontremoli, over poor pasture lands, and descending through olive groves to the sea, the shore of which it follows at the foot of the mountains, was not without danger. The country produces little grain of any kind. Corn was brought from abroad, at a great expense, in exchange for oil. The narrow space between the sea and the mountains was defended by a chain of fortresses, which might long stop the army on a coast where it would have experienced at the same time famine and the pestilential fever of Pietra-Santa. Pietro de' Medici, upon learning that the French were arrived at Sarzana, and perceiving the fermentation which the news of their approach excited at Florence, resolved to imitate that act of his father which he had heard the most praised—his visit to Ferdinand at Naples. He departed to meet Charles VIII. On his road he traversed a field of battle, where 300 Florentine soldiers had been cut to pieces by the French, who had refused to give quarter to a single one. Seized with terror, on being introduced to Charles, he, on the first summons, caused the fortresses of Sarzana and Sarzanello to be immediately surrendered. He afterwards gave up those of Librafratta, Pisa, and Leghorn; consenting that Charles should garrison and keep them until his return from Italy, or until peace was signed; and thus establishing the king of France in the heart of Tuscany. It was contrary to the wish of the Florentines that Medici had engaged in hostilities against the French, for whom they entertained an hereditary attachment; but the conduct of the chief of the state, who, after having drawn them into a war, delivered their fortresses, without authority, into the hands of the enemy whom he had provoked, appeared as disgraceful as it was criminal.

Pietro de' Medici, after this act of weakness, quitted Charles, to return in haste to Florence, where he arrived on the 8th of November, 1494. On his preparing, the next day, to visit the signoria, he found guards at the door of the palace, who refused him admittance. Astonished at this opposition, he returned home, to put himself under the protection of his brother-in-law, Paolo Orsini, a Roman noble, whom he had taken, with a troop of cavalry, into the pay of the republic. Supported by Orsini, the three brothers Medici rapidly traversed the streets, repeating the war cry of their family—"Palle! Palle!"—without exciting a single movement of the populace, upon whom they reckoned, in their favour. The friends of liberty, the Piagnoni, on the other hand, excited by the exhortations of Savonarola, assembled, and took arms. Their number continually increased. The Medici, terrified, left the city by the gate of San Gallo; traversed the Apennines; retired first to Bologna, then to Venice; and thus lost, without a struggle, a sovereignty which their family had already exercised sixty years.

The same day, the 19th of November, 1494, on which the Medici were driven out of Florence, the Florentines were driven out of Pisa. This latter city, which had been eighty-seven years under the dominion of her ancient rival, could not habituate herself to a state of subjection. Pisa had successively lost all that gave her prosperity or made her illustrious. She no longer had shipping, commerce, or wealth; the population diminished; agriculture was neglected throughout the Pisan territory; stagnant water began to infect the air; every profession which led to distinction was abandoned. There were no men of science or letters, no artists; there remained only soldiers; but with them, courage and the military spirit survived at Pisa in all their ancient splendour. Every noble served in the companies of adventure; every citizen and peasant exercised himself in arms, and on every occasion evinced a bravery which was beginning to be rare in Italy, and which commanded the respect of the French. Charles VIII, on receiving from Pietro de' Medici the fortresses of Librafratta, Pisa, and Leghorn, in the Pisan states, engaged to preserve to the Florentines the countries within the range of these fortresses, and to restore them at the conclusion of the war. But Charles had very confused notions of the rights of a country into which he carried war, and was by no means scrupulous as to keeping his word. When a deputation of Pisans represented to him the tyranny under which they groaned, and solicited from him the liberty of their country; he granted their request without hesitation, without even suspecting that he disposed of what was not his, or that he broke his word to the Florentines: he equally forgot every other engagement with them. Upon entering Florence, on the 17th of November, at the head of his army, he regarded himself as a conqueror, and therefore as dispensed from every promise which he had made to Pietro de' Medici—he hesitated only between restoring his conquest to Pietro, or retaining it himself. The magistrates in vain represented to him that he was the guest of the nation, and not its master; that the gates had been opened to him as a mark of respect, not from any fear; that the Florentines were far from feeling themselves conquered, whilst the palaces of Florence were occupied not only by the citizens but by the soldiers of the republic. Charles still insisted on disgraceful conditions, which his secretary read as his ultimatum. Pietro Capponi suddenly snatched the paper from the secretary's hand, and tearing it, exclaimed, "Well, if it be thus, sound your trumpets, and we will ring our bells!" This energetic movement daunted the French: Charles declared himself content with the subsidy offered by the republic, and engaged on his part to restore as soon as he had accomplished the conquest of Naples, or signed peace, or even consented to a long truce, all the fortresses which had been delivered to him by Medici. Charles after this convention departed from Florence, by the road to Sienna, on the 28th of November. The Neapolitan army evacuated Romagna, the patrimony of St. Peter, and Rome, in succession, as he advanced. He entered Rome on the 31st of December, without fighting a blow. The first resistance which he encountered was on the frontiers of the kingdom of Naples; and having there taken by assault two small towns, he massacred the inhabitants. This instance of ferocity struck Alphonso II with such terror, that he abdicated the crown in favour of his son, Ferdinand II, and retired with his treasure into Sicily. Ferdinand occupied Capua with his whole army, intending to defend the passage of the Vulturno. He left that city to appease a sedition which had broken out at Naples; Capua, during his absence, was given up through fear to the French, and he was himself forced, on the 21st of February, to embark for Ischia. All the barons, his vassals, all the provincial cities, sent deputations to Charles; and the whole kingdom of Naples was conquered without a single battle in its defence. The powers of the north of Italy regarded these important conquests with

a jealous eye: they, moreover, were already disgusted
by the insolence of the French, who had begun to conduct themselves as masters throughout the whole peninsula. The duke of Orleans, who had been left by
Charles at Asti, already declared his pretensions to the
duchy of Milan, as heir to his grandmother, Valentina
Visconti. Ludovico Sforza, upon this, contracted alliances with the Venetians, the pope, the king of Spain,
and the emperor Maximilian, for maintaining the independence of Italy; and the duke of Milan and the Venetians assembled near Parma a powerful army, under
the command of the marquis of Mantua.

Charles VIII had passed three months at Naples in
feasts and tournaments, while his lieutenants were subduing and disorganising the provinces. The news of
what was passing in northern Italy determined him on
returning to France with the half of his army. He departed from Naples, on the 20th of May, 1495, and
passed peaceably through Rome, whilst the pope shut
himself up in the castle of St. Angelo. From Sienna he
went to Pisa, and thence to Pontremoli, where he entered the Apennines. Gonzaga, marquis of Mantua,
awaited him at Fornovo, on the other side of that chain
of mountains. Charles passed the Taro, with the hope
of avoiding him; but was attacked on its borders by the
Italians, on the 6th of July. He was at the time in full
march; the divisions of his army were scattered, and at
some distance from each other. For some time his danger was imminent; but the impetuosity of the French,
and the obstinate valour of the Swiss, repaired the
fault of their general. A great number of the Italian men
at arms were thrown in the charges of the French cavalry, many others were brought down by the Swiss
halberts, and all were instantly put to death by the
servants of the army. Gonzaga left 3500 dead on the
field, and Charles continued his retreat. On his arrival
at Asti, he entered into treaty with Ludovico Sforza,
for the deliverance of the duke of Orleans, whom
Sforza besieged at Novara. He disbanded 20,000 Swiss,
who were brought to him from the mountains, but to

whose hands he would not venture to confide himself. On the 22d of October, 1495, he repassed the Alps, after having ravaged all Italy with the violence and rapidity of a hurricane. He had left his relative, Gilbert de Montpensier, viceroy at Naples, with the half of his army; but the people, already wearied with his yoke, recalled Ferdinand II. The French, after many battles, successively lost their conquests, and were at length forced to capitulate at Atella, on the 23d of July, 1496.

The invasion of the French not only spread terror from one extremity of Italy to the other, but changed the whole policy of that country, by rendering it dependent upon that of the transalpine nations. While Charles VIII pretended to be the legitimate heir of the kingdom of Naples, the duke of Orleans, who succeeded him under the name of Louis XII, called himself heir to the duchy of Milan. Maximilian, ambitious as he was inconsistent, claimed in the states of Italy prerogatives to which no emperor had pretended since the death of Frederick II in 1250. The Swiss had learnt, at the same time, that at the foot of their mountains there lay rich and feeble cities which they might pillage, and a delicious climate, which offered all the enjoyments of life; they saw neighbouring monarchs ready to pay them for exercising there their brigandage. Finally, Ferdinand and Isabella, monarchs of Aragon and Castile, announced their intention of defending the bastard branch of the house of Aragon, which reigned at Naples. But, already masters of Sicily, they purposed passing the strait and were secretly in treaty with Charles VIII, to divide with him the spoils of the relative whom they pretended to defend. Amidst these different pretensions and intrigues, in which Italian interests had no longer any share, the spirit of liberty revived in Tuscany once more, but only to exhaust itself in a new struggle between the Florentines and Pisans. The French garrisons which Charles had left in Pisa and Librafratta, instead of delivering them to the Florentines, according to his order, had given them up

to the Pisans themselves on the 1st of January, 1496.
The allies, who had fought Charles at Fornovo, reproached the Florentines with their attachment to that
monarch, and took part against them with the Pisans.
Ludovico Sforza, and the Venetians, sent reinforcements to the latter, and the emperor Maximilian himself brought them aid. Thus, the only Italians who had
at heart the honour and independence of Italy, exhausted themselves in unequal struggles and in fruitless attempts.

At the moment when Florence expelled the Medici,
that republic was bandied between three different parties. The first was that of the enthusiasts, directed by
Girolamo Savonarola; who promised the miraculous
protection of the Divinity for the reform of the church
and the establishment of liberty. These demanded a
democratic constitution—they were called the *Piagnoni*.
The second consisted of men who had shared power
with the Medici, but who had separated from them;
who wished to possess alone the powers and profits of
government, and who endeavoured to amuse the people
by dissipations and pleasures, in order to establish at
their ease an aristocracy—these were called the *Arabbiati*. The third party was composed of men who remained faithful to the Medici, but not daring to declare themselves, lived in retirement—they were called
Bigi. These three parties were so equally balanced in
the balia named by the parliament, on the 2d of December, 1494, that it soon became impossible to carry
on the government. Girolamo Savonarola took advantage of this state of affairs to urge that the people had
never delegated their power to a balia which did not
abuse the trust. "The people," he said, "would do much
better to reserve this power to themselves, and exercise
it by a council, into which all the citizens should be
admitted." His proposition was agreed to: more than
1800 Florentines furnished proof that either they, their
fathers, or their grandfathers, had sat in the magistracy;
they were consequently acknowledged citizens, and admitted to sit in the general council. This council was

declared sovereign, on the 1st of July, 1495; it was invested with the election of magistrates, hitherto chosen by lot, and a general amnesty was proclaimed, to bury in oblivion all the ancient dissensions of the Florentine republic.

So important a modification of the constitution seemed to promise this republic a happier futurity. The friar Savonarola, who had exercised such influence in the council, evinced at the same time an ardent love of mankind, deep respect for the rights of all, great sensibility, and an elevated mind. Though a zealous reformer of the church, and in this respect a precursor of Luther, who was destined to begin his mission twenty years later, he did not quit the pale of orthodoxy; he did not assume the right of examining doctrine; he limited his efforts to the restoration of discipline, the reformation of the morals of the clergy, and the recall of priests, as well as other citizens, to the practice of the gospel precepts: but his zeal was mixed with enthusiasm; he believed himself under the immediate inspiration of Providence; he took his own impulses for prophetic revelations, by which he directed the politics of his disciples, the Piagnoni. He had predicted to the Florentines the coming of the French into Italy; he had represented to them Charles VIII as an instrument by which the Divinity designed to chastise the crimes of the nation; he had counselled them to remain faithful to their alliance with that king, the instrument of Providence, even though his conduct, especially in reference to the affairs of Pisa, had been highly culpable. This alliance however ranged the Florentines among the enemies of pope Alexander VI, one of the founders of the league which had driven the French out of Italy; he accused them of being traitors to the church and to their country for their attachment to a foreign prince. Alexander, equally offended by the projects of reform and by the politics of Savonarola, denounced him to the church as a heretic, and interdicted him from preaching. The monk at first obeyed, and procured the appointment of his friend and disciple the Dominican

friar, Buonvicino of Pescia, as his successor in the
church of St. Mark; but on Christmas-day, 1497, he
declared from the pulpit that God had revealed to him,
that he ought not to submit to a corrupt tribunal; he
then openly took the sacrament with the monks of St.
Mark, and afterwards continued to preach. In the course
of his sermons, he more than once held up to reproba-
tion the scandalous conduct of the pope, whom the
public voice accused of every vice and every crime to
be expected in a libertine so depraved—a man so ambitious, perfidious, and cruel—a monarch and a priest
intoxicated with absolute power.

In the mean time, the rivalry encouraged by the
court of Rome between the religious orders soon procured the pope champions eager to combat Savonarola:
he was a Dominican, the general of the Augustines;
that order whence Martin Luther was soon to issue.
Friar Mariano di Ghinazzano signalised himself by his
zeal in opposing Savonarola. He presented to the pope,
friar Francis of Apulia, of the order of minor observan-
tines, who was sent to Florence to preach against the
Florentine monk, in the church of Santa Croce. This
preacher declared to his audience that he knew Savonarola pretended to support his doctrine by a miracle.
"For me," said he, "I am a sinner; I have not the presumption to perform miracles, nevertheless, let a fire
be lighted, and I am ready to enter it with him. I am
certain of perishing, but Christian charity teaches me
not to withhold my life, if, in sacrificing it, I might
precipitate into hell a heresiarch, who has already
drawn into it so many souls."

This strange proposition was rejected by Savonarola;
but his friend and disciple, friar Dominic Buonvicino,
eagerly accepted it. Francis of Apulia declared that he
would risk his life against Savonarola only. Meanwhile,
a crowd of monks, of the Dominican and Franciscan
orders, rivalled each other in their offers to prove by
the ordeal of fire, on one side the truth, on the other
the falsehood, of the new doctrine. Enthusiasm spread
beyond the two convents; many priests and seculars,

and even women and children, more especially on the
side of Savonarola, earnestly requested to be admitted
to the proof. The pope warmly testified his gratitude
to the Franciscans for their devotion. The signoria of
Florence consented that two monks only should devote
themselves for their respective orders, and directed the
pile to be prepared. The whole population of the town
and country, to which a signal miracle was promised,
received the announcement with transports of joy. On
the 17th of April, 1498, a scaffold, dreadful to look on,
was erected in the public square of Florence: two piles
of large pieces of wood, mixed with faggots and broom,
which should quickly take fire, extended each eighty
feet long, four feet thick, and five feet high; they were
separated by a narrow space of two feet, to serve as a
passage by which the two priests were to enter, and
pass the whole length of the piles during the fire. Every
window was full; every roof was covered with specta-
tors; almost the whole population of the republic was
collected round the place. The portico called the Loggia
de' Lanzi, divided in two by a partition, was assigned
to the two orders of monks. The Dominicans arrived at
their station chanting canticles, and bearing the holy
sacrament. The Franciscans immediately declared that
they would not permit the host to be carried amidst
flames. They insisted that the friar Buonvicino should
enter the fire, as their own champion was prepared to
do, without this divine safeguard. The Dominicans answered, that "they would not separate themselves from
their God at the moment when they implored his aid."
The dispute upon this point grew warm. Several hours
passed away. The multitude, which had waited long,
and begun to feel hunger and thirst, lost patience; a
deluge of rain suddenly fell upon the city, and descended in torrents from the roofs of the houses—all
present were drenched. The piles were so wet that
they could no longer be lighted; and the crowd, dis-
appointed of a miracle so impatiently looked for, separated, with the notion of having been unworthily trifled
with. Savonarola lost all his credit; he was henceforth

rather looked on as an impostor. Next day his convent was besieged by the Arrabbiati, eager to profit by the inconstancy of the multitude; he was arrested with his two friends, Domenico Buonvicino, and Silvestro Marruffi, and led to prison. The Piagnoni, his partisans, were exposed to every outrage from the populace—two of them were killed; their rivals and old enemies exciting the general ferment for their destruction. Even in the signoria, the majority was against them; and yielded to the pressing demands of the pope. The three imprisoned monks were subjected to a criminal prosecution. Alexander VI despatched judges from Rome, with orders to condemn the accused to death. Conformably with the laws of the church, the trial opened with the torture. Savonarola was too weak and nervous to support it: he avowed in his agony all that was imputed to him; and, with his two disciples, was condemned to death. The three monks were burnt alive, on the 23d of May, 1498, in the same square where, six weeks before, a pile had been raised to prepare them a triumph.

CHAPTER XIV

THE FRENCH MASTERS OF MILAN AND GENOA, AND THE SPANIARDS OF NAPLES   THE GONFALONIER SODERINI AT FLORENCE   LEAGUE OF CAMBRAY AGAINST VENICE   THE MEDICI RE-ESTABLISHED AT FLORENCE

THE expedition of Charles VIII against Naples had directed towards Italy the attention of all the western powers. The transalpine nations had learnt that they were strong enough to act as masters, and if they pleased as robbers, in this the richest and most civilised country of the earth. All the powers on the confines henceforth aspired to subject some part of Italy to their dominion. They coveted their share of tribute from a land so fruitful of impost, from those cities in which industry employed such numbers, and accumulated so much capital. Cupidity put arms in their hands, and smothered every generous feeling. The commanders were rapacious; the soldiers thought only of pillage. They regarded the Italians as a race abandoned to their extortions, and vied with each other in the barbarous methods which they invented for extorting money from the vanquished, until at last they completely destroyed the prosperity which had provoked their envy.

Charles VIII died at Amboise, on the 7th of April, 1498, the day destined at Florence for the trial by fire of the doctrine of Savonarola. Louis XII, who succeeded that monarch, claimed, as grandson of Valentina Visconti, to be the legitimate heir to the duchy of Milan, although, according to the law acknowledged by all Italy, and confirmed by the imperial investiture granted to the father of Valentina, females were excluded from all share in the succession. This monarch, at his coronation, took with the title of king of France those of duke of Milan and king of Naples and Jerusalem. It was to to the duchy of Milan that he seemed particularly attached, apparently as having been the object of his ambition before he came to the throne. He preserved during his whole reign, as if he were simply duke of Milan, a feudal respect for the emperor as lord paramount, which was as fatal to France as to Italy.

After having thus announced to the world his pretensions to the duchy of Milan, Louis hastened to secure his possession of it by arms. He easily separated his antagonist, Ludovico Sforza, from all his allies. The emperor Maximilian had married the niece of Ludovico, to whom he had granted the investiture of his duchy; but Maximilian forgot, with extreme levity, his promises and alliances. A new ambition, a supposed offence, even a whim, sufficed to make him abandon his most matured projects. The Swiss had just then excited his resentment; and to attack them the more effectually, he signed with Louis XII a truce, in which Ludovico Sforza was not included, and was therefore abandoned to his enemy. The Venetians were interested still more than the emperor in defending Ludovico, but were incensed against him; they accused him of having deceived them, as well in the war against Charles VIII as in that for the defence of Pisa. They suspected him of having suggested to Maximilian the claims which he had just made on all their conquests in Lombardy, as having previously appertained to the empire. They were obliged, moreover, to reserve all their resources to resist the most formidable of their enemies. Bajazet II had just declared war against them. Bands of robbers continually descended from the mountains of Turkish Albania to lay waste Venetian Dalmatia. The Turkish pachas offered their support to every traitor who attempted to take from the Venetians any of their stations in the Levant. Corfu very nearly fell into the hands of the Turks: at length hostilities openly began. The Turks attacked Zara; all the Venetian merchants established at Constantinople were put into irons, and Scander Bashaw, sangiak of Bosnia, passed the Isonzo on the 29th of September, 1499, with 7000 Turkish cavalry. He ravaged all the rich country which extends from that river to the Tagliamento, at the extremity of the Adriatic, and spread terror up to the lagune which surround Venice. Invaded by an enemy so formidable against whom they were destined to support, for seven years, a relentless war, the Venetians would not expose themselves to the danger of maintaining another war against the French. On the 15th of April, 1499, they signed, at Blois, with Louis, a treaty, by which they contracted an alliance against Ludovico Sforza, and abandoned the conquest of the Milanese to the king of France, reserving to themselves Cremona and the Ghiara d'Adda.

Ludovico Sforza found no allies in any other part of Italy. Since the execution of Savonarola at Florence, the faction of the Arabbiati had succeeded that of the Piagnoni in the administration, without changing its policy. The republic continued to guard against the intrigues of the Medici, who entered into an alliance with every enemy of their country, in order to bring it back under their yoke. Florence continued her efforts to subdue Pisa; but, fearing to excite the jealousy of the kings of France and Spain, did not assemble for that purpose either a numerous army or a great train of artillery. She contented herself with ravaging the Pisan territory every year, in order to reduce that city by famine. Even these expeditions were suspended when those powerful monarchs found it convenient to make a show of peace. The cities of Sienna, Lucca, and Genoa, actuated by their jealousy of Florence, sent succour to Pisa. Pope Alexander VI, who had been always the enemy of Charles VIII, now entered into an alliance with Louis XII; but on condition that Cæsar Borgia, son of Alexander, should be made duke of Valentinois in France and of Romagna in Italy—the French king assisting him against the petty princes, feudatories of the holy see, who were masters of that province. The king of Naples, Frederick, who had succeeded his nephew Ferdinand on the 7th of September, 1496, was well aware that he should, in his turn, be attacked by France; but although he merited, by his talents and virtues, the confidence of his subjects, he had great difficulty in re-establishing some order in his kingdom, which was ruined by war, and had neither an army nor an exchequer to succour his natural ally, the duke of Milan.

A powerful French army, commanded by the sires De Ligny and D'Aubigny, passed the Alps in the month of August, 1499. On the 13th of that month they attacked and took by assault the two petty fortresses of Arazzo and Annone, on the borders of the Tanaro; putting the garrisons, and almost all the inhabitants, to the sword. This ferocious proceeding spread terror among the troops of Ludovico Sforza. His army, the command of which he had given to Galeazzo San Severino, dispersed; and the duke, not venturing to remain at Milan, sought for himself, his children, and his treasure, refuge in Germany, with the emperor Maximilian. Louis XII, who arrived afterwards in Italy, made his entry into the forsaken capital of Ludovico on the 2d of October. The trembling people, wishing to conciliate their new master, saluted him with the title of duke of Milan, and expressed their joy in receiving him as their sovereign. The rest of Lombardy also submitted without resistance; and Genoa, which had placed itself under the protection of the duke of Milan, passed over to that of the king of France. Louis returned to Lyons before the end of the year: the fugitive hopes which he had excited already gave way to hatred. The insolence of the French, their violation of all national institutions, their contempt of Italian manners, the accumulation of taxes, and the irregularities in the administration, rendered their yoke insupportable. Ludovico Sforza was informed of the general ferment, and of the desire of his subjects for his return. He was on the Swiss frontier, with a considerable treasure: a brave but disorderly crowd of young men, ready to serve any one for pay, joined him. In a few days 500 cavalry and 8000 infantry assembled under his banner; and, in the month of February, 1500, he entered Lombardy at their head. Como, Milan, Parma, and Pavia immediately opened their gates to him: he next besieged Novara, which capitulated. Louis, meanwhile, displayed the greatest activity in suppressing the rebellion: his general, Louis de la Tremouille, arrived before Novara, in the beginning of April, with an army in which were reckoned 10,000 Swiss. The men of that nation in the two hostile camps, opposed to each other for hire, hesitated, parleyed, and finally took a resolution more fatal to their honour than a battle between fellow countrymen could have been. Those within Novara not only consented to withdraw themselves, but to give up to the French the Italian men at arms with whom they were incorporated, and who were immediately put to the sword or drowned in the river. They permitted La Tremouille to arrest in their ranks Ludovico Sforza, and the two brothers San Severino, who attempted to escape in disguise. They received from the French the wages thus basely won, and afterwards, rendered reckless by the sense of their infamy, they in their retreat seized Belinzona, which they ever after

retained. Thus, even the weakest of the neighbours of
Italy would have their share in her conquest. Ludovico
Sforza was conducted into France, and there condemned to a severe captivity, which, ten years afterwards, ended with his life. The Milanese remained
subject to the king of France from this period, to the
month of June, 1512.

The facility with which Louis had conquered the
duchy of Milan, must have led him to expect that he
should not meet with much more resistance from the
kingdom of Naples. Frederick also, sensible of this, demanded peace; and, to obtain it, offered to hold his
kingdom in fief, as tributary to France. He reckoned,
however, on the support of Ferdinand the Catholic, his
kinsman and neighbour, who had promised him powerful aid, and had given him a pledge of the future by
sending into Sicily his best general, Gonzalvo di Cordova, with sixty vessels and 8000 chosen infantry. But
Ferdinand had previously proposed to Louis a secret
understanding, to divide between them the spoils of
the unhappy Frederick. While the French entered on
the north to conquer the kingdom of Naples, he proposed that the Spaniards should enter on the south to
defend it; and that, on meeting, they, instead of giving battle, should shake hands on the partition of the
kingdom, each remaining master of one half. This was
the basis of the treaty of Grenada, signed on the 11th
of November, 1500. In the summer of 1501, the perfidious compact was executed by the two greatest monarchs of Europe.

The French army arrived at Rome on the 25th of
June; at the same time that the army of Gonzalvo di
Cordova landed in Calabria. The former, from the moment they passed the frontier, treated the Neapolitans
as rebels, and hanged the soldiers who surrendered to
them. Arrived before Capua, they entered that city
while the magistrates were signing the capitulation,
and massacred 7000 of the inhabitants. The treachery
of Ferdinand inspired the unhappy Frederick with still
more aversion than the ferocity of the French. Having

retired to the island of Ischia, he surrendered to Louis, and was sent to France, where he died, in a captivity by no means rigorous, three years afterwards. The Spaniards and French advanced towards each other, without encountering any resistance. They met on the limits which the treaty of Grenada had respectively assigned to them; but the moment the conquest was terminated, jealousy appeared. The duke de Nemours and Gonzalvo di Cordova disputed upon the division of the kingdom: each claimed for his master some province not named in the treaty. Hostilities at last began between them on the 19th of June, 1502, at Atripalda. Louis, while the negotiation was pending, delayed sending reinforcements to his general. After a struggle, not without glory, and in which La Palisse and Bayard first distinguished themselves, D'Aubigny was defeated at Seminara on the 21st of April, and Nemours at Cerignola on the 28th of the same month, 1503. The French army was entirely destroyed, and the kingdom of Naples lost to Louis XII. Louis had sent off, during the same campaign, a more powerful army than the first, to recover it; but, on arriving near Rome, news was received of the death of Alexander VI, which took place on the 18th of August, 1503. The cardinal d'Amboise, prime minister of Louis, detained the army there to support his intrigues in the conclave: when it renewed its march, in the month of October, the rainy season had commenced. Gonzalvo di Cordova had taken his position on the Garigliano, the passage of which he defended, amidst inundated plains, with a constancy and patience characteristic of the Spanish infantry. During more than two months the French suffered or perished in the marshes: a pestilential malady carried off the flower of the army, and damped the courage and confidence of the remainder. Gonzalvo, having at last passed the river himself, on the 27th of December, attacked and completely destroyed the French army. On the 1st of January, 1504, Gaëta surrendered to him; and the whole kingdom of Naples was now, like Sicily, but a Spanish possession.

Thus the greater part of Italy had already fallen under the yoke of the nations which the Italians denominated barbarian. The French were masters of the Milanese and of the whole of Liguria; the Spaniards of the Two Sicilies; even the Swiss had made some small conquests along the Lago Maggiore; and this was the moment in which Louis XII called the Germans also into Italy. On the 22d of September of the same year in which he lost Gaëta, his last hold in the kingdom of Naples, he signed the treaty of Blois, by which he divided with Maximilian the republic of Venice, as he had divided with Ferdinand the kingdom of Naples. Experience ought to have taught him that Maximilian, like Ferdinand, would reserve for himself the conquests made in common. The future ought to have alarmed him; for Charles, the grandson and heir of Maximilian of Austria, and of Ferdinand of Aragon, of Mary of Burgundy, and of Isabella of Castille, was already born. It was foreseen that he would unite under his sceptre the greatest monarchies in Europe; and Louis, instead of guarding against his future greatness, had promised to give him his daughter in marriage. It was the thoughtlessness of Maximilian, and not the prudence of Louis, that delayed, during four years, the execution of the treaty of Blois.

During this interval, Genoa—which had never ceased to consider herself a republic, although the signoria had been conferred first on Ludovico Sforza, and next on Louis XII as duke of Milan—learned from experience that a foreign monarch was incapable of comprehending either her laws or liberty. According to the capitulation, one half of the magistrates of Genoa should be noble, the other half plebeian. They were to be chosen by the suffrages of their fellow-citizens; they were to retain the government of the whole of Liguria, and the administration of their own finances, with the reservation of a fixed sum payable yearly to the king of France. But the French could never comprehend that nobles were on an equality with villains; that a king was bound by conditions imposed by his subjects; or that money could be refused to him who had force. All the capitulations of Genoa were successively violated; while the Genoese nobles ranged themselves on the side of a king against their country: they were known to carry insolently about them a dagger, on which was inscribed, "Chastise villains"; so impatient were they to separate themselves from the people, even by meanness and assassination. That people could not support the double yoke of a foreign master and of nobles who betrayed their country. On the 7th of February, 1507, they revolted, drove out the French, proclaimed the republic, and named a new doge; but time failed them to organise their defence. On the 3d of April, Louis advanced from Grenoble with a powerful army. He soon arrived before Genoa: the newly-raised militia, unable to withstand veteran troops, were defeated. Louis entered Genoa on the 29th of April; and immediately sent the doge and the greater number of the generous citizens, who had signalised themselves in the defence of their country, to the scaffold. .

Independent Italy now comprised only the states of the church, Tuscany, and the republic of Venice; and even these provinces were pressed by the transalpine nations on every side. The Spaniards and French alternately spread terror through Tuscany and the states of the church; the Germans and Turks held in awe the territories of Venice. The states of the church were at the same time a prey to the intrigues of the detestable Alexander, and his son Cæsar Borgia. More murders, more assassinations, more glaring acts of perfidy, were committed within a short space, than during the annals of the most depraved monarchies. Cæsar Borgia, whom his father created duke of Romagna in 1501, had previously despoiled and put to death the petty princes who reigned at Pesaro, Rimini, Forli, and Faenza. He had, in like manner, possessed himself of Piombino in Tuscany, the duchy of Urbino, and the little principalities of Camerino and Senegallia. He had caused to be strangled in this last city, on the 31st of December, 1502, four tyrants of the states of the church, who followed the trade of condottieri. These princes had served in his pay, and, alarmed by his intrigues, had taken arms against him; but, seduced by his artifices, they placed themselves voluntarily in his power. Cæsar Borgia had made himself master of Città do Castelli, and of Perugia; and was menacing Bologna, Sienna, and Florence, when, on the 18th of August, 1503, he and his father drank, by mistake, a poison which they had prepared for one of their guests. His father died of it, and Borgia himself was in extreme danger. In thirteen months he lost all his sovereignties, the fruits of so many crimes. Attacked in turn by pope Julius II, who had succeeded his father, and by Gonzalvo di Cordova, he was at last sent into Spain, where he died in battle, more honourably than he deserved.

In Tuscany, the republic of Florence found itself surrounded with enemies. The Medici, continuing exiles, had entered into alliances with all the tyrants in the pontifical states: they took part in every plot against their country; at the same time, they sought the friendship of the king of France, who was more disposed to favour a prince than a republic. Pietro de' Medici had accompanied the army sent, in 1503, against the kingdom of Naples, and lost his life at the defeat of the Garigliano. His death did not deliver Florence from the apprehension which he had inspired. His brothers Giovanni and Giuliano carried on their intrigues against their country. The war with Pisa, too, which still lasted, exhausted the finances of Florence. The Pisans had lost their commerce and manufactures; they saw their harvests, each year, destroyed by the Florentines: but they opposed to all these disasters a constancy and courage not to be subdued. The French, Germans, and Spaniards, in turn sent them succour; not from taking any interest in their cause, but with the view of profiting by the struggle which they protracted. Lucca and Sienna also, jealous of the Florentines, secretly assisted the Pisans; but only so far as they could do it without compromising themselves with neighbours whom they feared. Lucca fell, by degrees, into the hands of a narrow oligarchy. Sienna suffered itself to be enslaved by Pandolfo Petrucci, a citizen, whom it had named captain of the guard, and who commanded obedience, without departing from the manners and habits of republican equality.

In the new position of Italy, continually menaced by absolute princes, whose deliberations were secret, and who united perfidy with force, the Florentines became sensible that their government could not act with the requisite discretion and secrecy, while it continued to be changed every two months. Their allies even complained that no secret could be confided to them, without becoming known, at the same time, to the whole republic. They accordingly judged it necessary to place at the head of the state a single magistrate, who should be present at every council, and who should be the depositary of every communication requiring secrecy. This chief, who was to retain the name of gonfalonier, was elected, like the doge of Venice, for life; he was to be lodged in the palace, and to have a salary of 100 florins a month. The law which created a gonfalonier for life was voted on the 16th of August, 1502; but it was not till the 22d of September following that the grand council chose Pietro Soderini to fill that office. He was a man universally respected; of mature age, without ambition, without children; and the republic never had reason to repent its choice. The republic, at the same time, introduced the authority of a single man into the administration, and suppressed it in the tribunals. A law of the 15th of April, 1502, abolished the offices of podesta and of captain of justice, and supplied their places by the *ruota;* a tribunal composed of five judges, of whom four must agree in passing sentence: each, in his turn, was to be president of the tribunal for six months. This rotation caused the name of *ruota* to be given to the supreme courts of law at Rome and Florence.

The most important service expected from Soderini was that of subjecting Pisa anew to the Florentine republic: he did not accomplish this until 1509. That city had long been reduced to the last extremity: the inhabitants, thinned by war and famine, had no longer any hope of holding out; but Louis XII and Ferdinand of Aragon announced to the Florentines that they must be paid for the conquest which Florence was on the point of making. Pisa had been defended by them since 1507, but only to prevent its surrendering before the amount demanded was agreed on: it was at length fixed at 100,000 florins to be paid to the king of France, and 50,000 to the king of Aragon. This treaty was signed on the 13th of March; and on the 8th of June, 1509, Pisa, which had cruelly suffered from famine, opened its gates to the Florentine army: the occupying army was preceded by convoys of provisions, which the soldiers themselves distributed to the citizens. The signoria of Florence abolished all the confiscations pronounced against the Pisans since the year 1494; they restored to them all their property and privileges. They tried, in every way, to conciliate and attach that proud people; but nothing could overcome their deep resentment, and their regret for the loss of their independence. Almost every family, which had preserved any fortune, emigrated; and the population already so reduced by war, was still further diminished after the peace.

The republic of Venice was condemned, by the war which it had to support against the Turkish empire, from 1499 to 1503, to make no effort for maintaining the independence of Italy against France and Aragon. It had solicited the aid of all Christendom, as if for a holy war, against Bajazet II; and, in fact, alternately received assistance from the kings of France, Aragon, and Portugal, and from the pope: but these aids, limited to short services on great occasions, were of little real efficacy. They aggravated the misery of the Greeks among whom the war was carried on, caused little injury to the Turks, and were of but little service to the Venetians. The Mussulmans had made progress in naval discipline; the Venetian fleet could no longer cope

with theirs; and Antonio Grimani, its commander, till
then considered the most fortunate of the citizens of
Venice, already father of a cardinal, and destined, long
after, to be the doge of the republic, was, on his return to his country, loaded with irons. Lepanto, Pylos,
Modon, and Coron, were successively conquered from
the Venetians by the Turks; the former were glad at last
to accept a peace negotiated by Andrea Gritti, one of
their fellow-citizens, a captive at Constantinople. By
this peace they renounced all title to the places which
they had lost in the Peloponnesus, and restored to
Bajazet the island of Santa Maura, which they had,
on their side, conquered from the Turks. This peace
was signed in the month of November, 1503.

The period in which the republic of Venice was
delivered from the terror of the Turks was also that of
the death of Alexander VI, and of the ruin of his son
Cæsar Borgia. The opportunity appeared to the signoria favourable for extending its possessions in Romagna.
That province had been long the object of its ambition. Venice had acquired by treachery, on the 24th
of February, 1441, the principality of Ravenna, governed for 166 years by the house of Polenta. In 1463,
it had purchased Cervia, with its salt marshes, from
Malatesta IV, one of the princes of Rimini; upon the
death of Cæsar Borgia, it took possession of Faenza,
the principality of Manfredi; of Rimini, the principality
of Malatesta; and of several fortresses. Imola and
Forli, governed by the Alidosi and the Ordelaffi, alone
remained to be subdued, in order to make Venice mistress of the whole of Romagna. The Venetians offered
the pope the same submission, the same annual tribute,
for which those petty princes were acknowledged pontifical vicars. But Julius II, who had succeeded Borgia,
although violent and irascible, had a strong sense of
his duty as a pontiff and as an Italian. He was determined on preserving the states of the church intact for
his successors. He rejected all nepotism, all aggrandisement of his family; and would have accused himself
of unpardonable weakness, if he suffered others to

usurp what he refused to give his family. He haughtily exacted the restitution of all that the Venetians possessed in the states of the church; and as he could not obtain it from them, he consented to receive it from the hands of Louis and Maximilian, who combined to despoil the republic. He, however, communicated to the Venetians the projects formed against them, and it was not till they appeared resolved to restore him nothing, that he concluded his compact with their enemies.

The league against Venice, signed at Cambray, on the 10th of December, 1508, by Margaret of Austria, daughter of Maximilian, and the cardinal d'Amboise, prime minister of Louis, was only the completion of the secret treaty of Blois, of the 22d of September, 1504. No offence had been given, to justify this perfidious compact. Maximilian, who detested Louis, had the same year endeavoured to attack him in the Milanese; but the Venetians refused him a passage; and after three months' hostilities, the treaty between the emperor and the republic was renewed, on the 7th of June, 1508. Louis XII, whom the Venetians defended, and Maximilian, with whom they were reconciled, had no other complaint against them than that they had no king, and that their subjects thus excited the envy of those who had. The two monarchs agreed to divide between them all the *terra firma* of the Venetians, to abandon to Ferdinand all their fortresses in Apulia, to the pope the lordships in Romagna, to the houses of Este and Gonzaga the small districts near the Po; and thus to give all an interest in the destruction of the only state sufficiently strong to maintain the independence of Italy.

France was the first to declare war against the republic of Venice, in the month of January, 1509. Hostilities commenced on the 15th of April; on the 27th of the same month, the pope excommunicated the doge and the republic. The Venetians had assembled an army of 42,000 men, under the command of the impetuous Bartolomeo d'Alviano and the cautious Piti-

gliano. The disagreement between these two chiefs,
both able generals, caused the loss of the battle of
Aignadel, fought, on the 14th of May, 1509, with the
French, who did not exceed 30,000. Half only, or less,
of the Venetian army was engaged; but that part fought
heroically, and perished without falling back one step.
After this discomfiture, Bergamo, Brescia, Crema, and
Cremona, hastily surrendered to the conquerors, who
planted their banners on the border of Ghiaradadda,
the limits assigned by the treaty of partition. Louis
signalised this rapid conquest by atrocious cruelties: he
caused the Venetian governors of Caravaggio and of
Peschiera to be hanged, and the garrisons and inhabitants to be put to the sword; he ruined, by enormous
ransoms, all the Venetian nobles who fell into his
hands; seeking to vindicate to himself his unjust attack by the hatred which he studied to excite.

The French suspended their operations from the
31st of May; but the emperor, the pope, the duke of
Ferrara, the marquis of Mantua, and Ferdinand of
Aragon profited by the disasters of the republic to invade its provinces on all sides at once. The senate, in
the impossibility of making head against so many enemies, took the generous resolution of releasing all its
subjects from their oath of fidelity, and permitting
them to treat with the enemy, since it was no longer
in its power to defend them. In letting them feel the
weight of a foreign yoke, the senate knew that it only
rendered more dear the paternal authority of the republic; and, in fact, those citizens who had eagerly
opened their gates to the French, Germans, and Spaniards, soon contrasted, in despair, their tyranny with
the just and equal power which they had not had the
courage to defend. The Germans, above all, no sooner
entered the Venetian cities, than they plunged into the
most brutal debauchery; offending public decency, and
exercising their cruelty and rapacity on all those who
came within their reach. Notwithstanding this, the
native nobles joined them. They were eager to substitute monarchy for republican equality and freedom; but

their insolence only aggravated the hatred which the Germans inspired. The army of the republic had taken refuge at Mestre, on the borders of the Lagune, when suddenly the citizen evinced a courage which the soldier no longer possessed. Treviso, in the month of June, and Padua on the 17th of July, drove out the imperialists; and the banners of St. Mark, which had hitherto constantly retreated, began once again to advance.

The war of the league of Cambray showed the Italians, for the first time, what formidable forces the transalpine nations could bring against them. Maximilian arrived to besiege Padua in the month of September, 1509. He had in his army Germans, Swiss, French, Spaniards, Savoyards; troops of the pope, of the marquis of Mantua, and of the duke of Modena; in all more than 100,000 men, with 100 pieces of cannon. He was, notwithstanding, obliged to raise the siege, on the 3d of October, after many encounters, supported on each side with equal valour. But these barbarians, who came to dispute with the Italians the sovereignty of their country, did not need success to prove their ferocity. After having taken from the poor peasant, or the captive, all that he possessed, they put him to the torture to discover hidden treasure, or to extort ransom from the compassion of friends. In this abuse of brute force, the Germans showed themselves the most savage, the Spaniards the most coldly ferocious. Both were more odious than the French; although the last mentioned had bands called flayers (*écorcheurs*), formed in the English wars, and long trained to grind the people.

Pope Julius II soon began to hate his accomplices in the league of Cambray. Violent and irascible, he had often shown in his fits of passion that he could be as cruel as the worst of them. But he had the soul of an Italian. He could not brook the humiliation of his country, and its being enslaved by those whom he called barbarians. Having recovered the cities of Romagna, the subject of his quarrel with the Venetians, he began to make advances to them. At the end of the first campaign, he entered into negotiations; and on the

21st of February, 1510, granted them absolution. He was aware that he could never drive the barbarians out of Italy but by arming them against each other; and as the French were those whom he most feared, he had recourse to the Germans. It was necessary to begin with reconciling the Venetians to the emperor; but Maximilian, always ready to undertake every thing, and incapable of bringing any thing to a conclusion, would not relax in a single article of what he called his rights. As emperor, he considered himself monarch of all Italy; and although he was always stopped on its frontier, he refused to renounce the smallest part of what he had purposed conquering. He asserted that the whole Venetian territory had been usurped from the empire; and before granting peace to the republic, demanded almost its annihilation.

It was with the aid of the Swiss that the pope designed to liberate Italy. He admired the valour and piety of that warlike people: he saw, with pleasure, that cupidity had become their ruling passion. The Italians, who needed the defence of the Swiss, were rich enough to pay them; and a wise policy conspired for once with avarice; for the Swiss republics could not be safe if liberty were not re-established in Italy. Louis XII, by his prejudice in favour of nobility, had offended those proud mountaineers, whom, even in his own army, he considered only as revolted peasants. Julius II employed the bishop of Sion, whom he afterwards made cardinal, to irritate them still more against France. In the course of the summer of 1510, the French, according to the plan which Julius had formed, were attacked in the Milanese by the Swiss, in Genoa by the Genoese emigrants, at Modena by the pontifical troops, and at Verona by the Venetians; but, notwithstanding the profound secrecy in which the pope enveloped his negotiations and intrigues, he could not succeed, as he had hoped, in surprising the French every where at the same time. The four attacks were made successively, and repulsed. The sire de Chaumont, lieutenant of Louis in Lombardy, determined to avenge himself by besieging the pope in Bologna, in the month of October. Julius feigned a desire to purchase peace at any price; but, while negotiating, he caused troops to advance; and, on finding himself the stronger, suddenly changed his language, used threats, and made Chaumont retire. When Chaumont had placed his troops in winter quarters, the pope, during the greatest severity of the season, attacked the small state of Mirandola, which had put itself under the protection of France; and entered its capital by a breach, on the 20th of January, 1511.

The pope's troops, commanded by the duke of Urbino, experienced in the following campaign a signal defeat at Casalecchio, on the 21st of May, 1511. It was called "the day of the ass-drivers," because the French knights returned driving asses before them loaded with booty. The loss of Bologna followed; but Julius II was not discouraged. His legates laboured, throughout Europe, to raise enemies against France. They at last accomplished a league, which was signed on the 5th of October, and which was called Holy, because it was headed by the pope. It comprehended the kings of Spain and England, the Swiss, and the Venetians. Louis XII, to oppose an ecclesiastical authority to that of the pontiffs, convoked, in concert with Maximilian, whom he continued to consider his ally an œcumenical council. A few cardinals, who had separated from the pope, clothed it with their authority; and Florence dared not refuse to the two greatest monarchs of Europe the city of Pisa for its place of meeting, although the whole population beheld with dread this commencement of a new schism.

A powerful Spanish army meanwhile advanced from Naples, to the aid of the pope, under the command of Raymond de Cardona; and laid siege to Bologna on the 26th of January, 1512. The French had driven to despair, by their extortions, the people of the provinces which they had seized from Venice. On the 3d of February, Brescia revolted against them. Gaston de Foix, duc de Nemours, and nephew of Louis XII, had, at the

age of twenty-two, been just placed at the head of the
French army. With a rapidity ever memorable, he in
turn successfully opposed his two enemies. Having, on
the 5th of February, entered Bologna, he forced the
Spaniards to raise the siege, and make a precipitate
retreat through Romagna. He instantly returned to attack the Venetians, and on his road defeated one of
their armies. He retook Brescia by assault, on the 19th
of February, and punished that unhappy city by a
frightful massacre of its inhabitants; but pillage disorganised and corrupted his army, and six weeks elapsed
before he could return to Romagna, to oppose the
armies of Spain and of the pope, which had again advanced. He forced them to give battle, near Ravenna,
on Easter Sunday, the 11th of April, 1512. It was the
most murderous battle that Italy had yet seen: nearly
20,000 dead covered the plain on which it was fought.
Gaston de Foix was, for the last time, victorious. The
formidable Spanish infantry slowly retreated, without
permitting itself to be broken in any part. Gaston,
furious at its escaping him, made one last effort against
it, and was killed.

The death of Gaston proved the signal of the defeat
of the French in Italy. The ministers of Louis thought
they might, after the battle of Ravenna, safely dismiss
a part of their army; but Maximilian, betraying all his
engagements, abandoned the French to their enemies.
Without consenting to make peace with Venice, he
gave passage through his territory to 20,000 Swiss,
who were to join the Venetian army, in order to attack the French. He, at the same time, recalled all the
Germans who had enlisted under the banner of France.
Ferdinand of Aragon and Henry VIII of England almost simultaneously attacked Louis, who, to defend
himself, was obliged to recall his troops from Italy. In
the beginning of June, they evacuated the Milanese; of
which the Swiss took possession, in the name of Maximilian Sforza, son of Louis the Moor. On the 29th of the
same month, a revolution drove the French out of
Genoa; and the republic and a new doge were again

proclaimed. The possessions of France were soon reduced to a few small fortresses in that Italy which the
French thought they had subdued. But the Italians did
not recover their liberty by the defeat of only one of
their oppressors. From the yoke of France, they passed
under that of the Swiss, the Spaniards, and the Germans; and the last they endured always seemed the
most galling. To add to their humiliation, the victory
of the Holy League enslaved the last and only republic
truly free in Italy.

Florence was connected with France by a treaty concluded in concert with Ferdinand the Catholic. The
republic continued to observe it scrupulously, even after
Ferdinand had disengaged himself from it. Florence
had fulfilled towards all the belligerent powers the
duties of good neighbourhood and neutrality, and had
given offence to none: but the league, which had just
driven the French out of Italy, was already divided in
interest, and undecided on the plan which it should
pursue. It was agreed only on one point, that of obtaining money. The Swiss lived at discretion in Lombardy,
and levied in it the most ruinous contributions: the
Spaniards of Raymond de Cardona insisted also on
having a province abandoned to their inexorable avidity;
Tuscany was rich and not warlike. The victorious
powers who had assembled in congress at Mantua proposed to the Florentines to buy themselves off with a
contribution; but the Medici, who presented themselves at this congress, asked to be restored to their
country, asserting that they could extract much more
money by force, for the use of the holy league, than a
republican government could obtain from the people
by gentler means. Raymond de Cardona readily believed them, and in the month of August, 1512, accompanied them across the Apennines, with 5000
Spanish infantry as inaccessible to pity as to fear. Raymond sent forward to tell the Florentines, that if they
would preserve their liberty, they must recall the
Medici, displace the gonfalonier Soderini, and pay the
Spanish army 40,000 florins. He arrived at the same

time before the small town of Prato, which shut its
gates against him: it was well fortified, but defended
only by the *ordinanza*, or country militia. On the 30th
of August, the Spaniards made a breach in the wall,
which these peasants basely abandoned. The city was
taken by assault; the militia, which would have incurred less danger in fighting valiantly, were put to
the sword: 5000 citizens were afterwards massacred,
and others, divided among the victors, were put to
lingering tortures, either to force them to discover
where they had concealed their treasure, or to oblige
their kinsmen to ransom them out of pity; the Spaniards having already pillaged all they could discover
in holy as well as profane places.

The terror caused at Florence, by the news of the
massacre of Prato, produced next day a revolution. A
company of young nobles, belonging to the most illustrious families, who, under the title of Society of the
Garden Ruccellai, were noted for their love of the arts,
of luxury and pleasure, took possession, on the 31st of
August, of the public palace; they favoured the escape
of Soderini, and sent to tell Raymond de Cardona that
they were ready to accept the conditions which he
offered. But all treaties with tyrants are deceptions.
Giuliano de' Medici, the third son of Lorenzo, whose
character was gentle and conciliatory, entered Florence
on the 2d of September, and consented to leave many
of the liberties of the republic untouched. His brother,
the cardinal Giovanni, afterwards Leo X who did not
enter till the 14th of the same month, forced the signoria to call a parliament on the 16th. In this pretended
assembly of the sovereign people, few were admitted
except strangers and soldiers: all the laws enacted since
the expulsion of the Medici in 1494 were abolished.
A balia, composed only of the creatures of that family,
was invested with the sovereignty of the republic. This
balia showed itself abjectly subservient to the cardinal
Giovanni de' Medici, his brother Giuliano, and their
nephew Lorenzo, who now returned to Florence after
eighteen years of exile, during which they had lost ev-

ery republican habit, and all sympathy with their fellow-citizens. None of them had legitimate children; but they brought back with them three bastards—Giulio, afterwards Clement VII, Ippolito, and Alessandro—who had all a fatal influence on the destiny of their country. Their fortune, formerly colossal, was dissipated in their long exile; and their first care, on returning to Florence, was to raise money for themselves, as well as for the Spaniards, who had re-established their tyranny.

CHAPTER XV

CALAMITIES WITH WHICH THE FRENCH, SPANIARDS, AND GERMANS OVERWHELMED ITALY   PILLAGE AND RUIN OF THE GREATEST CITIES   OPPRESSION OF THE ITALIAN NATION, AND LOSS OF ITS INDEPENDENCE

THE three destructive wars comprised in the last chapter—viz. that of the French and Swiss in the Milanese, that of the French and Spaniards in the kingdom of Naples, that of the French, Spaniards, Germans, and Swiss, in the states of Venice—robbed Italy of her independence. The country to which Europe was indebted for its progress in every art and science, which had imparted to other nations the medical science of Salerno, the jurisprudence of Bologna, the theology of Rome, the philosophy, poetry, and fine arts of Florence, the tactics and strategy of the Bracceschi and Sforzeschi schools, the commerce and banks of the Lombards, the process of irrigation, the scientific cultivation both of hills and plains—that country now belonged no more to its own inhabitants! The struggle between the transalpine nations continued, with no other object than that of determining to which of them Italy should belong; and bequeathed nothing to that nation but long-enduring, hopeless agonies. Julius II in vain congratulated himself on having expelled the French, who had first imposed a foreign yoke on Italy; he vowed in vain that he would never rest till he had also driven out all the barbarians; but he deceived himself in his calculations: he did not drive out the barbarians, he only made them give way to other barbarians; and the new comers were ever the most oppressive and cruel. However, this project of national liberation, which the pope alone could still entertain in Italy with any prospect of success, was soon abandoned. Eight months after the expulsion of the French from the Milanese, and five months after the re-establishment of the Medici at Florence, Julius II, on the 21st of February, 1513, sank under an inflammatory disease. On the 11th of March, Giovanni de' Medici succeeded him, under the name of Leo X; eleven months after the latter had been made prisoner by the French at the battle of Ravenna, and six months after the Spanish arms had given him the sovereignty of his country, Florence.

It has been the singular good fortune of Leo X to have his name associated with the most brilliant epoch of letters and the arts since their revival. He has thus shared the glory of all the poets, philosophers, artists, men of learning and science, his contemporaries. He has been held up to posterity as one who formed and raised to eminence men who were in fact his elders, and who had attained celebrity before the epoch of his power. His merit consisted in showering his liberality on those whose works and whose fame had already deserved it. His reign, on the other hand, which lasted nine years, was marked by fearful calamities, which hastened the destruction of those arts and sciences to which alone the age of Leo owes its splendour. The misfortunes which he drew down on his successor were still more dreadful. The pope was himself a man of pleasure, easy, careless, prodigal; who expended in sumptuous feasts the immense treasures accumulated by his predecessor. He had the taste to adorn his palace with the finest works of antiquity, and the sense to enjoy the society of philosophers and poets; but he had never the elevation of soul to comprehend his duties, or to consult his conscience. His indecent conversation and licentious conduct scandalised the church; his

prodigality led him to encourage the shameful traffic
in indulgences, which gave rise to the schism of Luther;
his thoughtlessness and indifference to human suffering
made him light up wars the most ruinous, and which
he was utterly unable to carry on; he never thought of
securing the independence of Italy, or of expelling the
barbarians: it was simply for the aggrandisement of his
family, that he contracted or abandoned alliances with
the transalpine nations: he succeeded, indeed, in pro-
curing that his brother Giuliano should be named duc
de Nemours, and he created his nephew duke of Urbino; but he endeavoured also to erect for the former a
new state, composed of the districts of Parma, Placentia, Reggio, and Modena; for the latter, another, consisting of the several petty principalities which still
maintained themselves in the states of the church. His
tortuous policy to accomplish the first object, his perfidy
and cruelty to attain the second, deserved to be much
more severely branded by historians.

The sovereign pontiff and the republic of Venice
were the only powers in Italy that still preserved some
shadow of independence. Julius II had succeeded in
uniting Romagna, the March, the patrimony and campagna of Rome, to the holy see. Amongst all the vassals of the church, he had spared only his own
nephew, Gian Maria della Rovere, duke of Urbino. On
the defeat of the French, he further seized Parma and
Placentia, which he detached from the Milanese, without having the remotest title to their possession, as he
also took Modena from the duke of Ferrara, whom he
detested. Leo X found the holy see in possession of all
these states, and was at the same time himself all-
powerful at Florence. Even the moment of his elevation to the pontificate was marked by an event, which
showed that every vestige of liberty had disappeared
from that republic. The partisans of the Medici pretended to have discovered at Florence a conspiracy, of
which they produced no other proofs than some imprudent speeches, and some wishes uttered for liberty.
The most illustrious citizens were, nevertheless, ar-

rested; and Machiavelli, with several others, were put
to the torture. Pietro Boscoli and Agostino Capponi
were beheaded; and those who were called their accomplices exiled. The two republics of Sienna and
Lucca were in a state of trembling subjection to the
pontiff; so that all central Italy, peopled with about
4,000,000 inhabitants, was dependent on him: but the
court of Rome, since it had ceased to respect the ancient municipal liberties, never extended its authority
over a new province without ruining its population
and resources. Law and order seemed incompatible
with the government of priests: the laws gave way to
intrigue and favour; commerce gave way to monopoly.
Justice deserted the tribunals, foresight the councils,
and valour the armies. It was proverbially said, that
the arms of the church had no edge. The great name of
pope still moved Europe at a distance, but it brought
no real force to the allies whom he adopted.

The republic of Venice, with a smaller territory, and
a far less numerous population, was in reality much
more powerful than the church. Venetian subjects, if
they did not enjoy liberty, had at least a government
which maintained justice, order, and the law; their
material prosperity was judiciously protected. They in
return were contented, and proved themselves devotedly attached to their government; but the wars
raised by the league of Cambray overwhelmed that
republic with calamity. The city of Venice, secure
amidst the waters, alone escaped the invasion of the
barbarians; though, even there, the richest quarters had
been laid waste by an accidental fire. The country and
the provincial towns experienced in turn the ferocity
of the French, Swiss, Germans, and Spaniards. Three
centuries and a half had elapsed since this same Veronese march, the cradle of the Lombard league, had repelled the invasion of Frederick Barbarossa. But while
the world boasted a continual progress, since that period, in civilisation, while philosophy and justice had
better defined the rights of men, while the arts, literature, and poetry, had quickened the feelings, and ren-

dered man more susceptible of painful impressions, war was made with a ferocity at which men in an age of the darkest barbarism would have blushed. The massacre of all the inhabitants of a town taken by assault, the execution of whole garrisons which had surrendered at discretion, the giving up of prisoners to the conquering soldiers in order to be tortured into the confession of hidden treasure, became the common practice of war in the armies of Louis XII, Ferdinand, and Maximilian. Kings were haughty in proportion to their power; they considered themselves at so much the greater distance above human nature: they were the more offended at all resistance, the more incapable of compassion for sufferings which they did not see or did not comprehend. The misery which they caused presented itself to them more as an abstraction; they regarded masses, not individuals; they justified their cruelties by the name of offended majesty; they quieted remorse by considering themselves, not as men, but as scourges in the hand of God. Three centuries have elapsed, and civilisation has not ceased to march forward; the voice of humanity has continued to become more and more powerful; no one now dares to believe himself great enough to be dispensed from humanity; nevertheless, those who would shrink with horror from witnessing the putting to death of an individual, do not hesitate to condemn whole nations to execution. The crimes which remain for us to relate, do not merit more execration than those of which we are ourselves the witnesses at this day. Kings, in their detestation of freedom, let loose upon unhappy Italy, in the sixteenth century, famine, war, and pestilence; as, from the same motive in our time, they have loosed upon heroic Poland, famine, war, and the cholera.

Louis XII, after having lost the Milanese, through his infatuated ambition to reconquer the small province of the Cremonese, which he had himself ceded to the republic of Venice, felt anew the desire of being reconciled with that republic, his first ally in Italy. The Venetians, who knew that without their money, artillery,

and cavalry, the Swiss could never have faced the
French, much less have driven them out of Italy, saw
that their allies did not appreciate their efforts and
sacrifices. Maximilian, who in joining never granted
them peace, but only a truce, re-asserted his claims on
Verona and Vicenza, and would not consent to allow
the Venetians any states in Terra Firma but such as
they purchased from him at an enormous price. The
pope, to enforce the demands of Maximilian, threatened the Venetians with excommunication; and their
danger after victory appeared as great as after defeat.
Andrea Gritti, one of their senators—made prisoner after the battle of Aignadel, and the same who, during his
captivity at Constantinople, had signed the peace of
his country with the Turks—again took advantage of his
captivity in France to negotiate with Louis. He reconciled the republic with that monarch, who had been
the first to attack it; and a treaty of alliance was signed
at Blois, on the 24th of March, 1513. This was, however, a source of new calamity to Venice. A French
army, commanded by La Tremouille, entered the Milanese, and on its approach the Germans and Spaniards
retired. The Swiss, who gloried in having re-established
Maximilian Sforza on the throne of his ancestors, were,
however, resolved not to abandon him. They descended
from their mountains in numerous bodies, on the 6th of
June, 1513; attacked La Tremouille at the Riotta, near
Novara; defeated him, and drove him back with all the
French forces beyond the Alps. The Spaniards and the
soldiers of Leo X next attacked the Venetians without
any provocation: they were at peace with the republic,
but they invaded its territory in the name of their ally
Maximilian. They occupied the Paduan state, the Veronese, and that of Vicenza, from the 13th of June till the
end of autumn. It was during this invasion the Spaniards displayed that heartless cruelty which rendered
them the horror of Italy; that cupidity which multiplied
torture, and which invented sufferings more and more
atrocious, to extort gold from their prisoners. The Germans in the next campaign, over-ran the Venetian

provinces; and notwithstanding the savage cruelties and numerous crimes of which the country had just been the theatre, yet the German commander found means to signalise himself by his ferocity.

Francis I succeeded Louis XII on the 1st of January, 1515; on the 27th of June he renewed his predecessor's treaty of alliance with Venice; and on the 15th of August entered the plains of Lombardy, by the marquisate of Saluzzo, with a powerful army. He met but little resistance in the provinces south of the Po, but the Swiss meanwhile arrived in great force to defend Maximilian Sforza, whom, since they had reseated him on the throne, they regarded as their vassal. Francis in vain endeavoured to negotiate with them; they would not listen to the voice of their commanders; democracy had passed from their *landsgemeinde* into their armies, popular orators roused their passions; and on the 13th of September they impetuously left Milan to attack Francis I at Marignano. Deep ditches lined with soldiers bordered the causeway by which they advanced; their commanders wished by some manœuvre to get clear of them, or make the enemy change his position; but the Swiss, despising all the arts of war, expected to command success by mere intrepidity and bodily strength. They marched to the battery in full front; they repulsed the charge of the knights with their halberds, and threw themselves with fury into the ditches which barred their road. Some rushed on to the very mouths of the cannon, which guarded the king, and there fell. Night closed on the combatants; and the two armies mingled together fought on for four hours longer by moonlight. Complete darkness at length forced them to rest on their arms; but the king's trumpet continually sounded, to indicate to the bivouac where he was to be found; while the two famous horns of Uri and Unterwalden called the Swiss together. The battle was renewed on the 14th at daybreak: the unrelenting obstinacy was the same; but the French had taken advantage of the night to collect and fortify themselves. Marshal Trivulzio, who had been present at eighteen pitched battles, declared that every other seemed to him children's play in comparison with this "battle of giants," as he called it: 20,000 dead already covered the ground; of these two-thirds were Swiss. When the Swiss despaired of victory they retreated slowly, but menacing and terrible. The French did not dare to pursue them.

This horrible butchery, however, hastened the conclusion of the wars which arose from the league of Cambray. The Swiss were not sufficiently powerful to maintain their sway in Lombardy: eight of their cantons, on the 7th of November, signed, at Geneva, a treaty of peace with Francis I, who compensated, with considerable sums of money, all the claims which they consented to abandon. On the 29th of November, the other cantons acceded to this pacification, which took the name of "Paix perpétuelle," and France recovered the right of raising such infantry as she needed among the Swiss. Raymond de Cardona, alarmed at the retreat of the Swiss, evacuated Lombardy with the Spanish troops. The French recovered possession of the whole duchy of Milan. Maximilian Sforza abdicated the sovereignty for a revenue of 30,000 crowns secured to him in France. Leo X, ranging himself on the side of the victors, signed, at Viterbo, on the 13th of October, a treaty, by which he restored Parma and Placentia to the French. In a conference held with Francis at Bologna, between the 10th and 15th of the following December, Leo induced that monarch to sacrifice the liberties of the Gallican church by the concordat, to renounce the protection he had hitherto extended to the Florentines and to the duke of Urbino, although the former had always remained faithful to France. The pope seized the states of the duke of Urbino, and conferred them on his nephew, Lorenzo II de' Medici. Amidst these transactions, Ferdinand the Catholic died, on the 15th of January, 1516, and his grandson Charles succeeded to his Spanish kingdoms. On the 13th of August following, Charles signed, at Noyon, a treaty, by which Francis ceded to him all his right to the kingdom of Naples as the dower of a newborn daughter, whom he promised to Charles in marriage. From that time Maximilian remained singly at war with the republic of Venice and with France. During the campaign of 1516, his German army continued to commit the most enormous crimes in the Veronese march; but Maximilian had never money enough to carry on the war without the subsidies of his allies: remaining alone, he could no longer hope to be successful. On the 14th of December he consented to accede to the treaty of Noyon; he evacuated Verona, which he had till then occupied, and the Venetians were once more put by the French in possession of all the states of which the league of Cambray had proposed the partition: but their wealth was annihilated, their population reduced to one half, their constitution itself shaken, and they were never after in a state to make those efforts for the defence of the independence of Italy, which might have been expected from them before this devastating war.

Had Italy been allowed to repose after so many disasters, she might still have recovered her strength and population; and when the struggle should have recommenced with the transalpine nations, she would have been found prepared for battle; but the heartless levity and ambition of Leo did not give her time. While the family of the Medici was becoming extinct around him, he dreamt only of investing it with new dignities; he refused the Florentines permission to re-establish their republic, and offered his alliance to whatever foreign monarch would aid him in founding on its ruins a principality for the bastard Medici. His third brother Giuliano duc de Nemours, whom he had at first charged with the government of Florence, died on the 17th of March, 1516. Lorenzo II, son of his eldest brother Pietro, whom he had made duke of Urbino, and whom he sent to command at Florence after Giuliano rendered himself odious there by his pride and by his contemptible incapacity—he too died only three years afterwards, on the 28th of April, 1519. Leo supplied his place by

cardinal Giulio de' Medici, afterwards Clement VII.
This prelate was the natural son of the first Giuliano
killed in the Pazzi conspiracy of 1478. He was considered the most able of the pope's ministers, and the
most moderate of his lieutenants. Giuliano II had also
left an illegitimate son, Ippolito, afterwards cardinal;
and Lorenzo II had a legitimate daughter, Catherine,
afterwards queen of France, and an illegitimate son,
Alexander, destined to be the future tyrant of Florence.
Leo, whether desirous of establishing these descendants, or carried away by the restlessness and levity of
his character, sighed only for war.

The emperor Maximilian died on the 19th of January, 1519, leaving his hereditary states of Austria to
his grandson Charles, already sovereign of all Spain, of
the Two Sicilies, of the Low Countries, and of the
county of Burgundy. Charles and Francis both presented themselves as candidates for the imperial crown;
the electors gave it to the former, on the 28th of June,
1519: he was from that period named Charles V. Italy,
indeed the whole of Europe, was endangered by the
immeasurable growth of this young monarch's power.
The states of the church, over which he domineered
by means of his kingdom of the Two Sicilies, could not
hope to preserve any independence but through an alliance with France. Leo at first thought so, and signed
the preliminary articles of a league with Francis; but,
suddenly changing sides, he invited Charles V to join
him in driving the French out of Italy. A secret treaty
was signed between him and the emperor, on the 8th
of May, 1521. By this the duchy of Milan was to be
restored to Francesco Sforza, the second son of Louis
the Moor. Parma, Placentia, and Ferrara were to be
united to the holy see: a duchy in the kingdom of Naples was to be secured to the bastard Alexander de'
Medici. The pope united his army to that of the emperor in the kingdom of Naples; the command of it
was given jointly to Prospero Colonna and the marquis
Pescara: war was declared on the 1st of August, and
the imperial and pontifical troops entered Milan on the

19th of November: but in the midst of the joy of this first success, Leo X died unexpectedly, on the 1st of December, 1521.

Death opportunely delivered Leo from the dangers and anxieties into which he had thoughtlessly precipitated himself. His finances were exhausted; his prodigality had deprived him of every resource; and he had no means of carrying on a war which he had only just begun. He left his successors in a state of distress which was unjustly attributed to them, and which rendered them odious to the people; for the war into which he had plunged them, without any reasonable motive, was the most disastrous of all those which had yet afflicted unhappy Italy. There remained no power truly Italian that could take any part in it for her defence. Venice was so exhausted by the war of the league of Cambray, that she was forced to limit her efforts to the maintenance of her neutrality, and was hardly powerful enough to make even her neutral position respected. Florence remained subject to the cardinal Giulio de' Medici. The republics of Sienna and Lucca were tremblingly prepared to obey the strongest: all the rest depended on the transalpine power; for an unexpected election, on the 9th of January, 1522, had given a Flemish successor to Leo X, under the name of Adrian VI. This person had been the preceptor of Charles V, and had never seen Italy, where he was regarded as a barbarian. The kingdom of Naples was governed and plundered by the Spaniards. After the French had lost the duchy of Milan, Francesco Sforza, who had been brought back by the imperialists, possessed only the name of sovereign. He had never been for a moment independent; he had never been able to protect his subjects from the tyranny of the Spanish and German soldiers, who were his guards. Finally, the marquis de Montferrat and the duke of Savoy had allowed the French to become masters in their states, and had no power to refuse them passage to ravage oppressed Italy anew.

The marshal Lautrec, whom Francis I had charged
to defend the Milanese, and who still occupied the
greater part of the territory, was forced by the Swiss,
who formed the sinews of his army, to attack the imperialists on the 29th of April, 1522, at Bicocca. Prospero Colonna had taken up a strong position about
three or four miles from Milan, on the road to Monza:
he valued himself on making a defensive war—on being successful, without giving battle. The Swiss attacked him in front, throwing themselves, without listening to the voice of their commander, into a hollow
way which covered him, and where they perished, without the possibility of resistance. After having performed
prodigies of valour, the remainder were repulsed with
dreadful loss. In spite of the remonstrances of Lautrec,
they immediately departed for their mountains; and he
for his court, to justify himself. Lescuns, his successor
in the command, suffered the imperialists to surprise
and pillage Lodi; and was at last forced to capitulate
at Cremona on the 6th of May, and evacuate the rest
of Lombardy. Genoa was not comprehended in the
capitulation, and remained still in possession of the
French; but, on the 30th of May, that city also was
surprised by the Spaniards, and pillaged with all the
ferocity which signalised that nation. It was one of the
largest depots of commerce in the west, and the ruin
of so opulent a town shook the fortune of every merchant in Europe. The general of Charles then, judging
Lombardy too much exhausted to support his armies,
led them to live at discretion in the provinces of his
ally, the pope. They raised among the states still calling
themselves independent, enormous subsidies to pay the
soldiers, for which purpose Charles never sent money.
The plague, breaking out at the same time at Rome and
Florence, added to the calamities of Italy so much the
more that Adrian VI abolished, as pagan superstition
or acts of revolt against Providence, all the sanitary
measures of police which had been invented to stop
the spread of contagion. The pope died on the 14th of
September, 1523; and the Romans, who held him in

horror, crowned his physician with laurel, as the saviour of his country.

The death of Adrian, however, saved no one. The cardinal Giulio de' Medici was chosen his successor, on the 18th of November, under the name of Clement VII. This man had passed for an able minister under his cousin Leo X, because prosperity still endured, and the pontifical treasury was not exhausted; but when he had to struggle with a distress which he, however, had not caused, his ignorance in finance and administration, his sordid avarice, his pusillanimity, his imprudence, his sudden and ill considered resolutions, his long indecisions, made him alike odious and contemptible. He was not strong enough to resist the tide of adversity. He found himself, without money and without soldiers, engaged in a war without an object: he was incapable of commanding, and nowhere found obedience.

The French were not disposed to abandon their title to Lombardy, the possession of which they had just lost. Before the end of the campaign, Francis sent thither another army, commanded by his favourite, the admiral Bonnivet. This admiral entered Italy by Piedmont; passed the Ticino on the 14th of September, 1523; and marched on Milan. But Prospero Colonna, who had chosen, among the great men of antiquity, Fabius Cunctator for his model, was admirable in the art of stopping an army, of fatiguing it by slight checks, and at last forcing it to retreat without giving battle. Bonnivet, who maintained himself on the borders of Lombardy, was forced, in the month of May following, to open himself a passage to France by Ivrea and Mont St. Bernard. The chevalier Bayard was killed while protecting the retreat of Bonnivet, in the rear-guard. The imperialists had been joined, the preceding year, by a deserter of high importance, the constable Bourbon, one of the first princes of the blood in France, who was accompanied by many nobles. Charles V put him, jointly with Pescara, at the head of his army, and sent him into Provence in the month of July; but after having besieged Marseilles, he was soon constrained to retreat. Francis I, who had assembled a powerful army, again entered Lombardy, and made himself master of Milan: he next laid siege to Pavia, on the 28th of October. Some time was necessary for the imperialists to re-assemble their army, which the campaign of Provence had disorganised. At length it approached Pavia, which had resisted through the whole winter. The king of France was pressed by all his captains to raise the siege, and to march against the enemy; but he refused, declaring that it would be a compromise of the royal dignity, and foolishly remained within his lines. He was attacked by Pescara on the 24th of February, 1525; and, after a murderous battle, made prisoner.

For several months, while Francis I was besieging Pavia, he appeared the strongest power in Italy; and the pope and Venetians, alarmed at his proximity, had treated with him anew, and pledged themselves to remain neutral. The imperial generals, after their victory, declared that these treaties with the French were offences against their master, for which they should demand satisfaction. Always without money, and pressed by the avidity of their soldiers, they sought only to discover offenders, as a pretence to raise contributions, and to let their troops live at free quarters. The pope and the Venetians were at first disposed to join in a league for resisting these exactions; and they offered Louisa of Savoy, regent of France, their aid to set her son Francis at liberty. But Clement VII had not sufficient courage to sign this league: he preferred returning again to the alliance of the emperor and the duke of Milan, for which he paid a considerable sum. As soon as the imperial generals had received the money, they refused to execute the treaty which they had made with him, and the pope was obliged to go back to the Venetians and Louisa of Savoy. Meanwhile Jerome Morone, chancellor of the duke of Milan, an old man regarded as the most able politician of his time, made overtures, which revived the hope of arming all Italy for her independence. Francesco Sforza found himself treated by the Germans and Spaniards with the greatest indignity in his own palace: his subjects were exposed to every kind of insult from an unbridled soldiery; and when he endeavoured to protect them, the officers took pleasure in making him witness aggravations of injustice and outrage. The man, however, who made the German yoke press most severely on him was the marquis Pescara, an Italian, but descended from the Catalonian house of Avalos, established in the kingdom of Naples for more than a century. He manifested a sort of vanity in associating himself with the Spaniards: he commanded their infantry; he adopted the manners as well as pride of that nation. Morone, nevertheless, did not despair of awakening his patriotism, by exciting his ambition. The kingdom of Naples, which had flourished under the bastard branch of the house of Aragon when the family of Avalos first entered it, had sunk, since it had been united to Spain, into a state of the most grievous oppression. Morone determined on offering Pescara the crown of Naples, if he would join his efforts to those of all the other Italians, for the deliverance of his country. Success depended on him: he could distribute the imperial troops, which he commanded, in such a manner as that they could oppose no resistance. The duke of Milan had been warned that Charles V intended taking his duchy from him, to confer it on his brother Ferdinand of Austria. The kingdom of Naples and the duchy of Milan were ready to pass over from the emperor's party to that of France, provided the French king would renounce all his claims to both, acknowledge Pescara king of Naples, Francesco Sforza duke of Milan; and restore to Italy her independence, after having delivered her from her enemies.

This negotiation was at first successful: each of the governments to which the proposition of concurring in the independence of Italy was addressed, seemed to agree to it. France renounced all pretensions to Lombardy and the Two Sicilies; Switzerland promised to protect, on its side, the land of ancient liberty, and to furnish it with soldiers; Henry VIII of England promised money; Pescara coveted the crown, and Sforza was impatient to throw off a yoke which had become insupportable to him; but, unhappily the negotiation was entrusted to too many cabinets, all jealous, perfidious, and eager to obtain advantages for themselves by sacrificing their allies. Clement was desirous of obtaining from the emperor a more advantageous treaty, by threatening him with France; the queen regent of France endeavoured to engage Charles to relax his rigour towards her son, by threatening him with Italy; Pescara, reserving the choice of either betraying his master or his allies, as should prove most profitable to him, had warned Charles that he was engaged in a plot which he would reveal as soon as he had every clue to it. The duchess of Alençon, sister of Francis, sent by her mother to negotiate at Madrid, spoke still more clearly. She offered Charles to abandon Italy, the project respecting which she disclosed, provided the emperor, in restoring her brother to liberty, would renounce his purpose of making him purchase it at the price of one of the provinces of France. Pescara, finding that his court knew more than he had told, determined on adopting the part of provocative agent instead of rebel; he had only to choose between them. On the 14th of October, 1525, he invited Morone to a last conference in the castle of Novara. After having made him explain all his projects anew, while Spanish officers hid behind the arras heard them, he caused him to be arrested, seized all the fortresses in the state of Milan, and laid siege to the castle, in which the duke had shut himself up. He denounced to the emperor as traitors, the pope, and all the other Italians his accomplices; but while he played this odious part, he was attacked by a slow disease, of which he died on the 30th of November, 1525, at the age of thirty-six, abhorred by all Italy.

Charles, abusing the advantages which he had obtained, imposed on Francis the treaty of Madrid, signed on the 14th of January, 1526; by which the latter abandoned Italy and the duchy of Burgundy. He was set at liberty on the 18th of March following; and almost immediately declared to the Italians, that he did not regard himself bound by a treaty extorted from him by force. On the 22d of May, he signed a league for the liberty of Italy with Clement VII, the Venetians, and Francesco Sforza, but still did not abandon the policy of his mother: instead of thinking in earnest of restoring Italian independence, and thus securing the equilibrium of Europe, he had only one purpose—that of alarming Charles with the Italians; and was ready to sacrifice them as soon as the emperor should abandon Burgundy. At the same time, his supineness, love of pleasure, distrust of his fortune, and repugnance to violate the treaty of Madrid, hindered him from fulfilling any of the engagements which he had contracted towards the Italians; he sent them neither money, French cavalry, nor Swiss forces. Charles, on the other hand, sent no supplies to pay his armies to Antonio de Leyva, the constable Bourbon, and Hugo de Monçada, their commanders. These troops were therefore obliged to live at free quarters, and the oppression of the whole country was still more dreadful than it had ever yet been.

The defection of the duke of Milan, in particular, gave a pretence to Antonio de Leyva to treat the wretched Milanese with redoubled rigour, as if they could be responsible for what Leyva called the treachery of their master. The Spanish army was quartered on the citizens of Milan; and there was not a soldier who did not make his host a prisoner, keeping him bound at the foot of the bed, or in the cellar, for the purpose of having him daily at hand, to force him, by blows or fresh torture, to satisfy some new caprice. As soon as one wretched person died under his sufferings, or broke his bonds and ended his sufferings by voluntary death, either precipitating himself through a window or into a well, the Spaniard passed into another house to recommence on its proprietor the same torture. The Venetians and the pope had united their forces, under the command of the duke of Urbino, who, exaggerating the tactics of Prospero Colonna, was ambitious of no other success in war than that of avoiding battle. He announced to the senate of Venice, that he would not approach Milan till the French and Swiss, whose support he had been promised, joined him. His inaction, while witnessing so many horrors, reduced the Italians to despair. Sforza, who had been nine months blockaded in the castle of Milan, and who always hoped to be delivered by the duke of Urbino, whose colours were in sight, supported the last extremity of hunger before he surrendered to the Spaniards, on the 24th of July, 1526. The pope, meanwhile, was far from suspecting himself in any danger; but his personal enemy, Pompeo Colonna, took advantage of the name of the imperial party to raise in the papal state 8000 armed peasants, with whom, on the 20th of September, he surprised the Vatican, pillaged the palace, as well as the temple of St. Peter, and constrained the pope to abjure the alliance of France and Venice. About the same time, George de Frundsberg, a German condottiere, entered Lombardy with 13,000 adventurers, whom he had engaged to follow him, and serve the emperor without pay, contenting themselves with the pillage of that unhappy country.

The constable Bourbon, to whom Charles had given the chief command of his forces in Italy, determined to take advantage of this new army, and unite it to that for which at Milan he had now no further occasion; but it was not without great difficulty that he could persuade the Spaniards to quit that city where they enjoyed the savage pleasure of inflicting torture on their hosts. At length, however, he succeeded in leading them to Pavia. On the 30th of January, 1527, he joined Frundsberg, who died soon after of apoplexy. Bourbon now remained alone charged with the command of this formidable army, already exceeding 25,-000 men, and continually joined on its route by disbanded soldiers and brigands intent on pillage. The constable had neither money, equipments, nor artillery, and very few cavalry; every town shut its gates on his approach, and he was often on the point of wanting provisions. He took the road of southern Italy, and entered Tuscany, still uncertain whether he should pillage Florence or Rome. The marquis of Saluzzo, with a small army, retreated before him; the duke of Urbino followed in his rear, but always keeping out of reach of battle. At last, Bourbon took the road to Rome, by the valley of the Tiber. On the 5th of May, 1527, he arrived before the capital of Christendom. Clement, long alarmed at his march, had, on the 15th of March, signed a truce of eight months with the viceroy of Naples, and dismissed his troops, never imagining that one of the emperor's lieutenants would not respect the engagements of the other. On the approach of Bourbon, however, the walls of Rome were again mounted with engines of war. The next day, the 6th of May, this renegade prince led his troops to the assault of the city. He was killed near the Janiculum, while mounting the first scaling ladder. His fall did not stop the terrific band of robbers which he led. The victorious army scaled the walls, which were ill defended; and spread terror through the quarters of the Borgo, Vatican, and Trastevere. In a few hours they were masters of the whole city, Clement having neglected to destroy the bridges on the Tiber.

The capital of Christendom was then abandoned to a pillage unparalleled in the most calamitous period—that of the first triumph of barbarism over civilisation: neither Alaric the Goth nor Genseric the Vandal had treated it with like ferocity. Not only was all that could be seized in every house and every shop carried off, but the peasants of the fiefs of Colonna took possession of the heavy furniture which did not tempt the cupidity of the soldier. From the day on which these barbarians entered the city all personal protection was withdrawn; women were abandoned to the outrages of the victors; and sanctuaries, enriched by the veneration of Christendom for twelve centuries, were devoted to spoliation. The squares before the churches were strewed with the ornaments of the altar, relics,

and other sacred things, which the soldiers threw into
the street after having torn off the gold and silver
which adorned them. Men, women, and children were
seized, whenever their captors could flatter themselves
that they had concealed some treasure, or that there
was any one sufficiently interested for them to pay their
ransom. Every house resounded with the cries and
lamentations of wretched persons thus subjected to the
torture; and this dreadful state of crime and agony
lasted not merely days, but was prolonged for more
than nine months: it was not till the 17th of February,
1528, that the prince of Orange, one of the French lords
who had accompanied Bourbon in his rebellion, finally
withdrew from Rome all of this army that vice and disease had spared. The Germans, indeed, after the first
few days, had sheathed their swords, to plunge into
drunkenness and the most brutal debauchery; but the
Spaniards, up to the last hour of their stay in Rome,
indefatigable in their cold-blooded cruelty, continued
to invent fresh torture to extort new ransoms from all
who fell into their hands; even the plague, the consequence of so much suffering, moral and physical, which
broke out amidst all these horrors, did not make the
rapacious Spaniard loose his prey.

The struggle between the Italians, feebly seconded
by the French, and the generals of Charles V, was prolonged yet more than two years after the sack of Rome;
but it only added to the desolation of Italy, and destroyed alike in all the Italian provinces the last remains
of prosperity. On the 18th of August, 1527, Henry VIII
of England and Francis I contracted the treaty of
Amiens, for the deliverance, as the two sovereigns announced, of the pope. A powerful French army, commanded by Lautrec, entered Italy in the same month,
by the province of Alexandria. They surprised Pavia on
the 1st of October, and during eight days barbarously
pillaged that great city, under pretence of avenging the
defeat of their king under its walls. After this success,
Lautrec, instead of completing the conquest of Lombardy, directed his march towards the south; renewed

the alliance of France with the duke of Ferrara, to whose son was given in marriage a daughter of Louis XII, sister of the queen of France. He secured the friendship of the Florentine republic, which, on the 17th of the preceding May, had taken advantage of the distress and captivity of the pope, to recover its liberty, and to re-establish its government in the same form in which it stood in 1512. The pope, learning that Lautrec had arrived at Orvieto, escaped from the castle of St. Angelo on the 9th of December, and took refuge in the French camp. The Spaniard Alarcon had detained him captive, with thirteen cardinals, during six months, in that fortress; and, though the plague had broken out there, he did not relax in his severity. After having received 400,000 ducats for his ransom, instead of releasing him, as he had engaged to do the next day, it is probable that he suffered him to escape, lest his own soldiers should arrest him in order to extort a second ransom.

Lautrec passed the Tronto to enter the Abruzzi with his powerful army on the 10th of February, 1528. The banditti whom Charles V called his soldiers, whom he never paid, and who showed no disposition to obedience, were cantoned at Milan, Rome, and the principal cities in Italy: they divided their time between debauchery and the infliction of torture on their hosts; their officers were unable to induce them to leave the towns and advance towards the enemy. The people in the excess of suffering, met every change with eagerness, and received Lautrec as a deliverer. He would probably have obtained complete success, if Francis had not just at this moment withheld the monthly advance of money which he had promised. That monarch, identifying his pride of royalty with prodigality, exhausted his finances in pleasures and entertainments; his want of economy drew on him all his disasters. Lautrec, on his side, although he had many qualities of a good general, was harsh, proud, and obstinate: he piqued himself on doing always the opposite of what he was counselled. Disregarding the national peculiarities of the French, he attempted in war to discipline them in slow and regular movements. He lost valuable time in Apulia, where he took and sacked Melfi, on the 23d of March, with a barbarity worthy of his adversaries, the Spaniards: he did not arrive till the 1st of May before Naples. The prince of Orange had just entered that city with the army which had sacked Rome, but of which the greater part had been carried off by a dreadful mortality, the consequence and punishment of its vices and crimes. Instead of vigorously attacking them, Lautrec, in spite of the warm remonstrances of his officers, persisted in reducing Naples by blockade; thus exposing his army to the influence of a destructive climate. The imperial fleet was destroyed, on the 28th of May, in the gulf of Salerno, by Filippino Doria, who was in the pay of France. The inhabitants of Naples experienced the most cruel privations, and sickness soon made great havoc amongst them: but a malady not less fatal broke out at the same time in the French camp. The soldiers, under a burning sun, surrounded with putrid water, condemned to every kind of privation, harassed by the light cavalry of the enemy, infinitely superior to theirs, sank, one after the other, under pestilential fevers. In the middle of June, the French reckoned in their camp 25,000 men; by the 2d of August there did not remain 4000 fit for service. At this period all the springs were dry, and the troops began to suffer from hunger and thirst. Lautrec, ill as he was, had till then supported the army by his courage and invincible obstinacy; but, worn out at last, he expired in the night of the 15th of August:—almost all the other officers died in like manner. The marquis de Saluces, on whom the command of the army devolved, felt the necessity of a retreat, but knew not how to secure it in presence of such a superior force. He tried to escape from the imperialists, by taking advantage of a tremendous storm, in the night of the 29th of August; but was soon pursued, and overtaken at Aversa, where, on the 30th, he was forced to capitulate. The magazines and hospitals at Capua were, at the same time, given up to the Spaniards. The prisoners and the sick were crowded together in the stables of the Magdalen, where contagion acquired new force. The Spaniards foresaw it, and watched with indifference the agony and death of all; for nearly all of that brilliant army perished—a few invalids only ever returned to France.

During the same campaign another French army, conducted by François de Bourbon, count de St. Pol, had entered Lombardy, at the moment when Henry duke of Brunswick led thither a German army. Henry, finding nothing more to pillage, announced that his mission was to punish a rebellious nation, and put to the sword all the inhabitants of the villages through which he passed. Milan was at once a prey to famine and the plague, aggravated by the cupidity and cold-blooded ferocity of Leyva, who still commanded the Spanish garrison. Leyva seized all the provisions brought in from the country; and, to profit by the general misery, resold them at an enormous price. Genoa had remained subject to the French, and was little less oppressed; none of its republican institutions were any longer respected: but a great admiral still rendered it illustrious. Andrea Doria had collected a fleet, on board of which he summoned all the enterprising spirits of Liguria: his nephew Filippino, who had just gained a victory over the imperialists, was his lieutenant. The Dorias demanded the restoration of liberty to their country as the price of their services: unable to obtain it from the French, they passed over to the imperialists. Assured by the promises of Charles, they presented themselves, on the 12th of September, before Genoa, excited their countrymen to revolt, and constrained the French to evacuate the town: they made themselves masters of Savona on the 21st of October, and a few days afterwards of Castelletto. Doria then proclaimed the republic, and re-established once more the freedom of Genoa, at the moment when all freedom was near its end in Italy. The winter passed in suffering and inaction. The following year, Antonio de Leyva surprised the count de St. Pol at Landriano, on the

21st of June, 1529, and made him prisoner, with all the principal officers of the French army. The rest dispersed or returned to France. This was the last military incident in this dreadful war.

Peace was ardently desired on all sides; negotiations were actively carried on; but every potentate sought to deceive his ally in order to obtain better conditions from his adversary. Margaret of Austria, the sister of the emperor's father, and Louisa of Savoy, the mother of the king of France, met at Cambray; and in conference, to which no witnesses were admitted, arranged what was called *"Le traité des dames."* Clement VII had at the same time a nuncio at Barcelona, who negotiated with the emperor. The latter was impatient to arrange the affairs of Italy, in order to pass into Germany. Not only had Soliman invaded Austria, and, on the 13th of September, arrived under the walls of Vienna, but the reformation of Luther excited in all the north of Germany a continually increasing ferment. On the 20th of June, 1529, Charles signed at Barcelona a treaty of perpetual alliance with the pope: by it he engaged to sacrifice the republic of Florence to the pope's vengeance, and to place in the service of Clement, in order to accomplish it, all the brigands who had previously devastated Italy. Florence was to be given in sovereignty to the bastard Alexander de' Medici, who was to marry an illegitimate daughter of Charles V. On the 5th of August following, Louis and Margaret signed the treaty of Cambray, by which France abandoned, without reserve, all its Italian allies to the caprices of Charles; who, on his side, renounced Burgundy, and restored to Francis his two sons, who had been retained as hostages. Charles arrived at Genoa, on board the fleet of Andrea Doria, on the 12th of August. The pope awaited him at Bologna, into which he made his entry on the 5th of November. He summoned thither all the princes of Italy, or their deputies, and treated them with more moderation than might have been expected after the shameful abandonment of them by France. As he knew the health of

Francesco Sforza, duke of Milan, to be in a declining
state, which promised but few years of life, he
granted him the restitution of his duchy for the sum
of 900,000 ducats, which Sforza was to pay at different terms: they had not all fallen due when that
prince died, on the 24th of October, 1535, without
issue, and his estates escheated to the emperor. On the
23d of December, 1529, Charles granted peace to the
Venetians; who restored him only some places in
Apulia, and gave up Ravenna and Cervia to the pope.
On the 20th of March, Alphonso d'Este also signed a
treaty, by which he referred his differences with the
pope to the arbitration of the emperor. Charles did
not pronounce on them till the following year. He
conferred on Alphonso the possession of Modena,
Reggio, and Rubbiera, as fiefs of the empire; and he
made the pope give him the investiture of Ferrara. On
the 25th of March, 1530, a diploma of the emperor
raised the marquisate of Mantua to a duchy, in favour
of Frederick de Gonzaga. The duke of Savoy and the
marquis de Montferrat, till then protected by France,
arrived at Bologna, to place themselves under the protection of the emperor. The duke of Urbino was recommended to him by the Venetians, and obtained some
promises of favour. The republics of Genoa, Sienna,
and Lucca had permission to vegetate under the imperial protection; and Charles, having received from
the pope, at Bologna, on the 22d of February and 24th
of March, the two crowns of Lombardy and of the
empire, departed in the beginning of April for Germany, in order to escape witnessing the odious service
in which he consented that his troops should be employed against Florence.

CHAPTER XVI

OPPRESSION OF ITALY DURING THE THREE LAST CEN-
TURIES   SUCCESSIVE FALL OF ALL HER REPUBLICS
HER LAST CONVULSIONS

THE evil destiny of Italy was accomplished. Charles
VIII, when he first invaded that country, opened its
gates to all the transalpine nations: from that period
Italy was ravaged, during thirty-six years, by Germans,
French, Spaniards, Swiss, and even Turks. They inflicted on her calamities beyond example in history;
calamities so much the more keenly felt, as the sufferers were more civilised, and the authors more
barbarous. The French invasion ended in giving to
the greatest enemies of France the dominion of that
country, so rich, so industrious, and of which the possession was sought ardently by all. Never would the
house of Austria have achieved the conquest of Italy,
if Charles VIII, Louis XII, and Francis I had not
previously destroyed the wealth and military organisation of the nation; if they had not themselves introduced the Spaniards into the kingdom of Naples, and
the Germans into the states of Venice; forgetting that
both must soon after be subject to Charles V. The independence of Italy would have been beneficial to
France: the rapacious and improvident policy which
made France seek subjects where it should only have
sought allies, was the origin of a long train of disasters
to the French.

A period of three centuries of weakness, humiliation, and suffering, in Italy, began in the year 1530:
from that time she was always oppressed by foreigners,
and enervated and corrupted by her masters. These
last reproached her with the vices of which they were
themselves the authors. After having reduced her to
the impossibility of resisting, they accused her of
cowardice when she submitted, and of rebellion when
she made efforts to vindicate herself. The Italians, dur-

ing this long period of slavery, were agitated with the
desire of becoming once more a nation: as, however,
they had lost the direction of their own affairs, they
ceased to have any history which could be called
theirs; their misfortunes have become but episodes in
the histories of other nations. We should not, however,
look upon the task which we have imposed on ourselves as concluded, if we did not distinguish, amidst
this general subjugation, the particular calamities which
closed the existence of the republics which still remained independent after the coronation of Charles V.

The Florentines, who, from 1512, had been victims
of all the faults of Leo X and Clement VII, who had
been drawn into all the oscillations of their policy, and
called upon to make prodigious sacrifices of money
for projects with which they had not even been made
acquainted, were taught under these popes to detest
the yoke of the Medici. When the constable Bourbon
approached their walls in his march to Rome, on the
26th of April, 1527, they were on the point of recovering their liberty: the cardinal de Cortona, who commanded for the pope at Florence, had distributed arms
among the citizens for their defence; and they determined to employ them for their liberation: but the
terror which this army of brigands inspired did the
cardinal the service of repressing insurrection. When,
however, they heard soon after of the taking of Rome,
and of the captivity of the pope, all the most notable
citizens presented themselves in their civic dress to the
cardinal de Cortona; declared firmly, but with calmness, that they were henceforth free; and compelled
him, with the two bastard Medici whom he brought
up, to quit the city. It was on the 17th of May, 1527,
that the lieutenant of Clement obeyed; and the constitution, such as it existed in 1512, with its grand
council, was restored without change, except that the
office of gonfalonier was declared annual. The first
person invested with this charge was Nicolo Capponi,
a man enthusiastic in religion, and moderate in politics:
he was the son of Pietro Capponi, who had braved

Charles VIII. In 1529, he was succeeded by Baldas-
sare Carducci, whose character was more energetic, and
opinions more democratic. Carducci was succeeded, in
1530, by Raffaele Girolami, who witnessed the end of
the republic.

Florence, during the whole period of its glory and
power, had neglected the arts of war: it reckoned for
its defence on the adventurers whom its wealth could
summon from all parts to its service; and set but little
value on a courage which men, without any other
virtue, were so eager to sell to the highest bidder.
Since the transalpine nations had begun to subdue Italy
to their tyranny, these hireling arms sufficed no longer
for the public safety. Statesmen began to see the necessity of giving the republic a protection within itself.
Macchiavelli, who died on the 22d of June, 1527, six
weeks after the restoration of the popular government,
had been long engaged in persuading his fellow-citizens of the necessity of awakening a military spirit in
the people: it was he who caused the country militia,
named *l'ordinanza,* to be formed into regiments. A
body of mercenaries, organised by Giovanni de' Medici,
a distant kinsman of the popes, served at the time as
a military school for the Tuscans, among whom alone
the corps had been raised: it acquired a high reputation under the name of *bande nere.* No infantry
equalled it in courage and intelligence. Five thousand
of these warriors served under Lautrec in the kingdom of Naples, where they almost all perished. When,
towards the end of the year 1528, the Florentines perceived that their situation became more and more
critical, they formed, among those who enjoyed the
greatest privileges in their country, two bodies of
militia, which displayed the utmost valour for its defence. The first, consisting of 300 young men of noble
families, undertook the guard of the palace, and the
support of the constitution; the second, of 4000 soldiers
drawn only from among families having a right to sit
in the council-general, were called the civic militia:
both soon found opportunities of proving that gen-

erosity and patriotism suffice to create, in a very short period, the best soldiers. The illustrious Michael Angelo was charged to superintend the fortifications of Florence: they were completed in the month of April, 1529. Lastly, the ten commissioners of war chose for the command of the city Malatesta Baglioni of Perugia, who was recommended to them as much for his hatred of the Medici, who had unjustly put his father to death, as for his reputation for valour and military talent.

Clement VII sent against Florence, his native country, that very prince of Orange, the successor of Bourbon, who had made him prisoner at Rome; and with him that very army of robbers which had overwhelmed the holy see, and its subjects, with misery and every outrage. This army entered Tuscany in the month of September, 1529, and took possession of Cortona, Arezzo, and all the upper Val d'Arno. On the 14th of October the prince of Orange encamped in the plain of Ripoli, at the foot of the walls of Florence; and, towards the end of December, Ferdinand de Gonzaga led on the right bank of the Arno another imperial army, composed of 20,000 Spaniards and Germans, which occupied without resistance Pistoia and Prato. Notwithstanding the immense superiority of their forces, the imperialists did not attempt to make a breach in the walls of Florence; they resolved to make themselves masters of the city by blockade. The Florentines, on the contrary, animated by preachers who inherited the zeal of Savonarola, and who united liberty with religion as an object of their worship, were eager for battle: they made frequent attacks on the whole line of their enemies, led in turns by Malatesta Baglioni and Stefano Colonna. They made nightly sallies, covered with white shirts to distinguish each other in the dark, and successively surprised the posts of the imperialists: but the slight advantages, thus obtained, could not disguise the growing danger of the republic. France had abandoned them to their enemies; there remained not one ally either in Italy or the rest of Europe; while the army of the pope and emperor comprehended all the survivors of those soldiers who had so long been the terror of Italy by their courage and ferocity, and whose warlike ardour was now redoubled by the hope of the approaching pillage of the richest city in the West.

The Florentines had one solitary chance of deliverance. Francesco Ferrucci, one of their citizens, who had learned the art of war in the bande nere, and joined to a mind full of resources an unconquerable intrepidity and an ardent patriotism, was not shut up within the walls of Florence: he had been named commissary-general, with unlimited power over all that remained without the capital. Ferrucci was at first engaged in conveying provisions from Empoli to Florence: he afterwards took Volterra from the imperialists; and, having formed a small army, proposed to the signoria to seduce all the adventurers and brigands from the imperial army, by promising them another pillage of the pontifical court, and succeeding in that, to march at their head on Rome, frighten Clement, and force him to grant peace to their country. The signoria rejected this plan as too daring. Ferrucci then formed a second, which was little less bold. He departed from Volterra, made the tour of Tuscany, which the imperial troops traversed in every direction, collected at Leghorn, Pisa, the Val di Nievole, and in the mountains of Pistoia, every soldier, every man of courage, still devoted to the republic; and, after having thus increased his army, he intended to fall on the imperial camp before Florence and force the prince of Orange, who began to feel the want of money, to raise the siege. Ferrucci, with an intrepidity equal to his skill, led his little troop, from the 14th of July to the 2d of August, 1530, through numerous bodies of imperialists, who preceded, followed, and surrounded him on all sides, as far as Gavinana, four miles from San Marcello, in the mountains of Pistoia. He entered that village about mid-day, on the 2d of August, with 3000 infantry and 500 cavalry. The prince of Orange, at the same time, entered by another gate, with a part of the army which besieged Florence. The different corps, which had on every side harassed Ferrucci in his march, poured in upon him from all quarters: the battle instantly began, and was fought with relentless fury within the walls of Gavinana. Philibert de Challon, prince of Orange, in whom that house became extinct, was killed by a double shot, and his corps put to flight; but other bands of imperialists successively arrived, and continually renewed the attack on a small force exhausted with fatigue: 2000 Florentines were already stretched on the field of battle; when Ferrucci, pierced with several mortal wounds, was borne bleeding to the presence of his personal enemy, Fabrizio Maramaldi, a Calabrese, who commanded the light cavalry of the emperor. The Calabrese stabbed him several times in his rage; while Ferrucci calmly said, "Thou wouldst kill a dead man!" The republic perished with him.

When news of the disaster at Gavinana reached Florence, the consternation was extreme. Baglioni, who for some days had been in treaty with the prince of Orange, and who was accused of having given him notice of the project of Ferrucci, declared that a longer resistance was impossible, and that he was determined to save an imprudent city, which seemed bent upon its own ruin. On the 8th of August he opened the bastion, in which he was stationed, to an imperial captain, and planted his artillery so as to command the town. The citizens, in consternation, abandoned the defence of the walls, to employ themselves in concealing their valuable effects in the churches; and the signoria acquainted Ferdinand de Gonzaga, who had succeeded the prince of Orange in the command of the army, that they were ready to capitulate. The terms granted on the 12th of August, 1530, were less rigorous than the Florentines might have apprehended. They were to pay a gratuity of 80,000 crowns to the army which besieged them, and to recall the Medici. In return, a complete amnesty was to be granted to all who had acted against that family, the pope, or the emperor. But Clement had no intention to observe any of the engagements contracted in his name. On the 20th of August, he caused the parliament, in the name of the sovereign people, to create a balia, which was to execute the vengeance of which he would not himself take the responsibility: he subjected to the torture, and afterwards punished with exile or death, by means of this balia, all the patriots who had signalised themselves by their zeal for liberty. In the first month 150 illustrious citizens were banished; before the end of the year there were more than 1000 sufferers: every Florentine family, even among those most devoted to the Medici, had some one member among the proscribed.

Alexander, the bastard Medici, whom Clement had appointed chief of the Florentine republic in preference to his cousin Hyppolito, did not return to his country till the 5th of July, 1531: he was the bearer of a rescript from the emperor, which gave Florence a constitution nearly monarchical; but, so far from confining himself within the limits traced, Alexander oppressed the people with the most grievous tyranny. Cruelty, debauchery, and extortion marked him for public hatred. On the 10th of August, 1535, he caused to be poisoned his cousin, the cardinal Ippolito, who undertook the defence of his fellow-countrymen against him. He at last, on the 6th of January, 1537, was himself assassinated by his kinsman and companion in licentiousness, Lorenzino de' Medici.

But the death of Alexander did not restore freedom to his country. The agents of his tyranny, the most able but also the most odious of whom was the historian Guicciardini, needed a prince for their protector. They made choice of Cosmo de' Medici, a young man of nineteen, descended in the fourth generation from Lorenzo, the brother of the former Cosmo. On the 9th of January, 1537, they proclaimed him duke of Florence, hoping to guide him henceforth at their pleasure; but they were deceived. This man, false, cold-blooded, and ferocious, who had all the vices of

Filippo II, and who shrank from no crime, soon got rid of his counsellors, as well as of his adversaries. Cosmo I, in 1569, obtained from the pope Pius V the title of grand duke of Tuscany; a title that the emperor would not then acknowledge, though he afterwards, in 1575, granted it to the son of Cosmo. Seven grand dukes of that family reigned successively at Florence. The last, Gian Gastone, died on the 9th of July, 1737.

It was Cosmo I who abolished the name of republic at Sienna, as he had done at Florence. That city, so long faithful to the Ghibeline party, had evinced the same devotion to the emperor in the wars of the beginning of the century. Charles V took advantage of it to introduce into Sienna a Spanish garrison, destined to overawe Tuscany and the court of Rome; but the Spaniards showed there, as every where else, the characteristic pride, cupidity, and ferocity which had rendered them universally odious. On the 11th of August, 1552, the Siennese, unable to bear with them any longer, rose against them, drove them out, and introduced a French garrison in their stead. Cosmo pledged himself to remain neutral in the war lighted up anew between the French and the imperialists: he, nevertheless, on the 27th of January, 1554, attacked, without any declaration of war, the Siennese, whose city he hoped to take by surprise. Having failed in this attack, he gave the command of his army to the ferocious marquis de Marignano, who undertook to reduce it by famine. The first act of Marignano was to massacre without mercy all the women, children, aged, and sick, whom the Siennese, beginning to feel the want of provisions, had sent out of the town: every peasant discovered carrying provisions into Sienna was immediately hung before its gates. The villages and fortresses of the Siennese, for the most part, attempted to remain faithful to the republic; but in all those which held out until the cannon was planted against their walls, the inhabitants were inhumanly put to death. It was then that the edge of the sword or famine destroyed the rustic population, particularly that of the coast of Maremma, covered with forests at this day. The Maremmane fever over-ran that desolate district; and those who at the peace returned there to reap the inheritance of the victims of Marignano, soon fell themselves the victims of that disease. The city of Sienna at last capitulated, on the 2d of April, 1555; and its capitulation was not better respected than that of Florence. Death and exile were the lot of those generous citizens to whom an amnesty had been promised. The Spaniards retained possession of Sienna for two years; and did not surrender it to the duke of Florence until the 19th of July, 1557.

After the subjugation of Sienna, there remained in Italy only three republics, Lucca, Genoa, and Venice, unless it may be permitted to reckon San Marino, a free village, situated on the summit of a mountain of Romagna, which has alike escaped both usurpation and history until our own time.

In 1546, Lucca had a gonfalonier, named Francesco Burlamachi, who formed the bold project of restoring liberty to all the republics of Tuscany. The militia of Lucca, in number only 2000, were to be reviewed by him on a given day, after which he was to lead them suddenly across the mountains to Pisa, in order to rouse that warlike city to revolt: detachments were, at the same time, to be sent to excite similar insurrections at Pescia, Pistoia, Florence, Bologna, Sienna, and Perugia. Popular governments were every where to be organised, and the different towns were to form one confederation.

Charles V, then engaged in Germany in combating the league of Smalkalde, was supposed not to be in a situation to defend Italy. But the spies of Cosmo discovered the plot. The duke of Florence demanded the punishment of the conspirators from the magistrates of Lucca; who, trembling at the emperor's displeasure, delivered Burlamachi to the lieutenant of Charles at Milan. The first magistrate of a republic, calling itself still free, was tortured, and afterwards beheaded, by order of a foreign governor. From that period Lucca was ruled by a narrow aristocracy, called in derision *i signori del cerchiolino;* because the magistracies passed among them from one to the other in rotation as in a circle. The Martiniana law, proposed on the 9th of November, 1556, by the gonfalonier Martin Bernardini, excluded from office every man who was not descended from families which had an hereditary share in the sovereignty of the republic: of those there were not, in the year 1600, more than 168; and at the last enumeration, made in 1797, not more than 88. They were, nevertheless, to furnish a signoria, composed of a gonfalonier, nine anziani, a senate of thirty-six members, and a grand council of ninety. This jealous aristocracy, hated by the people, could not maintain itself from the moment it came in contact with the French of the revolution. These last took possession of Tuscany, on the 15th of October, 1800; on the 25th of December, 1801, the Lucchese gave themselves a representative constitution; and on the 4th of June, 1805, they demanded of Napoleon a sovereign of his family. His sister, the princess Elise, was, on the 23d of June following, invested with the principality of Lucca, but with laws which secured to the citizens and people more equality and freedom than they had for a long period enjoyed.

Andrea Doria restored the name of republic to Genoa, his native country, but with it he restored neither liberty nor independence. He constituted for the government of the republic a narrow aristocracy, which he continued to rule with his nephew Giannettino. He, at the same time, attached his country to the house of Austria, with a submission which the greater number of Genoese felt as the deepest humiliation. It was to throw off the double yoke of the Spaniards and of Doria that Gian Luigi de' Fieschi formed a conspiracy, celebrated alike in history and poetry. Fieschi brought down the vassals of his vast fiefs in the mountains; he had roused and inflamed the partisans of ancient freedom: he combined with all these the restless spirits which desired only confusion and a change. In fine, he secured the aid of France; and on the 2d of January, 1547, seized the port, fleet, and gates of the city. Giannettino Doria was killed as he endeavoured to appease the sedition. The aged Doria fled; the revolution was accomplished: but Gian Luigi de' Fieschi, who should direct its course, was nowhere to be found. In passing from one galley to another, he had fallen unperceived into the sea, and, being loaded with heavy armour, was drowned. His companions, without a chief, knew no longer what was to be done. Though victors, they already treated with the signoria as if vanquished; and contented themselves with the promise of an amnesty. The Dorias did not observe this pledge; all the conspirators whom they could seize were executed. It was not till after the death of Andrea Doria, which took place only on the 25th of November, 1560, that the Genoese limited, though in a small degree, the rights of the aristocracy; they admitted, on the 17th of March, 1576, a body of new nobles into the government. They also preserved, with jealousy, the little that remained of their independence. The court of Spain repeatedly endeavoured to suppress the name of republic, and to overawe them by a citadel; but they twice defeated its attempts, in 1548 and 1571.

The aristocracy of Genoa was again, in 1628, endangered by a conspiracy. The families inscribed on the golden book, and having the right to sit in council, including the new as well as ancient nobility, did not exceed in number 170; but there were in Liguria at least 450 families equally noble, decorated with titles, possessing fiefs, prelacies, commanderies, and hereditary wealth, who were excluded from all share in the government. Julius Cesar Vachero persuaded these to aid him in seizing a sovereignty from which they thought themselves unjustly excluded. Vachero was a merchant of immense wealth, who had adopted the Spanish manners, then predominant in Italy. His palace was always filled with bravos; he never walked out without having numbers in his train; whoever offended him immediately fell under the dagger of the assassin, who escaped from justice by intimidating the judges or witnesses with fresh crimes. All the families not inscribed on the golden book promised to unite their bravos to those of Vachero. On the 1st of April, 1628, they were to make a joint attack upon the public palace, massacre all the ancient nobility, and new-model the government, under the protection of the duke of Savoy: but the plot was discovered the evening preceding that destined for its execution. Vachero and several of his accomplices were arrested and executed.

The Genoese in the same century experienced a great calamity. On the 18th of May, 1684, their capital was bombarded by the fleet of Louis XIV; who felt his royal dignity offended by so small a people daring to resist his will. He demanded the establishment of a depot at Savona, to provision with salt and ammunition of war his fortress of Casal de Montferrat. The senate of Genoa refused their consent to an establishment alike contrary to their neutrality and independence. The marquis de Siegnelay punished them, by pouring on this city 14,000 bombs in three days: the public palace was more than half destroyed; and the whole town would have been ruined, if the doge had not consented to proceed to Paris with four senators to make his apology to the king.

. Dignity and grandeur still characterised the doge, even in his humiliation: but this proud, and perhaps noble, merit was all that remained to the Genoese aristocracy; it became more and more narrow and exclusive. It adopted the manners of the Spaniards, under whose protection it had risen. The Genoese nobles, like the grandees of Spain, always kept a band of assassins in their pay; and it was by the dagger alone that they sought to make themselves feared or respected. The sovereign nobility, prodigal and voracious, created by their pomp wants beyond their resources: accordingly, they stooped to the most disgraceful depredations to obtain money. The state could make no contract without being robbed; it was cheated in the victualling of fortresses, and of the navy, and in the payment of troops; every place was an object of sale, and justice was venal in the tribunals. The subjects of the eastern and western coasts, called the two *Riviere*, and of Corsica, frequently revolted in order to throw off a yoke which had become odious to them. In the eighteenth century, the Corsicans redoubled their efforts to rid themselves of the tyranny of Genoa. From the year 1730 to the 15th of May, 1768, Corsica maintained an obstinate war against the republic; which esteemed itself fortunate in prevailing on France to accept all its rights to that island in payment of a debt contracted with the French for the purpose of subduing its revolted subjects.

But the spirit of the ancient Italian republicans was not extinguished among the people of Genoa as among the nobles. The two branches of the house of Austria in Spain and Germany had become extinct; and, in the war of the Austrian succession, the Genoese had made alliance with the house of Bourbon, which disputed with Maria Theresa the inheritance of her father Charles VI. In this war the French, united with the Spaniards, were defeated and driven out of Lombardy. The Austrians appeared before Genoa; and the senate, which dared not arm the population, opened their gates to them, on the 6th of September, 1746. The Austrians abused, as they have ever done, the favours of fortune. They exacted from Genoa a contribution of 9,000,000 of florins of the empire, a sum which that city was not in a condition to pay. They seized all the money at the bank, all the plate of the churches, and even the property of individuals. They emptied the arsenals; and destined the artillery of Genoa to be employed in an attack which they meditated against Provence. They made the Genoese themselves draw the cannon of which they robbed them; and expecting to find in the Italians Austrian baseness and servility, they urged them in their labour with blows. A heavy mortar had stuck fast amidst the ruins of a narrow street, and a German serjeant raised his cane on a Genoese to make him draw with more force; the latter, seizing a stone, threw it at the head of the Austrian. The people collected, calling out, not "to arms!" for they had none, but to attack the Austrians with stones. The Genoese from every window showered on them the stones of walls which they demolished, or the tiles of houses which they unroofed. In those narrow and winding streets the soldiers could find no shelter. They could present themselves in no imposing masses. They fired on their assailants; and more than one house was full of dead: but as they could not see the fall of those whom they struck, they were not cheered by their success. Meanwhile the streets were soon covered with Austrian dead. The Austrians tried in vain to set fire to houses, in the construction of which there happened to be but few combustible materials. Terror at length seized them: they fled from the city. It was the 5th of December, 1746. The populace which had expelled them lost no time in lining the ramparts and gates with cannon. The marquess Botta Adorno, general of the Austrians, had established in Genoa all his magazines, with his park of artillery. The revolt which drove him out deprived him both of arms and provisions; and in the barren mountains which surround Genoa nothing was to be procured: he was accordingly, on the 10th of December, obliged to repass the Apennines. The peace of Aix-la-Chapelle, concluded two years afterwards, on the 18th of December, 1748, secured to the republic of Genoa the integrity of its territory, under the protection of France.

The expulsion of the Austrians was the last glorious event in the history of Genoa, as well as the last display of energy by the Italian nation, till the universal convulsion caused by the revolution of France. In the years 1794 and 1795, the senate of Genoa availed itself of the importance of its position to preserve its neutrality: its inclinations, however, sometimes prevailed over its interest, and not unfrequently exposed the French to outrages. These last postponed their demand of reparation, till the victory of Monte Notte, gained by Bonaparte over the Piedmontese and Austrians, on the 11th

of April, 1796, placed Genoa at their discretion. From
that time the partisans of democracy began to claim as
a right that all the inhabitants of Liguria should participate in the sovereignty. The nobles, seconded by
the clergy, had a numerous party on their side among
the people. On the 22d of May, 1797, they resorted to
arms; and 10,000 of the lowest class, collected by the
cry of *Viva Maria!* for a moment triumphed over the
friends of liberty. But this event itself furnished Bonaparte with an opportunity of interfering: he supported
the rights of the nation against the aristocracy, and
made the deputies of the senate sign, on the 6th of
June, 1797, the convention of Monte Bello, which
obliged the Genoese to adopt the name of the Ligurian
republic; the inhabitants of Liguria being all admitted
to a share in the sovereignty. The constitution of this
republic was proclaimed on the 14th of June, 1797; it
was modified on the 26th of June, 1802; and abolished
on the 8th of October, 1805, by the union of the state
of Genoa to France. Bonaparte had engaged the members of the government themselves to make the demand, on the 4th of June, 1805.

We have now to speak only of the decline and fall
of the republic of Venice, the state in Italy whose existence was of longest duration. As this republic was
the most powerful, the most wealthy, and the most
wisely administered of all the Italian states, it appeared,
even after the year 1530, when all Italy fell under the
yoke of Charles V, to have preserved some vigour and
independence. But the signoria of Venice did not share
in the illusion which it created abroad: it felt the nation's weakness and danger, and knew too well that
the vital principle was gone.

The whole of the 16th century was employed by the
Venetians in repairing the disasters of the league of
Cambray. They had to rebuild all the walls of their
city; to recover their reduced population; to re-
establish their manufactures and agriculture, and to
liquidate the enormous debt with which they were
loaded; besides being always menaced by the Turks,

against whom they had to support two disastrous wars: one from 1537 to 1540, which cost them their islands in the Archipelago, and their last fortresses in the Morea; the other from 1570 to 1573, which deprived them of the isle of Cyprus. They appeared in some degree sacred to the western people, who regarded them as their defenders against the infidels; they were moreover united by an identity of interests to the Roman empire—like them, menaced by the Mussulmans: they, consequently, drew closer their alliance with the house of Austria, and under that pretext withdrew themselves from every other participation in the general affairs of Europe.

But in the beginning of the seventeenth century the Mussulman empire no longer inspired so much terror. The yoke of Spain continued to grow more insupportable to Italy; while the development of the protestant party in Europe showed some prospect of throwing it off. The policy of the Venetian republic was, in fact, constantly to throw off the yoke of the house of Austria. But knowing its own weakness, and justly suspicious of allies who would abandon after compromising them, the Venetians contented themselves with giving succour to those whom they considered the defenders of European liberty, without openly making themselves a party in their leagues.

Venice was the first to acknowledge Henry IV, rejected by the catholic powers, and to negotiate his reconciliation with the pope. In 1617, it made alliance with the Dutch. During the thirty years' war, it gave succour to the protestants of Germany, to Bethlem Gabor, and to Ragotski, in Hungary. It supported the duke of Savoy against the king of Spain, and the protestant Grisons against the catholics of that canton.

At this period, when the republic was come almost to open hostility with the court of Spain, Philip III was represented in Italy by three powerful noblemen, ambitious, intriguing, and faithless—Don Pedro de Toledo, governor of Milan; the duke d'Ossuna, viceroy of Naples; and the marquis de Bedmar, ambassador at

Venice. In 1618, a project was formed between these three lords to destroy a republic which stood in the way of their ambition, and which had always thwarted the enterprises of Spain. Some French adventurers, who had signalised themselves in the armies and fleets of the republic, of whom the most illustrious were the corsair Jaques Pierre and Jaffier, dissatisfied with the rewards which they had obtained, offered their services to the marquis de Bedmar. The marquis encouraged them to enlist in their service the assassins, bravos, and robbers who, under the Spanish rule, always formed a part of the household of men of quality. It was agreed that, at a given signal, they should massacre the doge, senators, and nobles; that the city should afterwards be abandoned to their pillage; and that a general fire should veil their crimes. On the other side, it appears that Jaques Pierre gave early notice of this plot to the senate; that he carried it on by its order; that the senate made use of it to hide its secret intelligence with the duke d'Ossuna, with whom a project was entered into of nearly the same nature with that which had been proposed in the preceding century by Morone to Pescara. It was intended, with the aid of the senate, to re-establish the independence of all Italy, by driving the Spaniards out of Lombardy, and giving Ossuna the crown of Naples. Fresh disclosures of Antoine Jaffier apparently discovered to the Council of Ten that the conspirators preferred the pillage of Venice to the doubtful chances of a revolt at Naples; and that the information which they had given of their plot was destined only to deceive the vigilance of the state inquisitors. The republic, however, had embarked itself in intrigues which could not bear the light. On a certain morning, the inhabitants of Venice saw with horror the bodies of Jaques Pierre, Regnault, Boulant, and several others, hanging in the square of St. Mark. One hundred and sixty others were, it was affirmed, drowned in the grand canal; among them was Jaffier. No motive was assigned for these executions; no explanation was given to the public; no recrimination was addressed to the court of Spain. The Council of Ten desired, above all, the silence of terror; and the romantic history of this conspiracy, published by St. Réal in 1674, and the tragedy of *Venice Preserved*, by Otway, in 1682, were the only public documents of this catastrophe for a long time.

The Venetians were afterwards forced by the attacks of the Turks to make advances to the house of Austria, the enemy of their enemies. On the 23d of June, 1645, the sultan Ibrahim unexpectedly attacked the isle of Candia. The war which thus began was the longest and most ruinous that the republic had yet sustained against the Ottoman empire: it lasted twenty-five years. The Venetians displayed obstinate valour in defence of Candia. Courageous adventurers arrived from every part of the west to fight under their banner, as in a holy war. Their fleet twice destroyed that of the Mussulmans; but the forces of the republic were too disproportioned to those of the Turkish empire. Candia was forced to surrender on the 6th of September, 1669; and the senate of that colony, the reflected image of the republic, returned into the grand council of Venice, which had given it birth: peace followed this capitulation.

A second war between the Venetians and the Porte was, before the end of the century, crowned with more success. The republic engaged in it, in 1682, in concert with the emperor Leopold and John Sobieski, king of Poland. It conquered the Morea, Egina, Santa Maura, and several fortresses in Dalmatia, which were secured to it by the treaty of Carlowitz, signed on the 26th of January, 1699: but the Turks could not suffer so feeble an enemy to take from them one of their finest provinces. They might soon visibly convince themselves that the Venetians were no longer in a state to make a last effort to protect their conquests: the supreme power was concentrated in an oligarchy becoming daily more distracted. Half the nobility admitted to the grand council were reduced to the most extreme poverty. They lived on the bounty of the great, to whom they sold their suffrages. The families from among whom alone was selected the Council of Ten made every other tremble and obey. They regarded the state as a prey to be divided amongst themselves. Justice was venal; the finances dilapidated; the fortifications falling into ruin; the effective force of the army did not amount to one half of what appeared on the roll: every thing was to the Venetian noble an object of embezzlement and robbery. The oppression of the distant provinces was so great, that the eastern Christian subjects of the republic regretted the dominion of the Ottomans. The sultan, Achmet III, informed of this universal disorganisation, sent his army, on the 20th of June, 1714, into the Morea; and in a month conquered that peninsula, covered with fortresses, of which not one made any resistance. On the 27th of June, 1718, the republic abandoned, under the peace of Passarowitz, all its claims on the Morea. From that period it had no further war with the Turks.

The republic abstained, with the same timidity, from taking any part in the war of the succession, either in Spain or Austria, in the quadruple alliance, or in that of the election of Poland, which disturbed Italy during the first half of the eighteenth century. It could not even make its neutrality respected. Its territory, always open to every belligerent power, was often the theatre of their most obstinate warfare. Venice, with 3,000,000 of subjects, 14,000 troops of the line (of which one half was composed of excellent Sclavonian soldiers), twelve vessels of war, and the means of arming 50,000 men, was incapable of making herself respected, or of protecting her subjects, either by sea or land. Her debt, even in the bosom of peace, was always increasing; her manufactures always in decay; her territory was infested with robbers; every city was divided into factions, which the senate encouraged, in order to weaken its subjects. A suspicious and cruel government, which maintained itself only by the vigilance of spies, which had promoted immorality to enervate the people, which made the most profound secrecy its only safeguard, which did not tolerate even a question on public affairs, which deprived the accused of every protection before the tribunals, which acknowledged no other limit to the right of punishing by the dagger, by poison, or by the axe of the executioner, than that of the terror of its rulers—a government such as this became execrated by its subjects. It stained with the most odious tyranny the very name of republic.

The French revolution appeared to the Venetian aristocracy an enemy destined to destroy it: of all the governments which divided Europe, the Venetian was the most opposite in principle to that of the French; nevertheless, the senate refused to enter into the coalition against France, in 1792. Any display of force would have augmented its expenses, and diminished the spoils of provinces which the patricians divided amongst themselves. The same parsimony, the same sacrifice of the public to private interests, hindered Venice, when the victories of Bonaparte opened Lombardy to him, in April, 1796, from augmenting her army or provisioning her fortresses, in order to protect her territory from the two belligerent powers. The government, adopting a vacillating policy between the two parties, and awaiting events, laid aside its arms: this soon brought war into the states of the republic. The Austrians, always the first to violate neutral ground, traversed them in every direction: Beaulieu occupied Peschiera and Verona; Wurmser threw himself into Bassano, and passed through Vicenza and Padua; Alvinzi and the archduke Charles occupied Friuli and Palma Nova, up to the eastern limits of the republic. Napoleon successively drove the Austrians from each of these provinces; but, as the French occupied them, the spirit of reform in the tribunals and the laws, the spirit of publicity and equality, an impatience of every yoke—the spirit, in short, of the French—manifested itself, and the republic was at last made to understand how much it was detested by all those who had the least elevation of soul or cultivation of mind.

Others, it is true, of the lowest class (day-labourers

in towns, and peasants in the country), completely under the influence of priests, comprehending only what exists, fearing all change, and still deeply excited by the name of St. Mark, regarded France and every thing French with horror. The senate, relying on this party, whose fanaticism it excited, and hearing that Napoleon had passed the Piove on his march to Germany, on the 11th of March, 1797, gave orders to arrest at Bergamo fourteen of the principal inhabitants, who had declared themselves the most earnest in favour of the new doctrines. The patriots, warned in time, arrested the proveditor himself, raised the standard of revolt, and proclaimed the liberty of Bergamo: a few days afterwards, a similar revolution broke out at Brescia. Bonaparte had just defeated the archduke Charles at the Tagliamento, and was marching on Vienna. An Austrian column, commanded by Laudon, had meanwhile penetrated by the Tyrol into Italy; which he inundated with proclamations, announcing the defeat and destruction of the French army, and inviting the Italians to take arms to crush its fugitive remains. The senate, feeling that its position became daily more critical, believed the moment come for throwing off the mask and joining the Austrians. Emili, the proveditor of Verona, after having conferred with Laudon, ordered the tocsin to be rung, on the 17th of April, throughout the whole province; and joining 30,000 insurgents to 3000 soldiers, whom he commanded, every where attacked the French, massacred all those within his reach, and suffered the infuriated people to murder 400 sick in the hospitals. The next day preliminaries of peace between Austria and the French republic were signed at Leoben; and, on the 3d of May, 1797, Bonaparte, informed of the insurrection which had been organised in the rear of his army, and of the massacre of his sick, declared war against Venice from Palma Nova. The oligarchy, in consternation, implored the court of Vienna, which had drawn it into this imprudent attack, to include Venice in the suspension of arms and the negotiations for peace; but Austria refused all assistance: she had her own views on her ally, and Venice fell. The French general Baraguai d'Hilliers entered the city on the 16th of May, and planted unopposed the tricolour banner on St. Mark. The negotiations for peace, however, continued. Austria, beginning to recover from her panic, disputed the concessions demanded, and asked compensation out of the states of her ally. Hostilities were on the point of recommencing; but France did not yet find herself strong enough to liberate all Italy. On the 17th of October, 1797, Napoleon signed the treaty of Campo Formio, by which he secured the liberty of one half of the Venetian territory up to the Adige, which was united to the Cisalpine republic. The Ionian isles were, at the same time, united to France. Austria, on her side, took possession of Venice and the remainder of the Venetian states. The loss of liberty sustained by that part of the republic was, however, of no long duration: at the expiration of eighteen months the war was renewed; and, after the French had made themselves masters of Vienna, they obliged Austria to restore Venice and all her territory to the kingdom of Italy, under the treaty of Presburg, signed on the 26th of December, 1805.

It was thus that the invasion of the French, at the end of the eighteenth century, restored to Italy all the advantages of which their invasion at the end of the fifteenth had deprived her. When Charles VIII entered Naples with his victorious army, on the 22d of February, 1495, and overthrew the ancient system of Italian politics, he gave the signal for all the calamities which afterwards precipitated the peninsula under the yoke of the transalpine nations. The Italians continued to regard themselves as the first people in Europe, but they had almost every where lost their liberty: of the five republics which they could still reckon, four were narrow aristocracies. When Napoleon Bonaparte was appointed to the command of the French army in Italy, on the 23d of February, 1796, he began to effect a regeneration which gave to the Italian nation more liberty than it had lost. It is the participation of num-

bers in the government, and not the name of republic
as opposed to monarchy, that constitutes liberty: it is,
above all, the reign of the laws; publicity in the administration, as well as the tribunals; equality; the removal of all shackles on thought, on education, and on
religion. Five millions and a half of inhabitants in the
kingdom of Italy were put in possession of a constitution
which secured to them all these advantages, with a
participation in the legislature and in the vote of taxes.
They had recovered the glorious name of Italians; they
had a national army, the bravery of which rendered it
daily more illustrious. Six millions and a half inhabitants
of the kingdom of Naples received institutions less advanced, it is true; but even there the law had succeeded arbitrary power; public and oral evidence had
succeeded secret information and the torture; equality,
the feudal system; education, instead of retrograding,
had been rendered progressive, and thought, as well as
religious conscience, had recovered freedom: finally,
2,000,000 of Piedmontese, 500,000 Genoese, 500,000
Parmesans, and 2,500,000 Tuscans and Romans—in all,
5,500,000 Italians—were temporarily united to France.
They partook of all the privileges of the conquerors:
they became with them accustomed to the dominion
of the law, to freedom of thought, and to military virtue—secure that at no very distant period, when their
political education should be accomplished, they would
again be incorporated in that Italy to the future liberty
and glory of which they now directed their every
thought.

Such was the work which the French accomplished
by twenty years of victory: it was doubtless incomplete,
and left much to be desired; but it possessed in itself
the principle of greater advancement: it promised to
revive Italy, liberty, virtue, and glory. It has been the
work of the coalition to destroy all; to place Italy again
under the galling yoke of Austria; to take from her,
with political liberty, civil and religious freedom, and
even freedom of thought; to corrupt her morals; and to
heap upon her the utmost degree of humiliation. Italy

is unanimous in abhorring this ignominious yoke: Italy, to break it, has done all that could be expected of her. In a struggle between an established government and a nation, the former has all the advantages: it has in its favour rapidity of communication, certainty of information, soldiers, arsenals, fortresses, and finances. The people have only their unarmed hands and their masses unaccustomed to act together: nevertheless, in every struggle during these fifteen years in Italy, between the nation and its oppressors, the victory has remained with the people. At Naples, in Sicily, in Piedmont, in the states of the church, at Modena and Parma, unarmed masses have seized the arms of the soldiers; men chosen by the people have taken the places of the despots in their palaces. The Italians, every where victorious over their own tyrants, have, it is true, been every where forced back under the yoke with redoubled cruelty by the league of foreign despots. Attacked before they could have given themselves a government or formed a treasury, arsenals, or an army, by the sovereign of another nation, who reckons not less than 30,000,000 of subjects, they did not attempt a hopeless resistance, which would have deprived them of every chance for the future. Let those who demand more of them begin by doing as much themselves.

Italy is crushed; but her heart still beats with the love of liberty, virtue, and glory: she is chained and covered with blood; but she still knows her strength and her future destiny: she is insulted by those for whom she has opened the way to every improvement; but she feels that she is formed to take the lead again: and Europe will know no repose till the nation which, in the dark ages, lighted the torch of civilisation with that of liberty, shall be enabled herself to enjoy the light which she created.

INDEX

ANCHOR BOOKS

EUROPEAN HISTORY

MARX, KARL, & ENGELS, FRIEDRICH Basic Writings on Politics and Philosophy, A185

MEYERHOFF, HANS, ed. The Philosophy of History in Our Time, A164

MILL, JOHN STUART John Stuart Mill: Essays on Politics and Culture, ed. Himmelfarb, A373

MUELLER, WILLIAM A. Church and State in Luther and Calvin, A454

NAMIER, LEWIS 1848: The Revolution of the Intellectuals, A385

NEALE, J. E. Queen Elizabeth I, A105

NEVINS, ALLEN The Gateway to History, A314

OSTROGORSKI, M. Democracy and the Organization of Political Parties—Vol. I: England, ed. Lipset, A388a

PIRENNE, HENRI A History of Europe
  Vol. I—From the End of the Roman World in the West to the Beginnings of the Western States, A156a
  Vol. II—From the Thirteenth Century to the Renaissance and Reformation, A156b
  —— Medieval Cities, A82

SERGE, VICTOR The Case of Comrade Tulayev, A349

SHATTUCK, ROGER The Banquet Years, A238

STERN, FRITZ The Politics of Cultural Despair—A Study in the Rise of Germanic Ideology, A436

SYPHER, WYLIE Four Stages of Renaissance Style, A45

TOCQUEVILLE, ALEXIS DE The Old Regime and the French Revolution, A60

TREVELYAN, G. M. History of England
  Vol. I—From the Earliest Times to the Reformation, A22a
  Vol. II—The Tudors and the Stuart Era, A22b
  Vol. III—From Utrecht to Modern Times, A22c

TROTSKY, LEON The Russian Revolution, A170

VICO, GIAMBATTISTA The New Science of Giambattista Vico, trans. Bergin & Fisch, A254

WADDELL, HELEN The Wandering Scholars, A63

WANDRUSZKA, ADAM The House of Habsburg, trans. Epstein, A453

WEDGWOOD, C. V. The Thirty Years War, A249

WILLEY, BASIL The Seventeenth Century Background, A19

WILSON, EDMUND To the Finland Station, A6

ANCHOR BOOKS

ANCIENT CIVILIZATION

ALBRIGHT, WILLIAM FOXWELL From the Stone Age to Christianity, A100

ALLEGRO, JOHN MARCO The Treasure of the Copper Scroll, A416

ARISTOPHANES Five Comedies of Aristophanes, trans. Rogers, A57

CAMPBELL, EDWARD F., JR., & FREEDMAN, DAVID NOEL, eds. The Biblical Archaeologist Reader, Vol. II, A250a

COULANGES, FUSTEL DE The Ancient City, A76

CROSS, FRANK MOORE, JR. The Ancient Library of Qumran, A272

FORSTER, E. M. Alexandria: A History and a Guide, A231

FRANKFORT, HENRI The Birth of Civilization in the Near East, A89

FRAZER, J. G. The New Golden Bough, ed. Gaster, A270

GASTER, THEODOR H. The Dead Sea Scriptures (Revised edition), A378

—— Thespis: Ritual, Myth and Drama in the Ancient Near East, A230

HADAS, MOSES, trans. & ed. A History of Rome, A78

HOMER The Odyssey, trans. Fitzgerald, A333

KITTO, H. D. F. Greek Tragedy, A38

KRAMER, SAMUEL NOAH History Begins at Sumer, A175

——, ed. Mythologies of the Ancient World, A229

MOSCATI, SABATINO The Face of the Ancient Orient, A289

MURRAY, GILBERT Five Stages of Greek Religion, A51

NEHRU, JAWAHARLAL The Discovery of India, A200

PLAUTUS Six Plays of Plautus, trans. Casson, A367

SAPPHO Lyrics in the Original Greek with Translations by Willis Barnstone, A400

SOMERVILLE, JOHN, & SANTONI, RONALD, eds. Social and Political Philosophy: Readings from Plato to Gandhi, A370

TAYLOR, A. E. Socrates, A9

TREVELYAN, G. M. A History of England: Vol. I—From the Earliest Times to the Reformation, A22a

VIRGIL The Aeneid of Virgil, trans. Lewis, A20

—— The Eclogues and Georgics of Virgil. In the Original Latin with a Verse Translation by C. Day Lewis, A390

WALEY, ARTHUR Three Ways of Thought in Ancient China, A75

WRIGHT, G. ERNEST, ed. The Bible and the Ancient Near East, A431

——, & FREEDMAN, DAVID NOEL, eds. The Biblical Archaeologist Reader, Vol. I, A250a

ANCHOR BOOKS

BIOGRAPHY, AUTOBIOGRAPHY AND LETTERS

ANDRADE, E. N. da C. Rutherford and the Nature of the Atom, S35
—— Sir Isaac Newton, S42
BEETHOVEN, LUDWIG VAN Beethoven: Letters, Journals and Conversations, trans. & ed. Hamburger, A206
BENDIX, REINHARD Max Weber: An Intellectual Portrait, A281
CASALIS, GEORGES Portrait of Karl Barth, A422
COLETTE My Mother's House *and* The Vagabond, A62
DE BEER, SIR GAVIN Charles Darwin, N41
DICKINSON, EMILY Selected Poems and Letters of Emily Dickinson, ed. Linscott, A192
ESSLIN, MARTIN Brecht: The Man and His Work, A245
FULLER, MARGARET Margaret Fuller: American Romantic—A Selection from Her Writings and Correspondence, ed. Miller, A356
GATHERU, R. MUGO Child of Two Worlds, A468
GEIRINGER, KARL Brahms: His Life and Work, A245
—— Haydn, A361
GRAVES, ROBERT Good-Bye to All That, A123
GREVILLE, CHARLES CAVENDISH FULKE The Great World: Portraits and Scenes from Greville's Memoirs, ed. Kronenberger, A409
JONES, ERNEST The Life and Work of Sigmund Freud, ed. & abr. in 1 vol. Trilling & Marcus, A340
KENDALL, PAUL MURRAY Richard the Third, A455
LEWIS, W. H. The Sunset of the Splendid Century: The Life and Times of Louis Auguste de Bourbon, Duc du Maine, 1670–1736, A355
MAC DONALD, D. K. C. Faraday, Maxwell and Kelvin, S33
NEALE, J. E. Queen Elizabeth I, A105
NEWMAN, JAMES R. Science and Sensibility, A357
SHATTUCK, ROGER The Banquet Years, A238
TAYLOR, A. E. Socrates, A9

LINGUISTICS AND LANGUAGE

HALL, ROBERT A., JR. Linguistics and Your Language, A201
JESPERSEN, OTTO Growth and Structure of the English Language, A46

A 12a

ANCHOR BOOKS

MYTHOLOGY AND LEGEND

BEDIER, JOSEPH   The Romance of Tristan and Iseult, A2
COULANGES, FUSTEL DE   The Ancient City, A76
FRAZER, J. G.   The New Golden Bough, ed. Gaster, A270
KRAMER, SAMUEL NOAH, ed.   Mythologies of the Ancient World, A229
MALINOWSKI, BRONISLAW   Magic, Science and Religion, A23
MURRAY, GILBERT   Five Stages of Greek Religion, A51
VIRGIL   The Aeneid of Virgil, trans. Lewis, A20
WESTON, JESSIE L.   From Ritual to Romance, A125

ANTHROPOLOGY AND ARCHAEOLOGY

ALLEGRO, JOHN MARCO   The Treasure of the Copper Scroll, A412
ALBRIGHT, WILLIAM FOXWELL   From the Stone Age to Christianity, A100
BENDIX, REINHARD   Max Weber: An Intellectual Portrait, A281
BOHANNAN, LAURA MARIE   Return to Laughter, N36
BOHANNAN, PAUL J., & DALTON, GEORGE, eds.   Markets in Africa—Eight Subsistence Economies in Transition, N39
CAMPBELL, EDWARD F., JR., & FREEDMAN, DAVID NOEL, eds.   The Biblical Archaeologist Reader, Vol. II, A250b
COULANGES, FUSTEL DE   The Ancient City, A76
CROSS, FRANK MOORE, JR.   The Ancient Library of Qumran, A272
ELKIN, A. P.   The Australian Aborigines, N37
FEINSTEIN, OTTO, ed.   Two Worlds of Change, A396
FRANKFORT, HENRI   The Birth of Civilization in the Near East, A89
FRAZER, J. G.   The New Golden Bough, ed. Gaster, A270
GASTER, THEODOR H.   The Dead Sea Scriptures (Revised edition), A378
HOWELLS, WILLIAM   Back of History, N34
——   The Heathens, N19
KLUCKHOHN, CLYDE, & LEIGHTON, DOROTHEA   The Navaho (Revised edition), N28
KRAMER, SAMUEL NOAH   History Begins at Sumer, A175
——, ed.   Mythologies of the Ancient World, A229
MAC GOWAN, KENNETH, & HESTER, JOSEPH A., JR.   Early Man in the New World, N22
MALINOWSKI, BRONISLAW   Magic, Science and Religion, A23
MINER, HORACE   Primitive City of Timbuctoo, A456
OLIVER, DOUGLAS   The Pacific Islands, N14
SHAPIRO, HARRY L.   Heritage of the Bounty, N23
TURNBULL, COLIN   The Forest People, N27
——   The Lonely African, A374
WASHBURN, WILCOMB E.   The Indian and the White Man, AD2
WESTHEIM, PAUL   The Art of Ancient Mexico, trans. Bernard, A416
——   The Sculpture of Ancient Mexico/La Escultura Del Mexico Antiguo (Bilingual edition, trans. Bernard), A335
WESTON, JESSIE L.   From Ritual to Romance, A125
WHITEFORD, ANDREW H.   Two Cities of Latin America: A Comparative Description of Social Classes, A395
WRIGHT, G. ERNEST, ed.   The Bible and the Ancient Near East, A431
——, & FREEDMAN, DAVID NOEL, eds.   The Biblical Archaeologist Reader, Vol. I, A250a